THE PRACTICE OF INDUSTRIAL RELATIONS

SECOND EDITION

DAVID A. PEACH
Professor
School of Business Administration
The University of Western Ontario

DAVID KUECHLE
Professor
Graduate School of Education
Harvard University

McGraw-Hill Ryerson Limited

Toronto Montreal New York Auckland Bogotá Cairo Guatemala Hamburg Johannesburg Lisbon London Madrid Mexico New Delhi Panama Paris San Juan São Paulo Singapore Sydney Tokyo

The Practice of Industrial Relations, Second Edition

Copyright © McGraw-Hill Ryerson Limited, 1985, 1975.

ISBN 0-07-548909-0

1 2 3 4 5 6 7 8 9 0 AP 4 3 2 1 0 9 8 7 6 5

Care has been taken to trace ownership of copyright material contained in this text. The publishers will gladly take any information that will enable them to rectify any reference or credit in subsequent editions.

Canadian Cataloguing in Publication Data

Peach, David A., date
  The practice of industrial relations

Includes bibliographical references and index.
ISBN 0-07-548909-0.

1. Industrial relations — Canada. 2. Trade-unions — Canada. I. Kuechle, David.

HD8106.5.P4 1985   331'.0971   C85-098227-8

42,500

CONTENTS

Preface v

Chapter 1 An Introduction to Labour Relations 1

Chapter 2 A Capsule History of Canadian Labour Relations 22

Chapter 3 Labour Legislation — An Overview 44

Chapter 4 The Organizing Challenge 61
Cases:
Muskoka University (A) 82
Muskoka University (B) 84
Muskoka University (C) 101

Chapter 5 The Negotiation Challenge 134
Cases:
McDonald Containers (A) 168
McDonald Containers (B) 176
McDonald Containers (C) 180
McDonald Containers (D) 182
McDonald Containers (E) 183
McDonald Containers (F) 187
McDonald Containers (G) 191
McDonald Containers (H) 197
McDonald Containers (I) 200

Addington Chemical Company 208

Jones and Smart, Ltd. (A) 220
Jones and Smart, Ltd. (B) 229

Chapter 6　The Grievance Challenge　240
　　　　　　Cases:
　　　　　　Alexander Bert, Ltd.　270
　　　　　　The Apex Case　282
　　　　　　Beavair　286
　　　　　　Bucklin Corporation　289
　　　　　　Canwest Life Assurance Company　298
　　　　　　Great Northern Telephone Company Limited　306
　　　　　　John Hemstead & Sons Ltd.　311
　　　　　　MacIntosh Metal Company　318
　　　　　　Personal Paper Company　323
　　　　　　Port Erie Hydro　326
　　　　　　R. G. Williamson Company, Limited　335
　　　　　　Young Products Ltd.　339

　　　　　　Globe Electronics, Ltd. (A)　346
　　　　　　Globe Electronics, Ltd. (B)　352
　　　　　　Globe Electronics, Ltd. (C)　356

　　　　　　Great Lakes Iron and Steel (A)　359
　　　　　　Great Lakes Iron and Steel (B)　365

Chapter 7　Building an Industrial Relations System　369
　　　　　　Cases:
　　　　　　Darthom Industries Ltd. (A)　372
　　　　　　Darthom Industries Ltd. (B)　392

Index　407

PREFACE

This book describes industrial relations practice in Canada. It is written for managers and students of management. It is practical, not theoretical, in its approach. While its primary focus is on the Canadian scene, there are some references and comparisons to practices in the United States in an attempt to highlight the similarities and differences in labour-management experiences in the two countries.

For students of management, the book provides a learning vehicle for understanding industrial relations practices and for carrying on decision-making responsibilities in the field. For practising managers, it provides an informative documentary and practical reference manual. Our intent, particularly in the case studies, has been to highlight the important industrial relations issues facing contemporary Canadian managers. To the degree that this book leads to greater understanding of this complex and specialized field, our purposes are met.

A number of people have helped us along the way to the completion of this book. We are grateful to our teachers of labour relations at the Harvard Business School — James J. Healey, Thomas Kennedy, and E. Robert Livernash. They will no doubt find a great deal of themselves in this book. The School of Business Administration, The University of Western Ontario, has provided not only financial support for this endeavour, but also a climate which encouraged the development and use of the material. We wish to acknowledge our appreciation to Deans J. J. Wettlaufer and C. B. Johnston, and to Research Directors J. N. Fry, David C. Shaw, Alexander Mikalachki, and Terry Deutscher. The school's research efforts, including this one, have been generously financed by The Associates' Plan for Excellence. We are grateful to the individuals and companies who have supported this plan. We also owe a word of thanks to the many students who have helped in giving the contents a trial run in the classroom.

More specifically, we wish to acknowledge the assistance of Paul Bergman, David DeYoung, Peter Lawrie, James Mackay, and Robert Malanchuk in developing some of the materials in this book. We also offer thanks to Linda Minutillo and Lynn Maslen for their help in typing the final draft of the manuscript and to David Whitehead for his helpful comments on the penultimate draft.

Finally, we owe our thanks to a number of individuals, companies, and unions who provided the basis for the cases and research studies which gave rise to this book. We are deeply grateful for their help in providing examples of "the practice of industrial relations" which we hope will make the subject come alive for the reader.

1

AN INTRODUCTION TO
LABOUR RELATIONS

When the Union's inspiration through the workers' blood shall run,
There can be no power greater anywhere beneath the sun;
Yet what force on earth is weaker than the feeble strength of one?
Solidarity forever, Solidarity forever,
Solidarity forever, for the Union makes us strong.

With this rousing chorus, we begin. In it, is the *raison d'être* of the union movement:

> The fundamental reason for the existence of the trade union is that by it and
> through it workmen are enabled to deal collectively with their employers.
> Trade unionism thus recognizes that the destruction of the workingman is
> the individual bargain, and the salvation of the workingman is the joint,
> united, or collective bargain.[1]

In this quotation, two principal participants and the key process in what can be called an industrial relations system have been introduced. The notion of an industrial relations system is both simple and complex. The basic elements are few — five in fact. They are: 1) participants 2) interacting in 3) an environment in a way that produces 4) outcomes or results. The fifth element is an ideology which serves as the glue to bind the system together. The number of participants and the number of environmental factors and the potential interactions among them and the variety of resulting outcomes produces the complexity. The basic framework of an industrial relations system was developed by John T. Dunlop of Harvard University. He called the participants "actors," and the outcomes a "web of rules."[2]

The purpose of this book is to facilitate an understanding of how the Canadian Industrial System works *in practice*. It is oriented toward the practitioner — or the potential practitioner — in the system, and deals with how the day-to-day decisions in the collective bargaining process are made and how these decisions produce results.

This chapter will introduce the participants or parties of interest, suggest some basic ways in which they can relate to each other, explore how environmental factors can influence the collective bargaining process, and examine what role ideology plays in the process.

THE PARTIES OF INTEREST
The Labour Movement

In 1983, there were 3,563,000 union members in Canada. This amounted to 40 percent of the non-agricultural paid workers in the country. (This figure was down from the record 3,617,000 union members in 1982, a result of the severe recession of 1982–83, and a preliminary example of how the economic environment can affect labour relations.)[3] Obviously, not all workers have opted for the sentiments expressed in "Solidarity forever." To put these figures in perspective, in 1980 the percentage of wage earners who were union members in six other O.E.C.D. countries was: Australia 56.4 percent; United Kingdom 57.5 percent; United States 24.7 percent; and West Germany 42.5 percent.[4]

If a majority of Canadian workers are not members of labour unions and do not have their conditions of employment established through the process of collective bargaining, in many sectors of the economy unionization is extensive. Table 1–1 shows union membership in Canada as a percentage of the workforce by major industrial groups. In Public Administration, Forestry, Construction, Transportation, Communication and Utilities, as well as in many segments of manufacturing, unionization exceeds 50 percent of the workforce. In other segments of the economy such as agriculture, finance and trade, the degree of unionization is very low.

The degree of union influence over terms and conditions of employment in

Table 1–1
Union Membership in Canada as a Percentage of the Labour Force by Major Industrial Group, 1981

	Number	Union Membership	Union Membership as a Percent of the Workforce	Percentage of Paid Workers Unionized
	Labour Force			
Agriculture	481,275	330	.1	.3
Forestry	100,765	29,238	29.0	56.2
Fishing & Trapping	36,870	3,754	10.2	37.5
Mines, Quarries,				
Oil Wells	210,025	70,227	33.4	35.5
Metal Mines	78,815	40,397	51.3	
Mineral Fuels	61,600	14,315	23.0	

Table 1–1 (continued)

	Number	Union Membership	Union Membership as a Percent of the Workforce	Percentage of Paid Workers Unionized
Manufacturing	2,219,375	872,948	39.3	44.4
Food	306,085	131,292	42.9	
Tobacco	8,265	5,543	67.1	
Rubber & Plastics	69,060	25,110	36.4	
Leather	32,055	9,656	30.1	
Textiles, Knitting & Clothing	228,025	78,282	34.3	
Wood	150,810	55,675	36.9	
Furniture	69,055	14,133	20.5	
Paper	146,465	98,448	67.2	
Printing, Publishing	136,425	33,511	24.6	
Primary Metal	138,095	87,460	63.3	
Metal Fabricating	190,545	64,258	33.7	
Machinery	121,590	30,777	25.3	
Transportation Equipment	208,425	111,978	53.7	
Electrical Products	133,855	58,808	43.9	
Non-Metallic Mineral Products	69,560	30,410	43.7	
Petroleum & Coal Products	26,500	4,432	16.7	
Chemicals	100,305	19,816	19.8	
Miscellaneous	84,255	13,359	15.9	
Construction	752,365	278,003	37.0	54.0
Transportation, Communication & Other Industries	935,575	448,326	47.9	53.2
Transportation, Storage & Communication	805,260	385,551	47.9	
Gas, Water & Electric Utilities	130,315	62,775	48.2	
Trade	1,957,575	151,202	7.7	8.9
Wholesale	558,495	28,675	5.1	
Retail	1,399,090	122,526	8.8	
Finance, Insurance Real Estate	621,120	16,141	2.6	2.8
Service	3,399,435	737,482	21.7	25.6
Public Administration	886,605	507,494	57.2	69.1
Other (Pensions, Unemployed, etc.)	—	44,923	—	

Source: Labour Force, Statistics Canada, *1981 Census of Canada*, Population; Labour Force—Industry Trends (Volume 1—National Series, Catalogue 92–925), Ottawa, Minister of Supply and Services, 1983, pp. 1–10.
Union Membership and Percentage of Paid Workers Unionized: Statistics Canada, *Corporations and Labour Unions Returns Act, Report for 1981, Part II—Labour Unions*, Ottawa, Ministry of Supply and Services, 1983, p. 62. and p. 60.

Table 1–2

Collective Agreement Coverage by Industry Group in Canada
Percentage of Employees Covered

Industry	Office Employees	Non-Office Employees
Logging	16	86
Mining	10	77
Manufacturing	9	76
Food, Beverage	8	70
Tobacco	10	100
Rubber	4	94
Leather	2	58
Textiles, Knitting, Clothing	3	65
Wood and Wood Products	3	77
Furniture	4	57
Pulp and Paper	21	94
Printing	24	57
Primary Metal	14	81
Metal Fabricating	3	77
Machinery	7	73
Transportation Equipment	12	96
Electrical Products	17	74
Non-Metallic Mineral Products	8	73
Petroleum and Coal Products	1	51
Chemicals	3	53
Transportation, Communications, Utilities	46	91*
Air Transport	33	94*
Truck Transport	14	67*
Railway Transport	37	99*
Communication	51	91
Electric Power	63	93
Trade	4	37*
Finance	3	21
Service	31	64*
Public Administration	87	91*

*The Labour Canada data includes a category labelled "Other Employees." These include operating employees, such as pilots, truck drivers, ships officers and conductors in the transportation industry, sales staff in trade, nurses and technical staff in hospitals in the service industry, and policemen and firemen in public administration. In this table, these employees have been included in the non-office category.

Source: Labour Canada, *Working Conditions in Canadian Industry, 1982*. Ottawa: Minister of Supply and Services, 1983. Reproduced by permission of the Minister of Supply and Services Canada.

Canada can be seen even more clearly in Table 1–2, which shows the percentage of non-office and office employees who are covered by collective agreements. Not all employees who are covered by agreements are actual union members, even though the union bargains for them. Non-office employees are defined as "non-supervisory workers directly engaged in the production of goods or services and the provision of maintenance and auxiliary services closely associated

Table 1–3
Union Membership by Province 1981

Province	Union Membership	Percent of Total Union Membership
Newfoundland	77,026	2.4
Prince Edward Island	9,432	.3
Nova Scotia	87,637	2.8
New Brunswick	74,204	2.3
Quebec	880,199	27.9
Ontario	1,123,214	35.5
Manitoba	123,638	3.9
Saskatchewan	92,253	3.1
Alberta	230,124	7.3
British Columbia	450,750	14.3
Yukon	2,458	.1
Northwest Territories	4,121	.2
Total	3,160,068	100.0

Source: Statistics Canada, Corporations and Labour Unions Return Act, Report for 1981, Part II—Labour Unions, p. 36.

with production operations." Non-office employees are defined as "supervisory, professional and technical staff, and personnel engaged in clerical, accounting, secretarial, sales, executive and administrative activities."[5] The data shown is for establishments in Canada having 20 or more employees and indicates that in many areas of the economy, the percentage of non-office employees whose terms and conditions of employment are determined by collective bargaining is very high.

Geographically, union membership in Canada is concentrated in three provinces, Quebec, Ontario and British Columbia, with these provinces having 78 percent of the union membership in Canada. This, of course, reflects basic population trends as well as the concentration of Canadian industry. Table 1–3 provides a breakdown of union membership by province.

Union Organization

When union members speak of their union, they are often referring to their local union. Local unions are units of national or international unions and are the basic building blocks of the labour movement in North America. There are over 15,000 local unions in Canada.[6] Local unions often consist of the employees of a given employer who have been organized by a particular union in a single plant, or sometimes of several plants in a locality. In the construction industry, local unions are typically composed of all union members in a given city or area. The negotiation and administration of collective agreements generally but not always occurs at the local level. To be sure, assistance in bargaining is often provided to the local by the parent union (just as it is, and often with more control, by the parent corporate organization), but the contract is negotiated and administered by the local union.

National and International Unions

There are 146 national unions in Canada and 74 international unions. These unions contain 96 percent of the union membership in Canada. (There are 366 local unions directly chartered by the labour federations and 240 Independent Local Organizations which account for the other four percent of union membership).[7] National unions are unions who charter local unions only in Canada. International unions are unions which charter locals in both the United States and Canada.

One of the most significant events in Canadian labour relations in recent years has been the rise of national unions. Until the 1970s the majority of Canadian union members were members of international unions. For example, in 1972, 60 percent of Canadian union members were members of international unions.[8] By 1983, that percentage had declined to 41 percent, while the percentage of union members who were members of national unions stood at 55 percent.[9]

The increase in the percentage of workers belonging to national unions has largely been in the public sector. However, there has also been a significant amount of Canadianization of unions representing workers in the private sector as well. For example, The Oil, Chemical, and Atomic Workers Union, and the International Chemical Workers Union are both international unions no longer existing in Canada. The former merged with the Canadian Chemical Workers Union (which had earlier split from the International Chemical Workers Union) to form the Energy and Chemical Workers Union, while remnants of the latter were absorbed by the Teamsters Union. In 1974, the Canadian locals of the United Brewery, Flour, Cereal, Soft Drinks and Distillery workers broke away from the international union to form a separate national union, as did most of the locals of the United Paperworkers (to form the Canadian Paperworkers Union).

Not all of these and other splits occurred with rancour, as a number were blessed and even encouraged by the international unions involved, as a solution to increased demands for Canadian autonomy within the international union structure. Other international unions moved in the 1970s to create essentially autonomous Canadian divisions of the unions. These included the Office and Professional Employees International Union, The Brotherhood of Railway, Airline and Steamship Clerks and The Teamsters. International unions such as the Autoworkers and the Steelworkers have provided a significant degree of autonomy to their Canadian branches for many years.

Unions in Canada range in size from the four-member International Association of Siderographers* to the 293,000 member Canadian Union of Public Employees. Table 1–4 shows the distribution of national and international unions in Canada by size. In 1984, there were 33 unions in Canada with a membership of more than 25,000. These are listed in Table 1–5. Two-thirds of the union members in Canada are members of these 33 unions.

---

*Siderography is one of the trades in the printing industry.

Table 1–4
International and National Unions in Canada by Size, 1984

	International Unions		National Unions		Total	
Membership Range	No. of Unions	Membership	No. of Unions	Membership	No. of Unions	Membership
Under 100	5	254	1	86	6	340
100– 199	6	777	6	924	12	1,701
200– 499	1	222	13	4,699	14	4,921
500– 999	2	1,300	14	10,094	16	11,394
1,000– 2,499	8	13,782	26	44,859	34	58,641
2,500– 4,999	7	20,077	31	109,392	38	129,469
5,000– 9,999	9	64,987	24	170,908	33	235,895
10,000–14,999	7	89,059	7	82,379	14	171,438
15,000–19,999	8	134,060	9	162,982	17	297,042
20,000–29,999	3	74,800	6	156,780	9	231,580
30,000–39,999	4	133,900	6	209,844	10	343,744
40,000–49,999	1	41,399	1	40,000	2	81,399
50,000–99,999	7	489,076	4	297,622	11	786,698
100,000 and over	3	398,000	3	717,187	6	1,115,187
Total	71	1,461,693	151	2,007,756	222	3,469,449

Source: Labour Canada, *Directory of Labour Organizations in Canada, 1984.* Reproduced by permission of the Minister of Supply and Services Canada.

A look at the names of the unions listed in Table 1–5 shows that unions appear to be of two types, those representing workers with a particular skill or occupation, such as carpenters or labourers, and those representing workers in a particular industry, such as the Steelworkers, or the Canadian Union of Public Employees. The former are called *craft* unions, while the latter are called *industrial* unions.

The differences between these two types of unions are historical in nature and will be more fully discussed in the next chapter. However, we can note here that the differences between the two union types are no longer as distinct as they once were. Originally, the craft unions restricted themselves to representing workers in a particular trade, and several craft unions could be (and still are on occasion) found even within a particular plant operation. The industrial unions attempted to organize *all* the workers in a plant, and indeed, within an industry, into a single union—regardless of the type of work that an individual performed. Now, many "craft" unions, such as the Machinists and the International Brotherhood of Electrical Workers (IBEW), operate at least partially on an industrial basis, representing all the workers in a given plant. Industrial unions, on the other hand, have organized workers in industries other than the one in which and for which they were founded.

The Federations

Of the 220 national and international unions in Canada, 124 are members of one of the five federations of unions. These 124 unions have about 75 percent of the union membership in the country. The federations are associations of unions

Table 1–5
Unions with 25,000 or More Members, 1984

	Membership
1. Canadian Union of Public Employees (CLC)	293,709
2. National Union of Provincial Government Employees (CLC)	242,286
3. Public Service Alliance of Canada (CLC)	159,646
4. United Steelworkers of America (AFL-CIO/CLC)	148,000
5. United Food and Commercial Workers (AFL-CIO/CLC)	140,000
6. International Union, United Automobile, Aerospace and Agricultural Implement Workers of America (CLC)	110,000
7. Social Affairs Federation (CNTU) (Fédération des affaires sociales (CSN)	93,000
8. International Brotherhood of Teamsters, Chauffeurs, Warehousemen and Helpers of America (Ind.)	91,500
9. Quebec Teaching Congress (Ind.) (Centrale de l'enseignement du Québec)	86,200
10. United Brotherhood of Carpenters and Joiners of America (AFL-CIO)	85,000
11. International Brotherhood of Electrical Workers (AFL-CIO/CFL)	72,927
12. International Association of Machinists and Aerospace Workers (AFL-CIO/CLC)	66,558
13. Service Employees International Union (AFL-CIO/CLC)	65,000
14. Canadian Paperworkers Union (CLC)	63,180
15. Labourers' International Union of North America (AFL-CIO)	59,310
16. International Woodworkers of America (AFL-CIO/CLC)	59,600
17. Quebec Government Employees Union (Ind.) (Syndicat des Fonctionnaires provinciaux du Québec)	55,241
18. United Association of Journeymen and Apprentices of the Plumbing and Pipe Fitting Industry of the United States and Canada (AFL-CIO)	41,399
19. Communications, Electronic, Electrical, Technical and Salaried Workers of Canada (CLC)	40,000
20. Alberta Teachers Association (Ind.)	37,381
21. National Federation of Building and Wood Workers Inc. (CNTU) (Fédération nationale des syndicats du bâtiment et bois Inc.) (CSN)	37,400
22. Canadian Brotherhood of Railway, Transport and General Workers (CLC)	37,389
23. Ontario Nurses Association (Ind.)	36,800
24. Ontario Secondary School Teachers Federation (Ind.)	36,072
25. Hotel and Restaurant Employees and Bartenders Union (AFL-CIO/CLC)	35,500
26. Energy and Chemical Workers Union (CLC)	32,000
27. American Federation of Musicians of the United States and Canada (AFL-CIO/CLC)	31,000
28. Federation of Women Teachers' Association of Ontario (Ind.)	30,232
29. Amalgamated Clothing and Textile Workers Union (AFL-CIO/CLC)	30,000
30. British Columbia Teachers Federation (Ind.)	29,780
31. Federation of Public Service Employees Inc. (CNTU) (Fédération des employés de services publics, Inc.) (CSN)	28,000
32. Retail, Wholesale and Department Store Union (AFL-CIO/CLC)	28,000
33. Hospital Employees Union, Local 180 (Ind.)	25,000

Source: Labour Canada, *Directory of Labour Organizations in Canada*, 1984.

that are essentially instruments for interunion cooperation and coordination and are not directly associated with the negotiation and administration of collective agreements. The federations make representations to various levels of government to attempt to influence the formation and administration of public policy. The federations help settle jurisdictional disputes — conflicts between two or more unions as to who will represent a group of employees or as to which employees will perform a certain type of work. Sometimes organizing drives are coordinated by a federation.

The largest and best known of the labour federations is the Canadian Labour Congress (CLC). In its present form, the CLC dates from the 1956 merger of the Trades and Labour Congress and the Canadian Congress of Labour. Details on the predecessor organizations and their merger can be found in Chapter 2. Over half of the union members in Canada are affiliated with the CLC. Figure 1–1 (page 10) shows the structure of the CLC.

As Figure 1–1 indicates, there is a federation of labour organizations chartered by the CLC in each province, e.g., the Ontario Federation of Labour. On a local basis, there are 123 labour councils such as the Vancouver and District Labour Council.

The second largest labour federation in Canada is the Confederation of National Trade Unions (CNTU), or to use its French name, the Confédération du Syndicats Nationaux (CSN). This federation was established in 1921 and is composed of unions which operate almost exclusively in Quebec. A second Quebec Federation, the Congress of Democratic Unions, or Centrale des Syndicats Démocratiques (CSD), is composed of unions which split from the CNTU in 1972 over the issue of political action and affiliation.

The Canadian Federation of Labour was founded in 1982 and is composed of a

Table 1–6
Union Membership by Congress Affiliation, 1983

Congress Affiliation	Membership	
	Number	Percent
CLC	2,013,050	56.5
AFL-CIO/CLC	851,341	23.9
CLC only	1,161,709	32.6
CNTU	213,370	6.0
AFL-CIO/CFL	213,301	6.0
CSD	56,826	1.6
CCU	38,684	1.1
AFL-CIO only	167,515	4.7
Unaffiliated International Unions	104,268	2.9
Unaffiliated National Unions	654,034	18.4
Independent Local Organizations	101,751	2.8
Total	3,562,799	100.0

Source: Labour Canada, *Labour Organizations in Canada 1983*, p. 19. Reproduced by permission of the Minister of Supply and Services Canada.

group of international unions — generally related to the building trades, which were suspended from the CLC in 1981 for withholding dues. The nature of this dispute is discussed more fully in Chapter 2.

The fifth federation in Canada is the small, nationalist federation called the Confederation of Canadian Unions. Table 1–6 presents a breakdown of the membership of the various labour federations.

Figure 1–1 (continued)
Canadian Labour Congress

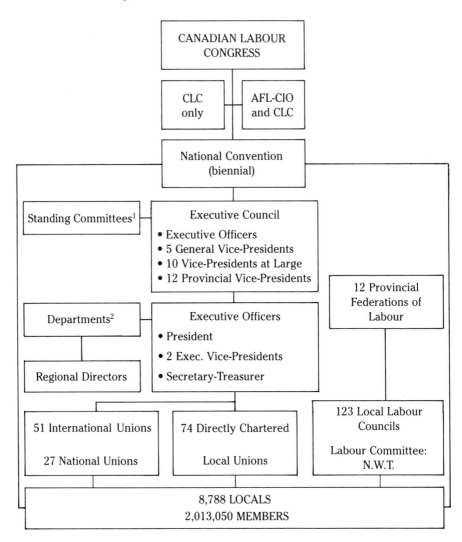

Source: Adapted from *The Current Industrial Relations Scene in Canada 1983*, W. D. Wood and Pradeep Kumar, eds. Kingston: Industrial Relations Centre, Queen's University.

Figure 1-1 (continued)

The U.S. labour federation is the AFL-CIO, which stands for American Federation of Labor — Congress of Industrial Organizations. This federation is a product of the merger of two federations in 1955, and is similar in nature and structure to the CLC. Many, but not all, of the international unions operating in Canada are members of both the CLC and the AFL-CIO. Some are members of one federation but not the other. For example, the United Electrical Workers (UE) are members of the CLC, but not of the AFL-CIO, while the Carpenters Unions are affiliated with the AFL-CIO but not with the CLC or any other Canadian Federation. Another large international union, the Teamsters, is not a member of either federation.

Employers and Their Organizations

The second set of "actors" in the industrial relations system are employers and their organizations. With a couple of notable exceptions, collective bargaining in Canada is conducted between a single employer and one or more unions. Roughly 80 percent of negotiations occur on this basis, with the majority occurring on a single-plant/single-union basis.[10] The notable exceptions to the single employer bargaining structure are the construction industry and the paper industry, where bargaining is generally done on an industry basis in Eastern and Western papermaking operations.

Where bargaining is done on an industry or provincial basis, the employer associations become important "actors" in the industrial relations system for the employers, as is the case, for example, with the Construction Labour Relations Association of British Columbia. Otherwise, employer associations have generally had a much lower profile with regard to labour relations than have the union federations. To be sure, organizations such as the Canadian Manufacturers Association, the Chamber of Commerce and the Canadian Federation of Independent Business speak out on labour relations and also do some research, but real decision making for employers is done at an enterprise level.

Given the data in the prior section on unions, and the above data on the single-site, single-employer nature of the bargaining structure, one obvious characteristic of collective bargaining in Canada (and in the U.S. as well) is its fragmented and decentralized nature. The nature of the North American industrial relations system in this sense is best seen in contrast to that in most of Western Europe where most of the key decisions are made centrally by government rather than by collective bargaining or by collective bargaining on a national basis (e.g., Sweden) or on industry basis (e.g., Germany). In North America, those decisions are made initially on an enterprise or single location basis. This extreme difference in structure may well account for the larger number of days lost due to strikes in Canada as compared to most of Western Europe. For a number of reasons, decentralized bargaining is likely to lead to more disputes than centralized bargaining; fewer disputes occur where terms and conditions of employment are set by government.[11]

Government

The third important member of the "actors" in the labour relations system is government. In the Canadian system, governments act both as employer and regulator, and this dual role makes government a very key player in the system. Under the Canadian Constitution the regulation of labour relations and employment in general is essentially the responsibility of the provinces. There is a federal jurisdiction, but it is relatively small in terms of the number of employees which are covered by federal regulations.

While the subject of labour legislation will be more fully explored in Chapter 3, we can note here that the governments have a role as "actors" in the labour relations system as the institution that establishes the basic parameters of the collective bargaining process via legislation. Through administrative agencies known as labour relations boards, the various pieces of legislation are administered, including most importantly the certification of unions as bargaining agents for groups of employees. The courts also serve as interpreters of legislation and final arbiters of the actions of administrative tribunals. Courts may also affect the behaviour of the parties through the use of injunctions, such as restricting the number of pickets during a strike.

The federal and provincial ministries of labour often play a major role in labour relations. They appoint conciliators and mediators to help resolve disputes arising during contract negotiations and at times arbitrators to resolve disputes over the application and interpretation of collective agreements. Minimum standards for wages, hours, and other conditions of employment are administered by the labour ministries and this activity often involves them in the workplace as do the activities of agencies such as human rights commissions, workmen's compensation boards, and occupational health and safety agencies.

ENVIRONMENTAL FACTORS

Every labour relations system operates in a context and is influenced by that context. The physical, economic, social, and political environments in which industrial relations systems operate help give them their unique characteristics. Changes in these environments often mean changes in the industrial relations system. As the world becomes more and more appropriately described as a "global village" the environmental factors of interest and concern to the participants in a labour relations system become global in nature. A complete discussion of environmental factors is not possible here, but some illustrations of various environmental factors and their impact on labour relations can begin to demonstrate the impact of these factors on the operation of the system.

Consider, for example, the physical environment, and one aspect of that environment, natural resources. At one time, a very high percentage of the world's nickel supply was mined and refined in Sudbury, Ontario. The discovery and development of other sources of nickel in other parts of the world have had a significant impact on the operation of the two major nickel companies in Sudbury, Inco and Falconbridge, and on labour relations in these companies. As another example, the availability of relatively inexpensive hydro-electric power in Quebec and British Columbia influences the location and international competitiveness of the aluminum industry which is concentrated in those locations. Finally, a climate in the Southern U.S. that contributes to the more rapid growth of trees for use in the manufacture of pulp and paper places Canadian producers at a relative competitive disadvantage and in turn influences the labour relations climate.

The economic environment is in many ways the most important of the sub-environments. The deep world-wide recession of the early 1980s meant extensive lay-offs, a reduction in dues-paying union members, pressure from employers to reduce costs through wage and work rule concessions, and an increased level of concern with job security in the workplace. Similarly, the effects of the high level of inflation experienced in the 1970s could be found in efforts to protect real incomes, chiefly via the increased use of cost of living adjustment clauses in collective agreements.

The size and dispersion of Canada's domestic market is an important factor in the nature of many of its economic institutions, as is its physical proximity to the U.S., which influences trading patterns and the importance of the relative competitiveness of its unit labour costs. The physical proximity of Canada to the U.S. was responsible for the presence of U.S. unions in Canada; consequently events in the U.S., such as developments in labour law, have been felt here. Presently, Canadian labour and employment law has become more adventuresome than that in the U.S. and we might well expect to see an increasing reverse flow of influence in the future.

A good example of what could be called a socio-economic environmental factor is the increased rate of participation by women in the labour force and the concomitant interest in women's rights. This is reflected in an increase in the number of union members who are women from 248,884 or 16.4 percent of union members in 1962 to 979,862 or 31 percent in 1981.[12] These changes are reflected in concerns for equality in pay and equal opportunity which can be seen in legislated requirements for "equal pay for equal work" and more recently "equal pay for work of equal value." The appointment of five special women vice-presidents by the CLC is a reflection of the changing sexual realities of the workplace, as is, in part, the rise to prominence of women labour leaders such as Grace Hartman and Shirley Carr.

In the early 1980s the change in the socio-political climate in the United States led to several important deregulatory changes in transportation and other industries. One of the results of the new competitive environment was reduction in wages for airline personnel, changes in work rules, and the development of a two-tier wage system in airlines and other forms of transport, all put into place with some severe stresses and strains via collective bargaining.

The incomes policies of the Federal Liberal government in 1975 for the economy as a whole with the attendant wage and price controls and the 6 and 5 controls program of the federal and most of the provincial governments in 1982 are perhaps the most vivid recent examples of how the political climate can affect labour relations.

IDEOLOGY

In Dunlop's industrial relations system model, ideology is defined as the glue that helps hold the system together. In Canada, the underlying political ideology is that of a parliamentary democracy. The dominant economic ideology is that of a mixed, regulated, capitalist, "free-enterprise" market-oriented economy, with all of the contradictions and tensions that this particular combination of words implies. The acceptance of these ideologies by the labour movement helps glue the system together. That acceptance, and the notion that unions ought to be chiefly oriented towards gains for their members at the bargaining table — of arguing about the relative size of the slices of pie rather than ownership of the pie — has been called "business unionism." This doctrine was first elaborated by Samuel Gompers, the first president of the AFL early in this century.

The espousal of the business unionism philosophy by North American unions is one of the distinguishing characteristics of the labour movement and the industrial relations system here. To be sure, Canadian unions are, in general, a little more militant and probably a little further to the left on the political spectrum than their U.S. counterparts. Some of the difference in political orientation can probably be attributed to the strong British tradition of the Canadian labour movement, and the Socialist history and orientation of that tradition. The adoption of the business unionism philosophy does not mean that labour in either Canada or the U.S. is adverse to political action. While unions can and do expect to make representations and to otherwise attempt to influence government, both federally and provincially, they can and do get involved directly in political action via support of political parties.

The traditional willingness of Canadian labour to deal with whatever government was in power was interrupted somewhat following the imposition of wage and price controls by the federal government in 1975. That move radicalized the relationship between the CLC and the federal government, and the following years were marked by a general refusal on the part of the CLC to deal with the federal government except in a fairly perfunctory manner and to refuse to cooperate with any government initiatives. The estrangement was broken somewhat in 1984 when the CLC agreed to participate in a federally funded productivity centre.

Historically, Canadian unions have shown more interest in affiliation with political parties than have their U.S. counterparts, where union support has tended to flow to candidates of the Democratic party. In 1921 the unions actually formed a party of their own, the Canadian Labour Party. However, many unions refused to participate, and the party was short-lived and unsuccessful.

Some unions, primarily industrial unions, affiliated with the Cooperative Commonwealth Federation (CCF) were instrumental in the formation of the New Democratic Party (NDP) in 1961. Some union members are directly affiliated with the party through their unions. However, this organizational support has not translated into rank-and-file support at the polls. Studies have consistently shown that in federal elections a majority of union members do not vote for NDP candidates. Provincially, the NDP has formed governments in only three provinces, and only one of them, British Columbia, can be considered to have a major industrial base and significant numbers of trade unionists. The NDP government of Dave Barrett in that province was short-lived. In Quebec the Parti Quebecois government was elected with strong support from the union movement in that province.

As was mentioned earlier, the political orientation of the CNTU caused the breakaway of some union groups to form the CSD. The split between the building trade unions and the CLC in 1981 no doubt reflected, at least indirectly, a more conservative political orientation on the part of the building trades unions than that prevalent in the CLC at the time.

THE WEB OF RULES

The outputs or results of the Canadian Industrial Relations System, or as Dunlop called them, the "Web of Rules" are many and, given the diversified and decentralized nature of the system, quite varied. The nature of the outputs and the way in which they are determined will be seen in later chapters and in fine detail in the case studies which follow. Developing an understanding of how labour relations systems function at an operational level is the basic intent of this book. The case studies, in particular, allow an examination of the system from a participant's view.

As a prelude to the detailed study of the system's operation, this final section will highlight some aspects of unions and management, and how they relate to each other, that are important in determining the nature and quality of the system's outputs.

The Nature of the Relationship

The basic day-to-day operational relationship between union and management can be characterized as a challenge-response process: union challenge and management response. There are three types of union challenge to management: the organizing challenge, the negotiating challenge, and the grievance challenge. The nature of the union challenge may be aggressively militant or quite non-militant. The nature of the management response can show similar variation. The exact nature of the challenge and the response is a function of how the parties use the power they have and how they relate to each other as organizations and as human beings. Given the variety possible in both the challenge and the response, the nature of the union management relationship can also show considerable variety.

Union management relationships can be arranged on a spectrum, as shown in Figure 1–2. The spectrum ranges from conflict to collusion, and any particular union-management relationship can be placed on this spectrum in relationship to certain key or benchmark relationships.[13]

Figure 1–2
The Spectrum of Union-Management Relations

	Containment–Aggression		Cooperation	
Conflict		Accommodation		

Conflict — In a relationship characterized as "conflict" the parties may be said to be engaged in a battle for survival. Both the challenge and the response are likely to be extremely militant. In this type of situation, management is strongly resisting the presence of a union in the workplace, and the union is responding in kind. Evidence of this kind of relationship is often found at the time when a union organizing attempt is underway or during some negotiations where management is attempting to break a strike, and, as a consequence, perhaps break the union.

Many of the activities which in earlier days used to characterize conflict relationships are now illegal: employer blacklists, yellow-dog contracts, the use of spies, or massive, violent picketing. The clarity of the law with regard to the fact that an employer must recognize and bargain with a union that can demonstrate that it represents the majority of employees and the repeated evidence that labour boards will take strong measures to enforce that law has largely discouraged extreme employer measures. However, those familiar with the Fleck Manufacturing and Radio Shack cases in Ontario will know that situations and relationships characterized as conflict can still be found.[14]

Containment-Aggression — In a relationship characterized as containment-aggression the parties tolerate the existence of one another — but just barely. In this type of relationship the union challenge and management response can be characterized as militant. Management acts in a way so as to minimize the degree of authority it shares with the union and to maximize the number of areas in which it can act unilaterally. In response, the union actively and aggressively works to increase the scope of its influence. This type of relationship tends to be very legalistic, and frequent recourse to arbitration is made in contract administration. Strikes are a frequent occurrence as contracts are negotiated. As an example of this type of relationship we can cite the relationship between Eastern Provincial Airlines and its pilots in the early 1980s which is a relationship that probably falls between conflict and containment on the spectrum.

Accommodation — Further along the spectrum is a relationship which is called accommodation. Here, while still watchful of their rights, the parties are actively attempting to adjust to (or accommodate) each other. This relationship is analogous to a lasting marriage; the parties are constantly adapting their relationship, although the relationship is not without the occasional "bad patch." The union and management are tolerant of each other, and the nature of both the challenge and the response can be described as moderate. Management tends to view the union as a channel of communication to employees rather than an obstacle. A fair amount of compromise characterizes the dealings of the parties in this type of relationship. The bargaining is conventional — for wages, benefits, working conditions — but management does not attempt to restrict the agenda for bargaining as it does under containment-aggression. Strikes can and do occur in accommodative relationships and there is recourse to arbitration in contract administration disputes, but the frequency of both is much lower than is the case with containment-aggression.

Cooperation — In a cooperative relationship the agenda for collective bargaining is very broad. It can include scheduling, prices, waste reduction, technological change, work measurement and methods analysis, and even such items as capital investment. In brief, the union and the workers it represents are seen as full partners in the enterprise. The orientation of both union and management is toward problem-solving. As a consequence, the relationship is non-legalistic. Formal grievances and strikes are rare. Companies and unions that have successfully adopted Scanlon Plans and other types of bonus and cost reduction or profit-sharing plans provide examples of cooperative relationships, as do sites where extensive quality-of-work-life efforts are in place. Although the number is probably growing, the number of union-management relationships that can be characterized as cooperative are relatively few.

Collusion — This final type of relationship is found where union and management are colluding to the detriment of another party. Sometimes those being harmed are the workers which the union supposedly represents. This type of unionism, known as "gangster" unionism or "predatory" unionism, is rare. The union (for a fee) signs a collective-bargaining agreement with the employer, and this effectively prevents another union from organizing employees (an existing contract is generally a bar to an organizing attempt). That agreement, called a "sweetheart contract," does not provide very significant benefits to the workers.

A legislative enquiry in Ontario in 1973 and 1974 heard testimony about union representatives receiving "payoffs" from companies in the Toronto construction industry to help ensure labour peace. These arrangements were similar to sweetheart agreements, and were, in many cases, extortion rackets masquerading as trade unions.

In another variant of a collusive relationship the union and the employer conspire to help themselves at the expense of other manufacturers and the general public. A classic case of this type of relationship occurred in New York City. There the union, the International Brotherhood of Electrical Workers, represented all the workers who installed and manufactured electrical equipment. The union workers refused to install any equipment not manufactured in New York City. This provided jobs for other union members and allowed the New York manufacturers to charge New York customers very high prices for the equipment. This practice was ruled illegal by the United States Supreme Court in a famous decision, "Allen Bradley Company v. Local No. 3, IBEW."[15]

There is probably no union-management relationship which fits neatly into one of the categories described above. Most collective bargaining relationships probably fall somewhere in between containment and accommodation. However, this brief enumeration shows that a variety of relationships are possible. The exact nature of the relationship is the responsibility of both union and management. Generally the parties get exactly the kind of relationship they deserve.

Other Factors — As the parties develop a relationship a number of factors which are under their control help influence that relationship. Four of these are particularly important in understanding labour relations and why certain outcomes occur. They will appear as factors in the cases which appear later in this book, and are identified here to provide some benchmarks for analyzing and understanding those cases.

Policy — Perhaps the most important determinants of the relationship between the parties are the policies adopted by union and management, or lack thereof. A policy is a statement as to how an organization will act in a given situation. While leaders of most organizations believe that their actions are policy-guided, those actions frequently are not, in fact, so guided. Actions are frequently impromptu and often made with short-run rather than long-run considerations in mind. Those companies with successful labour relations are successful because they manage by policy. The same is true for unions.

Management and the union face some fundamental policy decisions in their response to each other and to collective bargaining in general. What kind of a relationship do they want? How hard are they willing to work to achieve that relationship? In general, the tone of the relationship is the result of management initiative and not union initiative.

Both parties must make policy decisions concerning the content and administration of collective agreements. These decisions must encompass a host of specific subject areas, including wage payment systems, benefit level and structure, seniority systems and discipline. The parties must determine whether and to what extent they will use or resist pressure in the pursuit of their goals. Both sides must have implementing and procedural policies for translating their goals into action.

For example, management may decide to accept the union and to be "firm but fair" in dealing with it. In terms of discipline, this basic policy may give rise to a substantive policy of administering discipline for just cause. This policy may, in turn, be implemented by a policy of following a progressive disciplinary system. Detailed procedural policies would then follow to outline the specifics of the systems, such as the penalties associated with absenteeism.[16] A union could make a set of policies in the same way, policies which might include, for example, taking all discharge cases to arbitration.

History and Tradition — All union-management relationships must be viewed in a historical context. Even new relationships have a history that includes the union's organizational efforts and the response to them by the employer as well as the relationship between the employer and the employees prior to the establishment of the union.

The impact of history and tradition in a relationship can be seen in a number of ways. The parties may have a tradition of following certain wage settlements in other companies or industries in their own negotiations. Historically, certain work groups may have received a wage differential. Management may have responded only to the use of pressure tactics — wildcat strikes or slowdowns — by the union. Workers may traditionally have received a certain benefit, such as a coffee break or a Christmas bonus.

Insofar as history and tradition influence the parties' expectations about each other, rapid change cannot usually be accomplished without some upheaval. A company that has followed a set of policies designed to implement a containment-aggression relationship with the union could not logically expect to change that relationship to one of accommodation overnight. Mutual trust is earned over time.

Nature of Leadership — The personalities of leaders of both union and management and the type of leadership they provide are major determinants of a union-management relationship. Public focus on union leadership tends to be on those at the top of the heap, such as Dennis McDermott of the Autoworkers and the CLC, Robert White of the Autoworkers, Jean Claude Parrot of the Canadian Union of Postal Workers (CUPW), and John Freyer of the National Union of Provincial Government Employees (NUPGE). These are good examples of charismatic leaders who significantly influence relationships and events. Below the top level for both union and management are individuals who are equally responsible for shaping relationships. Those relationships are a function of their ability to relate to each other on a very personal basis, to sell their ideas, to lead their organizations. On a day-to-day basis, collective bargaining is an activity that is conducted between individuals, and the beliefs, attitudes, value systems, and abilities of those individuals influence outcomes very much.

Union Politics — The nature of leadership is particularly important within unions, because unions are democratic institutions. While the degree of democracy varies somewhat within unions, union officers must periodically stand for election and re-election. Officers who do not perform at a level consistent with the expectations of the membership face the prospect of opposition and defeat in the next election. Also, many unions require that new contracts be ratified by the membership before they become effective. In these instances, a membership dissatisfied with the deal their negotiators have made can reject it.

Within unions, special-interest groups may exist. This is particularly true of industrial unions where the goals and outlook of the skilled members such as electricians, or tool and die makers, may be different from those of the semi-skilled or non-skilled workers in the same local. Younger workers may have different interests than older workers. Female employees can at times be identified as a special-interest group. The union has the challenge of facing up to these often-conflicting demands of these special-interest groups in a manner that will satisfy the majority. Effective managers recognize the political pressures that union leaders and officers face and behave in a manner consistent with this reality.

Notes

1. John Mitchell, *Organized Labor*, Philadelphia American Book and Bible House, 1903, pp. 2–4.

2. John T. Dunlop, *Industrial Relations Systems*. New York: Holt, 1958.

3. Labour Canada, *Directory of Labour Organizations in Canada, 1983*. Ottawa: Minister of Supply and Services, 1983.

4. *The Current Industrial Relations Scene in Canada 1983*, W. D. Wood and Pradeep Kumar, eds. Kingston: Industrial Relations Centre, Queen's University, p. 241.

5. Labour Canada, *Working Conditions in Canadian Industry 1982*. Ottawa: Minister of Supply and Services, 1983, p. 102.

6. *Directory of Labour Organizations in Canada 1983*. P. 20.

7. Ibid.

8. *Labour Organizations in Canada, 1972*. Labour Canada, Economics and Research, p. xxv Table 3. Ottawa: Information Canada, 1973.

9. *Labour Organizations in Canada, 1983*.

10. John C. Anderson, "The Structure of Collective Bargaining," in *Union-Management Relations in Canada*, John Anderson and Morley Gunderson, eds. Don Mills, Ontario: Addison-Wesley, 1982, p. 179.

11. Roy J. Adams, "Industrial-Relations Systems in Europe and North America," in *Union-Management Relations in Canada*, pp. 469–72.

12. *Corporation and Labour Unions Act, Report for 1981, Part II Labour Unions*. Ottawa: Statistics Canada, 1983, p. 41.

13. Benjamin Selekman, Thomas Kennedy, Steven Fuller and John Baitsell, *Problems in Labor Relations*, Third Edition. New York: McGraw-Hill, Inc., 1965, pp. 1–11.

14. United Automobile Aerospace, and Agricultural Implement Workers of America (UAW) v. Fleck Manufacturing Company *et al.* LRB (Ontario). 78 CLLC, 16,159.

United Steelworkers of America v. Radio Shack (1980). LRB (Ontario). 80 CLLC, 16,003.

15. 252 U.S. 797 (1945).

16. Sumner H. Slichter, James J. Healy and E. Robert Livernish, *The Impact of Collective Bargaining on Management*. Washington, D.C.: The Broakings Institution, 1960, p. 880.

2

A CAPSULE HISTORY OF
CANADIAN LABOUR RELATIONS

A complete study of the development of the Canadian Industrial Relations System involves looking at the growth of the labour movement and its relationship to management in the context of the evolution of public policy and social and economic developments in Canada. This chapter will examine the growth and development of the Canadian labour movement and its often-stormy relationship with management, with only occasional references to labour legislation. Chapter 3 will examine the development of public policy. The two chapters, taken as a whole, should provide a basic framework for understanding how the industrial relations system has reached its current state of development.

EARLY HISTORY

The earliest recorded labour organization in Canada was a union of boot and shoe workers in Montreal in 1827, although there were probably antecedent organizations in Quebec and Nova Scotia. In the same year, the printers in Quebec formed a union, to be followed by those in Toronto in 1832 and in Hamilton and Montreal in 1833. These early unions were purely local associations, and the fact that they did not develop until the 1820s reflected the largely agricultural nature of the economy until that time.[1] Other early unions were formed in Ontario and Quebec among craft groups such as masons, carpenters, shipwrights, and coopers. Strikes of shoemakers and carpenters were reported in Toronto in the 1830s.[2]

The labour movement continued its slow growth into the 1850s on an exclusively local basis. By that time there were unions from coast to coast with coal miners organized — and striking — in British Columbia, and seal hunters organized in Newfoundland — and striking there as well. Shipwrights were organized in Victoria, B.C. and Newfoundland, and in Quebec, Halifax, and Saint John, New Brunswick.[3]

The first international unions made their appearance in Canada in the 1850s, when the British Amalgamated Society of Engineers established locals of machinists in Toronto, Hamilton, and Brantford in Ontario and in Montreal.[4] Beginning in 1871, the British Amalgamated Society of Carpenters and Joiners established locals in Toronto, Hamilton, Kingston, and St. Catharines. In 1861, the first U.S.-based international union, the Iron Moulders, appeared on the scene in Canada and established branches in Montreal, Toronto, Hamilton, London, and Brantford. This union was followed by the printers in 1865, and the Brotherhood of Locomotive Engineers in the same year.[5]

The Toronto Printers' Strike

The first real *association* of unions occurred in Toronto in 1871, when the Toronto Trades Assembly was formed. By 1872, there were 24 unions affiliated with the Assembly, which had set its sights on securing a nine-hour working day for workers.[6] Leading the way was the Toronto Typographical Society. In 1872 the printers represented by that society were working six days a week, ten hours a day, and decided on the following demands: "A week's work to consist of 54 hours, $10 per week, 25¢ per hour for job printers."[7]

Toronto's publishers, led by George Brown, editor of *The Globe and Banner*, and one of the fathers of Confederation, rejected the demand, stating that shorter hours were bad, that men would have more time to spend at home and would make a nuisance of themselves. The printers, in turn, went on strike.

Brown set out to break the strike. First he hired detectives to shadow the strikers. This resulted in several arrests on vagrancy charges and some trials on breach of contract charges wherein strikers were found guilty. Then Brown brought in strike breakers.

The next ten days provided the first real demonstration of labour solidarity in Canada's history. The Toronto Trades Assembly organized a Queen's Park demonstration for April 5 in order to rally the population against the employers. Trade unionists from the Iron Moulders, Bricklayers, Masons, Cigarmakers, Bakers, Machinists, Blacksmiths and many others joined together in a march along King Street to Yonge, north up Yonge Street to College, and west along College to Queen's Park. At Queen's Park 10,000 gathered and listened in apparent good spirits to a series of speeches — even while a snow storm began.[8]

The next day the employers struck back. They secured the arrest of the 24 members of the Printers Vigilance Committee, including John Armstrong, Vice-President of the Toronto Printers local and later president of the union, J. S. Williams, Toronto Trades Assembly Secretary, and Edward F. Clarke, later mayor of Toronto. Employers argued that the common law forbade combinations of labour, and Magistrate McNab agreed, finding all 24 guilty. He declared that they were members of an illegal body, a combination in restraint of trade.

News of the arrests and subsequent trial spread rapidly, and on April 17 around 4,000 persons gathered in Market Square. Excitement was high as speakers condemned the arrests and called for political action.

Meanwhile, in Ottawa Conservative Prime Minister Sir John A. Macdonald saw this as a chance to embarrass his political opponent, George Brown, and, perhaps, gain some votes in the federal elections which would take place in several months. On Thursday, April 18, Macdonald introduced emancipating legislation called the Trade Union Act which provided that combining to increase wages or to lower hours was not a conspiracy and did not violate the common law.

The employers were furious, but Macdonald's action, coupled with the persistence of the unions, resulted in substantial victories for the nine-hour movement. The Toronto Printers won their demands as did those in Hamilton. Later that year the Great Western Railway signed an agreement for "54 hours a week at 58½ hours pay," and the Grand Trunk Railway at Montreal instituted the nine-hour day and granted a general pay increase.

The Canadian Labour Union (CLU)

Following the Toronto Printers' strike of 1872 Canada's first trade union centre, The Canadian Labour Union (CLU), was born. The CLU was partly a product of worker solidarity demonstrated in Toronto. It was also a product of Confederation.

Confederation, in 1867, was a response to the fact that Canada's political structure had been unable to cope with the country's expanding economic forces. Railways and canals were needed, and dollars were needed to build them. In addition, there was a desire for greater independence from Britain and the United States. Confederation was followed by territorial unification brought about largely through railway building. Progress was swift, but there were serious shortcomings. Many of the immediate benefits went to large companies based in Toronto and Montreal, and inequities for employers and workers in other parts of the country were great. Thus there were moves to create a centralized labour movement to try to deal with those inequities.

Hamilton, Ontario trade unionists pioneered the movement, and on May 3, 1872 they hosted a conference of union delegates from Toronto, Brantford, and Montreal. This was probably Canada's first labour convention and resulted in the formation of the CLU. A follow-up convention was held in Toronto on September 23 at which a constitution was adopted with a preamble as follows:

> The working men of the Dominion of Canada, in common with intelligent producers of the world, feel the necessity of cooperation and harmonious action to secure their mutual interests and just compensation for their toil, and such limitation of the hours of labor that may tend to promote their physical and intellectual well being.[9]

The convention took up problems of shorter hours, immigration, convict and child labour, and organization of the unorganized. Rules of the CLU provided for annual meetings, with delegates elected from the unions. Per capita dues were fixed at 5 cents quarterly per member in the case of a directly chartered local and 50 cents per member for affiliated unions.[10]

The formation of the CLU, coupled with labour's victories in the nine-hour struggles, suggested that the labour movement in Canada was on the threshold of significant advances on behalf of the country's working population. However, this was not the case. Forty-one years later, in 1913, the labour movement had succeeded in organizing less than ten percent of the country's workers, contrasting sharply with Britain and Germany where over 22 percent of the working population had been organized. Predominant among the reasons for labour's slow growth in Canada were the following: (a) encumbering legal status, (b) confusions in the ideology of the movement, (c) a problem of public image, and (d) severe employer resistance.

(a) LEGAL STATUS OF UNIONS

The Trade Union Act of 1872 permitted groups of workers to join together for higher wages and lower hours. However, the government put another law on the statute books at the same time — The Criminal Law Amendment Act. This provided penalties for violence or intimidation during organizing campaigns and strikes; in addition, it provided that a union-management contract was not enforceable in a court of law. Soon thereafter, in 1873, a member of the Knights of St. Crispin, an early industrial union of shoemakers which operated in the U.S. and Canada, was arrested on a conspiracy charge under the Criminal Law Amendment Act for engaging in a strike. This was followed by more arrests and jail sentences, giving rise to demands by labour that the Act be repealed.

Unions were inhibited by the almost total absence, till World War II, of legislation protecting the right to organize and, once organized, to require employers to bargain. Social legislation was almost as slow in coming. Canada's first workmen's compensation bill was enacted in 1914 in the Province of Ontario. The first Unemployment Insurance Act was passed in 1940. There were no laws providing for old-age pensions or widows' allowances until World War II.

Instances of exploitation of women and children were rampant throughout the country. Two Royal Commissions, one in 1881, another in 1887, were appointed to inquire into conditions. They subsequently published reports of children working through the night in a glass factory, of a child of 8 toiling in a cotton mill earning wages of $92 a year, of brutal beatings without reasons, and of unjust fines. The worst instance of unjust fines may have been reached in one tobacco plant when a boy of 14 who had worked 40 hours for $1.60 was fined $1.75 and so ended up owing the company 15 cents. The boy's father saw no future in this business and demanded the fine be returned, but to no avail.[11]

Probably the principal reason for legislative inaction regarding social conditions was the continuing conflict of power between the federal and provincial governments. The federal government was reluctant to act on social matters, because there was general feeling that it lacked jurisdiction. As a result the responsibility fell on provincial governments, and they were slow to act. In 1880, Ontario adopted an Act regulating the hours of labour, but did not cover shops with fewer than 20 people, the places where abuses were most prevalent. Furthermore, no inspectors were appointed to enforce the Act until two years later, and no case of violation was brought to the courts for two more years.[12]

In Quebec, progress was even slower. In 1885 that province passed a Factory Act prohibiting labour for women and children beyond 12½ hours a day or 72 hours per week. Employment of boys under 12 and girls under 14 was prohibited, but provision for inspection was never made, so that violations continued virtually unchecked.[13]

(b) IDEOLOGY

Through the years the labour movement was consistently thwarted by confusion and disagreement about matters of ideology. Principal among the ideological issues were these two:
  —International vs national unions
  —Craft vs industrial organization

1. International Unionism[14]

Until the 1860s the labour movement in Canada had been almost exclusively Canadian. Then, in 1861, there was a significant move among some of the craft organizations to affiliate with U.S. unions. Among the crafts involved were the moulders and printers. The term "international union" referred almost exclusively to unions operating in both the United States and Canada, but nowhere else. In early years the relationship was fraternal; later it became a relationship of U.S. domination that transcended individual unions and influenced the development of national-level confederations.

There were many reasons for the early affiliation of Canadian unions with those in the U.S. The most important reasons were the following:
1. *The underdeveloped condition of the Canadian economy*, which gave rise to the desire of many Canadians to go to the United States for jobs. The union card helped. Before 1900 there was essentially unrestricted movement across the Canada–U.S. border.[15]
2. *Solidarity.* In the mid-1800s it was natural for members of crafts to seek out their own. At that time craft production was far more important than industrial production, so that members of a trade who wanted a strong union looked to members of the same trade in other locations rather than to members of other trades or unskilled workers in their own location. Most tradesmen, like carpenters, bricklayers, and painters, were relatively isolated, and their Canadian members were few. It made sense to become stronger by joining a larger organization of the same trades in the United States.
3. *Money.* Joining a large organization with more members paying dues meant greater financial security in the form of strike assistance in case of a bargaining impasse.
4. *Interflow of the United States and Canadian economies.* U.S.-dominated and U.S.-owned businesses were encouraged to set up operations in Canada in order to help develop the economy and create jobs. Many did so because of

the great supply of cheap natural resources and the availability of cheap labour. Labour and management both sought consistency in their relationships, and the presence of the same union in both countries was a comfortable means toward that end.

The merits of international unionism have provided subject matter for interminable debate. Some say it was a prime factor in speeding the growth of the Canadian trade union movement which, in turn, contributed to the rapid growth of the economy in general. Others say it impeded development of a national image; that for Canada a politically oriented, socialist-inclined, industrial form of unionism would have contributed to more rapid growth and a self-sufficient, individualistic economy.

These arguments will continue without resolution. However, it can safely be said that the international union setup was the most important single factor contributing to the nearly identical development of the U.S. and Canadian labour movements. In 1902, for example, the Trades and Labour Congress (TLC), Canada's oldest continuous labour organization, bowed to the wishes of the American Federation of Labor (AFL) and Samuel Gompers, AFL's president, in three actions at its Berlin (Kitchener), Ontario convention. In the first instance the convention refused to seat delegates from the Montreal Federated Trades Council, lifted that council's charter, and seated instead AFL-endorsed members. Then the convention adopted an amendment to the TLC constitution by a vote of 89 to 35 not to recognize a national union in a jurisdiction where an international union existed. This effectively excluded the Knights of Labor, an industrial organization whose membership included many different crafts. The Knights, who had been founded in the United States in 1869, were geared to unskilled workers and tended to organize on a plant, rather than craft, basis. This was directly contrary to the philosophy of the AFL, a craft-oriented organization. In 1886 the Knights had combined with various Canadian craft unions to form the TLC, thus making it an all-inclusive organization.

The TLC's action of 1902 was not only a stab in the back to the Knights but also represented one of the most important events in Canadian labour history, because this, the country's largest, most influential labour organization, had made a clear choice in favour of U.S. domination and abandoned, for the time being, one of its original reasons for being. This was punctuated by the convention's third act — the election of John Flett as president. Mr. Flett was a paid officer of an international union.[16] Because of the strength of the Knights of Labor in Quebec, some feel that the actions of 1902 were responsible for the ultimate development of a Quebec labour movement which was largely separate from that of the rest of the country.[17]

In 1938 the TLC made another decision which confirmed domination by the U.S.-based AFL. This involved expulsion of members affiliated with the Committee on Industrial Organization (CIO). In three years, Canadian union membership had increased from 280,648 in 1935 to 383,492 in 1937, the latter figure representing an all-time high for Canada. These increases were due largely to efforts of the CIO which had undertaken organization of the unorganized on an industry basis, spurred considerably by the depression of the 30s and a highly permissive political climate under U.S. President Franklin D. Roosevelt's New Deal. The CIO's efforts in the United States had carry-over effects into Canada.

The CIO was formed in 1935 when a large number of AFL affiliates, including the United Mine Workers of America, the International Typographical Union, and the Amalgamated Clothing Workers, split off from the AFL as a result of a convention fight. The fight centred on the issue of whether member unions should have the right to organize on an industrial basis. (The letters CIO originally stood for Committee on Industrial Organization; later they reflected the organization's success and a name change to Congress of Industrial Organizations). John L. Lewis, President of the United Mineworkers, led the fight, and the whole thing was brought to a head when at one point in the convention, Lewis walked across the floor and punched William Hutcheson, President of the United Brotherhood of Carpenters and Joiners, in the face. Lewis subsequently played a leading role in the formation of the Steelworkers Organizing Committee (SWOC) in a unionization drive against the major steel companies. Several new unions were formed as a result of the CIO's efforts. These included the United Steel Workers of America (USW), the United Automobile Workers of America (UAW), and the United Electrical, Radio and Machine Workers of America (UE).

In 1936 the AFL Executive Council suspended the CIO unions on grounds that they were fostering "dual unionism." Finally, in 1937, they were expelled. Throughout the 1930s the two organizations competed aggressively for members without particular regard for craft or industrial distinctions. By 1937 the CIO faction actually exceeded the AFL in membership by close to 300,000. In 1938 the CIO held a convention and formed a new federation, the Congress of Industrial Organizations. The first president of the organization was John L. Lewis.

CIO unions which were most active in Canada during the late 30s and early 40s were the USW and the UE. These and others, including national unions directly chartered by the TLC, were responsible for a dramatic increase in Canadian and TLC union membership, so that by 1948 there were 977,594 unionized workers in the country. In 1937 the CIO set up its first office in Canada, located in Toronto. At the same time the AFL was bringing pressure on the TLC executive council to follow the AFL's action of 1937 and expel all CIO affiliates. In the 1937 convention, TLC rejected the AFL's stance. However, in December of 1938 TLC's executive council met with the AFL executive council and was told that further delays in expulsion of CIO unions would almost certainly lead to the destruction of the TLC, because AFL unions would withdraw. TLC promptly suspended the CIO unions, thus depriving themselves of 11 international unions with around 22,000 members and succumbing once again to pressure from U.S. union headquarters.

Like the 1902 expulsion of the Knights of Labor, the TLC's 1938 action was an important crossroads decision in Canadian union life. In 1940 the 11 expelled unions joined the All-Canadian Congress of Labour, till then a small, relatively unimportant rival of TLC. At the 1940 convention the All-Canadian Congress constitution was changed, and a new name was adopted — the Canadian Congress of Labour (CCL). The CCL became the Canadian counterpart of the CIO.

The Canadian labour movement briefly asserted its sovereignty and independence in 1948 as a result of the Canadian Seamen's Union dispute, but soon after
that it reverted to its former pattern of U.S. domination and determinism. The
circumstances of the Seamen's dispute follow:

In December 1937 the AFL created the Seafarer's International Union (SIU) in
order to compete for bargaining rights on seagoing vessels with the National
Maritime Union (NMU), a CIO affiliate. The AFL convention ruled that SIU had
jurisdiction over seamen and fishermen in all waters of North America and
Canada. TLC's president, Percy Bengough, objected, telling AFL's president,
William Green, that this would create a dual representation situation, because
the Canadian Seamen's Union (CSU) had been chartered by that organization in
1936 and represented the same people as the SIU would represent.

While Green and Bengough bickered, Pat Sullivan, CSU president and TLC
secretary-treasurer, unexpectedly resigned both posts and organized another
union — the Canadian Lake Seamen's Union. Although they had contracts with
the CSU, Canadian ship owners signed a contract with Sullivan's union. This
caused a strike by the CSU, whose jurisdiction was confirmed by a federal
government commission. The strike started in June of 1948. The companies, in
turn, let loose violence on CSU members, bringing in gangsters and others to act
as strike breakers. This caused the TLC to call a mass trade union conference in
Ottawa to support the CSU. However, a group of Roadmen — full-time Canadian
vice-presidents of international unions — set up picket lines at the entrance to
the conference hall and subsequently told members of the press that the meeting was composed of 98 percent Communists and two percent fellow travellers.
The Roadmen were supporting SIU's entrance into the Canadian scene and
looked upon the Sullivan-CSU clash as an opening for them to wedge their way
into the picture.

On September 10, 1948, the executive council of TLC, its patience exhausted,
condemned the action of the Roadmen and suspended the Brotherhood of
Railway and Steamship Clerks (BRSC) whose leader, Frank Hall, was one of the
principal Roadmen.

BRSC's suspension was one of the important issues presented at the September 1948 TLC convention. BRSC had sponsored the SIU in spite of the clause in
TLC's constitution prohibiting affiliation of unions whose jurisdiction clashed
with existing affiliates. When a vote on the issue was taken the executive
council won support 545–198, indicating that in many cases the Roadmen were
not supported by their own delegates.[18]

After the convention the TLC executive council met with its AFL counterpart.
The AFL proposed revision of TLC's constitution so as to permit "each interna-
tional union to deliver a block vote at the convention through its Roadmen." The
TLC flatly refused, and on its return issued the oft-quoted statement; "Cooperation,
Yes, Domination, No!". Finally, the TLC had asserted its independence.

But the new-found independence of the Canadian labour movement was
short-lived, because in 1949 some strong-arm tactics by the AFL brought matters back into their former perspective. The scene was eastern Canada. Late in
1948 Canadian deep-sea shipping companies took a severe bargaining stance

with the CSU. They imposed a wage cut ranging from $20 to $50 a month and abolished the union hiring hall. The CSU, 6,500 strong, voted to strike, and the companies countered by terminating bargaining relationships with the CSU and signing contracts with the SIU. The SIU had virtually no Canadian members at the time, so it was glad to get anything and accepted the proposed wage cuts.

This represented collaborative action by the SIU and employers against an established Canadian union, a member of the TLC and certified by the Canada Labour Relations Board as the bargaining representative for the companies involved. On March 1, 1949, CSU picket lines in Halifax were broken by goons who boarded a Canadian National steamship and fired on the picket line from the ship. Eight striking seamen were injured.

CSU retaliated and by May of 1949 they had tied up ports around the world — in Great Britain, Western Europe, Latin America, Africa, and New Zealand. A sympathy stoppage in England by 50,000 dockers tied up 121 ships there for 74 days. Meanwhile the TLC, under severe pressure from its international union members, suspended the CSU, charging them with preventing members of affiliated unions from performing their normal work, therefore violating the sanctity of the contract. Less than one year after the "Cooperation, Yes, Domination, No!" doctrine was proclaimed, it died.[19]

2. Craft vs. Industrial Organizations

The ideological battle between those who favoured organization according to crafts and those favouring multicraft organization in single companies or industries has pervaded North American labour history since the early 1870s when the Knights of St. Crispin flourished in Canada. In the 1880s the Knights of Labor emerged. They were far bigger and more important than the Knights of St. Crispin, because they represented workers in many different industries. By 1886 the Knights of Labor had at least 158 local organizations in Canada and about 1,200 members. They were strongest in Quebec and Ontario, but their membership extended as far west as Nanaimo on Vancouver Island.

The Knights of Labor survived longer in Canada than in the United States, but their demise in both countries came about for the same reasons: too-rapid growth, vacillating leadership, and acceptance of nearly everyone as members, including radicals, socialists, and anarchists. The latter became involved in strikes and demonstrations of violence which not only served to give the Knights a poor image but quickly drained whatever financial strength the organization had built.

Chicago was a special Knights stronghold, and a major test for them occurred in the year 1886 as a result of the Haymarket Square riot. In that year the eight-hour movement was sweeping the United States. On May 1 upwards of 38,000 workers in Chicago staged a general strike in support of the movement. One company, McCormack Harvester, brought in Pinkerton guards and strikebreakers. On May 3 the strikers and strikebreakers clashed, bringing police to the scene. The subsequent fighting resulted in the deaths of four persons and 20 injuries. On May 4 a great protest meeting was held in Haymarket Square. More than 3,000 attended, including Chicago's mayor. Contrary to expectations the meeting was peaceful, and participants were dispersing when a detachment of 200 of Chicago's police arrived. Someone threw a bomb; the police fired. Eventually seven policemen were killed, 67 were injured. Four workers were killed and more than 50 were injured. The persons responsible were not immediately known, so the police combed the city for suspects. Eventually eight known anarchists were arrested and charged with murder. In an atmosphere of frenzy and fear they were immediately found guilty. Seven were sentenced to death, the eighth to 15 years imprisonment. There had been no evidence presented at the trials to connect the men with the bombing. In fact, all eight were pardoned six years later by Illinois Governor Peter Altgeld. However, when Terrence Powderly, leader of the Knights, was asked by a reporter for his reaction following the trial, Powderly said "The men are entitled to no more consideration than wild beasts." In taking this kind of position, Powderly put a knife into the back of the Chicago strike leaders, the eight-hour movement, and his own organization. With stronger leadership and discipline, the Knights might have emerged as the dominant labour force in North America. Instead they gradually faded away.

The industrial vs craft dispute came to the fore again following World War I. At that time there was industrial unrest and radicalization among workers, manifested, in part, by the emergence of several new movements. One such movement came from the 1918 TLC convention. Here delegates from the western provinces put forth a strong case for shifting the focus of the organization in order to promote industrial and Canadian unionism. They were summarily rebuffed, so following the convention they held a caucus of their own. This resulted in the Western Canada Labour Conference in March of 1919. Delegates to that conference agreed on a resolution which recommended severance of affiliation with international organizations and formation of an industrial organization. They called themselves the One Big Union (OBU).[20]

The terms of the conference resolution were ambiguous on two counts. It was not clear whether there should be secession from international unions, nor was it clear what attitude would be taken toward political action. Alberta's delegation had put forth a resolution calling for a united political party; however, the prevailing attitude on this score was, apparently, negative.

As preparations went forward to conduct a referendum regarding the Western Canada Labour Conference resolution, the Winnipeg General Strike began.[21] While the OBU did not start the strike they were active in it and reaped considerable strength from their involvement in it.

The Winnipeg General Strike reflected the general unrest which followed the war. It was not confined to Winnipeg but, at one point, became an interlocked general strike movement based in Winnipeg and extending west and east across Canada. The unrest was caused by the following factors: troops were returning from the War at the rate of 3,400 per month; unemployment rates were high; employers and landlords were basking in high profits from the War. The Canadian government had not released workers interned for antiwar activity but had rescinded its ban on free speech and free assembly. There were demands for the government to cut living costs and curb profiteers, all as part of a growing dissatisfaction with the social system. A kind of native Canadian socialism was developing which paralleled, in some respects, the Russian revolution of 1917.

The strike itself was set off as a result of a refusal by Winnipeg employers to deal with a newly formed metal trades council. The council was a conglomerate of various metal trades workers who had joined together to fight economic grievances. Their members at the time were earning $12 to $15 a week; but $1 in 1919 would buy only what 25 cents had bought before the war. A great number of immigrants were members of the council, many with strong socialist convictions.

The strike started on May 15 with these principal demands:
1. Recognition of the council,
2. an eight-hour day and a 44-hour (maximum) week,
3. double-time pay for overtime and one hour premium pay for nightshift work, and
4. 85 cents per hour for skilled workers and 25 cents for apprentices.

Within 48 hours, 35,000 persons in a city of 200,000 had succeeded in halting all construction and production. In addition, they froze all forms of transportation and communication. Hotels, banks, and most large buildings were closed and the supply of retail goods and food was sharply reduced.

The strike was administered by a Central Strike Committee consisting of 287 delegates, three from each of 94 union locals plus five from TLC. The principal role of delegates was to decide what industrial and civic activities would be allowed to continue during the strike and provide for essential services and supplies. They were to report back daily to their organizations.

Employers joined with governments at three levels (municipal, provincial, and federal) in order to end the strike. The mayor and the majority of Winnipeg council members were hostile, as were Premier Norris of Manitoba and Prime Minister Robert Borden. Borden, reflecting his fear that anarchy might prevail, said that this was an attempt at revolution — that public servants had no right to strike.

The federal government dispatched Royal Canadian Mounted Police to Winnipeg, and they were followed on May 22 by a battalion of troops and two Lewis machine guns. On May 25 the federal government ordered postal workers back to work and required them to sign an agreement never to stage a sympathetic strike in the future and to disaffiliate with the Winnipeg Trades and Labour Council. The provincial government delivered an identical ultimatum to telephone workers. The municipal government ordered police and firemen back to work, subject to dismissal. Postal workers and police defied the orders and, on June 9, 190 postal workers and all members of the police force were fired. Police were replaced the same day by around 2,000 "specials," an untrained, undisciplined group, some with police records. When they made their first appearance the specials, who had been cast in the role of strike-breakers, clashed with strikers. Soon a battle erupted, with strikers and ex-servicemen on one side and specials and RCMPs on the other. Antagonists hurled bottles, brickbats, and ashcan covers at each other. The specials proved to be inferior fighters and some were hit on the head with their own clubs.

On June 17 the main strike leaders were arrested. Rev. William Ivens, one of the leaders of the strike and editor of *The Strike Bulletin*, said the RCMP had descended on his home and dragged him away in the middle of the night while his children stood by crying. The leaders were hastily taken to the Stony Mountain Penitentiary. Bail was refused. This aroused militant action across Canada in defence of the strikers. Demonstrations took place in locations from Cape Breton to Vancouver Island. On June 20, the strike leaders were released, having spent 72 hours in jail. That afternoon a large crowd gathered near the city hall, including women, children, and exservicemen. The mayor read the Riot Act. At 2:30 p.m. approximately 50 mounted men, about half in red coats, half in khaki, approached the crowd swinging baseball bats. The crowd opened ranks and let them through. They stopped short, reversed direction and returned. On their return they were met by hisses, boos and a barrage of stones. With that, RCMPs and specials attacked, charging into the crowd firing revolvers. Two were killed, 30 injured. Winnipeg was placed under military control, and over 100 persons were arrested.

On June 26 the metal trades people went back to work. Others followed, but thousands were locked out, blacklisted, dismissed or otherwise discriminated against.

Aside from a compromise agreement on hours of work (from 55 a week to 50) the unions failed to attain any of their objectives, and losses were enormous. However, the Winnipeg General Strike had an important effect on Canadian labour history. It proved the folly of any general strike against the public in a free society as a means to get higher wages and fringes or improved working conditions. General strikes are most likely to be successful if their purpose is confined to dramatizing poor conditions; however, as soon as members of the public are inconvenienced by virtue of deprivation or discomfort the issue is complicated.

In a general strike the target is almost never frozen. The Winnipeg strike brought home that lesson, loud and clear. It pointed up the need for a strong union movement equipped to exercise economic power in selected situations on a case-by-case basis, and it provided strong impetus to the growth of the One Big Union. By the end of 1919 the OBU had 41,000 members, with 100 locals, eight central labour councils and two district boards, mostly in Western Canada. However, OBU had acquired a legacy during the Winnipeg General Strike which was eventually responsible for its undoing. This legacy involved an image of radicalism and revolution and subjected the organization to unreasonable resistance by employers, government and international unions. By 1921, its membership was less than 5,300, and it ceased to be a major force. In 1956, it was largely confined to a few local unions in Winnipeg, and what was left of it became part of the Canadian Labour Congress, CLC. Possibly the OBU had been a victim of the calendar, born one year too soon.

Between 1902 and 1967 eight trade union centres associated with international unions functioned in Canada alongside the TLC and, after 1940, the CCL. These included the One Big Union, the National Trades and Labour Congress of Canada, the Canadian Federation of Labour, the All-Canadian Congress of Labour, the Workers Unity League, the Canadian Congress of Labour, and the Federation of Catholic Workers of Canada (FCWC). All arose in connection with the revolt against international union domination and employer-union collaborations, and all were concerned with the issue of craft vs industrial organization.

Throughout the late 1930s and World War II, the crafts vs industrial issue became blurred. It was clear to both the AFL in the U.S. and the TLC in Canada that efforts of the CIO and CCL were reaping huge rewards through industrial organization, so they decided to compete. Union membership statistics in Canada show the results: 383,492 in 1937, 711,117 in 1945, 832,697 in 1946, 912,124 in 1947, and 977,594 in 1948. The AFL and TLC were organizing both crafts and industries; CIO and CCL were doing the same. Rival unions staged bitter fights for members as unions engaged in considerable raiding and crossing of each others' picket lines. This was especially prevalent in the building trades. Finally, in the early 50s, the going got tougher. The rate of growth in union membership had begun to decline in the United States during the war and in Canada in the late 1940s. During 1954 total union membership in Canada and the U.S. remained virtually unchanged from 1953. It seemed clear that hitherto rival organizations would have to cease fighting each other and pool their resources if they hoped to extend their organization efforts.

In June 1954, the AFL and CIO, under new presidents, George Meany and Walter Reuther, signed a two-year no-raiding pact. They had come to realize that the widely prevailing union piracy and consequent jurisdictional disputes had been a fruitless and costly exercise. By 1955, some 80 of the 110 AFL unions and 31 of the CIO's 33 unions had ratified the no-raiding agreement. Meanwhile the two federations operated a joint unity committee with Meany and Reuther playing dominant roles. There were also movements among some of the rival CIO and AFL international unions to consolidate. Then with apparent suddenness, on February 8, 1955, the joint committee announced that full agreement had been reached for the AFL and CIO to merge.

George Meany was elected president of the new organization, which then had a membership of over 15 million organized workers. Except for a statement by the president of the National Association of Manufacturers that the merger "should be outlawed" and an occasional expression of conservative fears that it would mean a labour monopoly, even the organs of the business community endorsed the move and expressed the belief that it would lead to greater industrial peace. The Wall Street Journal expressed the belief that the merger would not enhance the monopoly status of labour, and Nation's Business, while suggesting that it might mean "a political powerhouse," pointed out its potential advantage for industry in reducing the incidence of jurisdictional disputes.[22]

In April of 1956 the two principal rival federations of Canada also merged, forming the Canadian Labour Congress (CLC). The CLC brought together 111 international unions and 322 federal locals with a total membership of more than one million. Approximately 300,000 workers remained outside the CLC: 200,000 in independent, non-affiliated locals and 100,000 in the Confédération des Travailleurs Catholiques du Canada (CTCC). Then, in September, delegates to the CTCC convention voted to affiliate with CLC.[23] The affiliation never occurred as negotiations to merge the two federations failed.

Thus began an era in North American labour relations characterized by a shift of focus. The organizational activities and political manoeuvring continued, but raiding essentially stopped, and the principal attention of the union organizations switched to improvement of wages and working conditions for existing members.

In Canada, the birth of the CLC marked the beginnings of a truly independent labour movement. Although he was later to act as though he had never spoken these words, George Meany, as a guest of the CLC founding convention, called the organization a "free independent trade union centre for Canada. . . ."[24] The words proved prophetic. The CLC was an early proponent of the recognition of the Peoples Republic of China and its admission to the United Nations. The CLC also strongly condemned U.S. Policy in Vietnam in the 1960s. Both of these actions were in complete contrast to the Policies of the AFL-CIO.[25]

The rise of national unions in Canada was noted in Chapter 1, as was the fact that the majority of Canadian union members were members of the national rather than international unions. This reality has tended to support the independent stance of the CLC. Nevertheless, some residual of the historical friction between the CLC and the AFL-CIO, as well as that between craft and industrial unions and national and international unions remains. The most visible reminder of the past was the split between the craft oriented and international construction trade unions and the CLC in 1981. Ten of the thirteen unions suspended from the CLC formed the Canadian Federation of Labour in 1982. These unions were suspended because of their failure to pay dues. The dues were withheld because of a dispute between these unions and the CLC over voting at CLC conventions where each delegate has one vote rather than a vote proportional to the total membership of his or her union. At CLC conventions each local union affiliated with the congress is entitled to representation. The construction trades unions believed that these features of the CLC convention structure reduced their power and unfairly increased the power of large public sector unions like CUPE with many locals.

Also at issue was the chartering of a rival building trades construction department in Quebec by the Quebec Federation of Labour in 1981, which included a group which broke away from the IBEW over a pension-fund dispute. The CLC, despite protests from the building trades unions, refused to interfere in the matter. In the background were lingering problems over jurisdictional issues between the building trades and the Steelworkers and Woodworkers in British Columbia, and discomfort among the building trades over the political partisanship of the CLC in its alliance with the NDP and the nationalistic stance of some of the CLC unions.[26]

The constitution of the Canadian Federation of Labour reflected these concerns. It provided for proportional representation at the federation's conventions and committed the CFL to a non-partisan political stance.

At the time of the split, the CLC threatened to set up its own national building trades unions, but by 1984 had not done so. The federal government recognized the CFL, giving it, as well as the CLC, seats on the board of the national productivity centre established in 1984. There appeared to be an uneasy truce between the two federations, and the potential for future craft union versus industrial union disputes remained.

(c) PROBLEMS OF PUBLIC IMAGE

Labour's struggles were fraught with instances of violence which almost always were blamed on labour. No matter that self-serving interest groups tended to latch onto the labour movement as a convenient forum for airing their views and that members of these groups often provoked violence.[27] No matter that labour encountered repeated instances of hostility from employers, governments and the press. The fact remained that the labour movement was often equated in the public's mind with radicalism, strikes, violence and intimidation. For example, while only .36 percent of estimated working time was lost in strikes in the turbulent decade of the 1970s, the public hears considerably more about strikes and threatened strikes than about peaceful settlements. While all but a few strikes each year are conducted peacefully and without any hint of violence, those which result in violence promptly attract newspaper reporters, politicians and special interest groups looking for an opportunity to further their own interests.

Canadian labour history is dotted with instances of violence, much of it occurring in struggles for union recognition. In 1903, a four-month strike was held against the CPR, in which one picketer, Frank Rogers, was killed by gunfire. Rogers has been called the first of British Columbia's labour martyrs. In 1911 on Vancouver Island, a bitter srike started over the United Mineworkers attempt to organize the Dunsmuir Mines. The strike was to last two years, and ultimately involved 7,000 men. It was marked with outbreaks of violence and considerable property damage. Both provincial police and federal troops were used to maintain order. At one time over 250 miners were in jail.[28]

At about the same time, the United Mineworkers were involved in a similar dispute in Nova Scotia with the British Empire Steel and Coal Company (BESCO). The strikers were evicted from company-owned homes and food and fuel supplies were cut off. In the winter of 1909–10 many families lived in tents. A special police force was recruited by the company and the mine entrances were surrounded by barbed wire and electrical fences. Three people died as a result of accidental contact with the electrical fence. The strike was ultimately broken.[29] Violence broke out again in Cape Breton in 1922, between the Mineworkers and BESCO, this time over attempts to cut wages. Twelve thousand miners went on strike and succeeded in reducing the amount of the wage cut. In 1923 a recognition strike in the company's Sydney Steel plant saw the occupation of part of the plant by strikers. Two thousand troops were called in to put down the strike. In 1925, another attempt to reduce wages in the mines resulted in yet another strike. One miner was killed in a clash between company police and the strikers.[30]

The beginning of the depression brought more labour violence. In Estavan, Saskatchewan, violence occurred when 400 striking miners marched in defiance of an order not to stage a parade. Three miners were killed by police in the fighting which ensued.

A march from Vancouver to Ottawa by 2,000 unemployed workers led to a riot in Regina in 1935 when police attempted to arrest the leaders of the Workers Unity League, a communist organization, which was organizing the march at a rally on Dominion Day. Fighting broke out. A police detective was killed and over 100 people were injured. The Regina Riot was part of the chaos that was referred to in the slogan "King or Chaos" that helped the Liberals under Mackenzie King oust the Conservative government of R. B. Bennett.

In Ontario, Premier Mitchell Hepburn was violently opposed to the arrival of CIO organizers in that province. In 1937, when a strike of 400 workers occurred at the General Motors plant in Oshawa, Hepburn first called out the RCMP and then organized an armed volunteer force to deal with the situation. The strike, which was largely successful, was not marked by any violence, and Hepburn's volunteer force, dubbed "sons of Mitches" by the strikers, was not needed. Hepburn called the CIO organizers "foreign agitators and communists" and claimed that they were out to "smash our export business."[31] Hepburn won re-election in 1938 on an anti-CIO platform.

(d) SEVERE EMPLOYER RESISTANCE

The preceding section amply illustrates employer resistance to the union movement. This resistance was not confined to the bargaining table. Employers often attempted to head off unions before they ever gained a foothold, and their devices were many. Chief among them were misuse of immigrants, yellow-dog contracts, blacklists, detectives and labour spies.

1. Misuse of Immigrants

Sometimes employers gave immigrants false information when they hired them as strikebreakers. During a strike at the T. Eaton Company in Toronto, Alexander Redder, a cloakmaker, was brought in from Europe as a strikebreaker. Sometime later Redder discovered why he had been brought to Canada and requested money so that he could get back to New York. Eaton's agent refused, and Redder, in despair, took his own life.[32]

2. Yellow-dog Contracts and Blacklists

Two of the most notorious union busting devices were "yellow-dog" contracts and blacklists. Yellow-dog contracts were documents used initially by the railroads during their feverish construction days in the West. Later they were used by other industries as well and spread throughout North America. These were contracts stipulating as a condition of employment that the worker was not, and would not become, a member of a union. Any falsifications were met promptly with discharge when they were discovered. Many of the early railroad workers were oriental (yellow-skinned) and willing to work at substandard wages, thus excluding unionized workers looking for more money. These orientals came to be known as "yellow dogs."

Blacklists contained names of persons who were known to be members of unions. The lists were exchanged between employers, and if a person's name appeared on them his chances of obtaining employment were severely limited. The most prevalent use of blacklists was made by the National Metal Trades Association (NMTA), an organization of employers that featured a service to members by which individuals were traced from job to job through any number of name changes. One person was known to have gone through 12 job changes and seven aliases, and still he failed to escape the list. Members of NMTA were required to report any employees discharged for union activities; names of these employees were promptly published and issued to all other members of the association. The NMTA augmented the employer-reporting function with a tremendous detective staff that shadowed persons from place to place.

3. Labour Spies

Labour spies were frequently used. In 1900 the J. B. King Company of Toronto hired spies to work alongside regular workers and identify any union sympathizers. Once identified the sympathizers were fired. The Canadian Pacific Railway (CPR) went even further. They hired spies who worked their way into the union, took part in deliberations, even initiated new members. The CPR had many ways of locating "reliable" spies. In one case CPR officials succeeded in locating a lesser official of the United Brotherhood of Railway Engineers (UBRE) who was suffering financial difficulty, was in poor health, and was apparently uneasy about some past indiscretions. CPR detectives met him and threatened to expose him. His alternative was to sign on as a labour spy. This he did by signing the following statement:

I,_____, organizer of the UBRE, do hereby offer my services to the Special Service Department of The Canadian Pacific Railway Company.[33]

Private police were also used by some companies. The Dominion Iron and Steel Company employed them in 1912; the Ford Motor Company employed them in the 1920s and part way through the 1930s.

These various devices — yellow-dog contracts, blacklists, spies and the like — were not confined to earlier years. There is evidence that blacklists, and modern-day versions of yellow-dog contracts and spies are still used in Canada. Each year there are numerous instances of persons being discharged from employment as a result of union activity. Many of these instances have been documented as unfair labour practices, but many more have taken place without documentation.

The Province of Quebec

This brief history of the Canadian labour movement would not be complete without a discussion of the special situation in Quebec. The key differentiating feature of labour relations in Quebec was the development of the Roman Catholic labour movement.

This movement developed in the context of the unique nature of Quebec within the Canadian confederation. Institutionally Quebec has always had a high degree of autonomy. Culturally, the aim of generations of French Canadian leaders has been to maintain a French identity in the midst of an alien English-speaking society. The Catholic Church, with 85 percent of the population at least nominally affiliated with it, played a leading role in preserving and developing a strong separate French culture in Quebec. Prior to 1900, that culture was essentially rural and agricultural.

The twentieth century brought rapid industrialization to Quebec as well as other parts of the country, and changes to Quebec's way of life. The principal organizational structures of the new industrialism were introduced largely by English-speaking elements, Canadian, British and American. These included trade unions. The ownership and control of all major commercial, financial, and industrial operations were largely in the hands of the English-speaking (and Protestant) minority. French-Canadians were predominant in the ranks of farmers, blue collar workers, small shopkeepers, lower-paid white collar workers, civil servants, and the traditional professions of law, medicine and the priesthood.[34]

Prior to 1900, the development of the labour movement in Quebec was part of that in the rest of the country. The same unions were involved, which helps to explain why half of the unionized workers in Quebec are members of unions affiliated with the CLC and its provincial counterpart, the Quebec Federation of Labour.[35]

Roman Catholic Church leaders and lay nationalists in Quebec feared that they would lose their cultural identity as French Canadians if they acquired the expertise of the new industrialism and associated with the English-speaking factions. Since urbanization appeared to be unstoppable, the development of French Catholic trade unions was a natural solution to the problem of the preservation of French identity and culture.

Beginning in 1900 these unions were formed — not by the workers, but by the Church — with each having a chaplain appointed by the Bishop. The chaplains, in effect, became the chief executive officers of these unions, carrying out the normal functions of a trade union leader in organizing, negotiating, and administering collective agreements. The Jesuit Order became involved in the training of lay leaders for the movement through the École Sociale Populaire.[36]

In 1918, the various Catholic unions moved toward federation with the formation of the National Central Trades Council in Quebec City. Similar central councils were formed in other districts, and subsequent conferences were called to form a province-wide federation of Catholic unions. Finally in 1922 a permanent organization was established called Confédération des Travailleurs Catholiques du Canada (CTCC), known in English as the Canadian Catholic Confederation of Labour.

Throughout history the CTCC was a relatively small part of the Canadian labour movement. Its total membership never exceeded ten percent of all union members in the country. Even among French-speaking Catholic unionists, one-half to two-thirds generally belonged to non-Catholic unions. The rivalry between non-Catholic organizations, especially the TLC and the CCL, contributed materially to the survival and modest growth of the CTCC.

During and immediately after World War II, the CTCC experienced some important changes. Rapid industrial expansion drew large numbers of French Canadians into the cities where they came in contact with workers of other ethnic and religious backgrounds. Some CTCC unions ceased to be exclusively French-Canadian and Catholic, and new, aggressive lay leaders took top positions in the Federation, forcing out many of the Catholic clergy. There were glaring wage inequities between French-speaking and English-speaking workers, and the new leaders set forth to correct them. This, plus vigorous competition from CCL and TLC organizers, led to some of the most violent and spectacular labour disputes in Canada's history. The French-Catholic unions had converted from a mood of relative cooperation to aggressive militancy.

The event which marked the change in the nature of the Catholic labour movement in Quebec was the asbestos strike of 1949. Jean Marchand was the union leader. Pierre Trudeau was arrested for demonstrating on behalf of the strikers and later wrote the definitive study of the strike.[37] The strike began as a wildcat strike over wages and working conditions, but became a power struggle between organized labour and the provincial 'establishment' when Maurice Duplessis, the premier, sent in the QPP to protect strikebreakers who had been brought in by the companies. The four-month strike was marked by violence, and marked the emergence of the labour movement as a force to be reckoned with in Quebec. The strike was supported by important elements in the Church and demonstrated that the Church could no longer be counted on to maintain the Catholic syndicats as non-militant institutions.[38]

By 1960, the Church's connection had weakened, and in that year was officially broken. This event was marked by the change of the CTCC name to Confédération des Syndicats Nationaux (CSN). The year 1960 is often cited as the beginning of what has been called "the quiet revolution" in Quebec. Slogans of the revolution included "maîtres chez nous" and "ratapprege" — "masters in our own house" and "catching up."[39]

"Catching up" meant social and economic reform and a tremendous growth in education and health care. In 1964 a new liberal labour code was enacted, providing for collective bargaining and the right to strike for public sector employees. "Masters in our own house" meant that the CSN as a French Canadian trade movement had an advantage over the QFL during this period.

The CTCC had discussed merger with the newly-created CLC in 1956, but because of cultural and structural differences between the two organizations, the merger never occurred. In 1959, a strike of CBC personnel in Montreal, led by Réné Levesque, proved to be a turning point in the relationship between the two organizations. The hostility of CLC parent union executives toward their Montreal French-language locals during the strike caused them to break away from the CLC/QFL and join the CTCC, which in turn ended any possibility of merger between the two groups.[40]

Later as a cabinet minister in the Liberal Lesage government, Levesque was instrumental in the passage of the 1964 legislation which authorized collective bargaining in the public sector. Because that legislation prohibited affiliation of the public service unions with organizations with political ties, the legislation handed those unions to the CSN because the QFL was associated with the NDP.

The decade of the 1960s was marked by significant growth in the CSN and considerable conflict between it and the QFL. By the end of the decade changes in the leadership of both groups had helped reduce this conflict considerably. By 1972, the CSN, under the leadership of Marcel Pépin, and the QFL, under Louis Laberge, were combined with the major teachers union (Corporation des Enseignants du Québec — CEQ) in a "common front" to negotiate with the provincial government centrally over collective agreements in the public sector. The result of these negotiations was a major strike, back to work legislation, and the imprisonment of the three union leaders for counselling workers to disobey a court order.[41]

The year 1972 saw the break of a group of unions, with 75,000 members, away from the CSN to form the Centrale des Syndicats Democratiques (CSD). The split occurred because of increasing radicalism in the CSN. Publications like "Il n'y a plus d'aviner pour le Québec dans le system économique actuel" ("There is no longer a future for Quebec in the present economic system") and the marxist "Ne comptons que sur nos propres moyens" ("Let us rely on our own means"), while never becoming official CSN policy,[42] still served as an indication of the ideology of some important elements in the CSN.

The QFL and the CSN at this same time became increasingly nationalistic in their outlook. In 1976 and 1981, the QFL officially endorsed the separatist Parti Québécois in the provincial elections. The CSN did not officially endorse the PQ in an election, and this has been one of the sources of continuing differences between it and the QFL. These differences seem unlikely to disappear in the near future, and the situation appears likely to remain one of competition in some areas and cooperation in others, particularly in "common front" bargaining in the public sector.

Despite the QFL's affiliation with the CLC, language and cultural differences will continue to make Quebec a "special" labour relations situation. The QFL has, since 1974, had full control over labour education in Quebec, and has received funds from the CLC which members in Quebec contribute but for which they receive little benefit because of language or cultural differences. The QFL has also assumed full jurisdiction over local labour councils, their staffs and the funding for them. These arrangements are unique to the QFL and reflect requirements of trade unions in Quebec.[43]

Notes

1. Stewart Jamieson, *Industrial Relations in Canada*, Second Edition. Toronto: MacMillan, 1973, p. 12.

2. Jack Williams, *The Story of Unions in Canada*. Toronto: J. M. Dent & Sons (Canada) Limited, 1975, pp. 5–6.

3. Williams, pp. 7–8.

4. Edward E. Seymour, *An Illustrated History of Canadian Labour 1800–1974*. Ottawa: Canadian Labour Congress, 1974, p. 1.

5. Williams, pp. 10–11.

6. Seymour, p. 2.

7. Toronto Typographical Society, *Minutes*, February 17 and 24, 1872.

8. *Ontario Workman*, April 18, 1872.

9. Canadian Labour Union, *Proceedings*, September 1873.

10. Ibid.

11. Canada, Royal Commission on the Relations of Capital and Labour (Ottawa, 1889), *Evidence of Quebec*, pp. 21–148.

12. Ibid, *Evidence of Quebec*.

13. Ibid, *Evidence of Quebec*.

14. For an extensive study of international unionism in Canada, see John Crispo, *International Unionism*. McGraw-Hill, 1967.

15. H. C. Pentland, "The Canadian Industrial Relations System: Some Formative Factors," *Journal of Canadian Labour Studies*, Vol. 4, No. 4, 1979, p. 19.

16. Trades and Labour Congress of Canada, Seventeenth Annual Convention, 1902, *Proceedings*, pp. 46 and 73.

17. Pentland, p. 21

18. *Trades and Labour Congress Journal*, March 1949.

19. Charles Lipton, *The Trade Union Movement of Canada, 1827–1959*. Canadian Social Publications Ltd., 1963, pp. 280–2.

20. Western Canada Labour Conference, *Proceedings*, p. 27.

21. For a detailed account of the Winnipeg General Strike, see D. C. Masters, *The Winnipeg General Strike*. Toronto, 1950.

22. Foster Rhea Dulles, *Labor in America*. New York: Crowell, 1960, pp. 390–1.

23. *Montreal Star*, September 28, 1959, p. 1.

24. Canadian Labour Congress Convention, 1956, *Proceedings*.

25. Williams, *Unions in Canada*, p. 232.

26. For a full discussion of this dispute, see Joseph B. Rose, "Some Notes on the Building Trades—Canadian Labour Congress Dispute," *Industrial Relations*, Volume 22, No. 1, Winter 1983, pp. 87–93.

27. Some of the more notable special interest groups which latched onto the labour movement for their own self-interest were various anarchists, Marxian socialists, black internationalists, Lassaleans (who espoused direct overthrows of capitalism), women's rights advocates, and the international Communist movement.

28. Williams, pp. 84–88.

29. Seymour, pp. 12–13.

30. Seymour, pp. 24–25.

31. Jamieson, p. 89.

32. Trade and Labour Congress of Canada, Fourteenth Annual Convention, 1899, *Proceedings*, p. 7.

33. Canada, Royal Commission on Industrial Disputes in the Province of British Columbia, 1903, *Report*, p. 75.

34. Jamieson, p. 32

35. Shirley A. Goldenberg, *Industrial Relations in Quebec Past and Present*. Kingston: Industrial Relations Centre, Queen's University, 1975, p. 3.

36. Goldenberg, p. 4.

37. Pierre E. Trudeau, *La Grêve de l'amitante*. Montreal: Cite Libre, 1956.

38. Goldenberg, p. 7.

39. Goldenberg, p. 10.

40. Jamieson, p. 41.

41. Goldenberg, p. 17.

42. Jean Boivan, "Labour Relations in Quebec," in *Union–Management Relations in Canada*, John Anderson and Morley Gunderson, eds. Don Mills, Ontario: Addison-Wesley, 1982, p. 430.

43. Boivan, p. 433.

3

LABOUR LEGISLATION — AN OVERVIEW

A body of law built up through the years now provides a highly effective legislative, judicial and administrative framework for the industrial relations system, within which industrial relations practices take place. This chapter explores the principal components of that framework and looks at the historical development of Canadian labour law.

COMPONENTS OF A LEGAL FRAMEWORK FOR LABOUR RELATIONS

Three basic beliefs underlie the legal framework for labour relations in Canada (and the United States as well) and they are the central components of our industrial relations system:
1. Employees should be free to organize.
2. Representatives of employees should be able to engage employers in bargaining.
3. Employees and employers should be free to invoke meaningful sanctions in support of their positions: employees to withdraw services, employers to close their doors.

In Canada, until the latter part of the nineteenth century, all three of these components were illegal. By examining the development of labour legislation, the process by which each of them was legislated becomes clear.

The legal framework for labour relations in any country can be measured in two ways:
1. The degree of government intervention to define limits of the three components.
2. The kinds of legal substitution the government provides for use of sanctions.

EIGHT STAGES OF GOVERNMENT INTRUSION

Given the basic legal framework above, it is possible to trace the evolution of labour laws of any country through eight stages of government intervention or intrusion:

1. Adoption of a policy that employee organizations and collective bargaining are desirable;
2. removal of the three central components from legal disability;
3. creation of government offices of intervention to be available to parties on request (most frequently these offices take the form of mediation or conciliation);
4. imposition of government intervention as a condition-precedent to the exercise of sanctions (example: conciliation under the Canada Labour Code is a precondition to a legal strike or lockout);
5. imposition of public inquiry and publication of results (example: the Ontario Mediation and Conciliation Services provide for conciliation boards in some instances — these boards publish their findings and recommendations; also in Ontario, The School Boards and Teacher's Collective Negotiations Act provides for fact finding as one available dispute settlement procedure);
6. compulsory arbitration;
7. partial operation by the government;
8. seizure.

Through history, Canadian and U.S. labour relations have moved closer to the eighth degree of government intrusion. Instances of total seizure and operation of a company or industry by the government have been rare. So far, there have been no moves toward encompassing legislation to provide for seizure or partial seizure. However, there have been more and more laws in recent years calling for compulsory arbitration in certain instances as well as periods of wage control, particularly in the public sector.

In the remainder of this chapter, we will look at some landmark cases and legislation in the field of labour relations. We will consider both Canada and the United States, because the development of the legal framework in these two countries was intertwined as first one, then the other, moved ahead in protecting the rights of workers — and, later, in attempting to put controls on some of those rights.

Early Law

Regulations affecting the relationship between employer and employee can be traced back at least as far as the fourteenth century. At that time, the Black Death swept across Europe, leaving in its wake an extreme manpower shortage. This led to legislation in England which essentially put wage controls into effect and made it a crime to lure away another's workmen by offering higher wages.[1]

The advent of the industrial revolution in England in the eighteenth century saw the first real stirring of the labour movement. There the courts, and later parliament, responded to this situation by developing the doctrine of criminal conspiracy. In brief, this meant that labour unions were considered to be combinations in restraint of trade—a criminal act. The 1799 Combinations Act made it illegal for any worker to combine with any other worker to attempt to increase wages or reduce hours. It was also illegal to attempt, in any fashion, to encourage a worker to leave his work or to refuse to work with another person. The penalty for violation of the law was a three-month jail term.[2] The condition where trade union activity was an illegal criminal act was to prevail in Great Britain and Canada for 100 years.

The notion of using criminal law to enforce individual contracts of employment could be found in early Canadian legislation. The Master and Servant Act of 1859 made it a criminal offence to refuse to work or to obey lawful commands. It was also illegal for anyone to "induce" labourers to confederate for the purpose of demanding extravagant or high wages.[3] The extent to which this act discriminated against labour can be seen in the fact that breach of contract was a criminal offence for workers, whereas a contract breach was a civil offence for other persons.

The Trade Union Act of 1872

In 1871, the British parliament passed the Trade Union Act which exempted labour organizations from criminal prosecution for conspiracy, thus legalizing collective agreements. However, the act denied unions access to the courts for enforcement of those agreements. At the same time, amendments to the Criminal Law made it an illegal act, punishable by imprisonment, to use violence, or to intimidate or obstruct any person to attempt to coerce him or her to stop working, or to belong to a trade union.[4]

As was noted in Chapter 2, in response to the Toronto Printers' strike, the same two-part legislative package was passed by the Canadian Parliament in 1872. The exemption from the criminal conspiracy theory provided by the Trades Union Act was extended only to unions which registered with the government. Since very few unions registered, the Act was of little practical importance. The 1872 Criminal Law Provisions, which essentially prohibited peaceful picketing, was repealed in 1876.

In 1892, legislation was passed which exempted all unions from criminal prosecution for restraint of trade. However, at the same time, peaceful picketing was prohibited under the Criminal Code and was not legislatively sanctioned until 1934.[5]

Dispute-Settling Legislation

By the early 1900s, Canada was far ahead of the United States in dispute-settling legislation. In 1900, Parliament passed the Conciliation Act, modelled after earlier provincial legislation. The Act authorized the Minister of Labour to appoint conciliation officers or conciliation boards to help settle disputes when requested to do so by representatives of the employers or workers involved.

A more comprehensive act was passed in 1903 following a long strike of trackmen on the Canadian Pacific Railroad. The 1903 Act, known as the Railway Labour Disputes Act, was limited to coverage of railroad workers. It provided for a three-man conciliation board to serve in dispute situations: one nominee to be chosen by each party, the two nominees then to choose a chairman. The board had power to investigate the causes of dispute, to compel testimony under oath, and to require production of relevant documents.

If the conciliation board failed to bring about agreement, there was provision for arbitration. However, the power of arbitration boards was limited to making non-binding recommendations. The Act contained no restraints on strikes or lockouts; for this reason it was generally ineffective.

Provisions of the 1900 Conciliation Act and the Railway Labour Disputes Act of 1903 were combined and extended in the Conciliation and Labour Act of 1906. This, too, was inadequate and was succeeded in 1907 by the Industrial Disputes Investigation Act. The 1907 Act formed the backbone of Canadian labour legislation from that date till the present and is still on the books, mostly in its original form. It was copied in great part by the provinces, and, 19 years later, by the United States in that country's Railway Labor Act.

The Industrial Disputes Investigation Act (IDI) grew largely out of a rash of strikes. Perhaps the most influential of these was the eight-month strike of Lethbridge coal field workers in Alberta, which resulted in a winter fuel famine. Families suffered to the extent that they were forced to burn wood fence posts to keep warm. But that wasn't all: there were strikes of Manitoba and Ontario street railway workers and among employees of Quebec sawmills — giving rise to loud public outcries throughout the country for controlling legislation. At the time, most of Canada's workers were employed by public utility and transportation companies. In the ten years 1897–1906, one-seventh of all industrial disputes, accounting for over one-third of all striking workers, were in these industries. Consequently, the public enthusiastically backed the 1907 Act.

The new Act applied to disputes involving employees of ten or more persons engaging in mining, transport, communication, and public utility companies. The machinery it provided could be applied to any other industry if both parties consented. The philosophy underlying the Act was this: In any civilized community, private rights cease when they become public wrongs.

The Act provided for a tripartite Board of Conciliation and Investigation which had legal power to investigate disputes and compel submission of testimony and evidence. These features were derived from the 1903 Railway Labour Disputes Act. However, the new Act had a new and vitally important feature requiring postponement of any strike or lockout while investigations proceeded. Wages and working conditions were frozen during that time.

The main function of the tripartite board was to conciliate, that is, to act as a catalyst to try to get parties to come to a voluntary agreement. However, the Board had power beyond conciliation by virtue of a provision calling for it to make recommendations in the event conciliation failed. The Board's findings were to include "the cause of the dispute according to the merits and substantial justice of the case." In addition, the Act required that "the Board's recommendations . . . shall state in plain terms . . . what in the Board's opinion ought or ought not to be done by the respective parties concerned."

The 1907 Act had many weaknesses, but these were largely overcome because this Act had been substantially agreed upon in advance by labour and management. Consequently, representatives of both were committed to make it work. Its first test came shortly after its passage in 1907 when workers at the Montreal Point-St-Charles shops of The Grand Trunk Railway (now Canadian National) made plans to stage a strike in sympathy with fellow shopmen who had a dispute in Ontario. But that would have violated the IDI Act. So they didn't do it.

This and subsequent experiences caused labour to register increased coolness toward the Act. By 1916, the majority of members at the Trades and Labour Congress (TLC) convention voted for its repeal. Its biggest weakness was its failure to give protection to workers and unions against employers who took action to thwart unionization. There was no provision in the Act either protecting workers in their attempts to organize, or, once workers were organized, requiring employers to bargain.

Toronto Electric Commissioners vs. Snider[6]

The 1925 case of *Toronto Electric Commissioners versus Snider* was a court challenge to the 1907 Industrial Disputes Investigation Act based on grounds that the Dominion Government was acting beyond its proper constitutional jurisdiction. The Judicial Committee of the Privy Council of England, bypassing the Supreme Court of Canada, upheld the challenge, declaring the Act unconstitutional. The Committee reasoned that since the Act was concerned with civil rights of employers and employees in the respective provinces, there was a violation of Section 92 of the British North America Act which expressly assigned this function to the provinces.

The Canadian Parliament promptly amended the 1907 Act to restrict its application to disputes that were under the jurisdiction of the federal government. The amendment provided as well that the Act could extend to the provinces if they passed enabling legislation. Between 1925 and 1932, all provinces except Prince Edward Island did so. Two of them, Alberta and British Columbia, subsequently repealed their enabling acts and passed similar provincial laws of their own.

As a result of the Snider case, the Canadian provinces became the most significant makers and enforcers of labour laws in Canada. The Canada Labour Code (as amended) applied only to enumerated industries which crossed provincial lines. Crown corporations, railways, airlines, longshoring, and seafaring were among those industries which fell into this category.

Legislative Developments in the United States—1925–1940

From 1925 until 1940, the most significant legislative developments in North American labour law took place in the United States, starting with the Railway

Labor Act of 1926. Many of these had profound effects on subsequent Canadian legislation and serve, to this day, as bases for the existing legal framework for labour relations in both Canada and the United States.

1. THE RAILWAY LABOR ACT — 1926

The Railway Labor Act of 1926 represented the first and only piece of negotiated labour legislation in the history of U.S. labour relations. It was applied initially to the railroads, later to the airlines. It had many features that characterized Canada's Industrial Disputes Investigation Act. In addition, there were some significant differences. These included exclusive rights for unions representing a majority of members in a bargaining unit and compulsory features requiring employers to recognize and bargain with appropriate unions. Like the Industrial Disputes Investigation Act, the Railway Labor Act had many flaws, but it worked well for about ten years because labour and management were committed to it.

The Act set up machinery to deal both with disputes during a contract term and those arising after contract expiration and involving terms of a new agreement. Regarding the latter, the Act provided for a five-member National Mediation Board — the members to be appointed by the President. Disputes could be voluntarily submitted to the Board, or the Board could proffer its services if it found an emergency existed. In the event of an emergency, the Act provided a six-step procedure:

1. The National Mediation Board would meet with the parties and attempt to mediate — to secure a voluntary settlement;
2. if unsuccessful in mediation, the Board would attempt to induce the parties to submit items in dispute to binding arbitration;
3. if the parties refused arbitration, a 30-day moratorium would be declared regarding any changes in pay, work rules, working conditions, or established work practices; attempts at settlement would continue;
4. if there was still no settlement, and if the National Mediation Board believed the dispute would threaten to substantially interrupt interstate commerce, the Board was required to report to the President;
5. if the President shared the Board's viewpoint, he could create an investigatory board;
6. if an investigatory board was created, it had an additional 30 days to deliver a report, and the parties were barred from changing any of the conditions which gave rise to the dispute for 30 days after receiving the report.

After expiration of all these steps, or after Step 3 if Steps 4, 5, or 6 were not undertaken, there could be a strike or lockout.

2. NORRIS-LA-GUARDIA ACT — 1932

Since the early 1800s, workers had been repeatedly thwarted in their efforts to form unions and take collective action. Among their greatest enemies was the injunction, a remedy at law by which courts prohibited certain actions from being initiated or continuing on the grounds that there had been or could be a violation of the law. Violation of an injunction was dealt with through contempt-of-court proceedings.

The Norris-La-Guardia Act consisted of two important parts. The first part freed unions from the threat of anti-trust action. The second prohibited the use of the injunctive remedy in specified instances involving labour relations. Injunctions were barred as devices to prevent any of the following:
— strikes,
— payments of strike benefits,
— aid to individuals defending or prosecuting court action in labour disputes,
— non-violent picketing,
— peaceful assembly.

Thus, the injunction, long a scourge of worker organizations, was largely removed as a weapon. It would still be used in the event that unlawful acts were threatened or if there was likelihood of bodily injury or property damage and no adequate legal remedy was available. But framers of the act believed these instances would be rare.

The Norris-La-Guardia Act represented a significant step ahead of Canadian labour relations legislation in giving workers' organization significantly more freedom. It was not until 1968 that a stab at formulating similar anti-injunction legislation was taken in Canada. Until then, injunctions were used quite freely. At this writing, the continued absence of specific anti-injunction legislation permitted the spectre of uncertainty to persist.[7]

Mr. Justice Ivan Rand attempted to deal with injunctions in his report of 1968 which proposed changes in the Ontario Labour Relations Act. His suggestions were not adopted in legislative language. However, practices in the province (and, in general, elsewhere in Canada) have given them practical effect. Among the most important of Mr. Justice Rand's recommendations regarding injunctions were these:
1. Ex parte injunctions[8] should not be sanctioned — the alleged offender must be served notice and given an opportunity to defend himself;
2. in injunctive action, facts must be established by voice evidence, subject to cross examination, unless the alleged emergency is so great that there is not sufficient time to bring witnesses;
3. any misrepresentation or withholding of facts in injunctive action is punishable by contempt proceedings;
4. prior to issuance of an injunction, it must be shown that there have been reasonable efforts to obtain police assistance, to protect property, to permit lawful entry, and to prevent breach of peace. In addition, it must be shown that these efforts have failed.[9]

3. THE NATIONAL LABOR RELATIONS ACT (WAGNER ACT)—1936

The advent of the New Deal in the United States under President Franklin D. Roosevelt represented an almost revolutionary change in government attitude and policy toward organized labour.

The Wagner Act of 1936 applied to nearly all employees in the United States. Among its principal exclusions were those covered by the Railway Labor Act and agricultural employees. The Act reaffirmed three important principles established in the Railway Labor Act:
1. Workers shall have freedom to organize unions of their own choosing.
2. Workers shall be free from employer interference or domination.
3. Employers shall be required to recognize and bargain with appropriate unions.

In addition, the Wagner Act created a National Labor Relations Board to investigate complaints of unfair labour practices, to prosecute offenders and to conduct supervised elections to decide on the certification of unions representing the majority of workers in appropriate bargaining units.

The Wagner Act listed five unfair labour practices by managements:
1. Interference with workers' rights to organize;
2. domination of a labour organization;
3. discrimination for union activity;
4. discharge or discipline of an employee for filing charges under the Act;
5. refusal to bargain.

Through the years, the most frequent actions have been under the third and fifth items.

The Wagner Act did not provide for unfair labour practice actions against unions. This was intentional in order to give unions a relatively free path to massive organization. Economic recovery, according to Roosevelt's policy, depended on placing as much purchasing power as possible into the hands of the working population. It was not till 1947 that the pendulum shifted, and the Wagner Act was amended to provide for unfair labour practice actions against unions.

* * *

Passage of the Wagner Act in the United States led to strong agitation in Canada for similar legislation. At its convention of 1937, the TLC adopted a draft statute for the various provinces that was virtually identical to the Wagner Act. Within two years, all provinces except two had adopted variations of the draft. The two exceptions were Prince Edward Island and Ontario.

Social Legislation

Along with the move for enabling legislation for union organizing drives and dispute settling procedures, governments of Canada and the United States made rapid strides in the 1930s and 1940s toward enactment of much-needed social legislation. In the United States, the Fair Labor Standards Act of 1938 provided for minimum wages and maximum hours beyond which premium pay would be required. Standards applied both to union and non-union workers. Soon thereafter, Canada adopted standards as well — somewhat more liberal than those in the United States. In 1940, the federal government of Canada enacted the Unemployment Insurance Act, marking a major breakthrough in social legislation. This was followed, during World War II, by an Old Age Pension Act and a bill providing for widows' allowances.

Canadian Wartime Legislation

In 1940, as part of its war labour policy, the government of Canada issued a statement of principles which were put into operation by a series of subsequent orders-in-council. These orders prevailed until February 1944 when Wartime Labour Relations Regulations were proclaimed. These regulations represented Canada's first comprehensive labour policy since 1925 and had a direct impact on postwar legislation. Five provinces — British Columbia, Manitoba, New Brunswick, Nova Scotia and Ontario — suspended their provincial legislation and made the regulations operative as law. Ingredients of the regulations were these:

1. Workers would be free to organize;
2. employers would be compelled to engage in collective bargaining with representatives of a majority of their employees;
3. no strikes or lockouts could take place until a bargaining agent was certified and conciliation procedures were exhausted;
4. employers should be free from union interference in the discharge, transfer or layoff of employees for just cause;
5. unions should be free from interference or domination by employers;
6. employees should be free from discharge for union activity;
7. disputes regarding interpretation or alleged violation of a labour agreement must be settled through orderly arrangement of the parties;
8. internal affairs of unions should be exposed to members and to the public.

The final ingredient was to be implemented through requirements that unions file copies with the Department of Labour of their constitution, bylaws and lists of officers and that they must, in addition, provide members with up-to-date financial statements.

In 1943, the Province of Ontario adopted the Ontario Labour Relations Act, giving expression to the 1937 draft statute proposed by TLC and to the ingredients of the wartime labour regulations. One of the most important features of the 1943 Act was a new Court of Labour. The judge of the Labour Court would decide questions of union representation. Other features of the Act were these:

1. Repeal of the civil conspiracy doctrine;
2. declaration that restraint of trade would not, in itself, cause a union to be an unlawful entity;
3. declaration that a union was not a legal entity;
4. all disputes arising out of interpretation of the collective agreement would be settled ultimately by arbitration;
5. courts would give legal sanctity to collective agreements.

Wages during the war were regulated by Federal Government Order-in-Council 7440 issued in December of 1940. This provided that the 1926–1939 level would be the wartime norm for Canadian workers' wages. When wages went below this level, they could be raised, but the increase was limited to five percent for any one year. The order-in-council also provided for payment of a cost-of-living bonus. Additional restrictions were imposed by succeeding orders-in-council. In 1941, P.C. 8253 was passed. This provided for a National War Labour Board with powers of investigation and recommendation on wages and working conditions. Increases in basic wages were prohibited except by permission of the Board. Two years later, P.C. 9384 was enacted. This stipulated that a wage adjustment could be granted only where it was necessary in order to correct a gross inequity. Similar wartime restrictions were in effect in the United States. The labour movements in both countries had adopted a no-strike policy, and disputes over wages, hours or conditions were submitted to the respective country's War Labor Board for final and binding determination. Men who served on these boards obtained valuable experience which stood them in good stead as arbitrators and mediators after the war.

Following the war, there was considerable labour unrest caused by years of sacrifice. In 1945, the average hourly earnings for Canadian workers had been 69.4 cents per hour; the average hours worked per week was 44.3.[10] Strikes did occur during the war, but they were rare. So it was not surprising that labour sought to make up for the past six years in short order. It was stimulated in this mission by a situation of unprecedented prosperity. In late 1945, starting with the strike by the United Automobile Workers against the Ford Motor Company, unions began their drive. Chrysler Local 195 at Windsor, Ontario joined the strike. Demands included higher wages, a union shop,[11] seniority for returning servicemen, lay-off pay, and two weeks' vacation with pay.

There was considerable militancy. Mass picketing in Windsor led Labour Minister Humphrey Mitchell to believe a revolution was at hand. This view gained credence when the union withdrew members from operation of the power house, causing the Association of Insurance Underwriters of Ontario to express alarm to the Ontario Attorney-General that the property was in danger. Ontario Premier Drew asked Prime Minister Mackenzie King for help, and the next day, a group of Royal Canadian Mounted Police (RCMP) was sent to Windsor. The RCMP, joined by provincial and city police, attempted to open the picket lines so that company security police could enter the power house. This caused strikers to set up a blockade of automobiles around the plant. In some areas the blockade exceeded 20 blocks in depth. Consequently, the police never entered, and the company and government retreated. Mr. Justice Ivan Rand was appointed arbitrator in the dispute, and helped bring the negotiators together to hammer out an agreement. One product of the final settlement was a form of union security which required all employees represented by the union to pay dues, although union membership remained voluntary. This was called the "Rand formula" in Canada and the "agency shop" in the United States. It represented an advancement in union security, but still fell short of the union shop.[12]

The Ford Strike set the stage for 1946, when 139,474 workers went on strike in locations throughout Canada. Over 4.5 million man days of work were lost. These figures represented an all-time high for the country. The strike conditions were accompanied by an increase in union membership in 1946 exceeding 120,000.

In the United States, labour unrest was equally severe. Two nationwide coal strikes, a national railroad strike and countless others set off a wave of public opinion which applied pressure on the Congress to enact legislation which would temper the effects of the 1936 Wagner Act. This Act had given unions almost unencumbered freedom to organize and provided virtually no weapons for employers to resist effectively. Furthermore, there was considerable agitation for some form of emergency powers to be put in the hands of the federal government — similar to that which was provided in the Railway Labor Act — to intervene in disputes that threatened national health and welfare. Out of this scene, the Taft-Hartley Act emerged. This was an amendment to the Wagner Act and was passed in 1947 over President Harry Truman's veto. It set the pattern for U.S. and Canadian labour legislation for the next 25 years. The Taft-Hartley Act is still on the books, with no immediate prospects of major change. It is more formally known as the National Labor Relations Act.

Among the provisions of the Taft-Hartley Act was a listing of unfair labour practices which could be brought against unions. These were:
1. Restraint of employees in their rights to organize;
2. causing or attempting to cause an employer to discriminate against an employee, or to deny employment except for failure to pay dues;
3. refusal to bargain;
4. engaging in any of several forms of secondary boycott;
5. requiring excessive or discriminatory dues;
6. causing or attempting to cause an employer to pay for services not performed;
7. engaging in any of several forms of illegal picketing.

In addition to giving more power to management by virtue of these unfair labour practices, the Taft-Hartley Act gave additional rights to individuals irrespective of union representation. Under Section 9a of the Act, an individual could bring his own grievance to his employer and have the grievance adjusted without union intervention, provided the adjustment was consistent with the collective agreement and provided the union representative was given an opportunity to be present.

Perhaps the best-known sections of the Act were those dealing with emergency disputes, Sections 206–210. These gave the President of the United States power to delay a work stoppage for up to 80 days if he believed that it imperiled the national health and safety.

Postwar Canadian Labour Acts

Following the war and the expiration of the wartime legislation, jurisdiction over labour relations in Canada reverted to the provinces. A conference of Labour Ministers in 1946 urged that uniform collective bargaining legislation be adopted, and in 1948, the federal government passed The Industrial Relations and Disputes Investigation Act, which essentially re-worded the provisions of the 1944 regulations — without wage control.[13] This legislation was followed by all of the provinces, with relatively minor differences between the various acts. The uniformity in legislation was short-lived, however, and today there are significant differences in the legislative framework of the industrial relations system among the various jurisdictions.

In general, Canadian law has retained some similarity with the Wagner Act/Taft-Hartley elements of U.S. law, while differing from it in some important respects. The similarities are:
1. The three basic organizing and recognition principles exist in all jurisdictions.
2. With the exception of Quebec, all Canadian jurisdictions have labour relations boards to administer the legislation. Quebec has a three-tier system of commissioners which deal with certification and unfair labour practices and a Labour Court which acts in an appellate capacity over commission decisions as well as hearing prosecutions brought under the Labour Relations Act.
3. There are specified unfair labour practices for both unions and management in all jurisdictions.

The key differences between U.S. and Canadian law are:
1. With the exception of Alberta, British Columbia and Quebec, there are no provisions in Canadian law for emergency dispute resolution. Disputes in Canada are handled by *ad hoc* legislation.
2. In all jurisdictions, except Saskatchewan, conciliation is required before a strike or lockout can take place. Conciliation is voluntary in the U.S.
3. U.S. law does not mandate any particular provisions for collective agreements. In Canada, except for Saskatchewan, all ageements are required to have a provision banning strikes and lockouts during the term of an agreement and requiring all disputes to be submitted to arbitration. There are other required portions of collective agreements that vary by jurisdiction in Canada.
4. The U.S. law generally provides a greater degree of responsibility for unions to fairly represent employees (i.e., to represent them in a non-discriminating way), and safeguards to ensure democratic processes as well. Only four Canadian jurisdictions (federal, British Columbia, Ontario, and Quebec) have legislated fair representation requirements.
5. The role of the courts in issuing injunctions is clearly restricted by the Norris-La-Guardia Act in the U.S. In Canada, only British Columbia has acted to similarly restrict the use of injunctions by taking remedial power from the courts and giving it to the Labour Relations Board.[14] In other jurisdictions, the question of injunctive relief is far from clear. In general, injunctions will be issued by the courts in labour disputes where there is probability of property damage or personal injury, where unlawful acts are taking place or are threatened, or where no adequate remedy exists under the law. In other situations, the role of injunctions varies from jurisdiction to jurisdiction and situation to situation.

PUBLIC SECTOR LEGISLATION

In 1944, Saskatchewan became the first North American jurisdiction to give government employees collective bargaining rights. It did so with legislation that conferred those rights on *all* workers in the province and to this time has not made any legislative distinction between public-sector and private-sector employees. Saskatchewan is unique in this regard, however, as all other Canadian

Table 3–1
Labour Legislation in Canada

	Federal	Alberta	British Columbia	Manitoba	New Brunswick
Private Sector	Canada Labour Code	The Labour Relations Act	Labour Code	Labour Relations Act	Industrial Relations Act
Crown Corporations and Government Agencies	Canada Labour Code	Public Service Employees Relations Act	Essential Service Disputes Act — Labour Code	Labour Relations Act	Public Service Labour Relations Act
Civil Service	Public Service Staff Relations Act	Public Service Employees Relations Act	Public Service Labour Relations Act	Civil Service Act	Public Service Labour Relations Act
Municipal Workers	—	The Labour Relations Act	Labour Code	Labour Relations Act	Industrial Relations Act
Police	*	Firefighters' and Policemen's Labour Relations Act	Essential Service Disputes Act — Labour Code	Provincial Police Act	Public Service Labour Relations Act
Firefighters	Public Service Staff Relations Act	Firefighters' and Policemen's Labour Relations Act	Essential Service Disputes Act — Labour Code	Fire Department Arbitration Act	Public Service Labour Relations Act
Hospitals	Public Service Staff Relations Act	The Labour Relations Act	Essential Service Disputes Act —	Labour Relations Act	Public Service Labour Relations Act
Teachers	Public Service Staff Relations Act	The Labour Relations Act	School Act	Public Schools Act	Public Service Labour Relations Act

*The Royal Canadian Mounted Police are not given the right to collective bargaining.
**The structure of collective bargaining is governed by an Act respecting Management and Union Party
Organization in Collective Bargaining by the Sectors of Education, Social Affairs and Government Agencies.

Newfoundland	Nova Scotia	Ontario	Prince Edward Island	Quebec	Saskatchewan
Labour Relations Act 1977	Trade Union Act	Labour Relations Act	Labour Act	Labour Code	Trade Union Act
Public Service (Collective Bargaining) Act	Trade Union Act	Crown Employees Collective Bargaining Act	Civil Service Act	Labour Code — **	Trade Union Act
Public Service (Collective Bargaining) Act	Civil Service Collective Bargaining Act	Crown Employees Collective Bargaining Act	Civil Service Act	Civil Service Act — Labour Code	Trade Union Act
Labour Relations Act	Trade Union Act	Labour Relations Act	Labour Act	Civil Service Act — Labour Code	Trade Union Act
The Royal Newfoundland Constabulary Act	Trade Union Act	Police Act — Public Service Act (Provincial Police)	Labour Act	An Act respecting the syndicat plan of the Surete du Quebec	Police Act
St. John's Fire Department Act	Trade Union Act	Fire Department Act		Labour Code **	Trade Union Act
Public Service (Collective Bargaining) Act	Trade Union Act	Hospital Labour Disputes Arbitration Act	Hospitals Act	Labour Code **	Trade Union Act
Teacher Collective Bargaining Act	Teachers Collective Bargaining Act	School Boards and Teachers Collective Negotiation Act	School Act	Labour Code **	The Education Act

Source: *The Current Industrial Relations Scene in Canada 1983*, W.D. Wood and Pradeep Kumar, eds. Kingston: Industrial Relations Centre, Queen's University, pp. 107–111, 143–147.

jurisdictions have a variety of specific legislation covering public employees. The degree to which Canadian legislation permits collective bargaining in the public sector and allows for strikes by civil servants is another significant difference between Canada and the U.S., where, in addition to the federal government, only 28 of the 50 states have enacted labour relations legislation covering public-sector employees.

In 1964, revisions to the Quebec Labour Code gave all public employees, except for police and firefighters, the right to strike. In 1967, the federal government passed a Public Service Staff Relations Act. This act gave federal government employees the right to bargain for wages, hours and certain working conditions. It also gave them the right to strike. As bargaining units were certified to represent designated groups of employees, their leaders could elect one of two options at the start of each contract regarding the action to be taken in the event of an impasse at the end of the contract term. On one hand, they could elect to submit their dispute to conciliation which, if not successful, could give rise to a legal strike after a specified time period. On the other hand, they could forgo the right to strike, substituting compulsory binding arbitration of all issues in dispute. Most units have opted for arbitration of contract negotiation disputes.

The years following 1967 saw almost an explosion of collective bargaining legislation for employees in the public sector. By 1984, there were over 30 separate pieces of legislation regulating collective bargaining in the public sector. Table 3–1 (pages 56–57) summarizes Canadian labour relations legislation.

Table 3–1 provides visual evidence of the decentralized and fragmented nature of the legislative framework for collective bargaining in Canada. When the labour standards legislation and the occupational health and safety legislation in each jurisdiction are added to the acts listed in Table 3–1, one can easily conclude that a complete and detailed understanding of all this legislation is virtually impossible; particularly when the rules, procedures and decisions of labour relations boards, other administrative agencies and the courts must be taken into account in understanding the legislative/administrative framework within which industrial relations practitioners must operate.

This chapter has outlined the manner in which labour legislation has developed, and indicated the general nature of collective bargaining legislation. Subsequent chapters will provide some additional details on labour law, with particular reference to key differences between jurisdiction as these relate to union organizing, contract negotiation and contract administration. A complete explanation of the law, however, is beyond the scope of this book.

We close this chapter with a brief assessment of the decentralized nature of Canadian labour law. On the positive side, the law can be said to represent the diverse economic, social and political characteristics of Canada's provinces. In the U.S., where the basic legislation is national, a national consensus is needed before changes can be made. The difficulty in achieving such a consensus is reflected in the fact that there has been no important revision to the National Labor Relations Act in the U.S. since 1959. In Canada, change is much more frequent, and a legislative response to local and provincial problems and concerns is more likely to be an effective occurrence. Experimentation is more likely to occur.

On the negative side, because of the relative ease involved in amending legislation, there may be a tendency for the parties to spend their energy on influencing public policy rather than on attempting to work out effective relationships within an existing public policy framework. There are other costs to a fragmented approach to labour relations as well. George Adams, the former Chairman of the Ontario Labour Relations Board, described the Canadian approach to labour relations in this way:

> There are the substantial costs of duplication against the background of a scarcity of practitioners willing and able to serve the public as administrators. There is the complexity of regulation for any company wishing to do business in several of our provinces. There is also the potential for little reform in a province where collective bargaining lacks priority. And finally, there is the risk that the current framework is a substantial impediment to more centralized discussions and planning between labour and management with meaningful or desired trade-offs for their co-operation — the province lacking control over the key economic tools of government and the Federal Government having little say over the content of labour relations legislation. Clearly, these are issues that require the immediate attention of the key actors in the Canadian industrial relations system.[15]

Notes

1. Charles D. Gregory and Harold A. Katz, *Labor and the Law*, Third Edition. New York: W. W. Norton & Company, 1979, p. 13.

2. H. D. Woods, *Labour Policy in Canada*, Second Edition. Toronto: MacMillan of Canada, 1973, p. 34.

3. The Labor Relations Law Casebook Group, *Labour Relations Law*, Second Edition. Kingston: Industrial Relations Centre, Queen's University, 1974, pp. 8–9.

4. Woods, pp. 37–38.

5. Ibid., p. 41.

6. SSOLR 455(1924), 1 DLR 101 (1924), 2DLR 761 (1925), AC 396 (1925), 2 DLR 5(PC).

7. See A. W. R. Carrothers and E. E. Palmer, *Report of a Study on the Labour Injunction in Ontario*. Ontario Department of Labour, 1965.

8. Ex parte injunctions were used freely in Canada until the mid-1960s. These provided for issuance of prohibitive court orders based solely on the allegation of a violation of law or probable violation of law, or actual or probable damage or injury on sworn data by an alleged offended party. Such injunctions did not require the presence of the alleged offender.

9. Ivan C. Rand, *C.C. Report of the Royal Commission Inquiry into Labour Disputes*. Queen's Printer: Province of Ontario, 1968.

10. Charles Lipton, *The Trade Union Movement of Canada, 1927–1959.* Social Publications Ltd., 1960, p. 175.

11. Union Shops required that all employees join the union within a specified time period after hiring.

12. Lipton, pp. 270–271.

13. Woods, p. 98.

14. H. W. Arthurs, D. D. Carter and H. J. Glasbeek, *Labour Law and Industrial Relations in Canada.* Toronto: Butterworths, 1981, pp. 245–246.

15. George W. Adams, "Trends in Canadian Labour Law," *Proceedings* of the 17th Annual Meeting, Canadian Industrial Relations Association, 1980, p. 38.

4
THE ORGANIZING CHALLENGE

The organizing challenge is usually the first challenge which a union presents to management. Managements are very often unaware of union organizing until they receive a notice from the labour relations board that a union has applied to be certified as the representative of a specific group of employees.

In Chapter 3, we noted that one of the basic principles of North American labour law was that workers be free to form or join unions of their choice. All legislation provides for this right by establishing an administrative agency — the labour relations board* — to help insure that this occurs. The first part of this chapter will examine the legal framework within which union organization occurs. The second part will describe union organizing techniques.

THE LEGAL FRAMEWORK

Before the advent of collective bargaining legislation, unions had no easy way of being recognized for purposes of collective bargaining by employers. In general, the device most often used was the recognition strike which often led to bloody confrontations such as those described in Chapter 2. North American labour legislation has institutionalized the acquisition of bargaining rights, and as a result, recognition strikes are illegal. To acquire bargaining rights, a union simply

*All Canadian labour relations boards are appointed by the government (by order of the Governor General or Lieutenant General in Council). All have a chairman and one or more vice-chairmen. With the exception of the federal jurisdiction, Alberta and Prince Edward Island, the chairman and vice-chairmen are the only "neutrals," as the boards in all other jurisdictions are made up of an equal number of employer and employee representatives. Generally speaking, labour relations boards do not work as a whole but rather do their work in three-number panels.

applies to the labour relations board,** and if certain critical tests are met, is certified by the board as the exclusive bargaining agent for the employees in question. Once certification occurs, the employer is required to bargain with the union — and *only* with the union.

Exclusions from the Law

Not all employees are entitled to certification by labour relations boards. All legislation generally provides for specific exclusions from the labour relations legislation; that is, there are groups of individuals which the boards may not certify unions to represent. Table 4–1 provides a summary of excluded employee categories for each Canadian jurisdiction. In addition to those listed, groups such as teachers or firefighters are excluded from coverage by the act; specific collective bargaining legislation provides for them. (See Table 3–1).

Consistently excluded from coverage by legislation are managers and those employed in a confidential capacity by the employer in labour relations matters. Labour relations boards are frequently called on to decide whether particular individuals are managers or are employed in a confidential capacity in matters pertaining to labour relations. In general, boards do not rule on the basis of an individual's title but look closely at the functions which individuals actually perform. Very often, the boards examine the extent of authority an individual has over other employees, including the right to hire, fire or otherwise discipline employees and to appraise the work of those employees. Some boards have taken a very strict view of these requirements. For example, the Canadian Labour Relations Board has indicated that it was prepared to certify all employees in B.C. Telephone below the level of Vice-President, essentially because individuals below that level in the organization did not have real decision-making responsibilities.[2]

Appropriate Bargaining Unit

In the B.C. Telephone decision, the Canada Board indicated that while it would certify employees who would normally be considered managers, it would not certify them as part of another group of employees. They had to be in a separate bargaining unit. This is the approach generally taken by other boards.[3] The Public Service Staff Relations Act provides for certification of managers but requires that they be in a unit separate from other employees.[4]

The question of which group of employees is appropriate for collective bargaining is usually determined by agreement between the employer and the union. If they cannot agree, the labour board makes the determination. When a union applies for bargaining rights, it must state the group of employees that it seeks to represent.

**In Quebec, qualification applications are handled by certification agents and certification commissioners who work in much the same way as the labour boards in other jurisdictions.

Table 4–1[1]

Individuals Excluded from Coverage under Collective Bargaining Legislature

Jurisdiction	Exclusions
Federal	Those performing management functions or employed in a confidential capacity in matters relating to industrial relations.
Alberta	Those exercising managerial functions or employed in a confidential capacity in matters relating to labour relations. Members of the medical, dental, architectural, engineering or legal professions employed in their professional capacity, employees on a farm or ranch, domestic workers.
British Columbia	Those exercising the functions of a manager in the direction or control of employees or employed in a confidential planning or advisory position in the development of management policy or employed in a confidential capacity in matters relating to labour relations or personnel.
Manitoba	Those who perform management functions primarily or employed in a confidential capacity in matters relating to labour relations.
New Brunswick	Managers or superintendents or those who exercise management functions or those employed in a confidential capacity in matters relating to labour relations.
Newfoundland	Managers or superintendents or those who exercise management functions or those employed in a confidential capacity in matters relating to labour relations.
Nova Scotia	Managers or superintendents or those who exercise management functions or those employed in a confidential capacity in matters relating to labour relations. Members of engineering, architectural and legal professions who are employed in a professional capacity.
Ontario	Those who exercise managerial functions or employed in a confidential capacity in matters relating to labour relations. Members of the architectural, dental, land surveying, legal and medical professions employed in a professional capacity. Domestic employees. Persons employed in agriculture, hunting and trapping.
Prince Edward Island	Those who exercise managerial functions or employed in a confidential capacity in matters relating to labour relations. Members of the architectural, dental, engineering, legal and medical professions employed in a professional capacity.
Quebec	Those employed as managers, superintendents, foremen or representatives of the employer in relations with employees.
Saskatchewan	Those whose primary responsibility is to actually exercise authority and actually perform functions that are of a managerial character, those who are an integral part of the employees' management or those regularly acting in a confidential capacity in respect of industrial relations.

The term "bargaining unit" is used to describe a distinguishable group of employees capable of representation by a single union. Under some circumstances, primarily in the construction industry, some boards may certify a multiple union and/or multiple employer bargaining unit. More than one union may exist in a plant, each representing separate groups of employees and governed by a separate contract. Seagoing cargo vessels, as an example, are typically manned by representatives of six separate unions, some with only one or two members aboard but each with the power to deactivate the ship if his elected bargainers fail to come to an acceptable agreement. Crews on cross-country freight trains typically are comprised of representatives of four separate unions. Airline flight crews generally consist of representatives of three unions. Some manufacturing plants have as many as five separate bargaining units; more typically, those which are organized have two units of production employees, one or two units of distinguishable crafts, and an office workers group.

It is normal for a labour board to issue separate representation certificates to cover distinguishable employee units — even when applied for by the same union. However, in such instances, the union and company often agree in negotiation to bargain for all groups to be covered by the same contract.

In the absence of agreement on the bargaining unit by the employer and the union, the employers can have a significant influence in determining the appropriateness of a bargaining unit. However, challenges by employers are often looked upon with suspicion, because employers sometimes contest a unit merely as a means of gaining time to mount a campaign to defeat the union. If the employer's motives are sincere, and if his or her arguments are well presented, an employer can be reasonably certain that the following general guidelines will be used by the Board in determining the appropriateness of a proposed bargaining unit:

1. Is the proposed unit easily distinguishable geographically or by skill or craft?
2. Has the unit been agreed upon previously during an organizing drive?
3. Is there a clear community of interests among members of the bargaining unit?
4. Are typical lines of advancement or demotion in the organization substantially confined to the proposed unit?
5. Is the proposed unit typical?

In general, Canadian labour relations boards have tended to favour larger, more comprehensive bargaining units so as to avoid fragmentation of the bargaining structure. One group of employees that are almost always placed in a separate bargaining unit, though, is security guards and watchmen.

Another consideration in determining the composition of bargaining units may be the degree of ease or difficulty for employees in exercising the right to organize. Taking this into account, the Canada Labour Relations Board in 1977 reversed an earlier decision and ruled that employees in individual bank branches comprised an appropriate bargaining unit as opposed to employees in *all* branches in a bank. The Board's earlier position had made organization of bank employees a virtual impossibility.[5] While the Board's new position made certification much easier, it also served to fragment the post-organization bargaining in Canadian banks.

The board's rulings on the appropriateness of a bargaining unit are made as a result of a formal hearing, at which both the union and the employer may make representations. In making its decisions, the board may also receive factual information from its own staff, particularly from field officers who are empowered to investigate on behalf of the board. At the same hearing the board will hear evidence to determine if the union seeking certification is a *bona fide* bargaining agent as defined under the law.

Evidence of Membership

When a union applies for certification, it must submit evidence that employees in the proposed bargaining unit wish to be represented by that union. This evidence usually takes the form of membership cards signed by employees, along with a monetary payment of from $1.00 to $5.00.* Generally, the membership evidence must be timely; the card must have been signed within a specified time ranging from three months (Alberta, Newfoundland, Nova Scotia, Prince Edward Island) to six months (federal, Manitoba) to one year (Quebec). British Columbia, Ontario, and Saskatchewan have no specified time limits in their legislation.[6]

The board then checks and compares the membership cards against a list and sample signatures which the employer is required to submit to the board. If the union does not have the required number of signatures — usually expressed as a required percentage of the proposed bargaining unit — the board will dismiss the application. If the union has enough support, the board, after determining the appropriate bargaining unit and any other outstanding questions, will do one of two things:

1. It will either order an election among the affected employees as to whether they wish to be represented by a union, or
2. it will certify the union without an election.

Which course of action the board follows generally depends on the percentage of the bargaining unit that the union has signed. Table 4–2 summarizes the legislative provisions in each jurisdiction with regard to the percentage required for application and election or automatic certification. Most certifications in Canada occur without a vote.

The certification mechanism explains why most unions concentrate on organizing small cohesive groups of workers in a single location. Employers, on the other hand, faced with an application for certification, sometimes attempt to have the board define a bargaining unit of greater size than that applied for by the union. If successful with this strategy, the percentage of sign-ups required by the union would fall below that required for successful application to the board,

---

*Membership cards take many forms. An example is: "I, the undersigned employee of [company] wish to join the United Automobile, Aerospace and Agricultural Implement Workers of America, to abide by this organization's constitution and bylaws and to designate the organization as my exclusive bargaining agent."

Table 4–2
Certification Requirements

Jurisdiction	Membership Support Required for Application to Labour Board	Board Will Order an Election Where Indicated Support Is	Board Will Certify Automatically Where Membership Is	Percentage of Support Required in an Election***
Federal	none stated***	35%–50%	over 50%	majority of votes cast
Alberta	over 50%	*	over 50%	majority of votes cast
British Columbia	45%	45%–50%	over 55%	majority of votes cast
Manitoba	50%	*	*	majority of votes cast
New Brunswick	40%	40%–60%	more than 50%	more than 50% of those eligible to vote
Newfoundland	40%	40%–50%	over 50%	more than 50% of those eligible to vote
Nova Scotia	40%	40%	no provision	majority of votes cast
Ontario	45%**	45%–55%	more than 55%	majority of votes cast
Prince Edward Island	40%	*	more than 50%	majority of eligible employees or a majority of those voting if at least 75% of those eligible vote
Quebec	35%	35%–50%	more than 50%	majority of eligible employees
Saskatchewan	none stated	25%	no provision	majority of votes cast, if a majority of those eligible vote

* At the discretion of the board.
** 35% where a pre-hearing vote is requested.
***Federal legislation requires at least 35% of eligible employees to vote for the election to be valid. In British Columbia, if less than 55% vote, the board may order another election.

Source: *The Current Industrial Relations Scene in Canada 1983*, W. D. Wood and Pradeep Kumar, eds. Kingston: Industrial Relations Centre, Queen's University, pp. 112–115.

or at least would fall into the range where an election might be held, before which the employer might have the opportunity of influencing employee votes. Sometimes when they have a sufficiently large number of employees signed up, unions will move for a very comprehensive bargaining unit in order to include previously unsigned employees. Where union support is seen as overwhelming, employers will, at times, attempt to move for a smaller bargaining unit, excluding as many people as possible.[7]

Pre-hearing Vote

The possibility of delays in certification due to questions as to the appropriateness of the proposed bargaining unit or other matters has been handled in some jurisdictions by holding a pre-hearing vote. The provinces of Ontario and Prince Edward Island and the federal labour law provide for such a vote, which must be requested by the union at the time of application. The principal advantage to a pre-hearing vote, from a union's point of view, is that it allows minimal time for the employer to mount an effective drive to cause those who signed membership cards to change their minds about wanting a union.

There are two principal disadvantages:
1. If the employer successfully challenges the described bargaining unit, the results of the pre-hearing vote are invalid.
2. The organizer may need time after the application for certification to enlist more support.

Timeliness of Certification Application

Organizing drives of all kinds, whether a non-union company is involved or whether a raid on an established union by another is being attempted, must comply with specified laws regarding timing. If no trade union has been certified as a bargaining agent for the unit claimed by the union, the union may apply at any time. Some jurisdictions, including federal, British Columbia, Ontario and Quebec, have provisions which prevent repeated applications for certification within a limited time span. These jurisdictions can require a three to six months' interval between applications.[8]

Table 4–3[9]
Timeliness of Certification Applications

Jurisdiction	After Initial Certification Application From Another Union is Barred For	Where a Contract is in Force Application for Certification Will be Received
Federal	12 months	1. For agreements of two years or less, during the last three months of the term or the agreement. 2. For agreements of more than two years: a) in the 22–25 months of the agreement b) in the last three months of the year of the agreement c) in the last three months of the agreement.
Alberta	10 months	1. For agreements of two years or less, during the last two months of the term of the agreement. 2. For agreements of more than two years: a) the 11th and 12th months of the second and subsequent years of the agreement b) in the last two months of the agreement.

Table 4–3 (continued)

Jurisdiction	After Initial Certification Application From Another Union is Barred For	Where a Contract is in Force Application for Certification Will be Received
British Columbia	6 months	In the 7th and 8th month of each year of the agreement.
Manitoba	12 months	For agreements of 18 months or less, in the 7th, 8th and 9th months of the agreement. For agreements of more than 18 months: a) during the three months prior to the anniversary date on which the agreement took effect b) during the three months prior to the last three months of the agreement.
New Brunswick	12 months	For agreement of three years of less, the last two months of the agreement. For agreements of more than three years: a) the 35th and 36th months of the agreement b) the last two months of each year of the agreement c) the last two months of the agreement.
Nova Scotia	12 months	Same as New Brunswick except a three month "open session."
Ontario	12 months	For agreement of three years or less, the last two months of the agreement. For agreements of more than three years: a) the 35th and 36th months of the agreement b) the last two months of each year of the agreement c) the last two months of the agreement.
Prince Edward Island	10 months	1. For agreements of two years or less, during the last two months of the term of the agreement. 2. For agreements of more than two years: a) the 11th and 12th months of the second and subsequent years of the agreement b) the last two months of the agreement.
Quebec	6 months after parties have achieved a position to strike or lockout	The 90th to the 60th day prior to the expiration of an agreement or its renewal.
Saskatchewan	no specific provision; Board determines	No specific provision; Board determines.

In cases where a union has been certified, the labour boards will entertain an application from another union to represent the same group of employees but only at specified times. Such applications are often referred to as "raids." The general philosophy behind rules relating to raids by one union against another is that once certification is granted, the union and the employer ought to have an opportunity to negotiate a collective agreement free from the pressures of another organizing campaign. Once that agreement is signed, the parties should have an opportunity to build a working relationship. Consequently, the laws provide a bar to further raids while a contract is in effect. Table 4–3 provides a summary of the provisions in each jurisdiction for the acceptance of applications for certification where another union has previously been certified. British Columbia, Manitoba and Quebec legislation provides an "open season" at a time other than the period just before the expiry of a collective agreement. In these instances, the legislation reflects the belief that in the period just prior to the expiration of the collective agreement, the parties should be free of the pressure created by an application for certification so that they might devote their whole energy and attention to negotiating the provisions of the collective agreement.

Unfair Labour Practices

Unfair labour practices are actions by an employer or union which tend to inhibit a) an employee in his efforts to exercise freedom of choice regarding unionization, b) a union in representing that employee or, c) which tend to inhibit an employer in operating his business in a normal fashion, subject to laws permitting unionization and free collective bargaining.

A body of law has been built up through the years around unfair labour practices. A large majority of all unfair labour practice charges concern union organization campaigns and certification procedures. If charges are levied during an organization campaign, the investigation and hearing, if any, proceeds independently. The results of an unfair labour practice hearing could cause an election to be set aside. If the charges are serious enough, they could bar the union from further organizing for up to six months; if a company is found guilty, this could result in automatic certification of the union. The most frequent unfair labour practice charges fall into one of the following categories:
1. Intimidation, coercion, threats or promises to compel a person to join or not to join a union.
2. Persuasion of an employee during working hours to become or continue to be or refrain from becoming a member of a union.
3. Illegal strike or lockout or threat thereof.
4. Alteration of rates of pay or working conditions where the probable effect would be to cause an employee to refrain from joining or to quit membership in a union, unless such alteration is in the normal course of business.
5. Employer involvement or interference with a union.

Labour boards are given the jurisdiction to determine whether an unfair labour practice has occurred, and what, if any, remedy should be applied. Typically, the board's first response to a complaint is to assign a field officer to investigate and attempt to informally effect a settlement. If this fails, then the board will hold a hearing to decide if the charge has merit.

In deciding a case, the board will be influenced by many factors. Among these are the nearness of the incident to the time of election: the nearer, the more influence it is likely to have on an employee's vote; consequently, the more likely that the charge will be upheld. Another factor taken into consideration is the history of the employer's actions regarding union organizing attempts. If the employer has been known to make good on threats to discharge employees for union activity, then there is a greater likelihood that such threats would have an intimidating influence than if he had regularly retreated from threats in the past. Consequently, such an employer would be more vulnerable to an unfair practice charge.

Labour relations boards generally have wide ranging remedial powers to correct the effects of unfair labour practices. They can order reinstatement with full back pay to discharged employees. They can issue "cease and desist" orders and require the employer to compensate the union for the costs of an organizing campaign affected by unfair employer practices. In some cases, boards have required company presidents to publicly apologize to employees for unfair practices, and assure them that such acts would not be repeated.[10]

Violation of the various labour relations acts is also punishable by fines, although for this to occur the complainant must prosecute through the courts. In the federal and Ontario jurisdictions, such prosecutions can only occur with the consent of the Labour Relations Board, and such consent is not easily obtained. In any event, the fines specified in the legislation (e.g., in Ontario $1,000 per day for individuals; $10,000 per day for organizations)[11] do not go to a successful complainant, they go to the government, like a fine for a parking violation. Thus, despite provision for fines for unfair labour practices in legislation, this route is rarely taken by an aggrieved party, and where charges are laid, they almost always go to the labour boards and not the courts.

Other Issues

Voluntary Recognition

An employer may voluntarily recognize a union as the representative of his employees without the involvement of a labour relations board, and a collective agreement signed under such an agreement would be valid. However, if such voluntary recognition was secured at the expense of a union which could demonstrate that it represented a majority of employees, then recognition could be voided by a labour board, as could the voluntary recognition of a "union" that was formed with employer assistance or dominated by the employer. Ontario legislation provides for an "open season" throughout the first year of an agreement with a voluntarily recognized union as a safeguard against such situations.

Decertification

All Canadian jurisdictions have provisions for the termination of bargaining rights, or of "decertifying" a union. In general, the procedure for the termination of bargaining rights is the same as for certification. Labour boards generally look very carefully for evidence of employer involvement in any application for termination of bargaining rights that they receive. If any such involvement is found, the application is generally rejected. Applications for decertification will normally only be accepted by labour boards during the times when applications for certification would be acceptable when a collective agreement is in force. (See Table 4–3.)

Successor Rights

Canadian legislatures have generally moved to give the collective bargaining rights acquired by unions through the certification process some permanence by providing that such rights continue to exist where a business is sold or transferred. Where a contract is in effect, the new owner of a business must continue to follow the terms of the collective agreement. Where no agreement is in effect, the new owner has the same duty to bargain in good faith as did the old owner. While the notion of preserving bargaining rights is a simple one, difficulties are often involved in its application. These difficulties include questions as to whether a sale or transfer actually occurred, what to do if there is an intermingling of employees of the old employer with those of the new, and whether the bargaining rights remain if the character of the business has changed. Labour boards generally have the authority to investigate and resolve any questions that relate to the status of bargaining rights in the event of a sale or transfer.[12]

ORGANIZING TECHNIQUES

All major unions employ field organizers. These are men and women who spend most of their time going from company to company attempting to organize workers. Their skills are finely honed. In general, their knowledge of the relevant laws is complete. They vary their techniques as the composition of the workforce and problems of the employment relationship dictate.

This section is written from the viewpoint of a union organizer, not because the authors necessarily sympathize with the union point of view but because we believe that intricacies of an organizing drive can be understood best by viewing them through the eyes of one who is most frequently involved.

Some organizers are specialists within their profession. One union, for example, employs a man in Canada who specializes in organizing workers of Italian origin. He is Italian himself, speaks the language and appreciates the special problems of this ethnic minority. Others specialize in organizing blacks, women, or white collar professionals. Some are especially adept in organizing miners, others in organizing lumbermen.

Organizers are not elected to their positions. They are full-time union employees whose tenure often transcends that of elected officers. Some of them have, themselves, formed unions to bargain for wages, hours and working conditions with their employer — the union. Now, at a time in history when vistas for new organizing activity have narrowed, the skills of organizing are more finely tuned than ever before.

The Contact

Most union organizing drives start with a few disgruntled workers who have compared their wages and working conditions with those of other workers in the community. Typically, one or two of them call or visit the local office of a union, possibly learning about it from a friend or a newspaper article. While unions carry identifying names that tend to associate them with a certain group of workers, the competitive nature of most unions will lead them to express interest in any group of workers indicating a genuine desire to organize. Many unlikely associations have developed through the years as a result of this competitiveness. The Playboy Club bunnies in New York City, for example, have been represented by the Teamsters Union—known generally as an organization for truck drivers; District 50 of the United Mineworkers represent the dormitory maids at Yale University, and the United Steelworkers represent bartenders in Timmins, Ontario.

On initial contact, the union official will assess the situation; if it looks reasonably promising, the organizer will take the names, addresses and phone numbers of the interested employees and assign an organizer to contact them. From this time on, the organizer works as strategist, educator, counsellor and companion to members of the work force in an effort to enlist enough support to secure certification, provided, of course, that he or she believes there is a reasonable probability that the workers can be organized.

Sometimes union organizers themselves will take the initiative in attempting to enlist a group of workers, even if there has been no contact from members of the workforce. This sort of action is most common in communities where one or two well-known non-union companies operate amid a preponderance of unionized firms. Such companies are often a source of embarrassment and unrest for a local organizer, for one or both of two reasons. Either the managements are so enlightened that workers believe their non-union situation is better than being unionized, causing envy among unionized workers, or the management has been successful in thwarting union organizing drives in the past through well-executed battle techniques and represents a seductive challenge to the union man to try again. The Dominion Foundry and Steel Company (DOFASCO) of Hamilton, Ontario represented a challenge to the United Steelworkers of America, who represent a large number of workers in this highly organized industrial community. DOFASCO has remained unorganized through the years by maintaining a record of progressive labour relations practices and keeping their wage and fringe benefit packages at least equal to and sometimes ahead of the union pattern. Time and time again, organizers have mounted campaigns at DOFASCO, and time and time again, they have been thwarted, sometimes as a result of poor organizing techniques, more often as a result of a lack of interest among employees.

One of the organizer's first tasks is to form a nucleus of committed employees who will be willing to work long hours for no compensation and sometimes at considerable risk to themselves. Quite naturally, this nucleus is usually made up of people suggested by those who made the initial contact. However, experienced organizers usually insist on meeting all members of the nucleus group for the first time in person. This way, a more accurate assessment can be made as to whether the person can do the job; those who seem reluctant are promptly dropped.

While the law prohibits discrimination against employees for union activity, an employer may discharge a worker and then sit back and wait for the long cumbersome process of unfair labour practice action to take its course. In general, labour boards hold any discharge during a union campaign as based on anti-union bias unless there is evidence to the contrary, so that the employee is likely to prevail and be awarded his job plus full back pay. However, the union campaign might well be a matter of history. For this reason, organizers are careful to spell out the risks involved and to point out the desirability of keeping the campaign quiet, at least in the early stages.

Most organizers prefer to work with a group of no more than four or five highly committed workers who can be trusted to maintain confidentiality. With information gathered from those workers about the company, its history, its personalities, its products, customers and practices giving rise to the desire to organize, the union organizer can plot the campaign.

Axiomatic with all campaigns is the need for an up-to-date, accurate list of all employees in the bargaining unit. Obtaining such a list without the knowledge of the employer is difficult, so organizers resort to many devices. One of the crudest, but sometimes necessary as a last resort, is to write down the licence plate numbers of all cars in the company parking lot, and then to make a request to the Ministry of Transportation and Communications to furnish the names of the owners. This provides a starting point.

Having obtained a list, the organizer then attempts to learn as much as possible about each person — age, seniority, work classification, ethnic background and attitude toward a union. A worker's attitude toward unionization may be unknown at the outset of the campaign, but as time progresses, the position will become known. Also, the organizer tries to learn about any disagreeable working conditions, or bull-headed supervisors, and about how the company stacks up against other companies in the community in terms of wages and benefits. Most of this information can be secured from the workers who made the original approach, but an organizer is well advised to check out all information carefully, because disgruntled workers do not always see things accurately.

Competent organizers have a good knowledge of the community, its politics, the attitude of the police force, the record of courts regarding issuance of injunctions, other unions in the area, and the nature of the news media. All of these become important as the campaign progresses.

Sign-Ups

Perhaps the most difficult job of an organizer is to get employees signed to membership cards as soon as possible, but quietly. Probably the best way to secure committed signatures is to visit each employee at his or her home, but such visits are extremely time consuming. They should never seem hurried, and for maximum effectiveness, the organizer should call at a convenient time, avoiding meal hours, and including the whole family in the conversation. The organizer should be willing to talk about all sorts of subjects including Wayne Gretzky's scoring record and the Prime Minister's latest pronouncement. All this means at least an hour with each employee and, possibly, a follow-up visit. Most organizers consider four or five visits a day to be the maximum possible.

By developing a nucleus of committed employees who are willing and able to make house visits, the organizer can gain considerable effectiveness and speed. Effectiveness comes from familiarity; workers will generally respond most favourably to someone they know or with whom they share a workplace. However, there are risks in having fellow employees make house calls. One is that they may be unable to give satisfactory answers to questions about the union. Another risk is that they may "blow" the sales pitch through lack of sophistication, trying to hog the conversation, engaging in heated arguments or putting on pressure. For these reasons, the organizer must do a hard-nosed educating job and screen out those who lack the necessary skills. For these reasons, as well, house-to-house sign-ups are not usually undertaken, except in special cases where a particular employee's signature is considered "key" to the campaign's success. Rather, the organizer and a small nucleus of employees seek to sign up people on company premises during lunch, coffee and break periods or while they are coming to or going from work. Signatures are obtained most rapidly this way, but managements also find out about the organizing drive most rapidly this way.

The first approach to sign a union card is normally made to those employees who are believed to be most in favour of the union. This helps build enthusiasm. It also increases the probability of maintaining secrecy longer, because these employees are least likely to disclose the fact that organizing is taking place.

The organizer aims for 70 to 80 percent sign-ups and automatic certification. All organizers try to give the impression that the union is there to stay, that there is no intention of pulling out, even if the going gets tough. And they make it clear that organizing is risky — that the employer might retaliate. They set up a procedure by which authorization cards can be turned in to the organizer or to the union office as they are collected. This way the cards can be carefully checked to be sure that they are properly filled out.

Union organizers are constantly on the alert for forged cards. In Canadian jurisdictions, one forged card, regardless of the number of valid cards, could cause the union to lose its organizing rights at the company involved. In the United States, the knowing submission of a forged card to the National Labor Relations Board is a federal offence, and the forger may be punished by up to five years in jail and a $10,000 fine.

One way to minimize the incident of forgeries is for the organizer to insist that employees who collect signatures write their own name on each card as a witness. Presumably, a person will be reluctant to forge a card bearing his name.

Generally, organizers do not divulge the number of sign-ups to anyone until they have a substantial majority. There are two reasons for this: first the employer might use the information in planning a campaign to defeat the union; and second, it might cause discouragement, if the number is low, or laxity, if it is high, among members of the organizing committee.

Resistance

Most organizing drives encounter resistance after an early surge of sign-ups. Usually this comes when the organizing committee moves from securing signatures of those favourable to the union to those who are less certain. Here, more than at the earlier stages, the organizer must use his or her knowledge about the company and its problems and the union and its ability to cope with those problems. The organizer takes on the role of salesperson; one who knows the customer best and is well acquainted with the commodity being sold—the union — usually succeeds best. It is at this stage in the campaign that the organizer often chooses to come out in the open. This is done because the employer is likely to find out anyhow, since employees with doubts often go to him with questions; and because a wide-open, above-the-board campaign can sometimes yield a fair number of sign-up cards caused by a bandwagon effect, especially if there is a large, enthusiastic base of employees who have already signed.

Sign-ups usually continue throughout the campaign. A rule of organizing is that no more than one organizer should ever approach an employee at one time — lest there be an impression of intimidation. Most often the sign-up campaign is augmented by distributing leaflets at plant gates, by announcements of the drive through the media and sometimes by scheduling an open meeting.

One veteran organizer said that he often used the "rainy day" technique to sign up recalcitrant, but "key," employees. This involved making house contacts on cold, rainy, miserable days. If done with humility and sincerity the worker sometimes signs a card out of sympathy, expressing the belief that if someone believes in the union so much that he is willing to go out on such a miserable night, it must be worth signing.

General Meetings

Open general meetings are held less frequently in modern organizing drives than they were in the 1930s and 40s. This is because in today's sprawling cities, they are usually poorly attended, and a sparsely populated meeting often dampens enthusiasm. Even with a good turnout, there is a danger that some formerly enthusiastic employees will lose their enthusiasm — especially if they are forced to listen to a number of long-winded speeches. Veteran organizers have a series of rules that help guide them in holding general meetings. These include the following:
1. Don't hold a meeting unless you are sure of a good turnout.
2. If there are speeches, be sure the speaker talks sincerely, with a simple vocabulary.

3. Be sure speakers refrain from telling off-colour jokes or jokes with racial or ethnic overtones.
4. Maintain a "togetherness" atmosphere, never using the phrase "you people" or the word "you."
5. Don't make wild promises.

The final item regarding wild promises reflects a material departure from earlier organizing drives. It was possible to promise a great deal in the early days because conditions were often bad and could be improved substantially in a short time. In addition, workers were less sophisticated then and perhaps more gullible. Now, workers are far more knowledgeable and skeptical. They trust understatement before they trust flamboyance.

Perhaps the most important reason for avoiding wild promises is to avert subsequent disappointment. If a group of workers becomes certified and then starts bargaining with hopes of fulfilling all their promises at once, the employer is likely to resist, even to the point of refusing to sign a contract. If this happens in a first negotiation, the newly formed union could be destroyed.

Employer Tactics

From an employer's viewpoint, the best tactic for avoiding a union is to create and maintain working conditions such that employees believe they are best off without a union. Nearly every work force has members who espouse unionization, no matter how good the working conditions, but these people are easily overcome by the majority if it can be shown that wages and working conditions are as good or better than those at any union shop. These facts should be matters of constant awareness among members of the workforce, not items that are brought up only when the union organizing drive becomes evident.

There are many devices that employers can use to thwart an organizing drive, some of them legal and some of them not, but the effect of these devices is likely to be temporary unless the employer sincerely builds toward a relationship where unions are deemed unnecessary. There are consultants who specialize in helping employers keep unions out both by designing short-term tactics and helping to build a long-term, progressive relationship. Some of these consultants are highly effective, sometimes going so far as to knowingly violate the law where it will gain them a momentary advantage, aware that risks are involved but believing the risks are low as compared to the benefits of keeping the union out. Union organizers are well aware of the tactics used by these consultants, and they have devised tactics of their own in defence. Among the employer-consultant tactics described most often by union organizers are the following:
1. Discharging or disciplining known union agitators;
2. the use of doctored statistics, such as selective wage surveys, to make employees believe conditions are better than they are;
3. making threats or promises contingent upon victory or defeat of the union;
4. secretly promoting the formation of an employees' association and encouraging the association itself to apply for certification.
(Items 1, 3, and 4 are generally considered by boards to be unfair labour practices.)

A shrewd union organizer will anticipate these tactics and warn members of the workforce to be on the lookout for them. Then, if they are used, the organizer can say: "I told you so." If they are not used, he can always hold out the possibility that they might be.

Some employers make sudden changes when threatened by organization. These may indicate genuine new-found awareness that problems exist and a sincere desire to do something about them, or, on the other hand, they may represent a flurry to take the immediate sting out of the union drive. Among such changes are insurance programs, and opening up the doors of executive offices to listen to employee committees to create lines of communication. All these devices involve risks, even if attempted in good faith, because union leaders can claim that their mere presence caused the improvements to happen, asking workers to imagine how much more could be accomplished if the union were there all the time. In addition, the devices may be costly, well beyond the price of the improvement itself, because if the union drive is successful, the existing wages, fringe benefits and working conditions become the base on which negotiation demands are built.

The most frequent tactics used by employers to thwart unionization are those which delay certification procedures, giving the company more time to mount a campaign of its own designed to cause employees to vote "no union" in the election. One of the most frequently used delay tactics is a challenge of the proposed bargaining unit, contending for any number of reasons that it is not appropriate for bargaining, that it should be enlarged or reduced. Employers are ill-advised to use this kind of tactic unless they are prepared to live with the unit they propose, because union organizers may accede to their wishes knowing they have enough signed cards to win outright certification or an election even if the unit is changed. If the union agrees to a revised unit, the issue is generally solved without board interference. If they do not, the board might prescribe the unit as the employer proposed it, and if the union is certified, this then becomes a unit from which it is almost impossible to retreat. Records are heavy with cases where employers sought to change the composition of a bargaining unit so as to include assistant supervisors, leadhands, sales personnel or inspectors and won their point only to wind up with these groups organized, against the desire of both the employer and members of the included groups. Similarly, employers have succeeded in reducing the size of a proposed unit only to find the employees who are left out forming another unit of their own, covered by a separate contract.

Employer's Rights

Laws governing union organizing are aimed toward an ideal where there can be a genuine expression of employee preference without either party resorting to illegal or questionable tactics. A realistic employer who wishes for stability in employee relations will hope for an overwhelming victory or defeat in the organizing attempt; this will help insure that the union clearly represents the employees, or, on the other hand, that there are not many unhappy employees as a result of the union's defeat. To win or lose by a close margin means that regardless of the outcome, there are a substantial number of disgruntled employees.

If an employer learns that a substantial majority of his employees wish to join a union, he should seriously consider granting voluntary recognition, so that the parties can get on quickly with the job of collective bargaining. However, he should recognize that voluntary recognition may be tenuous. If the true wishes of employees have not been represented, there is a danger that the agreement to recognize may be challenged. If a challenge is raised at any time during the first year by an employee or another union, most Canadian labour laws place the onus on the parties to the agreement to establish that the recognized union is entitled to represent the employees. Failure to uphold the onus could result in throwing out any collective agreement which has been reached.[13] In addition, the challenging union could win certification.

Employers have demonstrated repeatedly their lack of knowledge about their rights and obligations under the labour laws, and about those of employees and unions as well. Many times they make serious errors, committing blatant violations of the law and causing employees to swarm to the arms of a union. Then, finally, when they seek expert advice, it is too late — the game is lost.

On the other hand, many employers, when faced with an organizing drive, act as if the jig is up: because they do not know their rights, they surrender without a whimper. When confronted with an organizing campaign, the first step a company should take is to obtain good legal counsel. Following is a list of some of the things an employer may do under the law. All of these are predicated on an employee's right under the law not to join, as well as to join, a union.

1. Employers have a right to express their opinions, views and sentiments regarding unions in general and the organizing union in particular. This is one of the most potent weapons employers can use; yet, strangely, it is seldom utilized.
2. Employers may state their position on whether employees should or should not vote for the union, or on any other matters involved in the organizing campaign.
3. Employers may prohibit solicitation for the union on their own property on company time. Generally, they must allow solicitation on free time, subject to reasonable regulations respecting safety and proper conduct.
4. Employers may prohibit distribution of union literature on premises, provided that they customarily prohibit distribution of all forms of literature.
5. Employers may increase wages, make promotions and take other personnel action if they would do so anyway in the normal course of business and in accordance with established policy.
6. Employers may assemble employees during working hours and state opinions respecting the election, as long as they avoid threats and promises.[14] However, if an employer does this in Ontario during the 72-hour period preceeding an election or in the United States in the 24-hour period before an election, the election itself may be set aside. Employers have no obligation to give the union the same opportunity.

The following actions by an employer are illegal and could cause automatic certification or setting aside of an election if the employer wins:
1. Promise of improvements in wages or working conditions contingent on the defeat of the union;
2. threat to move or close the business or to reduce wages or beneficial working conditions;
3. granting of wage increases or making other personnel changes that are *not* in the normal course of business;
4. taking any action which the Board believes deceived the employees on vital issues to the degree that they were unable to vote freely.

Labour boards will look at all employer actions in the context of the employer's total response to the organizing campaign. Where that campaign involves elements of strong anti-union propaganda, for example, what might ordinarily appear to be innocent language or actions might be viewed by the Board as less than benign.

While some employers give up the ghost when the union appears, others overreact. Suddenly the door to the front office opens, golf dates are cancelled and afternoon cocktails are postponed. The foremen become more friendly, more interested in the employees and their problems; personal letters from the president are prepared and sent to the homes of employees stating that after an honest, thorough study, the president believes, in the best interests of all concerned, that there is no advantage in having a union. An employee committee is organized to convince the workers that they already have an organization.

All these are legal, but if they happen suddenly they are likely to seem insincere. Alert union organizers are ready for such moves and often make fairly standard, but effective, countermoves. For example, if an employee committee has been formed, the union will most likely attempt to force that committee to solve a knotty problem, like reorganization of a seniority system for handling promotions and lay-offs, or the design of a liberal pension plan. When this happens the committee often collapses.

Collective Bargaining

During the later stages of an organizing campaign, the union organizer usually gathers a committee of employees together to start working on bargaining demands. This helps maintain enthusiasm after most of the card signing is done and while formal certification processes are taking place. In addition to keeping the workers interested, it makes for preparedness when the time for bargaining arrives. According to the law in all jurisdictions, the union is required to make the first move toward bargaining following certification, by giving the employer written notice. Then the law requires the parties to meet within a stipulated time period of the giving of notice or within such further period as parties agree upon. The law requires, in addition, that they shall bargain in good faith and make every reasonable effort to make a collective agreement. In all jurisdictions, once certification is made, the employer is prohibited by law from changing rates of pay and other terms of employment.

Once certification is secured the union organizer normally leaves the scene and puts his newly formed bargaining committee into the hands of an area representative or business agent whose job it is to negotiate contracts or to serve as adviser to local negotiating teams. In a smooth-running union, the transition is easy. The organizer has refrained from wild promises and has kept the expectations of the new union members within reason. With luck, the organizer has established a businesslike relationship with the employer so that the company and union can operate with respect for each other and genuine concern for each other's problems. However, not all unions are smooth-running, and union organizers do not always approach the job on a businesslike basis. All too often, the organization phase of labour-management relations results in frayed nerves and, sometimes, violence, as parties look upon the organizing drive as a battle to be won or lost. Whatever its outcome, if the organizing drive is based on less-than-honourable intentions or if antagonisms develop during the campaign, there is likely to be a deleterious effect on the relationship for many succeeding years.

Notes

1. Federal: Canada Labour Code, R.S.C. 1970, C L-1, Sec. 107; Alberta: Labour Relations Act, R.S.A. C. 1-1.1, Sec. 1 (k); British Columbia: Labour Code, R.S.B.C., 1972, C. 212, Sec. 1(2); Manitoba: Labour Relations Act, C.C.S.M., C. L10, Sec. 1(k); New Brunswick: Industrial Relations Act, R.S.N.B., 1973, C. I-14, Sec. 1; Newfoundland: The Labour Relations Act, 1977, S.M. 1977, C.64, Sec. 2(M); Nova Scotia: Trade Union Act, S.N.S. 1972, C. 19, Sec. 2; Ontario: Labour Relations Act, R.S.O. 1980, C. 228, Sec. 2; Prince Edward Island: Labour Act, R.S.P.E.I. 1974, C. L-1, Sec. 7(2); Quebec: Labour Code, R.S.Q., 1977, C. C-27, Sec. 1(1); Saskatchewan: Trade Union Act, R.S.S. 1978, C. T-17, Sec. 2(f).

2. [1976] 1 C.L.R.B.R. 273.

3. H. W. Arthurs, D. D. Carter and H. J. Glasbeek, *Labour Law and Industrial Relations in Canada.* Toronto: Butterworths, 1981, p. 178.

4. R.S.C. 1970 S. 26(1), (4).

5. Canadian Imperial Bank of Commerce [1977] C.L.R.B.R. 99.

6. *The Current Industrial Relations Scene in Canada 1983*, W. D. Wood and Pradeep Kumar, eds. Kingston: Industrial Relations Centre, Queen's University, pp. 119–120.

7. H. W. Arthurs *et al*, p. 174.

8. Ibid., p. 172.

9. Canada Labour Code, Sec. 124(2); Alberta Labour Relations Act, Sec. 34(3); British Columbia Labour Code, Sec. 39; Manitoba Labour Relations Act, Sec. 26; New Brunswick Industrial Relations Act, Sec. 10 (3)(5)(6)(7); Newfoundland Labour Relations Act, Sec. 36 (3)(4); Nova Scotia Trade Union Act, Sec. 22 (3)(4)(5); Ontario Labour Relations Act, Sec. 5 (2)(4)(5); Prince Edward Island Labour Act, Sec. 11 (3)(4)(5)(6); Quebec Labour Code, Sec. 22; Saskatchewan Trade Union Act, Sec. 5.

10. See Canadian Imperial Bank of Commerce 80 C.L.L.C. 16,002 and Radio Shack 1980 1 C.L.R.B.R. 99.

11. The Labour Relations Act (R.S.O. 1980) Sec. 96.

12. H. W. Arthurs *et al*, pp. 181–183.

13. The Labour Relations Act (R.S.O., 1980) Sec. 60(3).

14. See, for example, Ex-Cello Corporation [1977] 2 C.L.R.B.R. 233.

MUSKOKA UNIVERSITY (A)

Mr. Henry Talbot, Personnel Manager for the library at Muskoka University, was troubled about the conversation he had overheard earlier that morning between two employees in the Binding Department. There was a rumour circulating that a union organization drive was about to commence.

Muskoka University was a medium sized university with approximately 6,000 students, 1,000 of which were graduate students. There were five faculties at the university, Engineering, Law, Fine Arts, Arts and Science, and Business Administration. The university was located in Bradley, Ontario, which was approximately 150 miles north of Toronto. Bradley had a population of 120,000 and many of the residents were employees of the Federal or Provincial governments, or the Canadian National Railways. The city was a major rail centre, and both Federal and Provincial governments had established regional headquarters in Bradley. The city was often described as a "university and government town."

The library employed 130 people, plus professional librarians in the main library and the various faculty and departmental libraries. The university, in total, employed approximately 1,200 clerical and support people. In addition, there were five cafeterias and one tavern on the campus.

The university, like most others in Ontario, was under severe pressure to restrict and meet budgets in the wake of recent provincial government announcements of reduced spending in the education field. There had been some staff reductions already and it was likely there would be more, affecting virtually all areas of the university.

Mr. Talbot, 31 years old, had been hired just eight months before, in January, to formulate a new classification and pay rate system, and to administrate all matters pertaining to library personnel. He had had six years experience in university library administration, mostly at McMaster University in Hamilton. He had been hired by Dr. Ronald Butler, the chief librarian and Mr. Bill Masters, Personnel Director for Muskoka University.

Dr. Butler had also recently come to Muskoka. He was 42 years old and had sixteen years of library experience. He had been hired nine months before Mr. Talbot's appointment. Mr. Talbot described him as "a dynamic and aggressive man." Dr. Butler felt the previous administration had been sloppy and too informal; he was planning to make major changes in the organization of the library. The university was in the process of completing a new, much larger library complex which would be finished in December and available for occupancy in the early spring. Dr. Butler wanted to complete all the organizational changes so that he could implement them when the library moved into its new building. Thus, Mr. Talbot was hired to organize and implement all changes which would directly involve employee relations in the library, leaving Dr. Butler free to concentrate on other facets of the preparations for the library move.

Mr. Talbot began by reviewing Muskoka Library personnel procedures and records. He was initially distressed with the unusual mixture of employees;

there seemed to be a number of young political radicals and militants, people who had a history of staying at the same job for only one or two years at a time, as well as a number of long-term employees who were mostly middle aged and older women. There were also several professional librarians; many employees had one or more university degrees. He soon found out that the university personnel office had the attitude that if people applying for a job were not accepted in other university departments, they would send them to the library. The situation had developed into an office joke.

Mr. Talbot continued reviewing the records and interviewing staff for approximately four months and then in early May began to isolate problems and potential causes, and formulate some tentative solutions. In June he prepared a questionnaire to be given to each employee, requesting them to describe the job they were performing, and to discuss any problems they were encountering. By mid-July he received the tabulated results of the questionnaire and studied them carefully. The problems that concerned the employees were consistent with the major problems that he previously had identified: arbitrary pay increases and promotions, no job descriptions, little relationship between responsibility exercised and pay, and low job security. Mr. Talbot was encouraged by the cooperation and the number of responses he had received through the questionnaire.

In August, after studying the results of the questionnaire, Mr. Talbot began to interview employees and library departmental supervisors, and to write more formal job descriptions. In late August, the university administration awarded a general and substantial wage increase to all of its clerical staff in order to keep in line with overall community rates. This increase was given quite independently from the work that Mr. Talbot was doing. As August was ending and September beginning, however, the new job description and classification system were beginning to take shape, and Mr. Talbot was confident that he would be able to give Dr. Butler a report with recommendations for substantial changes, some time in November.

In mid-September, just as students were returning to classes for the fall term, Mr. Talbot overheard two employees in the Binding Department talking about a small group of employees, who, allegedly, had contacted a union, the Canadian Union of Public Employees (CUPE), and had asked it to try to organize the library staff. Mr. Talbot was concerned about the rumour and what effect a union drive might have on the fate of his upcoming report. He wondered how to go about getting more information, and if a union was going to try, what staff members they would want to organize. He tried to anticipate the implications of running a unionized university library, both advantages and disadvantages. If there was a union drive beginning he wondered what position should he take and what policy should he follow when responding to the union bid. Mr. Talbot was concerned as to how to proceed.

MUSKOKA UNIVERSITY (B)

During the first week in October, Mr. Talbot, the personnel manager of Muskoka University Library, was trying to complete his report on the new employee classification and pay rate system that he had developed. He was hoping to finish the report by the end of the month. Mr. Talbot had worked long and hard in recent weeks. He was very concerned with the rumours of a possible union organization drive by the Canadian Union of Public Employees (CUPE) for the library staff at Muskoka University. He had overheard two employees talking about it in mid-September, and had decided to ignore the rumour until it was substantiated. In the meantime, he decided he would try to complete his report as quickly as possible. However, the rumours had become more prolific since the beginning of October, to the point where employees had allegedly received a letter from CUPE. Mr. Talbot, his concern renewed, intensified his efforts to complete his report. In mid-October, somebody slipped a letter and pamphlet under Mr. Talbot's office door. The letter is reproduced as Exhibit I.

The pamphlet described how a library worker represented by CUPE won reinstatement for unjust dismissal as a result of a grievance filed under a Collective Agreement. The pamphlet featured a picture of the cheque for back pay in the amount of $5,000, which the employee received as a result of the grievance settlement.

EXHIBIT I

CANADIAN UNION OF PUBLIC EMPLOYEES

October 14th.

To: All the Employees of the Faculty of the Library
Muskoka University

Greetings:

Well as I stated in my letter of October 1st, that a great number of calls were received at this office asking what could be done to make working for Muskoka a more rewarding experience. These are people, like you, who are aware of the fine tradition of the University. But, they believe that dignity of the University does nothing to give dignity to their work.

They have found that the dignity of the University can't be cashed at the Bank. Can't give them Job Security. Can't improve their Fringe Benefits.

Library and clerical workers in the Faculty of the Library have expressed a great interest in somehow joining together to present to the University Management, proposals for improving wages, working conditions, fringe benefits and methods of classifying jobs. Your response has been most gratifying. Keep those cards coming.

In Ontario, C.U.P.E. already represents University employees at Carleton, Brock, Windsor, Guelph, Waterloo, Toronto, Queens, Boards of Education, Municipal, Library,

C.B.C. employees, Professional Librarians and support staffs at City of London, North York, East York, Toronto and Bradley. C.U.P.E. represents approximately 90,000 here in Ontario. These people felt the same frustrations and needs now being expressed by your fellow Muskoka workers. They felt, as you do, the financial pinch caused by the rising costs of living. They began working to improve their conditions by joining together as a Local of C.U.P.E.

The Ontario Labour Law says specifically that you can be represented by C.U.P.E. only after a majority 55% sign C.U.P.E. Membership Cards. Once that happens you decide for yourself what type of improvements you would like to see made. C.U.P.E., with it's trained, highly skilled Representatives will assist you in your bargaining. He will be backed up by the C.U.P.E. Research Statistics Department as well as the C.U.P.E. Legislative and Public Relations experts.

YOU and the other members of your Local have the final say on what you will finally accept as your conditions of work and wages, and your present amicable relationship with your employer will not change. In fact, a contract (which is a legal document) will define the channels of communications, clarifying the procedures you would take for grievances, requests, etc. A contract will also put an end to arbitrary decisions often made by those in charge.

Enclosed is a Membership Card. Please follow instructions closely:

(1) On line B fill in the amount of One Dollar ($1.00).

(2) On the line where the word "Signed" appears *Sign* — do not print your name. Sign as you would on your pay cheque.

(3) On bottom line enter the date.

(4) The two blank lines immediately above the date are to be filled in by the Union Representative.

(5) On the reverse side of the Application Card, enter your name in block capitals with your last name on top row. Fill in your full address, phone number and occupation.

(6) Seal the card in an envelope with One Dollar ($1.00) initiation fee and mail to the Canadian Union of Public Employees, 420 Maple Street, Bradley or phone 442-6666 and we will arrange to pick up your card.

Persons who fill out the application card will receive a receipt by mail.

This correspondence should be treated as confidential. The Union does not reveal the names of persons who sign applications nor does The Labour Relations Board.

The Employer cannot know who signs applications unless such persons themselves reveal the fact. We suggest you govern yourself accordingly.

Yours truly,

Syd Hall

Sydney Hall,
Canadian Union of Public Employees,
Organizing Staff.

SH/pb
cc: F. Bain

After reading the union literature, Mr. Talbot phoned Dr. Butler and set up an appointment for later in the morning. At their meeting they decided the first step to be taken was to consult the lawyer that the university retained, Mr. George Wixter, from the firm of Wixter, Wineapple and Jensen in Toronto.

Mr. Wixter had been retained by the university for several years. In the past three years, the university had called upon Mr. Wixter twice for consulting services regarding union organizing drives. Three years ago CUPE had attempted to organize the Building and Maintenance employees at Muskoka University and had failed. One year ago CUPE had attempted to organize the Kitchen and Services employees and had failed. In both previous organization efforts the union organizers had claimed that two major reasons for their failures were university administration interference, which they were not able to prove, and choices of bargaining units by the union that were too unweildy and too spread out for effective concentrated drives.

Mr. Talbot contacted Mr. Wixter and informed him of the contents of the materials that were slipped under his door. Mr. Wixter explained that the organizing drive, the third in three years for CUPE at Muskoka University, was a very important attempt for the union. They would likely view it as a last attempt for some time if unsuccessful, or the start of many if successful. In the course of the discussion Mr. Wixter advised Mr. Talbot on some of the subtle aspects of what constituted an unfair labour practice and what the repercussions would be; he also advised Mr. Talbot of the administration's right to present its own point of view. He concluded the conversation with a warning that if the administration decided to be aggressive and was found guilty of an unfair labour practice, the union could likely be automatically certified without a vote, which was neither a good idea for the administration nor fair for the employees. Therefore, if employees came into Mr. Talbot's office to discuss the union organizing efforts, Mr. Wixter advised Mr. Talbot to call in his secretary, or someone else who was trustworthy, to be a witness to the conversation. A common ploy of many unions was to send in union supporters posing as anti-union employees, and to ask the administration for advice on how to oppose the union. If the administration made any kind of suggestion, the employees would report it to the organizer and likely testify in an unfair labour practice suit.

Mr. Talbot concluded his conversation with Mr. Wixter by promising to keep him informed of events as they occurred and to consult him before taking any action.

Mr. Talbot related his conversation with Mr. Wixter to Dr. Butler. The two men were concerned how they should approach the problem. The university administration had a record of defeating organization drives, but it was not clear if it had been done deliberately. Mr. Talbot saw how a responsible and strong union could help to force and hasten more formal employee relations, and might even add more importance to his own report. On the other hand, Dr. Butler pointed out that CUPE had demonstrated a militant tendency in some organizations recently, and the university could be virtually paralyzed if faced with a strike during the Christmas or final exams some year. The likelihood of a strike might be increased in view of the tighter government budgets, and the consequent

EXHIBIT II

CANADIAN UNION OF PUBLIC EMPLOYEES

October 20th.

To: All the Employees of the Faculty of the Library
Muskoka University

Greetings:

You are invited to attend a special meeting to be held on Thursday night next, October 28th.

If you want to learn more about the Canadian Union of Public Employees and what we have been able to do for other University employees such as yourselves across Canada, then start planning to-day to take time out of your busy schedule to help yourself by attending this very important meeting.

Plan to bring a friend from the Faculty of the Library with you.

Place:	Y.M.C.A. Maple & Talbot Avenue Room 201 A
Date:	October 28th.
Time:	8:00p.m.

I hope to see you next Thursday, October 28th.

Yours truly,

Syd Hall

Sydney Hall,
Organizing Staff. C.U.P.E.

cc: F. Bain

---

inability of the university to meet union demands. No conclusions were reached at the meeting.

Once or twice a week union literature found its way onto Mr. Talbot's desk. Soon after he received his first employee letter and pamphlet another set arrived (Exhibit II). Mr. Talbot had been impressed with the sophistication of the national headquarters' literature, but was curious what effect the local literature, written by the local organizer, was having. He thought that it was less sophisticated, and might even alienate some of the more educated and conservative employees.

Although Mr. Talbot had never met Mr. Sydney Hall, the local organizer, he had heard from various sources that he was a former high school custodian in Toronto. He had worked his way up the union ranks, and at 39, was reportedly hoping that the library organizing at Muskoka University, if successful, would

MUSKOKA FACULTY OF
LIBRARY STAFF:

Many librarians at the Muskoka University have asked the Canadian Union of Public Employees to upgrade wages and working conditions, just as they did for the 160 library employees at Kings University, Queenston earlier this year.

Consider some of the following things that CUPE was able to negotiate with the Kings University management and then ask yourself if your future shouldn't lie in CUPE.

* A complete reclassification of all positions.

* General wage increases ranging from 25 to 78 per cent over one year.

* Three hours leave per week with pay to attend university courses.

* The university pays for health and welfare insurance during maternity leave.

* A female employee is guaranteed a maternity leave of up to six months without loss of seniority.

* Three weeks vacation after one year of work.

* The university will pay for transportation of all employees, male and female, if they are required to work after 11 p.m.

JOIN CUPE — It's in all your best interests.

THE CANADIAN UNION OF PUBLIC EMPLOYEES - 60 MAPLE STREET, No. I
442-8177

draw attention to himself in view of the previous two failures of his predecessors. Mr. Hall had less education than many of the library employees that he was trying to organize, and probably hoped to prove, to the national officers, that he had an ability to deal with white collar workers. This speculation was reasonable to Mr. Talbot because of CUPE's recent thrusts to expand their white collar representation.

Mr. Talbot finished his report and recommendations for a new classification and pay rate system in the first week of November. Included in his report were detailed job descriptions, and a new wage schedule outlining proposed minimums, maximums and increments for each employee classification. The report was the product of almost 10 months of intensive study, questionnaires, and interviews.

EXHIBIT III

CANADIAN UNION OF PUBLIC EMPLOYEES

November 3rd.

To: The Employees of the Faculty of the Library
Muskoka University

Greetings:

At the last meeting held on Thursday night last, October 28th, many of you asked various questions. One of them being, if we join a Union and are Certified under the Labour Relations Act of Ontario, will we lose any of our present benefits, privileges, rights etc.

THE ANSWER IS SIMPLY NO.

You are protected by the Labour Laws of the Province of Ontario.

Many employees have told us about the Unfair Job Titling System that has employees doing the same work but under different Job Titles earning vastly different amounts of money.

We have heard complaints about the arbitrary way in which pay increases are decided and how some people get increases and others don't — and with no Right of Appeal.

This will not happen if you join the All Canadian Union, the Canadian Union of Public Employees. When we are Certified we will bargain collectively for all the employees in the Faculty of the Library as required by the Labour Relations Act.

Enclosed is a Wage Schedule of the Bradley Public Library.

Within the next few days one of the volunteer organizers will approach you with a Canadian Union of Public Employees Membership Card.

I hope you will join your fellow workers soon.

Yours truly,

Syd Hall

Sydney Hall,
Organizer C.U.P.E.

SH/pb
cc: F. Bain

EXHIBIT III (Continued)

Clerical Employees

Category	Job Title	Rates Per Week
C10		$510.00
C20		600.00
C30	Repair Clerk	684.00
	Plastikleer Technician	
C40	Clerk Typist, Historical Museums	684.00
	Clerk Typist, Catalogue Preparation	
	Clerk Typist, Art Museum	
C50	Agency Library Clerk	770.00
	Library Clerk, Circulation	
	Order Clerk	
	Library Clerk, Adult Services	
	Typist, Adult Services	
	Offset & Duplicating Machine Operator	
	Clerk, Historical Museums	
	Film Technician	
C60	Clerk Typist, Community Rel.	770.00
	Films-Music Clerk	
	Senior Steno Clerk, Art Museum	
	Graphic Artist	
C70	Head, Order Department	856.00
	Senior Clerk Typist, Catalogue Preparation	
	Senior Library Clerk, Children's Services	
C80		856.00
C90	Head, Circulation Department	942.00

Professional Employees

Category	Job Title	
L10		$ 942.00
L20		1026.00
L30	Librarian, Pub. Service	1026.00
	Asst. Curator, Education	
	Asst. Curator, Historical Museum	
	Librarian, Technical Services	
	Adult Education Officer	
	Asst. Curator, Installations	
L40	Head, Small Branch	1026.00
	Asst. Curator, Registration	
L50	Regional Film Librarian	1026.00
L60	Head, Arts & Science Dept.	1197.00
	Head, Humanities Dept.	
	Head, Mobile Library Services	
	Head, Large Branch	
	Supervisor, Historical Museums	
L70	Community Relations & Education Officer	1197.00

The recommendations called for major changes in the organization of the library staff, substantial wage increases for many employees, a limited number of staff reductions, and a new and more formal supervisor/employee relationship which excluded opportunities for arbitrary promotions and raises.

The day after completing the report and submitting it to Dr. Butler, Mr. Talbot was given a copy of the letter which Mr. Hall had sent to employees that morning (Exibit III).

Mr. Talbot was furious. He was certain that the rates quoted in the letter for the Bradley Public Library were far overstated. He believed it was a deliberate attempt to mislead employees at Muskoka University. Also, he felt that many of the principal complaints allegedly voiced at the union meeting had been thoroughly and satisfactorily dealt with in his report. He contacted the Bradley Public Library to check the rates that the union had quoted, and he was sent, in the mail, a section of the Bradley Public Library's collective agreement with CUPE. The correct wage schedule is reproduced as Exhibit IV. When he studied this information he realized that what the union had quoted as the Bradley Library employees' weekly salaries were, in fact, the employees' yearly increments for each category. The figures quoted by the union had absolutely no relationship to weekly wages.

Mr. Talbot immediately contacted Dr. Butler and Mr. Masters, the university's Personnel Director, and discussed the problem of dealing with clearly incorrect

EXHIBIT IV

Bradley Public Library
Wage Schedule

Category	Minimum Salary	Maximum Salary	6 mos.	Yearly Increment 1 yr.	2 yrs. and Beyond
10	10863	14454	255	255	510
20	12414	16614	300	300	600
30	13968	18756	342	342	684
40	15516	20304	342	342	684
50	17067	22464	385	385	770
60	18624	24021	385	385	770
70	20172	26157	428	428	856
80	21723	27708	428	428	856
90	23774	29868	471	471	942
10	22110	24936	471	471	942
20	24441	32499	513	513	1026
30	27540	35748	513	513	1026
40	28710	36918	513	513	1026
50	29871	38079	513	513	1026
60	31032	40608	598	598	1197
70	32196	41772	598	598	1197

and misleading union information. Already the union had said, in a previous letter, 55 percent of the employees were required to sign up before they could be certified. This was an error, intentionally or unintentionally, and in the

EXHIBIT V

November 10th.

NOTHING TOO SERIOUS THOUGH

To: The Employees of the Faculty of the Library
Muskoka University

Greetings:

Remember that letter you got dated November 3rd, the one that had enclosed a wage schedule of the Bradley Public Library Board? On the front page was rates for Clerical employees *Per Week*.

WELL THAT'S WRONG

Not the message inside. That still goes.

We here at the C.U.P.E. office, were very gratified, that so many of you read your mail and responded by pointing out to us that you felt we had goofed.

The rates quoted are correct, but should have read *Bi-Weekly* rather than *per week*. I hope you will forgive us for the goof, but we would still like you to compare your *Rates Now* with the ones quoted for the employees at the London Library Board who are members of C.U.P.E.

The only way for you to help yourself is still by joining together to form a Union.

All across Canada public employees are realizing they can make their jobs more profitable and more rewarding by joining C.U.P.E.

Isn't it time you joined?

Yours truly,

Syd Hall

Sydney Hall,
Organizing Staff, C.U.P.E

SH/ed
cc: F. Bain

most recent letter the very serious and obvious wage mistake was made. The three men decided that the administration would pursue a policy of formally correcting any significant false claims it encountered from the union. They decided to send a letter to all library employees.

The same day that Dr. Butler and Mr. Masters were preparing a letter to the employees responding to these false claims by the union, the employees received the following letter and circular from Mr. Hall, the CUPE organizer (Exhibit V).

continued ...

MUSKOKA FACULTY OF LIBRARY STAFF:

MAYBE YOU NEVER THOUGHT

OF YOURSELF AS A

UNION MEMBER ...

NEITHER DID MANY OF THE
50,000 OFFICE, TECHNICAL AND
LIBRARY EMPLOYEES WHO ARE
NOW CUPE MEMBERS.

Many clerical and library employees think unions are just for people who work in factories. Well, that's the way it used to be.

But in recent years thousands of office, technical and library employees have realized they too can win the wages, working conditions and dignity they need and deserve by forming together as a union.

Many of the 50,000 members of the Canadian Union of Public Employees who are clerical workers thought of themselves as non-union types.

Then they began to look around. They saw that people with less responsibility and training were getting a better deal in wages and working conditions.

They realized they had to more or less take whatever came their way when it came to getting a raise or improving their working conditions. They saw they had no fair system of sharing the work-load or deciding who gets a promotion or preventing unfair lay-offs.

Then they decided to act.

(Once the decision to act is made you need not fear any reprisals from the employer. This is prevented by the laws of the province.)

They gained status as union members. They then had a system of seeing that their wages and working conditions matched up to their level of education and degree of responsibility. They began doing something about adequate maternity leave.

They worked with the CUPE well-trained, highly skilled representatives and the CUPE experts in research, law, public relations and education to make things better for themselves and their families.

They began working toward better pay, an end to office favoritism, a fair promotion system, equitable distribution of the work-load, overtime pay, sick leave credits, a system of straightening out complaints, and a way of upgrading their skills.

This is what most Ontario university library employees and other clerical, technical and library employees have done.

Library employees at Kings University and Bradley (Public Library) are already CUPE members. Isn't it time you joined them?

COME WITH CUPE

THE CANADIAN UNION OF PUBLIC EMPLOYEES

560 MAPLE ST.   442-8177

Mr. Talbot was even more furious because although the union correction brought the quoted wages almost in line with the actual wages, the error had still not been corrected. The quoted amounts were still the yearly increments, not the biweekly wages. Dr. Butler, Mr. Talbot, and Mr. Masters decided they would still send their prepared letter the next day. They consulted with Mr. Wixter, the attorney, and sent the letter which is reproduced as Exhibit VI.

EXHIBIT VI

Muskoka University, Bradley, Ontario, Canada

The Libraries

November 11.

Dear Library Staff Member:

The University has been aware for some time of the attempts of an outside union to establish itself as the bargaining agent for the University's library staff. It will be *your* decision, not the union's or the University's. To organize and be represented by a union or an association is your right which is protected by the Ontario Labour Relations Act. However, whenever those external to the University attempt to persuade you to their point of view by the use of incorrect or misleading facts and information, the University will challenge such statements and urge you to examine them critically.

The enclosure accompanying the union letter of November 3, purporting to set out the Bradley Public Library weekly rates for this year and the next is a *misrepresentation of the facts!*

The rates claimed by the union bear no relationship to the rates paid by the Bradley Public Library and are *substantially* higher than the rates currently in effect there.

The following chart outlines a sample comparison of major job classifications at the Bradley Public Library.

Sample of Rates Claimed by Union
Compared with Actual Rates in Effect

Category	Job Title	Rate Claimed By Union	Union Claim Overstated By: Min.	Max.
C.40	Clerk-typist Catalogue Preparation	684 week $35,568 year	129%	75%
C.50	Library Clerk Circulation	770 week $40,040 year	134%	78%

L.30	Technical Services Librarian	1,026 week $53,352 year	94%	49%
L.60	Department Head	1,197 week $62,244 year	101%	53%

These are not the only inaccuracies. In a recent letter the union stated it can be certified *only* after 55% sign membership cards. This is only partially true. If the Ontario Labour Relations Board directs that a vote be taken, the union may be certified if they receive more than 50% of the eligible votes. If 55% of those eligible sign union membership cards, the union will be certified *without a vote!*

If you wish further clarification of this information please feel free to discuss same with Henry Talbot, Library Personnel Officer.

Yours very truly,

B. Masters

Bill Masters,
Director of Personnel.

R. Butler

Ronald Butler,
Chief Librarian.

There were no union responses to Mr. Masters' and Dr. Butler's letter for approximately two weeks. In fact, there appeared to be no union communication to the employees at all during this period. Mr. Talbot wondered why there was a sudden quiet interval when during the preceding six weeks it had been hectic to keep up with the union literature. Finally, a letter appeared from a Mr. Carl McNab who was a library employee (Exhibit VII).

EXHIBIT VII

November 24th.

Dear Fellow Employees:

As you know, an organizing campaign is now underway to unionize the support staff of the University Library system. This campaign was **initiated** by a number of Library employees, who **invited** the Canadian Union of Public Employees (C.U.P.E.) to organize a union local at the Library.

Why do we want a union at the Library? First, there exists no organization to systematically gather our grievances and represent our needs to the Library Administration. We haven't heard from the University Staff Association in months; unfortunately it was never in a position to act effectively for us. C.U.P.E. can provide us with an organization and resources far superior to any staff association. Second, we are facing a number of problems which we could deal with much more effectively if we were organized in a union. Wages are of primary concern to most of us. **Last August** many of us were dissatisfied with our salary increases but there was little we could do except to complain individually. Unless we establish an organization that will represent all of us to Management, our position isn't going to get any stronger. Let's face it, University revenues are being **reduced** by the government; whatever the intention of the Library Administration, the chances of us getting the sizable wage increases we need are lessening. Now is the time in which we need to be organized so that we can express our individual needs in a collective way. Consider the gains of other Library employees who have joined C.U.P.E. Support staff members at the Bradley Public Library who are represented by C.U.P.E. receive $1,000.00 per year, or more, than Library employees at the University for doing equivalent jobs. King's University Library employees recently joined C.U.P.E.; they won a pay increase of 25% in some job categories in their first contract. There is no doubt that by joining C.U.P.E. we can get sizeable salary increases.

However, wage rates is only one area of many in which we can help ourselves by joining C.U.P.E. For example, the University currently pays 50% of our Health Insurance Benefits. In other Universities where C.U.P.E. represents Library employees, 75% to 100% of these benefits are paid by the University. In addition, C.U.P.E. could certainly help us to improve our pension and life insurance plans.

At present we have no job security at the Library. For many of us with families this is a precarious position to be in, considering how scarce jobs are becoming these days. By joining C.U.P.E. we can provide ourselves with job security and set up a fair system for promotions.

Recently, the Library Management has been cutting the number of full-time employees by not hiring replacements for staff members who have quit or who have been promoted. The number of full-time support staff in some departments has been reduced by as much as 50%. At the same time the work-load in every department is steadily increasing; the result is that we are **doing more work for the same pay**. We could end this Management policy if we joined C.U.P.E. and established a work contract between ourselves and the Library Administration.

Time and again we have been assured that the job evaluation and classification programme that is now underway will improve things for all of us. Unfortunately, now that we have filled out our questionnaires, we have absolutely no influence in the important decisions to be made affecting our jobs, wages and working conditions. If we were unionized and were working under a collective agreement job classification would not be the sole responsibility of Management, but would be carried out by Management and by ourselves as part of a contract.

Finally, it is important to remember that all the benefits that we can gain by joining C.U.P.E. need not be won at the expense of our holidays, our coffee breaks and other features of our jobs which we want to retain. As members of C.U.P.E. the process which we will follow to decide what we want to request from Management is absolutely democratic. We all have an equal voice and equal vote in deciding what improvements we want and in declaring what parts of our jobs we wish to remain the same. In short, we don't have to give up our holidays and other benefits to get higher wages, improved fringe benefits, job security and so on.

Recently many of us have received a letter from Dr. Butler stating that an "outside union" is attempting "to establish itself as the bargaining agent for the University's Library staff." As we stated earlier, **C.U.P.E. only began** an organizing campaign when a **number of us requested** it to do so. In fact, **Library staff members have done much of the organizing and campaigning for C.U.P.E.** Dr. Butler's letter implies that an outside group is trying to impose itself on us but the opposite is the case. We want to belong to C.U.P.E. and we are constantly being reassured by the growing number of our fellow employees who agree with us.

When we succeed in making C.U.P.E. our legally certified bargaining agent, **we** will have control of the C.U.P.E. local at the University Library. C.U.P.E.'s Constitution ensures that each unit controls it's own affairs and is in no way "directed" by an outside organization.

Dr. Butler's letter also implies that C.U.P.E. tried to mislead us by falsely inflating the wage rates at the Bradley Public Library. We emphasize that in re-typing the salary scales at the Public Library a mistake was made; "Rates Per Week" should have read "Rates Bi-Weekly". There was no attempt at falsification and C.U.P.E.'s correction was mailed **before** Dr. Butler's letter.

I have written to you on behalf of the many Library employees who have already joined C.U.P.E. in order to correct some misconceptions about the Union. Right now, there are C.U.P.E. members in **every Department** and in **almost every branch** Library. Remember also that no one can be fired, or punished in any way by the Library for attending a Union meeting or for signing a Union card. **Your protection lies within the Ontario Labour Relations Act.**

In order that there will be no misunderstanding, I must make it quite clear that this letter and it's contents have been produced by myself and other interested employees of the Library. It is not a creation of C.U.P.E. I believe however, C.U.P.E. will agree with the position we have taken.

We are beginning an intensive campaign to gather as many new C.U.P.E. members as possible. Help yourselves and your fellow workers by joining C.U.P.E. **now.**

Sincerely yours,

Carl McNab

Carl McNab

A few days after Carl NcNab's letter Mr. Hall sent a memo informing employees about a meeting in early December at the Holiday Inn downtown. The day after the memo inviting the employees to the general meeting, Mr. Hall sent another letter (Exhibit VIII).

In early December Dr. Butler and Mr. Masters approved Mr. Talbot's report on the classification and pay rate system in principle. However, Mr. Masters was concerned with the timing of the report in view of the union activity. He was worried that immediate implementation, including the pay raise, would be misconstrued by the union and might unfairly prejudice employees when considering the pros and cons of union membership.

Mr. Talbot pondered the problems of union organizing, the fate of his report, and the timing of the implementation. He was certain that many problems would be solved if his report could be implemented. Another intriguing problem that Mr. Talbot could not settle was concerning Mr. Hall, the CUPE organizer.

He had suspected earlier that Mr. Hall had been running into problems trying to organize a group with so many diverse backgrounds and education levels. Recently, he had been told by a reliable source that Mr. Hall was being criticized by younger militants who felt he wasn't communicating enough, nor being aggressive enough. There was a very guarded rumour circulating, that these militants, perhaps under the leadership of Carl McNab, had contacted Ottawa to ask that a new organizer replace Mr. Hall. Mr. Talbot wondered if the quiet period in November had any relationship to these rumours. All of this was very speculative and totally unsubstantiated, and Mr. Talbot even wondered whether it was deliberately planted information which was hoped to make him relax a bit and, perhaps, to be caught off guard. He wondered whether this rumour of a rift in the ranks had been completely fabricated.

One morning in mid-December, just as Christmas holidays were approaching, Mrs. Anna Banks burst into Mr. Talbot's office. She was visibly upset and on the verge of tears. Mrs. Banks was in her late forties and had worked in the library for eleven years. Although Mr. Talbot did not know her too well, he did remember that her employee record card had been particularly impressive. She had

EXHIBIT VIII

CANADIAN UNION OF PUBLIC EMPLOYEES

November 30th.

To: All the Employees of the University
of the Library System

Greetings:

Since our last letter of November 10th, a few things have happened at the Muskoka Library.

Dr. Butler and Mr. Henry Talbot, your friendly Personnel Officer have finally become aware of the support staff of the Library System. Perhaps now both of these gentlemen will give serious consideration to granting that long awaited pay raise promised. Surely they can't deny that in most cases the Public employee doing similar jobs in the Bradley area are getting approximately $3,000.00 more per year than the employees of the Library at Muskoka University.

Could it be that they don't consider that the Public is the real employer, and that you work for a public institution?

Dr. Butler and your friendly personnel officer are paid to operate the Library as cheaply as they can. This is their job. They cannot belong to the Union. Naturally, they will try and talk you people out of joining, because if you are represented collectively by the Union, that makes you equal with them and your rights are protected by Provincial Law.

We have been told that the Personnel Department has informed some people in the Supervisory capacity that they cannot belong to the Union. *This is wrong.* The University or the Union does not decide who is employed in a Confidential capacity or who exercises Managerial functions. *The Department of Labour will decide,* so don't be fooled. It's your right to be represented by a Union of your choice if you so wish. The University could be penalized for actions such as this.

Some of the long term employees whose jobs are deleted haven't as of this date been told whether they can look forward to a demotion, promotion, or dismissal. This could never happen if you had C.U.P.E. as your Representative.

We feel it would be nice if Dr. Butler granted you that pay raise before we are certified by the Ontario Labour Relations Board, so Gentlemen you had better get started.

Keep signing those C.U.P.E. Membership cards and we will get you that contract that so many of you desire.

Yours truly,

Syd Hall

SH/ed
cc: F Bain

Sydney Hall
Organizing Staff, C.U.P.E.

---

always been an excellent employee, and her supervisors spoke highly of her. In her eleven years of service she had worked in many different departments and had accumulated valuable general experience. She had two sons; her oldest was a freshman at Muskoka University; her husband was an assistant department manager in the local office of the provincial government.

Mr. Talbot tried to calm Mrs. Banks down in an effort to find out what had upset her. She blurted out that she thought it was unfair for people to keep pestering her to join the union. She did not want to join a union, and in fact, there was no way anyone could make her join. She didn't think it was right that a bunch of draft dodgers, who weren't even eligible to vote in government elections, could vote to have a union and ruin everything for people, Canadian citizens, who didn't want to be in a union. She was very upset that Mr. Talbot and Dr. Butler weren't seeming to care; they just weren't doing anything to stop the union. It looked like either the university wanted a union, or they were just too afraid to say anything. She asked if it was true that the library administration was considering giving everybody a big raise, and if it was, it might be enough to stop the union. She continued on for almost twenty minutes denouncing the unfairness of having to have a union, and begging Mr. Talbot to do something, to tell her what she could do to stop the union.

Mr. Talbot was in a quandary. He didn't know whether he should press Dr. Butler to give the wage increase immediately and to implement his recommendations. He was concerned because he hadn't thought that the organizing drive was so extensive and deeply rooted that it would upset people like

Mrs. Banks. He wondered how many more of his employees had reached, or were approaching, the stage Mrs. Banks had reached. He was even considering using informers by soliciting the help of trusted employees to keep him up to date with union activities. He didn't know what to say to Mrs. Banks in his office, and didn't know what, if anything, he could do during the Christmas holidays to alleviate union pressures.

MUSKOKA UNIVERSITY (C)

After Mr. Talbot returned to work from his Christmas Holidays he reviewed the hectic four months preceding Christmas. He had been deeply involved with completing his report on the restructuring of the library classification and pay system; at the same time he had been trying to keep up with union activities. He was concerned because he was not aware of the general sentiments of most employees toward the union efforts. He was curious about the tone and composition of the off-campus union meetings, and still wondered if the rumours regarding the growing rift in the organization campaign were true. He recalled his encounter with Mrs. Banks just before the Christmas break, and wondered if she had been sincere or a union plant. He had told her that it was an employee's right to join a union if he or she wanted to, and it was not the administration's decision. He had also told her that an employee, if upset with union practices, could inform the administration and could also voice his or her opinions to the Ontario Labour Relations Board. She had left the office considerably more calm than she had entered, but Mr. Talbot had felt she had not been very satisfied with his answers.

During the Christmas break, Dr. Butler, the Chief Librarian, and Mr. Masters, Personnel Director for Muskoka University, had decided to implement Mr. Talbot's recommendations as quickly as possible, including an immediate wage increase where appropriate. The decision had been difficult in view of the anticipated union reactions, but Dr. Butler had prevailed and insisted that the original objective of the report was to develop a new system to implement before the library moved to its new facilities, and union or no union he had wanted it done as they had initially planned. Preparations for the move were beginning to be stepped up and involved many departmental meetings and briefings. Dr. Butler had felt that it would be an opportune climate, when employees were having required changes explained and were engaging in frequent meetings, to include discussions on the new classification and pay rate system. He felt the wage increases would contribute to the employees' acceptance of the plan. Thus, Mr. Talbot, in early January began to prepare for departmental meetings at which he would discuss the implications and philosophy of the new system, and solicit questions and potential problems from the employees.

On the 8th of January, Mr. Talbot saw an article in the local city newspaper, *The Bradley Banner*, which is reproduced as Exhibit I.

Three days later the Muskoka University *Martlet*, a student newspaper, printed an editorial (Exhibit II).

Mr. Talbot read the articles with interest and was a little amazed at how quickly the facts had become confused. Mr. Masters appeared to have been caught in an interview unprepared, and Mr. Hall was calling the December wage increase an administration trick. The Banner reporter also had linked previous CUPE attempts and their failures to the present library organizing campaign, and implied that the implementation of Mr. Talbot's recommendations was just another aspect of the university administration's determination to stop unioniz-

EXHIBIT I

The Bradley Banner, January 8

CUPE WOULD ORGANIZE LIBRARY STAFF AT MUSKOKA UNIVERSITY

By Linda Smith
of The Bradley Banner

The Canadian Union of Public Employees, one of the country's largest unions, has tried unsuccessfully over the past three years to organize the more than 1200 staff employees at Muskoka University.

Reasons given for its failure to do so involve 11th-hour pay increases by the university and the complexity of trying to satisfy the variety of interests found among support staff groups.

Now, CUPE has set its sights on a smaller, though not insignificant target — the more than 130 staff employees in the university's vast library system, in addition to the professional employees of the library.

Sydney Hall, chief CUPE organizer at the university, said four organizational meetings have been held since the union first began efforts in September. There have also been a number of small group meetings.

Should CUPE be successful in its application for certification, it would be the first foothold a major union has ever achieved at the university.

The main dispute between the library workers and the administration seems to be salary, despite what one employee called an "average $2,400 increase" granted just before Christmas.

Bill Masters, university personnel officer, said he could not say exactly what the increase was but that it was associated with a complete job reclassification among the library support staff.

He said the majority of support staff members received increases as a result of the reclassification.

Most of those persons employed as support staff in Muskoka's library system this year will receive salaries ranging from $11,500 to $22,000 according to a proposed salary schedule.

CUPE representatives said the increase still leaves Muskoka library employees well below their counterparts at the Bradley Public Library.

The union, which is already the bargaining agent for Bradley Public Library employees, claims that increase was an attempt by the university to keep the union out.

"But the dissatisfaction is still there," Mr. Hall said.

According to him, the next step is to meet with the employees again to determine whether they wish the union to proceed with its application for certification.

One employee representative, who said he would not speak for his fellow workers, said he is optimistic certification will be achieved. He said his optimism is based on the general feeling amongst the staff.

"We haven't really picked up on the campaign," he said. "We've been away over Christmas. But we're going ahead with it."

In addition to the fact library workers do not have an internal organization of their own, CUPE has another advantage.

The Muskoka staff association, according to its chairman, Douglas White, has no interest in performing as a union in representing its membership.

He said there are plans to redraft the association's constitution to "make it perfectly clear the staff association will never faintly resemble a union organization."

Mr. White suggested the association should be a social and cultural organization.

Fred Bain, national representative for CUPE in the Bradley area, said certification will not likely be automatic.

He said he believes the professional employees of the library are against unionization, "but if it came to a vote I think they'd vote for the union because they know the support staff needs it."

Both Mr. Bain and Mr. Hall said the union will be in a position to apply for certification but they would not say when the application will be made.

ation. Mr. Talbot felt badly since he had not written his report with those objectives in mind.

EXHIBIT II

Muskoka University Martlet
Editorial — January 11

B MOVIE

The Canadian Union of Public Employees has recently been trying to gain a foothold on the campus and at present is trying to organize the employees of the university library. In a story recently in the Bradley Banner the reasons for CUPE's failure to organize the library staff were attributed to an 11th hour pay raise by the University administration.

It sounds like the plot for a grade B movie, but the locale isn't Muskoka.

When Dr. Ronald Butler took over as chief librarian a year and a half ago he set as one of his major priorities the reorganization of the support staff within the library system. The University personnel office had long realized that a re-evaluation of the support staff was necessary and last year hired Henry Talbot as a new personnel officer to be specifically responsible for the library. His initial task was to do this re-evaluation.

After several months of work with the staff, department heads and administration, the work began to show what needed to be done. The process was to be completed by July but became a longer job than first expected. Over 25 other libraries were contacted, information was analyzed, and job descriptions drawn up.

After a great deal of discussion between the various concerned groups it was finished and new pay scales and classifications became effective just before Christmas with the result that various members of staff received raises through this reclassification.

Any suggestion at all that this was an 11th hour operation is unbased and the library and the university administration are due for credit in completing this operation which at last brings library salaries into line with the rest of the field and brings Muskoka's library salary policy out of the Dark Ages.

EXHIBIT III

January 19th.

Dear Fellow Employees:

Over the past few weeks those of us who have been active in campaigning for the Canadian Union of Public Employees have been asked a number of questions by other Library staff members. These questions have concerned our reaction to the new job classifications and salary schedules. We hope that this letter will answer your questions and will explain the future course of unionization at the Library.

We were not surprised by the timing of the salary increases, and in fact we had discussed the probability of there being a minimal adjustment in wages in order to lessen the appeal of the union for Library employees. It is a traditional tactic of employers, when a union campaign is underway, to offer an increase in salary that falls below the level a Union could establish, in the hope that staff members will abandon unionization. For example, Megalife Insurance Company suddenly introduced pay increases for its employees soon after C.L.C. announced its intention to unionize staff there. Rather than deal with a united staff and face the necessity of granting salary increases on a regular basis, it is to the advantage of the Library, and ultimately the University, to make a re-adjustment now and hope that we will accept it and eventually reject unionization. We have the choice either of accepting irregular wage increases every two, three, or five years, or of unionizing and guaranteeing ourselves regular salary raises, improved fringe benefits, and a collective voice in our own affairs.

If we unionize, the Library and the University administration will be forced to manage their spiralling budgets. Millions of dollars are spent on monumental buildings and equipment, and bureaucracies are set up, while every last penny paid to us is examined and re-examined. We understand necessary expansion in a growing University, but we also believe that no matter how great and complex is the institution, the needs of the individual employee must take precedent over the organizational structure.

The adjusted pay levels are hardly impressive. A few staff members in some departments received substantial increases, but these hardly compensate for the time worked at the ridiculous amounts formerly paid. And most of us still receive a good deal less than we could earn if we established C.U.P.E. as our Union. For example, employees at Circulation now receive $14,500 per year; the amount paid for an equivalent job at the Bradley Public Library, where employees are represented by C.U.P.E., is $16,000 per year. In addition, the Circulation staff has been cut in half over the last year, while the work-load has increased. In this department, at least, the Library administration is actually saving money paid in wages even with the salary increases given to employees.

The purpose of salary re-scheduling was to bring our wage levels into line with those of other University Libraries. The fact that many of us in most Library departments are required to do additional work raises an entirely separate issue. More work without adequate compensation is equivalent to a wage cut. With C.U.P.E. as our bargaining agent we could establish the principle of uniform work loads as part of a contract with the library. And if we were unionized we could expect regular and substantial salary increases with each new contract.

Salary scheduling is only one area in which unionization would benefit us. At the Library we need a sensible policy providing job security and, at the same time, guaranteeing that a fair procedure for promotions will be followed. As individuals we have little chance of influencing the Library and the University on these issues, as active members of a union we could establish procedures to deal with such problems as part of our contractual relationship with our employer.

At present, the University arbitrarily establishes the amount we pay for Life, Health and Medical Insurance benefits that we receive. For its members the Canadian Union of Public Employees has a program providing greater benefits at less cost. C.U.P.E. would bargain for 100 percent payment of all our insurance policies by the University, and for a medical plan paid entirely by the University. This program would pay all drug costs of employees and all medical payments not covered by the new Ontario Health

Insurance plan. Thus the fringe benefits we receive could be vastly improved if we made C.U.P.E. our bargaining agent.

In addition there are any number of other areas in which C.U.P.E. could better our position as employees at the Library. For instance, because of a lack of time or money, many of us cannot take courses which would improve our skills, educational status, and, eventually, our salaries. At King's University C.U.P.E. has won for employees the right to be absent from work with pay for three hours per week to attend technical and general courses.

Some of you have expressed the fear that membership in a union would endanger those parts of your jobs which you now enjoy. Ontario Labour Law stipulates that immediately upon certification of a Union, every aspect of the work situation must remain constant until after a collective agreement is negotiated and voted on by the staff membership. And there is no "outside control" of what makes up the Union contract. The C.U.P.E. constitution guarantees that the members of each local unit are in charge of their own affairs. If we join together in a C.U.P.E. local, we decide what we want from the Library, C.U.P.E.'s experienced bargaining agents and lawyers negotiate for us, and we vote on the proposals which the Library puts foward. In short, we have much to gain and nothing to lose by joining C.U.P.E.

We are resuming our door-to-door campaign of Library employees, because we have found that this is the best way to explain the necessity of unionization. In considering the Union, we urge those of you who, for one reason or another, feel no need for improved salary and benefits, to consider other staff members who are raising families and who will be working at the Library for some time to come. Please feel free to call any of us about any aspect of C.U.P.E. or our organizing campaign. You can be assured that your questions will be held in the strictest confidence.

Sincerely yours,

Mr. Robert Simon — 1209-305 Grand St.	442-2419
Mr. Carl McNab — 479 Southern St.	663-6449
Mr. David Tanner — 54 Baseline St. Apt. 3	663-1195
Mr. Bob Duncan — 118 Maple St.	663-1097
Mr. Dave Skilling — 1079 Ridgedale Road	663-4442

Mr. Talbot noted that the letter was sent from Mr. Carl McNab and friends, and wondered whether Mr. Hall was encountering difficulties. There was a rumour that the union had sent out a scathing letter a few days before claiming that the wage increase was a deliberate attempt to interfere with an employee's decision regarding unionization. He had not been able to get a copy, but he suspected that if such a letter had been sent it might have upset a few people.

On February 8th a letter announcing a general union meeting, and a pamphlet were sent from Mr. Hall to all library employees (Exhibit IV).

Mr. Talbot was again very impressed with the sophistication of the national organization's literature and the apparent financial support they were giving the Muskoka Library campaign. Mr. Talbot wondered what the outcome of the general meeting would be. It seemed that the union was preparing to make an announcement since it was going to summarize the campaign's progress, and time was probably becoming a problem to the organizing committee.

On February 11th *The Martlet* published an article which is reproduced as Exhibit V.

EXHIBIT IV

C.U.P.E. Pamphlet Contents

THERE ARE MORE THAN 50,000 CLERICAL "STORIES" IN THE CANADIAN UNION OF PUBLIC EMPLOYEES... HERE ARE JUST SIX OF THEM.

THE WOMEN LISTED HERE ARE ALL EMPLOYED IN THE LIBRARY AT KINGS UNIVERSITY, QUEENSTON ONT. AND MEMBERS OF CUPE LOCAL 6887. READ BELOW WHY THEY ARE HAPPY TO BE CUPE MEMBERS.

* * * * * * * * * * * *

Besides a hefty retroactive cheque, CUPE had my job reclassified as well. As a result my employer began paying me for the work I was doing and my increase in two years amounted to $8,000. A clause in our contract states the principle of equal pay for equal work shall apply regardless of sex. In other words, CUPE promised equal pay for equal work and delivered the goods.

Myra Balsam

My husband Tom was already a member of CUPE working for the city. When he heard we were interested in joining a union he convinced me that CUPE was for us. It's all-Canadian and represents 160,000 Canadians doing all kinds of different jobs.

Jane Lind

As a supervisor of about 20 other employees I didn't think CUPE was for me. However I was left in the bargaining unit and CUPE negotiated for me just as they did for all the other members. Now, I don't find being a member of CUPE interferes with my job in the least.

Nancy Drake

We negotiated an "earn while you learn" clause in our agreement. The university agreed to us choosing a course, attending classes and being paid while we were in the classroom. Although I have a university degree, I welcomed this opportunity to continue my education.

Emily Dickens

Continued 2 ...

... 2 Continued

I began working three months before CUPE negotiated our first agreement
so my retroactive cheque was small. However, the union protested that
the job I was doing should be paid at a higher rate and we won the case.
After being properly classified my increase over the term of the agreement was $3000.

Margie Anderson.

As president of our local union, I'm really proud to be a member of CUPE.
Since we joined CUPE, a number of pleasant things have happened. We have
a union-management committee to discuss problems of mutual concern. Complaints that have arisen have been settled smoothly with the help of our
CUPE representative Ed Scott. Also with an end to office favouritism
the petty jealousies that such favouritism creates have ended too.

Doris Thompson

EXHIBIT V

The Martlet, February 11

LIBRARY UNION COMING FAST

By Hal Bodoni

The Canadian Union of Public Employees (CUPE) will apply to the Ontario Board of Labour for accreditation as the bargaining agent for about 130 library workers.

Sydney Hall, union representative, said Monday he hopes to make the application within the next two weeks.

CUPE will call a meeting of the library employees Thursday Feb. 17 to discuss the accreditation.

Hall said he hopes the accreditation will be automatic.

To obtain automatic accreditation, the union must have the written support of 55 percent of the workers involved.

With less than 55 percent, accreditation cannot take place until a vote has been taken among the employees. The union has to win 55 percent of the workers' votes.

"They could have been a lot tougher than they were," Hall said of the university management.

Bill Masters, personnel manager of the University said it is the right of the library staff to form a union if they so desire.

"It's the peoples choice," he said.

Fred Bain, national representative of CUPE, said Monday unionizing the library is the first step in unionizing all university employees.

He said an attempt was considered before, but it was decided there were too many employees to organize at once.

Library staff approached CUPE in September. Carl McNab, one of the ten employees who went to see CUPE originally said the problem in September was wages.

The problem stemmed from the July review of wages. At that time wage increases were promised which were not fulfilled, McNab said.

"We weren't being realistic in our promises," said Masters.

"It was more than that," Bob Simon, another library employee said. "There would be meetings (with employees) for weeks and weeks, then the policy would be handed down. We lack a voice in anything that happens to us."

The organization of employees has been done by the Library workers themselves. Most

CHAPTER 4   THE ORGANIZING CHALLENGE   107

of the talking was done in employees' homes. "The response was very good," McNab said. "Discontent was widespread."

CUPE seems to be the best union available, he added.

He dismissed the idea of forming a separate union, because of the cost.

The advantages of joining the union, said Bain, are job security and general improvement in working conditions.

"Vacations and sick time are pretty good," Hall said, "but we offer job security and better insurance benefits."

Masters said there has been a general improvement in wages and conditions.

"We hope this would indicate a serious effort on our part to involve each staff member in a team effort approach to the library organization," he said

McNab said the CUPE insurance plans are cheaper than those presently offered through the library by the London Life insurance company.

Employees leaving some departments have not been replaced, McNab said, leaving more work for those left. With the union, he said, this wouldn't happen.

A January general wage raise for the library workers has caused speculation on all sides.

Without consulting library workers, CUPE put out a pamphlet claiming the raise was directly due to the threat of the union coming in.

Simon said that although the raise was substantial, it was still not on par with the public library.

"Someone in circulation there gets $16,500 a year. In circulation here they get $14,500, and it used to be $11,000," he said.

Masters said there was no way of comparing the wage scales as the library structure at the university is different from that downtown.

"We've always tried for comparative wages," Masters said.

Masters explained the wage increase was the result of a survey undertaken last May and June to restructure the library employment and pay scales.

"A lot of hours went into the restructuring," he said, explaining the delay in implementing the new scale.

Masters said the university has a "moral obligation to the taxpayers not to lead the field in wages."

On February 16th, the day before the general meeting downtown, Mr. Hall sent out another letter (Exhibit VI).

On the same day the university received notification from the Ontario Labour Relations Board, via registered mail, of the union's application for certification. The union's application was dated February 14, and in it they applied for the following bargaining unit:

> All non-professional employees including unit-head of the Respondent at Muskoka University Libraries (Bradley), save and except Department Heads, those above the rank of Department Head, Professional Librarians, persons covered by subsisting collective agreement with the Canadian Union of Operating Engineers, employees working less than 24 hours per week, and students employed during the school vacation.

The union requested a pre-hearing vote be taken.

The Board fixed February 23 as the terminal date for the application, and requested the university to provide by that date:

a) a list of all the employees in the proposed bargaining unit as of February 14, and

b) a specimen (from existing employee records) of the signature of each employee in the proposed bargaining unit.

Mr. Talbot began preparing the list of all employees in the proposed bargaining unit, and posted the notices about the application which the Board had sent and required to be "posted in conspicuous places where they are most likely to come

EXHIBIT VI

February 16th.

To: All the Support Staff Employees of
the Muskoka University Libraries

Greetings:

Your response over the last few weeks has been most encouraging and I am pleased to inform you that the Canadian Union of Public Employees have now made application for Certification on your behalf to the Ontario Labour Relations Board.

I hope you will now join your fellow employees, and fill out the enclosed application for membership card, if you have not as yet joined. I would ask you to sign this card, complete the back of it and return it to this office *no later than the morning of February 22nd*, along with the initiation fee of $1.00. This is the only payment necessary until an acceptable Collective Agreement has been negotiated on your behalf.

February 22nd is the deadline
for submitting additional cards.

Thank you for your interest and co-operation.

Yours very truly,

Syd Hall

Sydney Hall,
Organizer,
SH/pb   Canadian Union of Public Employees,

·

to the attention of all employees who may be affected by the application." A meeting with Mr. Wixter, the university's lawyer, was also scheduled by Mr. Talbot which was to include Mr. Masters and Dr. Butler.

On February 16th, Mrs. Banks, who had burst into Mr. Talbot's office just before Christmas break, sent a letter to Mr. Steele, in the Provincial Department of Labour (Exhibit VII).

She received in reply a letter reproduced as Exhibit VIII.

On February 24, Mrs. Banks wrote a brief hand written letter to the Registrar of the Ontario Labour Relations Board. She explained who she was and that she had previously written a letter to Mr. Steele on February 15. She then enclosed a copy of the letter she had written to Mr. Steele, and also a copy of the newspaper clipping she had sent Mr. Steele.

On February 25, the university administration and the union met in Toronto at the Labour Board Offices. At this meeting the administration indicated that it was opposed to the proposed bargaining unit. The Board requested that the discussion be restricted to determining whether there should be a pre-hearing vote and if so, should there be any ballots segregated. The administration initially challenged eleven names; eventually, however, the parties agreed that a pre-hearing vote would be appropriate, and that four ballots should be segregated, the slide librarian, two library assistants, and a Research Assistant. The parties

EXHIBIT VII

1012 Maple Ridge Avenue,
Bradley, Ontario.
15th February.

Mr. Steele
Department of Labour,
Parliament Buildings,
Toronto 182, Ontario.

Dear Mr. Steele:

Last December I was talking to you by telephone about CUPE's campaign to enroll the employees of the libraries at the Muskoka University. The enclosed clippings from the Muskoka Martlet of 11th February and the Bradley banner of 12th February, indicate their progress.

In spite of CUPE's claims, there are many of us who do not want any union at all. We feel that the Provincial laws concerning unions are most undemocratic. They do not allow the opponents of the union any opportunity to oppose it actively. Management's hands are tied by the law. Our officials obeyed the rules and for this have been derided as "not tough." The union used outside professional organizers and had considerable funds at their disposal. Where could we get either to help us in our efforts to resist? There seems to be nothing to stop the union — not even a time limit. It can persist until it rolls right over us!

In the larger clipping, the pro-unionists admit that just ten people approached the union. There were far more than ten who definitely did not want a union, but to whom could they appeal?

The original ten, backed by the militant union, spent six months hammering at us, coaxing and pestering us to sign up. If the majority really wanted the union, it would not have taken so long.

Since a number of those who favour CUPE are draft-dodgers from the United States, they are not eligible to vote in Canadian Federal, Provincial or Municipal elections. We wonder why they should be permitted to vote in a union certification, thus committing Canadian citizens of long standing to a situation they do not want?

A high percentage of the support staff of the University Libraries are immigrants who have not yet become Canadian citizens. Frequently they

have said that they are not sufficiently familiar with our Canadian customs, politics, etc., to understand what is involved in the present situation. It hardly seems fair to put them in a position of having to vote on such an important issue as union certification.

There are many short term employees on the staff of the library. They may vote the long term employees into the union, then leave soon after. There is no provision for a later vote to see if the majority still want the union. Then too, we are not permitted to remain outside of the union if we wish.

Because the main library is at present in the process of introducing a new system of procedure, and also is in the awkward position of being half-moved into a new building, the staff is experiencing considerable turmoil and consequent dissatisfaction. Some of us feel that the union deliberately chose the library for its campaign, so that it could take advantage of this period of dissatisfaction for its own ends.

We also wonder why people with one, two or three university degrees should be required to belong to a union. While only a few of us are actually librarians, many of us have university degrees and some have post-graduate degrees. It is obvious from talking to the outside union organizers that they do not understand that the university library is quite different from a public library and even more different from a business office.

We have heard that the union plans to strike as soon as possible after certification. Possibly that could take place during the university's final examinations, causing great difficulty for the students; or during the moving to the new building, scheduled for May, which would also be inconsiderate.

Although the increases in December were high, the malcontents still want more money. This seems outrageous to us, since the university is not a profit-making institution. Also these malcontents apparently refuse to see that there is far more provision for expression of opinion and choice under the new administration.

Another point we dislike is the union's contribution of funds to one political party, even though the majority of union members do not support that party at the polls, as demonstrated in the recent provincial election. There must be many unwilling union members!

For these reasons we think that the laws regarding unions should be amended and that the Ontario Labour Relations Board should take our concern into consideration when dealing with CUPE's application for certification.

Yours sincerely,

Anna Banks

Enclosures — 2

(Mrs. J. B. Banks)

EXHIBIT VII (Continued)

The Bradley Banner — Feb. 12

MUSKOKA LIBRARIANS TO VOTE

The Canadian Union of Public Employees has applied for a pre-hearing vote in its attempt to become the bargaining agent for the more than 130 staff employees in the Muskoka University's library system.

The vote is to be conducted by the Ontario department of labour, but no date has been set.

Sydney Hall, chief CUPE organizer at the university, said 50 percent plus one vote for the union will bring certification, he said. "The situation looks good," he said. "If everyone who has signed up votes, then we'll have more than 50 percent."

A hearing before the Ontario Labour Relations Board will be held in Toronto Feb. 24.

EXHIBIT VIII

DEPARTMENT OF LABOUR
LEGAL BRANCH

DEPARTMENTAL SOLICITOR

James Steele, Q.C.

400 UNIVERSITY AVENUE
TORONTO, ONTARIO
TELEPHONE: 365-6625

February 17.

Mrs. J. B. Banks,
1012 Maple Ridge Avenue,
Bradley, Ontario.

Dear Mrs. Banks:

I acknowledge your letter of February 15th and newspaper clippings. Since it appears that a vote has been ordered by the Labour Relations Board the result of whether or not C.U.P.E. is to be certified is dependent on the vote and you or any other members are entitled to vote as you see fit.

If C.U.P.E. receives the majority of the votes it may be certified as the bargaining unit for the employees in the unit.

In any event you and others who support you can intervene in the application before the Labour Board and dispute the arguments by C.U.P.E. that it represents a majority of the staff members, or that certain staff members have withdrawn from membership in C.U.P.E.

The Board will determine who is entitled to vote or who should be deemed to be members of the bargaining unit and its decision will depend upon the argument advanced to it and the evidence that is presented.

I can therefore only suggest that you make efforts to have your point of view represented at any hearing before the Board.

Yours truly,

James Steele

JS/ms

James Steele

EXHIBIT IX

ONTARIO LABOUR RELATIONS BOARD

IN YOUR REPLY, PLEASE REFER TO OUR
FILE NO. 1599-71-R
Registered

400 UNIVERSITY AVENUE
TORONTO, ONTARIO
365-4151

February 25.

Anna Banks,
1012 Maple Ridge Avenue,
Bradley, Ontario.

Dear Madam:

Re: Canadian Union of Public Employees, and Muskoka University

I am returning herwith a handwritten letter of the 24th instant together with a photostat typewritten letter of the 15th instant, both signed by yourself a person purporting to be an employee of the Respondent in this matter.

It would appear from an examination of the envelope that the aforementioned documents were not mailed by registered mail and were received by the Board on February 25, after the terminal date fixed for this Application, namely February 23.

Your attention in this regard is directed to Sections 48 and 50 of the Board's Rules of Procedure, a copy of which is enclosed herewith, together with a copy of the Labour Relations Act.

Very truly yours,

V. McLeod

VM/ms
Enclosure.

V. McLeod
Deputy Registrar.

expressed their preference to hold the vote over a two day period in the latter half of March.

On February 26, Mrs. Banks received a reply from the Deputy Registrar (Exhibit IX).

Mrs. Banks was furious and virtually exploded into Mr. Talbot's office. Mrs. Banks was looked up to by many of her fellow employees, and she exercised a great deal of influence with the employees in her department. She lashed out at Mr. Talbot saying she had done what he had said, and it hadn't done any good. She also said that as much as she was not wanting a union, maybe a union was the only way to get things done around the library. She had believed in and trusted the administration, and they had let her down. Not only were they not trying to fight the union, but they were even building false hopes for those few employees that had remained loyal. She said that she was beginning to think that a union would serve the whole damn administration right for not having enough guts to stand up to it. And with that comment she stormed out of the room, not even

EXHIBIT X

Muskoka University, Bradley, Ontario, Canada

The Libraries

February 28.

NOTICE

The union made application for all non-professional university library staff employed in the main library, the divisional/professional libraries, and the departmental libraries.

At a meeting in Toronto yesterday convened by the Ontario Labour Relations Board the union records disclose that approximately 38% of the persons in the bargaining unit as proposed by the union have signed union application cards within the last six months. Under the new Ontario Labour Relations Act a vote has been ordered to determine the true wishes of the employees.

The University pressed for an early vote date and we are hopeful that the vote will be held on March 14 and 15 or March 21 and 22.

Watch this board for further details.

Henry Talbot

Henry Talbot,
Library Personnel Officer.

allowing Mr. Talbot to reply. Mr. Talbot thought he had better let things simmer down a bit before trying to approach Mrs. Banks again.

On February 28, following the hearing at the Ontario Labour Relations Board a notice was posted by Mr. Talbot (Exhibit X). Mr. Talbot was not sure whether this notice prompted or merely coincided with the barrage of posters, pamphlets, and letters that started the same day. The two posters labeled Exhibit

EXHIBIT XI

MUSKOKA LIBRARY EMPLOYEES
NOW ALL IT TAKES
IS YOUR X.

Thanks to library workers at Muskoka, the Canadian Union of Public Employees has won a vote to be held later this month. This means the Ontario Labour Relations Board is satisfied a good proportion of the Muskoka library workers want to be represented by CUPE.

Now all it takes is your X to put CUPE in a position to improve your wages and working conditions.
Many university employees in Ontario and throughout Canada are already members of CUPE. These are people who discovered the only way to ensure fair treatment was to join with other employees and bargain collectively with management.

Like these people, you work hard. You hold responsible jobs. Accordingly you deserve to have a say in determining your wages, working conditions and fringe benefits. But, as you've already learned, nobody is going to hand you these things on a silver platter.

You can take a big first step towards improved pay and decent working conditions once you are certified as a local of CUPE.

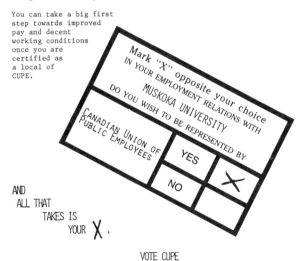

Mark "X" opposite your choice IN YOUR EMPLOYMENT RELATIONS WITH MUSKOKA UNIVERSITY DO YOU WISH TO BE REPRESENTED BY CANADIAN UNION OF PUBLIC EMPLOYEES

YES	
NO	X

AND
ALL THAT
TAKES IS
YOUR X.

VOTE CUPE

XI immediately were posted in the library. Mr. Talbot recognized the artwork of the second one as that of one of the employees in the inter-university loan department.

As Mr. Talbot went across the street to lunch at the faculty club during noon hour he noticed literally hundreds of posters (Exhibit XII). They were on the ground and taped up on building walls and on lamp posts. He noticed a group of

EXHIBIT XI (Continued)

We Can Make Our Voices Heard!
Together with C.U.P.E.

- **WAGES**
  A LEGAL CONTRACT WITH THE
  LIBRARY WOULD MEAN BETTER WAGES
  WITH GUARANTEED ANNUAL INCREMENTS.

- **GRIEVANCES**
  PROCEDURES WOULD BE LAID
  DOWN IN A UNION CONTRACT FOR
  EFFECTIVELY GUARANTEEING FAIRNESS.

- **ADVANCEMENT**
  UNIONIZED LIBRARIES HAVE VACANCIES
  POSTED; PROMOTIONS ARE BASED
  ON SENIORITY, NOT FAVOURITISM.

- **MEDICAL, INSURANCE & PENSION SCHEMES**
  THE BRADLEY PUBLIC LIBRARY HAS
  AGREED TO PAY 100% OF OHIP OF GROUP
  AND
  100% LIFE INSURANCE FOR LIBRARY WORKERS.

- **SICK DAYS & MATERNITY LEAVE**
  WORKERS AT BRADLEY PUBLIC LIBRARY
  & KINGS UNIVERSITY LIBRARY (BOTH
  WITH UNIONS) HAVE:
  .PAID SICK DAYS THAT ACCUMULATE YR TO YR.,
  .SIX MONTHS MATERNITY LEAVE,
  .PAID TIME OFF FOR JURY DUTY, AND IN
  TIMES OF BEREAVEMENT.

**A VOTE for the UNION
~IS A VOTE for ACTION**

C.U.P.E.

students standing outside the cafeteria handing them out and went over to ask them what it was all about. They did not appear to recognize him, and said they were members of the Canadian Labour Party, and that students and workers must unite against imperialistic administrations of capitalistic institutions. Mr. Talbot wondered how these people had got involved and whether the union had solicited outside help.

EXHIBIT XII

SUPPORT LIBRARY UNION

The coming vote for union certification of library workers is the first step towards better wages and working conditions in the library. Little job security, staff reductions, heavier workloads, plus low wages face all campus workers, from the cafeteria staff to the library workers. The present union drive to change these conditions in the library is not the first one at Muskoka. But, the university administration has a history of smashing every previous unionizing attempt. Covert threats, intimidating letters, shifting work hours, and firings have all been used. Similar tactics are being employed at the library now. The university administration is showing itself to be no different than any other boss in its dislike of organized workers.

The Board of Governors at Muskoka, besides employing thousands of workers at the university, represents a total of 70 corporations, who make tremendous profits from university contracts (OGEL Construction, Megalife, Addington Chemical). They scream about inflationary wages, when in fact, corporate profits continue to rise (30% in the last quarter) and real wages for working people continue to fall. Muskoka's personnel manager, Miserly Masters, apologizes for the low wages by saying the "university has a duty to the tax-payers, not to lead in wages." Who is he trying to fool? In fact, it is the administrators at Muskoka who are earning upwards of $60,000/year while the majority of tax-payers including the library workers at Muskoka earn only around 15 to 18 thousand a year.

There is no doubt that the workers in the library are getting a raw deal. Couple the indecently low wages and speed-up with intimidation when they try to improve their situation, and you have the situation the library workers are in. The workers are showing they are willing to fight the reactionary administration; now students should show that they are not going to accept union harrassment by the administration. Students can support the workers by signing and circulating a petition, writing to the Martlet, and coming to a support RALLY, on WEDNESDAY, MARCH 8TH, AT 12:30 in front of LEVINSEN HALL.

INFO: 442-8602
12:30 Wednesday, March 8
LEVINSEN HALL

On March 3, two letters and a pamphlet were circulated to all library employees (Exhibit XIII).

EXHIBIT XIII (Continued)

March 3rd.

Dear Fellow Employees:

As many of you already know, a vote will be held on March 14th and 15th to determine whether or not we will have a union at the Library. This vote will be in the form of a secret ballot and will be conducted by the Ontario Department of Labour. All non-professional staff members, with the exception of several department heads and secretaries to administrators, are eligible to vote. If more than 50% of those who vote support the union on their ballots, legal certification of C.U.P.E. as our bargaining agent will follow.

Those of us who have worked for unionization from the start advised C.U.P.E. to apply for a vote on our behalf in order to speed certification of the union. Consequently, we are no longer collecting union cards; instead, we are now campaigning to ensure that all of you who have signed union cards vote for the union in the upcoming election. And we are urging those of you who have not signed cards to vote with us for C.U.P.E.

Throughout the unionization campaign, the University and Library administrations have claimed to be neutral and impartial towards a union for employees. In the November 11th letter which they wrote to us, both Dr. Butler and Mr. Masters (the University Personnel Officer) stated that it was our right to organize a union and that the University would take no part in the decision. We know now that these claims were false and that the University and Library administrations are actively working against our unionization. When Library employees received wage increases at Christmas we pointed out that the rescheduling of salaries *in between* budgets was unprecedented at the University. We stated that the University, by giving us pay raises in the middle of a union campaign, was obviously trying to influence staff members not to join the union. Despite these salary increases, the rate at which people have joined the union has increased since Christmas.

It has been in the last few weeks, however, that the true intent of the University and Library administrations has become evident. Recently, the Ontario Labour Relations Board held a "pre-vote hearing" to verify our application for a vote. For the hearing the University hired a management labour relations lawyer from Toronto expressly to try to defeat our application. At this hearing the University's lawyer made several attempts to convince the Board that we didn't have enough union members to require a vote. Their lawyer argued that a number of union members who are supervisors are part of the management of the Library, and therefore not eligible to belong to C.U.P.E. Then the University argued that the professional librarians should be included in our union; from the start we have not attempted to organize professionals because they indicated to us that they did not want to unionize.

Either of these tactics, if they had been recognized by the Labour Board, could have resulted in the disqualification of our application. This is what the University and Library administrators desired, but their efforts failed and we got our vote.

Now we are being subjected to "rumours" spread either by the administrators or by those few staff members working with them. One such rumour concerns union dues. It has been alleged that the fees we will be paying to C.U.P.E. will be $45.00 per month. This is absolutely false. First, we decide collectively the amount we wish to pay as union dues; second, most C.U.P.E. locals set their dues rates at $15.00 per month or less. And we will save more than that amount by taking advantage of C.U.P.E.'s life and disability insurance plans instead of the Megalife schemes we now pay for. Another rumour has it that the Library administration has a list of union members and can act against people who have joined C.U.P.E. However, the fact is that the Labour Relations Board maintains total secrecy about who has signed union cards. This rumour is merely an attempt to intimidate those who are union members. But this rumour will not work either. It is illegal to punish or discriminate against anyone who has joined a union. Many of us have openly stated that we are C.U.P.E members in order to counteract rumours like this one. However, if anyone fears repercussions from the administration, the best way to ensure that we are all treated equally and fairly is to vote for the union. Remember that it will be a secret ballot and no one can possibly determine how individuals vote.

It is not surprising that the University and Library administrations are actively opposing our attempt to unionize. Unionization will guarantee regular pay increases and vastly improved benefits. Part of the job of the administration is to keep expenses down. In addition, our unionization will force the Library administration to correct some pressing problems such as increasing work-loads, staff shortages, promotion procedures and so on. In short unionization will establish a legal contract providing a fair deal for all of us and a means by which we can influence Library policies which affect us.

It's no accident that now, with the union vote a few days away, meetings are suddenly being called in many departments to discuss Library "problems". The Library administration doesn't want to deal with employees unified in a union. University administrators definitely don't want a union at the Library because they know that the unionization of all other campus employees will soon follow. In fact, since it has been announced that we are having a union vote, C.U.P.E. has received calls from a number of other campus employees inquiring how they too can organize.

We aren't deterred in the least by the attitude of the University and Library administrations. Instead, we believe that their actions will convince more staff members of the absolute necessity of unionization. The administrators are merely proving what we've been saying all along. Let's not forget that we have the support of many campus employees. And both faculty and students are circulating petitions which endorse our effect to join C.U.P.E.

Finally, we want to emphasize once more the importance of your vote for the union on March 14th-15th. We are certain that we can win the vote, but it is necessary that everyone who has signed a card or has otherwise indicated support for C.U.P.E. votes with us. Prior to the election, we will personally contact you to inform you further about voting and to answer any of your questions. We have lots of literature about C.U.P.E. including copies of contracts which C.U.P.E. has won for library employees at other universities, statements from C.U.P.E. members at university libraries and so on.

EXHIBIT XIII (Continued)

We believe that our campaign has, at the very least, brought many of us together to discuss common problems. This in itself has made it all worthwhile. Let's make certain that we keep working together by voting together for C.U.P.E. on March 14th-15th.

Sincerely yours,

Carl McNab —663-6449
Dave Skilling —663-4442
Bob Duncan —663-1047
Maureen Mann —663-6031
Robert Simon —442-2419
Jan Fair —442-9344
Myrna Hastings
Gerry Black
Mary Bell
Judy Rise
Bob Tourney
Carol Call
Anna Banks

EXHIBIT XIII (Continued)

CANADIAN UNION OF PUBLIC EMPLOYEES

Ref: K.2.3.

March 3rd.

To: All the Support Staff Employees of
the Muskoka University Libraries

Greetings:

Finally our Battle is almost over. The Ontario Labour Relations Board will probably order a representation vote and you can confirm your desire to be represented by the Canadian Union of Public Employees.

As you are no doubt aware, on February 14th, we made application for Certification on your behalf to the Ontario Labour Relations Board.

A Mr. W. G. Allen was appointed as Examiner by the Ontario Labour Relations Board and was authorized to confer with parties as to the description and composition of an appropriate Bargaining Unit.

A meeting was held at Toronto on Monday, February 28th, in attendance was Mr. Wixter, Council, Mr. Masters and Mr. Talbot for the University, and Mr. W. A. Lison,

Assistant Regional Director for Ontario and S. Hall for the Canadian Union of Public Employees.

It was agreed that matters in dispute have now been resolved, except that the University is maintaining that the Library does not constitute an appropriate Collective Bargaining Unit.

This matter will be dealt with by the Ontario Labour Relations Board after the vote has been taken. A number of precedents already have been established and proven that the University is wrong, such as, Kings University and Toronto University.

Tentative arrangements have been made for a certification vote to be held on Tuesday, March 14th and Wednesday, March 15th, alternate dates suggested by both parties are Tuesday, March 21st and Wednesday, March 22nd.

This is subject to confirmation by the Ontario Labour Relations Board whose officials will be conducting the vote. As soon as the date has been confirmed we will advise you as to the time and location. In any event the voting will be conducted on the Campus and you will be given an opportunity to cast your ballot during working hours.

I would like to thank you for your patience and ask you to start giving consideration to what you want negotiated on your behalf.

Yours truly,

Syd Hall

Sydney Hall,
SH/rds   Representative,
cc: F. Bain   Canadian Union of Public Employees,

EXHIBIT XIII (Continued)

CUPE BELONGS IN YOUR LIBRARY

PROFESSIONAL DIGNITY

Ask a librarian who is a union member where to find professional dignity and he will direct you to the section marked CUPE.

The direction comes naturally to the union librarian because CUPE has brought dignity into his working life.

CUPE stands for The Canadian Union of Public Employees, and a good deal more.

For the library staff member CUPE stands for winning — and keeping — professional standards for professional people.

For the library staff member who has been told repeatedly that he is a professional, but cannot expect professional wages and working conditions, CUPE stands for a new and better way of life.

With ever greater frequency, librarians in all parts of the country are turning to trade unionism as the avenue to this better life.

Librarians are not the only professionals who have embarked on the collective journey to union membership.

Newspaper reporters and writers, for instance, have grown tired of working for half of the pay and none of the security and other benefits of their "back shop" co-workers who were organized. Under the leadership of outstanding professionals such as Heywood Broun, newspapermen formed a union and soon were enjoying greater wages and benefits. Teachers, engineers, musicians, actors, pilots and other professionals found the same instrument for expression in the labour movement.

These professionals are realizing their goals by participating in the special union best attuned to their specific needs.

THE LIBRARIANS' UNION

Library employees are being motivated towards the labour movement because they are discovering that unionism has many advantages that they cannot find in their professional societies.

They are finding that CUPE serves them as a bargaining agent that inspires confidence in their ranks, respect from administrators and the goodwill of the public. Because CUPE is best equipped to insure librarians the attainment of security and recognition of personal worth, it is the special union of and for library employees.

Librarians now affiliated with CUPE realize that their union encourages the highest professional service standards by emphasizing the dignity of library employment.

CUPE IN YOUR LIBRARY

CUPE representation can bring a new sense of personal worth to you and your fellow employees.

WHAT CAN YOU EXPECT FROM CUPE?

First you will be associated with thousands of career librarians throughout the nation banded together in an organization that understand the fundamental problems confronting them.

You will be part of an organization which advocates community libraries.

You will have an opportunity to upgrade your own professional status.

You will find that collective effort through CUPE is an effective way to attain public support of better facilities — and bigger budgets.

You will find that the conditions created by union representation will help attract the most talented young people to your career.

You will be part of a union which carries on an aggressive program of fostering and promoting a better understanding between those it represents and the public.

You will belong to a union which advocates a library union entirely independent of, but cooperative with, administration in the belief that such independence provides a clear and responsible channel for employee expression.

You will share in the improved working conditions, wages and numerous other benefits which CUPE has demonstrated can be gained by the public librarian.

You will be provided machinery for employee consultation and representation on matters of policy affecting librarians' welfare.

By joining with thousands of library employees now being helped by CUPE, you will become a part of the collective effort to help yourself, your fellow worker, your library and your community.

Mr. Talbot noticed Mrs. Banks' name on the letter and felt guilty because he was probably the one who had alienated her. He wondered whether Mrs. Banks had gone around the library proclaiming her story to try to persuade other employees to vote for the union. Mr. Talbot, Dr. Butler and Mr. Masters were becoming concerned with the recent influx of union literature, and the effect it might have on the library employees.

The union had requested and received permission for a pre-hearing vote. Before the meeting with OLRB on February 25 for authorization of a pre-hearing vote, Mr. Masters, Dr. Butler, Mr. Talbot and Mr. Wixter, the lawyer retained by the university, had met to discuss the union situation. They were very concerned that the union, by organizing solely library employees, was attempting to fragment the university employee structure in an effort to gain a foothold at Muskoka. To the administrators it was not sensible to have different union locals in each building representing similar kinds of employees and classification groups. It was decided at the meeting that the university would attempt to propose a different bargaining unit. Mr. Wixter suggested that the university should propose a bargaining unit of all clerks and support staff. This would increase the bargaining unit to approximately 1200 members. If the proposal was accepted, the Ontario Labour Relations Board would nullify the pre-hearing vote and the union would have to attempt to organize the larger unit. However, if the union was successful in their campaign with the larger unit the university might encounter greater problems with their contract negotiations.

Mr. Talbot and Dr. Butler were worried that the overwhelming amount of union literature might be unfairly confusing employees, and, after consulting with Mr. Wixter, they sent a letter to library employees (Exhibit XIV).

Full page advertisements began appearing in *The Martlet* in each issue, and it was apparent that students were becoming increasingly interested in the situation from the many letters to the editor that were published. On March 8 the Canadian Labour Party held their advertised rally and demonstration and *The Martlet* recorded the event with the article reproduced in Exhibit XV.

On March 11, a leaflet was circulated through the library (Exhibit XVI).

EXHIBIT XIV

Muskoka University, Bradley, Ontario, Canada

The Libraries

March 6.

Dear Library staff member:

The Ontario Labour Relations Board has ordered a vote to determine whether you and other staff members wish to be represented by The Canadian Union of Public Employees.

The purpose of the vote is to give you the opportunity of deciding whether it is in your best interests to be represented by a union in your employment relations with the University or to continue to deal directly with us.

The vote is by secret ballot. The Ontario Labour Relations Board protects your ballot so that no one could know how you voted. You can mark your ballot exactly as you wish. *For example, it does not matter whether you have signed a Union card, you can still vote for or against the Union.*

The decision is yours!

The vote will probably be held on March 14 and 15 *or* March 21 and 22. We will advise you of the other details such as the poll locations and the hours of voting as soon as we are notified by the Board.

H. Talbot,
Library Personnel Officer.

R. Butler,
Chief Librarian.

EXHIBIT XV

March 10
Muskoka Martlet

CPL DEMONSTRATES SUPPORT FOR LIBRARY WORKERS

By Hal Bodoni

About a dozen students turned out for a demonstration, organized by members of the Canadian Party of Labour, to support Muskoka library workers in their attempt to unionize.

They withstood the cold in front of Levinson Hall for about 15 minutes before adjourning to the Student Union Building. Short speeches were made in the downstairs hall of the SUB.

Clerical library workers will vote on March 21–22 on having the Canadian Union of Public Employees (CUPE) act as bargaining agent for about 130 library workers.

Bill Masters, University personnel manager, grinned as he commented on the demonstration.

"With six people? . . . Do I have to say anything?"

Syd Hall, the library's CUPE organizer, refused to comment on the demonstration.

Fred Bain, national organizer of CUPE, said last week that CUPE has no communist affiliation.

Bain said a demonstration by the CPL would not help the unionizing attempt.

Hall said if students want to support the

union, it is "strictly up to them."

"We can't do anything about it if they want to demonstrate up there", he said.

Interviews

The Martlet, interested in Library employees' reactions to the demonstrations, interviewed a number of employees. Most employees preferred to remain anonymous, but some of the more prevalent opinions were:

"A cheap trick by the administration to smear CUPE's image."

"I think its dreadful! CUPE members didn't tell us that they had communist support."

"I think the administration engineered the whole thing. That's even more reason why we should have a union to protect us against such a deceiptful bunch of Mother . . . . . .!"

"I don't think the students should have any say in what happens here in the library. They always stick their noses into everybody else's affairs".

"I figure it's a joke; so why sweat it?"

Mr. Talbot, Mr. Masters and Dr. Butler had a meeting on March 12. They met because all were concerned with the apparent new tone of the campaign. Much of the literature was becoming very amateurish and emotional. The Canadian Labour Party demonstration and the consequent *Martlet* employee interviews had added a new and very different element to the organization efforts. The men were upset that some of the library employees could feel so strongly against the administration that they would suspect the university of prompting the rally to taint the union image. There were a number of fallacies perpetrated by the union that still had not been challenged by the administration. One, recently, that had bothered the administrators was the union claim that the university had sought to include the professional librarians in the bargaining unit when in fact, the university had presented a very strong case against the union's proposal to include them. The three men at the meeting decided that the administration should publish a fact sheet in which they would challenge the major false claims by the union. They composed a very long letter which responded to every incorrect union statement that they were aware of. They then decided to cut out parts of the letter because it was too long, and on March 13 sent the letter to the library employees (Exhibit XVII).

On March 15, Mr. Talbot posted a notice on the bulletin boards (Exhibit XVIII).

EXHIBIT XVI

MUSKOKA LIBRARY EMPLOYEES

YOU WOULDN'T VOTE

AGAINST YOURSELF.

But that's exactly what will happen if you don't vote for the Canadian Union of Public Employees or if you fail to vote at all.

The Ontario Labour Relations Board has ordered a vote for all library employees at the Muskoka University to determine whether or not you want CUPE to be your bargaining agent.

The Board already knows a large percentage of you want to join CUPE -- they just want to make sure a majority of Muskoka library employees want CUPE on campus.

The exact date of the vote is unknown but will probably be held the second or third week of March. You will be informed of the date and the voting locations just as quickly as they are known.

In the meantime consider some of the advantages that membership in CUPE would bring you and your co-workers:

> . An opportunity to negotiate a sound job
> security clause.

> . A chance to introduce a system of fair
> promotions, a complete job evaluation
> program with representation from the
> employees as well as management.

> . An occasion to press for improved fringe
> benefits to keep up with other Canadian
> workers and their families.

As most of you are already aware CUPE is the largest national union in Canada with 275,000 members. CUPE members include municipal employees, hospital workers, board of education employees, hydro workers, CBC employees as well as university employees.

Remember also that new CUPE locals set their own dues. The average dues rate for CUPE members is $15 a month. That's a small price to pay for the benefits which will accrue from being a member of the Canadian Union of Public Employees.

VOTE CUPE

EXHIBIT XVII

Muskoka University, Bradley, Ontario, Canada

The Libraries

March 13.

Dear Library Staff Member:

As stated in our letter dated November 11, the University will challenge incorrect or misleading facts and information used in an attempt by others to persuade you to their point of view. Recent claims by the union applying for your bargaining rights, and by a small group of sympathetic employees must not go unanswered.

What follows are *FACTS* answering some of the claims made by these people.

1. **Claim** *(union letter November 3)*
"Enclosed is a Wage Schedule of the Bradley Public Library."

   Fact
   The rates quoted were *annual increments*, **not** weekly rates as first claimed by the union or bi-weekly rates as offered in their attempt to correct their initial error. This *FACT* is confirmed in Appendix A — Salaries of the Bradley Public Library's current Collection Agreement with the union.

2. **CLAIM** *(Muskoka Martlet, March 3)*
"Bain (representative of C.U.P.E.) accused W. Masters, University Personnel Director of trying to include professional librarians in the union application for certification."

   (employee-signed letter, March 3)
   "Then the University argued that the professional librarians should be included in our union, from the start we have not attempted to organize professionals because they indicated to us that they did not want to unionize."

   Fact
   Although the Union sought the membership of the professional librarians in their letters November 3 and November 30, the University quite clearly sought their exclusion at an Ontario Labour Relations Board examination meeting in Toronto on February 28 — a meeting which Mr. Bain did not attend.

3. **Claim** *(employee-signed letter January 19)*
"It is a traditional tactic of employers, when a union campaign is underway, to offer an increase in salary . . . in the hope that staff members will abandon unionization."

   Fact
   The reclassifications and salary revisions announced in December were the result of a program initiated prior to July 1. A committee composed of

members of staff of the Library met frequently during the late spring and early summer and suggested a new salary administration program which included a job reclassification segment. As you know, each staff member participated in the reclassification procedures by answering an extensive questionnaire which was reviewed by their supervisor, the University Personnel Department, the Assistant Directors and the Director. Where a staff member believed the resultant classification to be incorrect, the duties were reviewed and in some cases the individual was interviewed personally to determine an even more detailed explanation of his/her responsibilities.

The reclassification provided the basis for a complete revision of salaries, totally unrelated to the union's bid for representation.

We have now presented you with the *FACTS* relating to the more serious claims made by the union and its sympathizers.

We conclude by emphasizing the importance of your right to vote and encourage you to do so. We only ask that you mark your ballot according to what you believe will be in the best interest of yourself and those dependent on you.

W. Masters,
Director of Personnel.

R. Butler,
Chief Librarian.

EXHIBIT XVIII

Muskoka University, Bradley, Ontario, Canada

The Libraries

March 15.

NOTICE

The University has just been informed by the Ontario Labour Relations Board that the Board will conduct a pre-hearing vote on March 21 and 22.

As mentioned earlier, this vote has been ordered to determine the true wishes of staff regarding union representation.

The university will continue to inform you of developments — watch this location for further details.

H. Talbot,
Library Personnel Officer.

This notice prompted another rash of literature, both pro- and anti-union. Samples of the literature are reproduced as Exhibit XIX.

EXHIBIT XIX

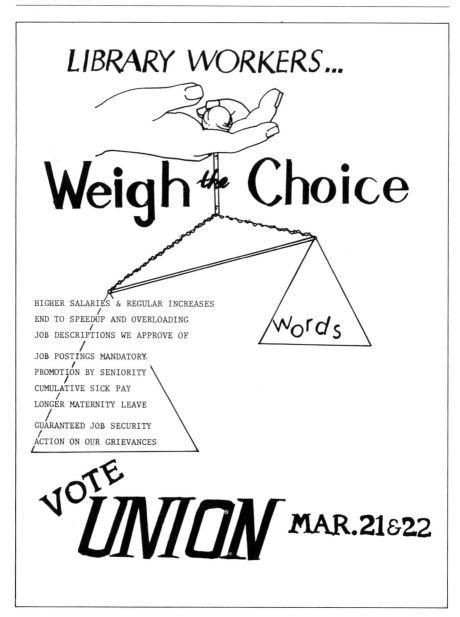

EXHIBIT XIX (Continued)

MARCH 21 AND 22
ARE THE DAYS
MAKE YOUR VOTE
COUNT WITH CUPE

The secret ballot ordered by the Ontario Labour Relations Board
will be March 21 and 22.

The Board already knows a large percentage of you want to join
CUPE-- they just want to make sure a majority of Muskoka library
employees want CUPE on campus.

Consider some of the advantages that membership in CUPE would bring
you and your co-workers:

. An opportunity to negotiate a sound job security clause.
. A chance to introduce a system of fair promotions, a
  complete job evaluation program with representation
  from the employees as well as management.
. An occasion to press for improved fringe benefits
  to keep up with other Canadian workers and their
  families.

As most of you are already aware, CUPE is the largest union in Canada
with 280,000 members. CUPE members include municipal employees, hospital
workers, board of education employees, hydro workers, CBC employees as
well as university employees.

After March 22 you can become part of CUPE and start working for the
things you deserve.

VOTE CUPE
CANADIAN UNION OF PUBLIC EMPLOYEES

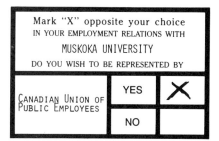

Some of the literature was disclaimed by both the union and the administration. The last week became very confusing, with each side accusing the other of distributing false literature and the other side pleading ignorance or denying it and counter charging. An example of one of the confusing letters and accompanying posters is contained in Exhibit XX. No one knew who A. Earnshaw was or why he was involved.

On March 21 and 22 the vote was held under the supervision of the Ontario Labour Relations Board. On March 23, Mr. Talbot sent a memorandum to department heads, Departmental libraries and senior administrators of the University and Muskoka Library System (Exhibit XIX).

Mr. Talbot began preparing for the upcoming meeting, in April, with the Labour Board Examiner. He had heard numerous rumours as to the likely outcome of the vote. Many of the rumours indicated that the union would win by a significant majority; others claimed it would be very close. The university in the pre-vote hearing with the board had indicated that they were going to challenge the bargaining unit. Two universities in Ontario already had attempted to propose larger bargaining units in response to CUPE library organizing drives and the Board had ruled against one administration but in favour of the other administration. The bargaining unit which had voted at Muskoka was all non-professional librarians which included library clerks and support personnel.

EXHIBIT XX

Bradley, Ontario.
Today.

My Friend:

A few words about the enclosed, which will I hope, make them a little more meaningful.

The newspaper clipping and it's attendant questions really need no explanation. It is quite true that at least this much of your money, (assuming you are a member of a Canadian Union, affiliated with either the Canadian Labour Congress or an American Union) — does in fact cross into the United States each year. Some of it is also used to provide generous salaries and expense accounts, tax free, for the officers and employees of the various Unions concerned.

The little sketch of the Chemistry (?) bit endeavours to depict graphically the various ways your money is divided, spent or otherwise disposed of, regardless of how *you* might wish to see it used.

I believe that I am reasonably well informed on the subject, having been involved with Unions, as well as Associations of Government Employees, for many years. You may believe, therefore, that I am not putting out half-baked ideas, but am speaking of something I know.

For some time now, you have been bombarded with Union literature, promising many things. Perhaps the first and most important is 'a voice in the determination of your own salaries, working conditions, fringe benefits and etc.' Is it possible that an Association of University Employees could present your case to Management much more clearly and knowledgeably than an employee of a Labor Union who has no personal interest in the matter other than his own salary? Think about it.

If your group becomes Unionized on the basis of the coming vote, it has been rumoured that you will be required to strike almost immediately for higher wages. Will the newly formed Union group pay Strike Pay? Since you are in effect your own employer, (University funds come mainly from the taxpayer), all expenses of such a strike, together with pay increases resulting, if any, must come out of your own pocket, at least in part.

It is my suggestion that it is better to support as strongly as is in your power, an Association of University Employees. Such an Association can elect representatives from within your own group, to speak with authority on all questions relating to conditions of employment. It is probably true, also, that Management would receive such representations with a greater degree of good will, than it would if the same representations are made by the paid representative of a large Union.

Finally, I should say that my interest in this matter is entirely due to my interest in my fellow men; and women. Having lived through many similar experiences, the ideas I offer are based thereon.

Sincerely,

A. Earnshaw, Past President,
Civil Service Association of Alberta.

P.S. Remember, **Do Vote**. A vote not used is in effect a vote for the Union.

EXHIBIT XX (Continued)

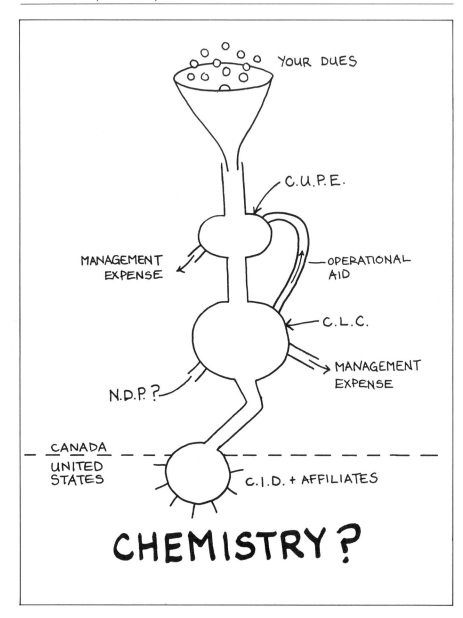

EXHIBIT XXI

Muskoka University, Library System

Memorandum   March 23.

To: Dr. Butler, W. Masters,
         All Library Department Heads and all Departmental Libraries

From: Henry Talbot, Personnel Officer

Subject: Muskoka Libraries
         Labour Relations Vote

The vote conducted by the Ontario Labour Relations Board this week resulted in a turnout of approximately 92% of eligible voters. Only a few problems were encountered during the voting and these were subsequently settled.

With the sealing of the ballot boxes at 6 p.m. yesterday, plans were made for a Board examiner to meet with representatives of both sides on April 6. At that time the Board will begin discussions regarding the union's application for certification.

Counting of the ballots cast on March 21 and 22 awaits the decision of the Ontario Labour Relations Board on the application for certification.

As further details become available they will be announced.

Henry Talbot

H. Talbot,
Personnel Officer.

Discussion Questions

1. Assume you are Mr. Talbot. Formulate what you think is an appropriate bargaining unit for Muskoka University and prepare your arguments for presentation to the Labour Board Examiner. Consider the long run implications for your solution.

2. What other problems might you anticipate before the board's hearing? What would your response be?

3. Evaluate the actions of the university and the union during the campaign. If you were in charge, what, if anything, would you have done differently? Why?

4. What do you think the results of the election would be? Why?

5
THE NEGOTIATION CHALLENGE

The second challenge which a union presents to management is the negotiation challenge. This is a recurring challenge. The typical Canadian collective agreement is for two years, with minimum permissible term under most legislation being one year and the maximum found in practice being three years.[1]

The negotiation of collective agreements is the most visible activity in industrial relations, the one which attracts the most attention from the media — particularly when negotiation involves a strike rather than a settlement without a strike. With regard to the negotiation of collective agreements, the general perception is somewhat at odds with reality. The parties spend much more time and energy in administering a collective agreement than they do negotiating it. The outcome of negotiations is most often, and by a wide margin, a settlement without a strike. The public focus on negotiations seems to stress monetary issues; in reality, non-monetary issues are at least as important. The perception that labour negotiations are adversarial in nature often is only partially correct.

The negotiation of collective agreements is a complex activity, and one which in North America exhibits a great deal of diversity in structure, content, and process. Consequently, this chapter can serve only as an introduction to the subject, but one which will allow the reader to gain some understanding and appreciation of the activity.

The Legal Framework

Once a union is certified by the labour relations board, the employer is required *by law* to meet with the union, and to make every reasonable effort to develop a collective agreement. Thus the law initiates the negotiation procedure. The law also imposes some general and specific requirements on the parties and we will begin the examination of negotiation procedures by looking at those legal requirements.

The Good Faith Requirement

All Canadian jurisdictions except Saskatchewan have a specific requirement for bargaining in "good faith" by both parties. There is not a great deal of jurisprudence on the meaning of "good faith bargaining" in Canada. Even in the U.S., where there have been more court and labour decisions, the concept of "good faith" in bargaining has been elusive.

One of the reasons for the relative lack of jurisprudence in Canada has been the lack of an effective remedy. Until relatively recently, the only remedy available was to seek a consent to prosecute order from the board and attempt to get a court to impose fines for the failure to obey the law. Obviously, this option is time consuming, and not particularly useful. Now, complaints about a lack of good faith bargaining can be taken directly to the labour board in the federal jurisdiction as well as in British Columbia, Ontario, and Quebec. Where boards have become involved in a determination of good faith bargaining, their focus has generally been on the process of negotiations rather than their content. Failure to agree on an item has not been found to be evidence of "bad faith" bargaining, but refusal to meet or refusal to fully discuss an item has been. In the U.S., the labour boards have ruled that bargaining on some subjects is mandatory while on others it is voluntary. Canadian boards have not made such distinctions. The only bargaining demands or positions which Canadian boards have found to be evidence of a lack of good faith, and for which they issued "cease and desist" orders (the standard remedy for good faith complaints), are those which are illegal under the labour relations act or other legislation.[2]

THE CONTENT OF COLLECTIVE AGREEMENTS

While labour boards in Canada have been reluctant to require the parties to agree on subjects for negotiation, some items are required by legislation to be part of the collective agreement. The following items are mandatory inclusions in collective agreements:

1. Arbitration Clauses With the exception of Saskatchewan, all Canadian jurisdictions require a clause in the collective agreement providing for the final and binding arbitration of all disputes arising during the term of a collective agreement over the application, interpretation or administration of that agreement. As part of its arbitration requirement, the British Columbia legislation requires a clause specifying that the employer will discipline or discharge employees only for "just cause."

2. No Strike or Lockout Provisions Given that disputes which arise during the term of collective agreements are required to be settled by arbitration, all Canadian jurisdictions except Saskatchewan also prohibit strikes and lockouts during the term of a collective agreement, and collective agreements in New Brunswick, Ontario, and Prince Edward Island must contain clauses to that effect. In other jurisdictions, the required arbitration clause must have a "no cessation of work" provision.

3. Union Security Union Security clauses in collective agreements are clauses which relate to requirements for union membership in and the payment and collection of union dues by members of the bargaining unit. When unions are certified as the representative of a group of employees, they are required to represent, i.e., bargain and handle grievances for, all members of that bargaining unit, *regardless of whether an employee is actually a member of the union.* Unions have taken the position that since they are required to represent all employees, membership in the union or at least payment of dues to the union should be required of all employees in the bargaining unit.

Union Security provisions can take a variety of forms. A *closed shop* provision provides that the employer will only hire or employ union members, i.e., union membership is required *before* employment. Such agreements are typically found in the construction or longshoring industries. They are illegal in the U.S., but permitted in Canada.

A *Union Shop* clause requires all members of the bargaining unit to become and remain members of the union *after employment* or after a probationary period. Under such a clause, the employer would not be permitted to continue to employ an employee who refused to join the union. Such clauses are legal in Canada. In the U.S., the federal legislation allows individual states to prohibit these clauses. Where such clauses are prohibited, the state laws doing so are called "right to work" laws. In Canada and the U.S., where union shop clauses are allowed, unions are generally prohibited from refusing to accept or maintain employees as members except for failure to tender dues. In Canada, British Columbia, Manitoba, Ontario, and Saskatchewan allow for exemption from union shop clauses for employees who object to union membership on religious grounds.

The *Modified Union Shop* (or *maintenance of membership*) is a type of union security arrangement that is a common variation on union shop clauses. This arrangement provides that all employees who are currently members of the union must maintain their membership and that all new employees must join the union. Such a clause allows employees who were strongly opposed to the union during its organized campaign to avoid membership.

The *Agency Shop* or *Rand Formula* (the former term is commonly used in the U.S., the latter in Canada, after it was proposed by Mr. Justice Ivan Rand as a way of resolving a dispute at the Ford Motor Company after World War II) are union security arrangements that do not require union membership, but require all members of a bargaining unit to pay dues to the union.

An *open shop* is a situation where there are no requirements for union membership or dues payments.

Checkoff is the process by which union dues are collected by the employer via payroll deduction and then remitted to the union. Checkoff provisions may be used with any of the other union security provisions. All Canadian jurisdictions provide that the employer must checkoff union dues when authorized to do so by the employee.[3] Thus all collective agreements in Canada have *de facto* checkoff clauses in them. In five Canadian jurisdictions — British Columbia, Manitoba, Ontario, Quebec, and the federal jurisdiction — the employer must deduct union dues from all employees in the bargaining unit and remit them to the union. Thus, in these jurisdictions, the *minimum* union security provision in collective agreements is the Rand Formula.

4. **Term** All Canadian jurisdictions specify that the minimum permissible term for a collective agreement is one year. There must be an article in the contract which specifies the date that the contract comes into effect and when it expires.[4]

5. **Technological Change** The British Columbia Labour Code[5] requires that all collective agreements in that province contain provisions providing for the arbitration of disputes relating to technological change which occur during the term of the agreement. The Canada Labour Code and the statutes in Manitoba and Saskatchewan[6] encourage the insertion of provisions dealing with the effects of technological change by providing that the union may reopen the collective agreement in mid-term if such provisions are not present in the agreement.

6. **Recognition** Ontario and New Brunswick require a clause in the collective agreement recognizing the union as the exclusive bargaining agent for the employees in the bargaining unit specified in the board's certification order. In all jurisdictions, the certification order forms the basis for the negotiation of the collective agreement, and a recognition clause is generally included in collective agreements where it is not required by law, so as to provide a clear indication in the contract of the group to whom the contract applies. The parties may agree to amend the certification order to add or delete employees, and the recognition clause would reflect this.

Exclusions from Collective Agreements

While the various items listed above are required to be part of collective agreements, there are also provisions which provide that some items cannot be part of collective agreements. In all jurisdictions, a contract cannot provide for wages, hours, and working conditions which are less than those provided by the labour standards legislation in each jurisdiction. Where wage restraint legislation has been in place, as was the case nationally in 1975–78, and in the federal and some provincial civil service sectors during the "6 and 5" program in 1982–83, the amount of wage increases permitted in renegotiation of collective agreements is controlled, and clauses which provide for wage increases above a specified level are prohibited.

The legislation which most severely restricts the content of collective agreements by proscribing items which are not subject to negotiation is found in the public sector. The federal Public Service Staff Relations Act excludes items covered by other legislation and thus excludes hiring, merit rating, classification, promotions, demotions, transfer, lay-off, and release — all covered by the Public Service Employment Act. Pensions are covered by the Public Service Superannuation Act. Legislation covering provincial employers in Nova Scotia, Ontario, and Quebec contains similar exclusions. Other provinces do not have such restrictions.

BARGAINING STRUCTURE

Even though unions are certified as bargaining agents for particular groups of workers, actual negotiations may take place in a structure different from these certified units. A negotiation involving a multiplant employer might involve only one union, but several different "bargaining units," since the union might well be certified as the bargaining agent for employees on a plant-by-plant basis. Thus labour board certification for bargaining purposes does not necessarily define the scope of the actual negotiations. The "election district" may be different from the "negotiating unit."[7]

In general, Canadian legislation is permissive regarding bargaining structure. As was noted in Chapter 1, the most prevalent form of bargaining is single employer, single plant, single union bargaining. The next most prevalent is single employer, multiplant, single union bargaining. There are also examples of single employer, single plant, multiunion bargaining structures as well as single employer, multiplant, multiunion bargaining, although these are much less frequent than the first two single employer variations.[8] There are also structures involving multiemployer structures with either a single union (a structure found in the trucking and fishing industries) or multiple unions (as is the case of the construction industry). British Columbia has the greatest incidence of the latter type of bargaining. About one third of union members are covered by agreement negotiated with employer associations.

Where the parties are free to develop the most appropriate bargaining structure, a number of factors — economic, geographical, historical, and tactical — are responsible for the structure that evolves. A full discussion of these factors is beyond the scope of this book,[9] but we can examine some legislative and administrative attempts to determine bargaining structures which will be illustrative of some of the concerns involved in the establishment of bargaining structures. These will be examined in the context of three key work situations: construction, railroads, and the public sector.

Construction

Historically, one of the most fragmented bargaining structures existed in the construction industry, an industry characterized by a large number of small employers and unions which organized employees on a craft basis. The unions were able to play "divide and conquer" with the weak, undercapitalized employers and with their associations as well. The result was a situation which one knowledgeable observer described as "chaotic," with a high level of strike activity and excessive wage escalation.[10]

Almost all Canadian jurisdictions have attempted to deal with the construction industry by encouraging or requiring province-wide bargaining for the entire industry at once or on a province-wide craft-by-craft basis. The most controlled situation is found in Quebec, where, since 1968, under the Construction Industry Labour Relations Act, bargaining has been required on a province-wide basis between the Association of Building Contractors of Quebec (ABCQ) and the union federation representing a majority of employees in the industry which, at the time of this writing, was the Quebec Federation of Labour. Furthermore, the terms and conditions established in these negotiations are then put into effect in the rest of the industry (i.e., the non-union segment) by government decree.[11]

In Ontario and Saskatchewan, province-wide bargaining by construction trade is required. The employers are represented by an employers' association and deal separately with each union (i.e., carpenters, electricians). There is no requirement that bargaining be coordinated on an industry-wide basis.[12] The British Columbia Labour Relations Board has the power under Section 57 of the British Columbia Labour Code to order the formation of a council of trade unions as a bargaining agent. Given this power, and a declaration by the board that it was prepared to use its power to form a council of trade unions in the construction industry, the craft unions in British Columbia formed a council. Now bargaining in B.C. construction is conducted on an industry basis. Elsewhere in Canada, industry-wide bargaining in construction is encouraged, but not required by law.

Railroads

Bargaining in Canadian railroads involves 18 unions and several major employers. The federal government has attempted to informally influence the bargaining structure to encourage industry bargaining. This process came closest to fruition in 1979, but since that time bargaining has become somewhat fragmented with negotiations for some employees on an industry basis; for example, the employers represented by the Railway Association of Canada, the unions by the Canadian Council of Shopcraft employees and the Associated Non-operating Railway Unions bargaining together on an industry basis. Other negotiations involve specific companies, such as CN and specific craft groups, such as engineers. In general, stronger coordination between the companies has resulted in broader-based bargaining than that which existed prior to 1979.

The British Columbia Labour Board used its powers under the Labour Code to impose a bargaining structure on the B.C. Railway, imposing a council of trade unions as the bargaining agent for the Crown Corporation employees. In doing so, the board cited the chaotic history of union representation, the trend to leapfrogging in bargaining, and the inability of the parties to settle their own disputes.[13]

The Public Sector

The most mandatory bargaining structures have been created in the public sector. The federal Public Service Staff Relations Act divides federal employees into five occupational categories which are then subdivided into 100 different occupational groups.[14] Under the act, the Treasury Board acts as the official "employer." At the other end of the spectrum is Alberta, where all provincial civil servants are in a single bargaining unit.[15]

Civil servants in British Columbia are divided into three bargaining units: licensed professionals, registered nurses, and all others. A two-tier bargaining structure has been developed there. The first tier covers basic terms and conditions of employment for all members of the bargaining unit; the second tier covers those terms and conditions which are unique to employees in a specific occupational group.[16]

Quebec also has a unique structure. Within this structure are four groups of employees: provincial civil servants, hospital and health care employees, education employees, and provincial employees in Crown Corporations and government agencies. The province negotiates directly with its civil servants (in eight bargaining units). Representatives of the health and social affairs ministers act as co-employers with hospitals and school boards and sit at the bargaining table. Major provisions such as wages are bargained provincially, while others are negotiated locally. The provincial agencies negotiate separately, but the Quebec Treasury Board must approve their settlement. This formal structure has been paired with an informal structure since 1972 wherein the public sector unions formed a common front to negotiate basic issues (essentially wages) directly with the government while at the same time dealing with issues specific to a particular sector (e.g., education) at a separate bargaining table.[17]

The bargaining in health and education in other provinces is much more decentralized than in Quebec. Saskatchewan and Newfoundland require province-wide bargaining in education, while in Ontario and elsewhere the process is decentralized. In Ontario there are separate negotiations for public and separate schools and for primary and secondary teachers in each school district except in Metro Toronto, where school boards have been required by law to negotiate together.

DISPUTE RESOLUTION

The most detailed legislative provisions relating to the negotiation process involve procedures for dispute or impasse resolution. The two procedures most often provided for in legislation are conciliation (or mediation) and arbitration.

Conciliation and Mediation

The dictionary definition of these two words is identical. They both mean "to reconcile," and in practical use they describe a process by which a neutral third party attempts to help union and management reach agreement over items in dispute or over which an impasse has occurred during bargaining. Sometimes the words are used separately to describe different stages of third party intervention, with conciliation usually the first stage and mediation the second.

Mandatory conciliation has been a prerequisite to strikes and lockouts in Canada since the Industrial Disputes Investigation Act of 1907, and as was outlined in Chapter 3, existed in other legislative forms prior to that time. In the U.S., conciliation has always been voluntary, and there appears to be a trend in Canada to move toward the use of conciliation on a voluntary basis. At one time, conciliation was *required* before a strike or lockout could occur in all jurisdictions except Saskatchewan. Now, in addition, Alberta, Manitoba, and Quebec have essentially voluntary conciliation.

Nevertheless, conciliation is still required in a majority of Canadian jurisdictions before the right to strike or lockout vests. In addition, most jurisdictions provide for a second stage of conciliation via conciliation boards. This basic two-step model for conciliation is found in the federal jurisdiction and in New Brunswick, Newfoundland, Nova Scotia, Ontario, and Prince Edward Island. Under this other model, at the request of either party, or, on his own volition, the labour minister may appoint a conciliation officer who meets with the parties and attempts to affect a settlement. The officer (who is a government employee — all jurisdictions have conciliators in their employ even where the process is voluntary) reports back to the minister whether he or she has been able to affect a settlement. If the officer has not been able to affect a settlement, the minister may appoint a conciliation board, typically composed of one nominee from each party and a neutral chairman chosen by the nominees. The board has power to hold hearings, gather evidence, and issue a report recommending the terms of settlement. Conciliation boards are rarely used now even though provision for them is still on the statute books. Usually upon receipt of a report from a conciliation officer stating that he or she has been unable to affect a settlement, the labour minister issues a "no board" report. Such a report is formal notice to the parties that the minister is not going to name a conciliation board. Following the issuing of a "no board" report, the right to strike or lockout vests in 7 days in the federal and New Brunswick jurisdictions, 14 days in Nova Scotia, Ontario, and Prince Edward Island, and 15 days in Newfoundland.[18] If a conciliation board is named, the right to strike or lockout vests 7 days after the receipt of the board's report in the above-named jurisdictions with the exception of Nova Scotia where the time period is 14 days.

In New Brunswick, Ontario, and Prince Edward Island, as well as in the federal jurisdiction, the minister may appoint a mediator after the report of a conciliation officer has been received. (In the federal jurisdiction, the individual is called a conciliation commissioner.) The report of this individual takes the place of a conciliation board.

British Columbia's legislation makes no provision for the appointment of conciliation boards. That legislation provides for a mediation officer, which the Labour Relations Board may appoint. If an officer is appointed, the parties do not acquire the right to strike or lockout until the officer's report has been received.

In Alberta, the parties may request the services of a mediator, but do not have to do so before acquiring the right to strike. The minister has the power to appoint a Disputes Inquiry Board (similar to a conciliation board). If such a board is established before a strike or lockout occurs, a strike or lockout may not occur until 10 days after its report. If the Board is appointed after a strike or lockout begins, its operations do not affect the strike or lockout.

In Manitoba, a conciliation officer, a mediator of the parties' choice, or a conciliation board may be appointed by the minister at the request of the parties, but such an appointment does not affect the right to strike or lockout. The same conditions essentially apply in Saskatchewan. Quebec legislation only provides for a conciliation officer to be appointed, but such an appointment and the report of the officer does not affect the right to strike or lockout.

Other Requirements

In Alberta, British Columbia, New Brunswick, Nova Scotia, and Prince Edward Island, a strike vote must be taken and a majority of those in the bargaining unit must approve of strike action before a legal strike can occur. In Alberta, the vote must be supervised by the Labour Relations Board. British Columbia and Alberta require that 72 hours notice of the strike or lockout be given. Nova Scotia requires that 48 hours notice be given to the Minister of Labour and Alberta requires that 72 hours notice be given to the province's Director of Mediation Services. In Manitoba, the parties are required to give the minister notice of strike or lockout action at least 14 days prior to the start of the action. In Newfoundland, the minister may order a strike or lockout vote taken when he or she believes that such action might be harmful to an industry or a section of the province. In Ontario, the employer may request the Board to order a vote on the last employer offer either before or after a strike has commenced.

Arbitration

Arbitration is a quasi-judicial procedure by which disputes are settled by a single arbitrator or a board of arbitration. The arbitration of disputes relating to the *content* of collective agreements, i.e., those arising during contract negotiations, is called *interests arbitration*. The arbitration of disputes which arise over the application, interpretation, or administration of existing collective agreements is called *rights arbitration*. Earlier in the chapter we noted that almost all Canadian contracts are required to have a clause requiring rights arbitration. This type of arbitration will be extensively discussed in Chapter 6.

Arbitration as a means of settling disputes or impasses during contract negotiations is required in a number of areas. It is often required where strikes are prohibited. At other times it is offered to the parties as an alternative to a strike or lockout. Table 5–1 outlines the employee groups who are forbidden by law to strike, and for whom arbitration is offered as an alternative. In these situations, conciliation is usually required before arbitration can commence.

The federal Public Service Staff Relations Act requires that each union bargaining unit irrevocably select either arbitration or conciliation/strike as a means of dispute resolution, should negotiations reach an impasse.[19] The New Brunswick Public Service Labour Relations Act provides for the same alternatives except that under this statute, a choice is made when an impasse is reached.[20]

Table 5–1
Employee Groups for which Interest Arbitration
Is Specified in lieu of Strike or Lockout

Jurisdiction	Employees
Alberta	Public Servants Firefighters Police Officers
*British Columbia	School Teachers
Manitoba	School Teachers
Newfoundland	Firefighters Police Officers
Nova Scotia	Civil Service
Ontario	Civil Servants Crown Corporation Employees Hospital Employees Firefighters Police Officers
Prince Edward Island	Civil Servants Hospital Employees School Teachers
*Quebec	Police Officers Firefighters

*British Columbia and Quebec have requirements in their legislation for the preservation of essential services which can be used to prevent strikes by certain groups of employees in health, safety, communication, and transportation. In B.C., unions of policemen, firefighters, and health care have access to arbitration if they request it.

The Ontario School Boards and Teachers Collective Negotiations Act provides a variety of impasse resolution procedures. Teachers are allowed to strike (and School Boards to lock out), but before this is permitted, fact finding and mediation must occur. Fact finding is conducted by a person appointed by the Education Relations Commission, which administers the Act. The fact finder can make recommendations (which are made public) for the settlement of items in disputes. If these procedures fail to produce agreement, the parties may agree to one of two types of arbitration: conventional, where the arbitrator makes whatever decision he or she believes appropriate on the items submitted; or final offer selection, where the parties develop final offers on all items in dispute and where the arbitrator must select one offer or the other.

Final offer selection is also used in settling salary disputes in major league baseball and in some U.S. public sector jurisdictions. When the idea of final offer selection was developed it was viewed as a device that would improve the likelihood of a negotiated settlement,[21] but in practice there is no evidence to support this view. It has not been used extensively.[22]

ARBITRATION IN FIRST NEGOTIATION IMPASSES

An important recent development in Canada is the use of arbitration in the settlement of disputes in the first negotiation following certification. Historically, employer resistance to the presence of a union in the workplace has at times extended beyond the certification stage to the negotiation stage, where some employers have essentially refused to negotiate a "reasonable" collective agreement. Four Canadian jurisdictions, the federal, British Columbia, Manitoba, and Quebec, now have provisions which permit the labour relations board, upon the application of either party, to impose a first agreement on the parties.[23] In general, the boards have not provided such a remedy automatically, but only after careful study of the situation, so as to determine whether such a contract imposition is appropriate.[24]

Pros and Cons of Arbitration

Where compulsory interests arbitration is provided for by legislation in North America, the assumption is that the public interest precludes any interruption of production or delivery of a service that would be caused by a strike or a lockout. Where there is no public interest involved (and both labour and management generally argue that this is true of most disputes in the private sector of the economy) both parties are generally opposed to interests arbitration, particularly when it is compulsory.

Many arguments are advanced against compulsory interests arbitration. Opponents claim that it destroys the bargaining process: "If the parties are not faced with the consequences of refusing to settle, their desire, determination, or even ability to settle dwindles."[25] Interest disputes are complex, and no clear criteria exist for third parties. For example, what should wages be? What seniority system is appropriate? Is there any objective way of determining these issues?[26] The decisions reached under compulsory arbitration are said to be subject to political pressure.[27] Compulsory arbitration may not prevent strikes, and may actually result in an increase in strike activity; strike activity is higher in Australia under compulsory arbitration than it is in the United States or Canada where the use of interests arbitration is infrequent.[28]

Not all of the evidence is against compulsory interests arbitration. Under the operation of the Ontario Hospital Disputes Arbitration Act, there is evidence that the operation of compulsory arbitration has not led to the breakdown of collective bargaining in that industry.[29] There have, however, been complaints about the length of time needed under this system to get a contract settlement. One study of the arbitration of teachers' disputes in British Columbia indicated that there was no "narcotic" effect on bargaining.[30] However, a study in other areas of B.C. found such an effect.[31] A study of arbitration under the Public Service Staff Relations Act also found evidence that arbitration does have a chilling effect on negotiations.[32]

Standards

Compulsory interests arbitration is part of the North American labour relations scene, and will probably continue to be so. Even though interests disputes are complex, and the criteria for decisions are often ambiguous and conflicting, such criteria do exist and have been used. Of course, the standards to be used by arbitrators can be set by statute or they can be agreed upon by the parties prior to arbitration. Where these conditions do not exist, the arbitrator must determine the criteria for making the decision, and the parties' arguments would include reference to the suitability of particular criteria.

The Public Service Staff Relations Act provides that the following factors shall be considered by the arbitration tribunal:

a) The needs of the Public Service for qualified employees;
b) the conditions of employment in similar occupations outside the Public Service, including such geographic, industrial or other variations as the Arbitration Tribunal may consider relevant;
c) the need to maintain appropriate relationships in the conditions of employment as between different grade levels within an occupation and as between occupations in the Public Service;
d) the need to establish terms and conditions of employment that are fair and reasonable in relation to the qualifications required, the work performed, the responsibility assumed and the nature of services rendered; and
e) any other factor that appears to be relevant to the matter in dispute.

Other criteria which have been used in interests arbitration include:

1. The prevailing practice in an industry, a similar industry, in a geographic area or in an industry in a given geographic area;
2. the cost of living;
3. a living wage;
4. the ability of the employer to pay;
5. the competition faced by the employer in both wage and product markets;
6. general wage movements, i.e., the percentage wage increase granted in an industry or in general;
7. productivity;
8. past practice;
9. expectations of the parties as evidenced by their negotiating positions;
10. the public interest.

THE BARGAINING PROCESS

While the legal framework within which negotiation occurs clearly influences and, at times, constrains the process, particularly in the private sector of the economy, there is such diversity that it is quite safe to say that no two negotiations are exactly alike, particularly in the private sector of the economy. Nevertheless, all negotiations involve some general types of activity and they follow some typical patterns.

Walton and McKersie[33] have identified four basic subprocesses that occur during negotiations. These subprocesses are: distributive bargaining, integrative bargaining, intra-organizational bargaining, and attitudinal structuring. We will use this framework to examine the negotiation process.

DISTRIBUTIVE BARGAINING

This is the type of bargaining that is most associated with labour negotiations, at least in the public mind. Distributive bargaining is that bargaining which involves the allocation of a fixed amount of resources and/or conflicting interests. This type of bargaining is involved in wage and benefit level determination and is thus central to labour negotiations.

Distributive bargaining has been examined from a number of theoretical perspectives, both economic and behavioural.[34] We will not attempt to review all of them here but will use a simple model to examine the process, a model which reflects recent thinking with regard to distributive bargaining.

Figure 5–1
Bargaining Positions

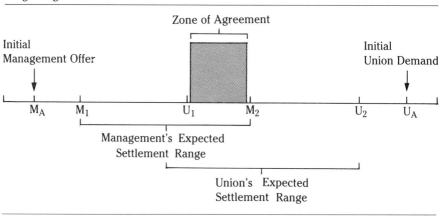

Figure 5–1 depicts the bargaining position of the two parties. Both parties have, at the beginning of the negotiation process, a general notion of their "bottom line": for management, this represents the largest settlement it is prepared to give, for the union, the "bottom line" describes the minimum settlement it will accept. These points are represented by (M2) and (U1) on Figure 5–1, and are sometimes called resistance points. Management also has a minimum expected settlement level, (M1), and the union has a maximum settlement level, (U2), the minimums and maximums defining their expected settlement ranges. The parties would begin bargaining by making offers or demands below and above these points, at (MA) and (MB). If the settlement ranges and, most importantly, the resistance points overlap, there is potential for a settlement. If they do not overlap, a strike or lockout is inevitable, unless the resistance points change during negotiations.[35]

The bargaining process is one in which each party is constantly assessing its own bargaining goals in terms of the cost of achieving those goals. Costs are assessed, in part, by attempting to determine the opponent's goals and the extent to which the opponent will resist particular settlements. Each negotiator attempts to make his or her goals attractive to the opponent, and to reduce the importance of the opponent's goal in the opponent's view. Each also may influence the opponent's perception of possible resistance to the opponent's bargaining goals. All of this is done while concealing or attempting to conceal the negotiator's own goals from the opponent. Under the pressure of a strike deadline (or a strike) this delicate ballet involving gradual concessions usually results in a contract settlement.

Bargaining Power

Distributive bargaining involves the use, the implied use, or the potential use of power. A showdown of power is latent in every negotiation.[36] While we normally think of labour negotiations in terms of economic power (the use of the strike or lockout), moral, legal, or political power can also be brought to bear in labour negotiations. Power need not be directed toward conflict; it can be a force behind cooperation as well. In any event, to consider labour negotiations without considering the potential use of power by other parties and its influence on the process is to have a naive and erroneous notion of the process.

The concept of bargaining power was formulated by Neil Chamberlain. He described the relative power in a two party relationship as follows:

$$\text{Bargaining Power of A} = \frac{\text{Cost to B of disagreeing with A's terms}}{\text{Cost to B of agreeing with A's terms}}$$

$$\text{Bargaining Power of B} = \frac{\text{Cost to A of disagreeing with B's terms}}{\text{Cost to A of agreeing with B's terms}}$$

If A is the employer, the greater the costs associated with disagreeing with the union's (B's) terms, that is, taking a strike, as opposed to agreeing with the union's terms, the greater the union's bargaining power. If the cost to one side of disagreeing with the other's terms is equal to or greater than agreeing to those terms, then the settlement is likely to be on the basis of the terms offered by the opposing side.[37]

The theory of bargaining power does not lend itself to a detailed calculation of the exact terms of settlement, in part because bargaining power is based on the perceived cost of agreeing or disagreeing. These perceptions are difficult to measure and keep changing as bargaining progresses. However, the notion of bargaining power is useful in understanding the collective bargaining process.

Bargaining power in a large part determines how and why negotiations turn out as they do. Why, for example, have wage settlements in the construction industry been as high as they have? In large part, because construction firms are small and undercapitalized and cannot survive a strike. The cost of disagreeing with the union's demands is high. At the same time, of course, construction firms have been able to pass on cost increases to consumers, and the cost to construction firms of agreeing to the union's terms has not been high. The rise of non-union contractors has helped to change the bargaining power equation, however.

Situations in which management bargaining power is high can be seen in refineries and similar processing operations and in many public utilities. In these operations management can frequently continue to run the operations in the event of a strike. For example, a 1973 strike by employees of Ontario Hydro lasted for several months. Service to equipment was impaired but not eliminated; power supplies were not interrupted and the union settled for the amount that was offered prior to the strike. In these circumstances, the cost to the company of disagreeing with the union offer (or demand) was low. There have been no subsequent strikes at Ontario Hydro at the time of this writing.

The concept of bargaining power also helps to explain some of the activities of the parties prior to and during negotiations. Each party will try to maximize its bargaining power and to influence the opponent's perceptions of that bargaining power. The activities of each party will be designed to minimize the actual and the perceived costs to the opposing party of agreeing with the opposition, and to maximize the costs of disagreeing.

In practice, these attempts to influence the outcome of negotiations take a variety of forms. In firms or industries with seasonal variations in production, efforts to influence bargaining power may revolve around manipulating the contract expiration date. Unions often try to have the contract expire just prior to the seasonal upswing in production. Companies in turn attempt to have the contract expire near the bottom of the seasonal cycle.

Companies may attempt to have large inventories or to have large stocks in the hands of customers prior to the strike deadline. Unions may resist such efforts by refusing to work overtime or setting up a picket line which effectively stops shipments after a strike begins. Unions attempt to build a strike fund to provide some income for members during a strike. The strike fund may be a major element in the union's bargaining power. Unions will also attempt to ensure that other unions will respect their picket lines during a strike. The extent to which picket lines are respected is also a major factor influencing union bargaining power.

These examples illustrate the attempts of the parties to enhance their bargaining power. Many other examples could be cited. The point has been made, though, that the parties will employ strategies built around increasing their own bargaining power and reducing their opponent's as part of the negotiation process, in an attempt to secure a settlement close to what they believe is appropriate.

Boulwarism

One interesting strategy in distributive bargaining has been practised by General Electric among others. It has been called Boulwarism, after the man, Lemuel Boulware, who developed it.

One essential feature of G.E.'s policy was effective two-way communication. The company constantly presented its views directly to its employees, and constantly sought feedback from them. During bargaining, the company listened to the union's proposals and the complete arguments behind these proposals.

The company then made an offer—essentially a final offer—the terms of which were released to the employees as well as to their union representatives. The offer was generally quite attractive, although probably not close to the union's goals for maximum success. While the company would rearrange some of the components of its offer, the size of the package would not be increased. The union could accept these terms or strike; the company would not change its position. Even after a 100-day strike in 1969–70, General Electric moved only a very small distance, if even that, from its offer.

Boulwarism represented an almost perfect example of commitment tactics. The unions which bargained with G.E. bitterly resented what they called the company's take-it-or-leave-it style of bargaining. The U.S. National Labor Relations Board ruled that in practising Boulwarism the company did not bargain in "good faith," but the board and the unions were unsuccessful in attempting to force the company to change its tactics, in part because the U.S. courts refused to find that best-offer-first bargaining was illegal.

The practice of Boulwarism appears deceptively easy. In truth, it requires a great deal of skill and effort. Assessing employee desires, attractively packaging the offer, and communicating not only the offer but also a host of day-to-day matters to employees is a time-consuming and difficult job.[38]

NTEGRATIVE BARGAINING

ntegrative bargaining is bargaining which does not involve conflicts of interest, ut problems which can be solved to the parties' joint advantage. An example of in integrative bargaining subject would be the design of a seniority system vhich could meet the needs of employees for job security and the needs of nanagement for flexibility in job assignment.

If the integrative bargaining process is to be successful, the parties must see ssues as having the potential for integration — not as win-lose propositions — ind they must have time to define or identify the problem, to search for alterna- ive solutions, and to explore their preference for particular solutions. For this eason, integrative items are often dealt with before monetary items in negotia- ions. Sometimes they are dealt with away from the main bargaining table, and ometimes they are dealt with on a continuous basis rather than just during the egotiation of a collective agreement. This continuous bargaining process has een used at B.C. Hydro and Ontario Hydro.[39] Labatts Breweries have used a egotiation approach called "single team bargaining" which features informal eating arrangements, a focus on problem-solving, off the record discussions, nd wide participation.[40]

The "principled negotiation" process developed by Roger Fisher and William Jry of the Harvard Negotiation Project and published in their book, *Getting* ɔ *Yes*, is particularly (but not exclusively) suited to the integrative bargaining rocess. A recapitulation of their formula for effective bargaining is not possible ere, but the reader who would like to study negotiation tactics is directed to ɔis excellent book.[41]

INTRA-ORGANIZATIONAL BARGAINING

Intra-organizational bargaining is that bargaining which occurs *within* the union and management organizations. It is, essentially, the process by which consensus is achieved within each organization.

Experienced negotiators can generally predict the outcome of negotiations quite accurately before negotiations begin, and, left to their own devices, the chief negotiator for a union and management could, in many cases, achieve a settlement quite quickly. Why, then, is negotiation often a long drawn-out process? The answer, in large part, lies in the fact that it is necessary for the chief negotiator for each side to achieve a consensus, on his or her own team and within his or her organization, and a belief that the best possible bargain has been obtained. An early conclusion to negotiations might be viewed by some as an indication that not enough had been gained or too much given away.

Neither unions nor managements are monolithic or homogeneous organizations. Unions are democratic organizations composed of members with both common and conflicting interests. The goals and preferences of skilled and unskilled, old and young, senior and junior, male and female employees are often not the same, and a gain for one group may well mean a loss for another. Similarly, the views of production, sales, finance, and employee relations personnel within a company are often at odds. The development of priorities and the resolution of differences among the members of each side are major functions of the negotiation process. As Derek Bok and John Dunlop put it:

> The process of accommodation within labor and management is central to collective bargaining. It should not be disparaged as merely a matter of internal politics on either side. In working out these internal adjustments in a viable way, collective bargaining serves a social purpose of enormous significance. The effective resolution of these problems is essential to the strength of leadership and to the continued vitality of both the company and the union.[42]

ATTITUDINAL STRUCTURING

The fourth subprocess which comprises labour-management negotiations is attitudinal structuring. This process involves influencing the basic relationship between the parties. The nature of union-management relationships was discussed in Chapter 1. The nature of the relationship clearly affects the nature of the negotiation process. However, the nature of the negotiation process also influences the union-management relationship.

The negotiation process can affirm or change beliefs and perceptions the parties have of each other. The negotiation process can condition attitudes and behaviour involving friendliness (or hostility), trust, respect, and openness between the parties. Difficulties in the negotiation of contracts often continue to manifest themselves in the administration of those agreements. Very often a difficult set of negotiations and a strike or lockout marks a watershed in the relationship between a union and management. This may serve as a kind of catharsis and induce the parties to seek ways of improving the way that they relate to each other.

These four bargaining processes occur every time that union and management seat themselves at the bargaining table. Successful and experienced negotiators are aware of the complex nature of bargaining, of long-run and short-run issues, of mutual and conflicting interests. Successful negotiation is not unlike juggling — keeping four processes in the air. It is, indeed, more of an art than a science.

NEGOTIATION PRACTICE
Preparing for Bargaining[43]

The negotiation process does not begin at the point at which the parties sit down at the table. Both unions and management devote a great deal of time and energy to preparing for negotiations. Events at the bargaining table are shaped by these efforts, and the negotiation process can properly be said to begin with these preparations. One study has shown that preparation and planning skills are the most important characteristics for a negotiator to have.[44]

In a sense, the preparation process is almost continuous. Once an agreement is negotiated, and the parties begin to live with or administer that agreement, problems may emerge that suggest possible revisions in the contract. Frequently the individuals responsible for negotiating agreements do not have the further responsibility of administering the agreement. Discussion of problems with the existing agreement with those who must live with the contract on a day-to-day basis is an important first step in preparing to negotiate another.

For the union, suggestions for revision as well as new demands will be solicited from shop stewards and members, sometimes in open union meetings. Some unions have special groups, such as wage-policy committees, to develop demands. Other union demands may emerge from policy resolutions passed by national or international union conventions. Management negotiators will seek the opinions of foremen and other line managers. Both sides will look at the grievance and arbitration records under the existing contract. Grievances can pinpoint trouble spots, and the losing side in an arbitration case may well wish to have the contract changed, to nullify the application of an arbitrator's award in the future.

During preparations, each side will not only develop its own demands but will also attempt to anticipate the demands which the other side is likely to make. With these in hand, cost data and counterarguments based on the anticipated consequences of implementing these demands can also be planned. For example, in 1955, the Ford Motor Company knew that it would again be faced with a demand from the auto workers for a guaranteed annual income. Prior to the negotiations, the company assigned a task force to the job of developing a proposal to provide an income guarantee in a way acceptable to itself. The result was the Supplemental Unemployment Benefit (SUB) Plan which was incorporated into the agreement and remains in effect (with important modifications, including short work week benefits) today. The union refers to the plan as Guaranteed Annual Income, which is now provided for employees with more than seven years' service.

Another task which faces the parties prior to actual negotiations is the assembly of a bargaining team. While each side is represented by a principal negotiator, he or she will be joined by other individuals representing each organization. These representatives serve several functions. For one, they can provide expertise on particular subjects or problem areas. The presence of these individuals allows the bargaining agenda to be divided into segments and discussed in subcommittees. Members of the bargaining team can also serve as representatives of special-interest groups in each organization. For example, a union bargaining team might include a representative of a skilled trades group, and a management team might include a representative of a production-line management. Individuals having particular influence in the two organizations might be chosen as members of the bargaining team, as might individuals who are well trusted by the other side.

The group that sits down with the chief negotiator at the bargaining table represents the varied, and sometimes conflicting, interests within each organization. This group must emerge satisfied with the negotiator's bargaining ability and also with the final settlement. It can help assure acceptance of the settlement in the wider constituency. Ultimate acceptance by that wider constituency is one reason for the large number of demands which are actually placed on the bargaining table. Acceptance of the final agreement is more likely if the members of each side believe that their problems and proposals have at least been presented and argued, even if they are not incorporated in the final agreement. A large number of issues on the table is also useful in the actual bargaining process, as we shall see shortly.

The chief negotiator for each side is usually quite experienced in negotiations. The chief negotiator for management is frequently an industrial relations staff specialist. Some small companies hire lawyers or other professional negotiators to negotiate for them. While members of the local union are generally involved in negotiations, frequently the chief negotiator for the union is a specialist or the staff of the national or international union. Where the chief negotiator is an "outsider," the bargaining team can help to keep the chief negotiator in tune with the realities of the workplace.

At the Bargaining Table

As they approach the bargaining table, each side has, either explicitly or implicitly, a list of demands, an estimate of the opponent's demands, and goals that define complete success and minimum success in the process that is to follow. Each side has an estimate of its own and the opponent's strengths and weaknesses and the strategies and tactics the opposition is likely to follow.

The first item of business is usually a quick run through of each side's proposals. Sometimes elaborate presentations are made at this point. The purpose here is to present demands and allow for enough discussion so that they are fully understood. During the initial presentation, all proposals may be represented as being equally important — vital to a reasonable settlement.

Each negotiator is, at this point, not only presenting the demands of the various interest groups which he represents but is likely to conceal his or her perceptions of the minimum acceptable settlement. Unions do not always make specific monetary demands at first. Rather they ask for a "substantial" wage increase or for a "significant" increase in pension benefits. Such non-specific demands not only conceal the union's minimum position from management but also reduce the likelihood of establishing unrealistic, unachievable goals in the minds of the membership, and preserve flexibility to respond to changing conditions as negotiating time goes on.

Some of the demands are made to facilitate future bargaining. The initial appearance of a demand from one side of the bargaining table can usually be expected to receive a cool reception from the other side. With an eye to a continuing relationship and to future bargaining, a demand may be introduced with the thought that it will not be granted during the present negotiation, but that it will seem less novel (and perhaps less outrageous) during the negotiation of the next contract.[45]

The guaranteed annual income demand made by Walter Reuther in the early 1950s is an example of a demand which was originally made to facilitate future bargaining. The auto workers also made a demand for a company-paid dental care plan for several negotiations prior to the 1973 sessions in which a company-paid dental plan was added to the agreement.

The next stage of the negotiation process sees the parties beginning to explore each other's proposals and attempting to find out how important each proposal is to the other side while still attempting to hide the relative importance of their own proposals. A negotiator may attempt to show his opponent that one of the latter's proposals is not important or is too costly. Where facts are in dispute, an effort will be made at this point to establish mutually acceptable data.

Some clues as to the perimeters of the settlement will begin to emerge at this stage, particularly to the experienced negotiator. The tone of voice, the selection of words, the arch of an eyebrow can all serve to provide clues to one's intentions. Phrases like, "I think we can work something out on that," when compared to phrases like, "We will never agree to that!" can provide indications as to the importance of particular positions. Minor concessions may also be made at this point, as evidence of good faith and to indicate progress.

The real positions of the parties are still far from clear, however. Both sides may still be bluffing on some issues. The degree of commitment of each side to particular issues may not yet be established. In fact, attempts by one side to commit itself to achieving a particular goal may be ignored by the other side in order to keep the negotiations flexible.

At this stage of negotiations, the size of the bargaining teams may be reduced. Subcommittees may be forced to consider some proposals or problems and to work out solutions or compromises for the consideration of the whole group. As the strike deadline approaches, the first "package" offers appear. Demands are dropped, sometimes not very loudly. The party may simply fail to mention an earlier demand when presenting a proposed package.

Initially, package offers may be tentative: "What would you think if . . ." "If we give this, would you be willing to drop this demand?" or, "Does this proposal seem fair to you?". Agreement may be reached on some issues, pending the settlement of other more important issues, such as the size of the monetary package.

Frequently, these package offers may not be made initially at the bargaining table, particularly as the parties move closer to a settlement. "Off the record" discussions between the principal negotiators, over drinks or dinner, in the hall or even in the washroom, may produce the first and final firm offers of settlement.[46] Sometimes when settlement is reached, one party may produce one final demand, as a "sweetener." While this is sometimes successful, it rarely works more than once.

When agreement is reached, it must be reduced to writing and signed by the parties. Very often agreement is reached "in principle" with the details left for the drafting session, although at times the parties will agree to a draft of a clause at the bargaining table. In these situations, as parts of agreements are reached they are put into writing, initialled, and then set aside until final agreement is reached on the whole package. If a final agreement is not reached, then all agreements previously reached are "off," as the parties will then attempt to put together a "new" and more acceptable package. Sometimes the drafting of the actual agreement is left to the lawyers of each side after negotiations have been completed.

Throughout the negotiating process each negotiator must constantly assess his own goals, the probable cost of achieving them, the goals of the other side, and the degree to which he will resist those goals. The negotiator must decide on tactics for communicating with and eliciting information from the other side. He must decide at what point to make concessions, at what point to appear firm, and how to appear to his own side to be holding out for a particular proposal while signalling to the opposing negotiator that he will drop the demand eventually. He must decide whether to and how to commit himself (and to what extent) to a particular position.

If a negotiator desires a particular settlement which he knows the other side will accept, but only with extreme reluctance, he can attempt to commit himself irrevocably to achieving that objective. He can do this, for example, through promises to his own team or statements to the press. If he can commit himself, he may force the other side to grant that demand.[47] A union negotiator may attempt to do this by making a clear statement to the membership. He may say, for example: "I will refuse to accept a wage increase of less than $1.00 an hour." Of course, if he misjudges the willingness of the opposition to grant the demand, he may find himself out on a limb. When a negotiator has done this, his opposite number must find a way to help the opposition back down gracefully. The behaviour of a negotiator must also be designed to help his opposition sell the settlement to his negotiating team.

Every negotiator faces a continual three-fold choice in negotiations; accept the available terms, attempt to improve the available terms through further bargaining, or break off negotiations with no intention of resuming them.[48] In labour negotiations, the strike deadline strongly influences the negotiator in his choice of a particular alternative.

The Strike Deadline

As the strike deadline approaches, the chances that an improved offer will be forthcoming become increasingly less likely. The strike deadline forces each side to reassess their position and move toward a final offer. As the strike deadline nears, the tactic of bluffing becomes less tenable. At the zero hour there must be either a settlement or a strike. Thus, the popular picture of the parties emerging from an all-night final bargaining session has a basis in reality; a lot of action occurs in the short time before a strike deadline.

In terms of the three-fold choice, if the parties do not accept the agreement they must continue bargaining under the duress of the economic sanctions imposed by the work stoppage. At the time of the strike, one of the parties may state that his position on an issue is, indeed, final. He has no intention of ever making a concession on the point; he will engage in no further bargaining no matter what penalties are invoked. The decision on the three-fold choice is never easy to make, but the strike deadline forces that decision to be made.

Sometimes, if agreement is near or appears within reach, the parties will extend the deadline. Frequently, however, there comes a time when the strike cannot be postponed any longer.

> Each side must make certain technical and organizational arrangements if there is to be a work stoppage; management must arrange for an orderly cessation of work . . . Plans must be made for essential orders. Goods in process and shipments must be rescheduled. Arrangements must be made for maintenance and repair. Supervision must be alerted and scheduled to perform some of these emergency functions. Unions in turn have to organize picket lines, banners and information about the strike must be prepared with the union and the community.[49]

Beyond a certain point, these procedures cannot be delayed any longer. The preparations must be implemented and the work stoppage begun.

Another decision which each side must make is how visible it wishes its strike preparations to become. Unions frequently take strike votes, which authorize work stoppage if there is no settlement. These are such a matter of form that they are not necessarily seen as a real threat, although they are frequently used as threats during negotiations and not merely as a device for determining the views of the union membership. Other more credible union strike threats might include the renting of a strike headquarters or the open solicitation of support from other unions. Management can ship goods, make arrangements to service customers from other plants, and increase security arrangements. Visible preparations for a strike may well bring charges of "bad faith" bargaining. They may also cause the other side to conclude that a work stoppage is inevitable, no matter what occurs at the bargaining table, thus bringing an end to effective bargaining.

Of course, if the preparations are a bluff, a threat that a party has no intention of carrying through, their credibility may be lost for future negotiations.

Strike Preparations

In the course of some negotiations, the parties turn their attention to the subject of strike preparations and conduct. While this bargaining is often tacit, at times it is quite explicit. A great deal of care is required in shutting down some production operations, such as a steel mill or petrochemical refinery, or a paper mill. If a strike is to begin, the parties will discuss the procedure for the orderly closing down of operations. The question of management access to the plant may also be discussed. Another question which frequently occurs is the payment of premiums on employee health and insurance plans. In some instances the union will take over the payment of these premiums from the company. On more than one occasion, when the union has been short of cash, the company has continued to pay these premiums, in effect making a loan to the union.

The union-management relationships which are characterized by arrangements such as those mentioned above are relationships in which the parties are committed to a reasonably satisfactory long-term relationship. While disagreement exists in the short run, and economic pressure in the form of a strike (and the corresponding willingness to take a strike) is being applied, the intent of that pressure is to impel an agreement so that a mutually profitable relationship can continue. The parties negotiate strike arrangements which will help preserve that long-term relationship.

One critical decision which every management must consider in terms of strike preparation is whether to attempt to continue operations during a strike. In some situations, such as electric utilities and refineries, supervisory personnel can be used to continue production. In other operations, replacements must be found for the striking employees; the employer can keep his doors open and urge the strikers to return to work, or he can hire replacements — strikebreakers, or "scabs" as they are called by unions.

The most critical factor influencing this decision is the probable union response. History shows that attempts to continue operations in the face of a strike often lead to violence. Unions have generally been successful in developing the ethic that picket lines are not to be crossed. When peaceful picket lines are crossed, striking employees may well attempt to forcefully prohibit entry to the struck premises.

This union reponse is understandable, since in many instances an attempt by an employer to continue operations is an attempt to do away with the union. At a minimum, an employer who can continue to operate during a strike is not being affected by that strike, and the union cannot hope to achieve its strike goals unless the employer is shut down.

THE LAWS REGARDING STRIKEBREAKERS

Quebec legislation is unique in North America in prohibiting the use of strikebreakers (or "scabs" as they are called by unions). In 1977, amendments to the

Labour Code forbade the use of strikebreakers, including the use of bargaining-unit employees who refuse to strike and employees from other employer work sites. However, the law does allow the employer to take steps which would prevent the destruction or deterioration of plant and equipment.[50]

British Columbia and Ontario both prohibit the use of professional strikebreakers by including their use under unfair labour practices.[51] The B.C. legislation defines a professional strikebreaker as a person not involved in a labour dispute "whose primary object in the Board's opinion is (a) to prevent, interfere with or break up a lawful strike or (b) to assist an employer in a lockout."[52]

Ontario also prohibits "strike related misconduct on the part of employers or their agents." This is described in the act as ". . . a course of conduct of incitement, intimidation, coercion, undue influence, provocation, infiltration, surveillance or any other like course of conduct intended to interfere with, obstruct, prevent, restrain or disrupt the exercise of any right under this Act in anticipation of, or during, a lawful strike or lock-out."[53]

Picketing

The subject of picketing is complex and legally unclear in most jurisdictions. Under the Labour Code of British Columbia, picketing is controlled by the Labour Relations Board, and the rules governing it are fairly clear. Picketing in B.C. is allowed at all employer sites of business — even those that are not the site of a strike. Picketing is also permitted at the business site of an employer's ally, i.e., someone who is helping the employer to resist a strike or helping in a lockout. Where more than one employer is involved on a single site, as is the case in construction, the Board may restrict picketing so that it does not affect employees other than those engaged in a strike or lockout. In any event, the only picketing allowed in B.C. is that connected with a legal strike or lockout. No picketing is allowed to blockade (prohibit entry or exit from) an employer's premises.[54]

The same rules generally apply in other jurisdictions, except that picketing is regulated by the courts through the use of injunctions enforced by officers of law (i.e., police officers) and not by the labour board. In general, any picketing in connection with an illegal strike can be enjoined, i.e., prohibited. Also, the number of pickets can be restricted through an injunction so as to allow entry to and exit from a site. Picketers may not engage in illegal acts such as damage to property or assault, and picketers committing such acts are liable for arrest and conviction.

Conciliation

A special problem for Canadian negotiators is the question of how to deal with the conciliation process. Most jurisdictions in Canada require conciliation before a work stoppage takes place. Some parties make conciliation a mere formality by meeting with the conciliation officer early in negotiations, simply to fulfill the statutory requirement. Others wait until the strike deadline is near and then use the help of a conciliation officer to help reach an agreement. Others reserve their final offers until after the conciliation process. A variety of approaches to conciliation are possible, but the use of the process in negotiation must be considered by every negotiator.

The process of conciliation or mediation is initiated most often when a representative of labour or management contacts the Director of the Mediation and Conciliation Service having jurisdiction over the negotiations and asks for help. The Director then assigns a conciliation officer or mediator to the parties. Most often assignments are made on a rotating basis in order to give the officers a roughly equivalent work load. Sometimes they are assigned because they have expertise in the industry involved or with the issues in dispute. Less often they are assigned on the basis of the parties' request for a particular individual. For purposes of this section, we will use the term mediator to describe both the mediators and conciliators.

Following appointment the mediator normally contacts the parties and arranges for a meeting at a mutually convenient time and place, not too far in the future. In Canadian jurisdictions a strike countdown begins only after a first-stage mediator has delivered his report. Thus first-stage mediation is not likely to be accompanied by much sense of urgency. In later stages there is considerably more urgency, because there is greater likelihood that a strike is either imminent or in progress. Under United States law there is no provision for first-stage mediation, so that a sense of urgency is more likely to accompany mediation in the United States.

Some mediators enter their first meeting with no advance preparation. Others research the industry, the parties and the issues before going in. There are legitimate arguments for either approach. Some believe that advance preparation tends to colour the mediator's opinion about what the settlement terms ought to be, that he or she should enter negotiations with a fresh, open mind. Others believe that mediators can be most helpful in the shortest possible time if they have advance knowledge of the particular problems facing the parties.

The first meeting is likely to be short. Here an experienced mediator determines the roles that he or she is expected to play. Usually the parties want him or her to act as a leader in helping them come to an agreement. Sometimes, they simply wish to go through the motions of mediation in order to fulfill statutory obligations and start the countdown toward a strike deadline.

If the mediator believes there is a desire for settlement, he or she will determine what issues still need to be resolved and the parties' present position on each of those issues. Having done this, he or she normally moves to separate meetings with each bargaining team.

The purpose of the separate meetings, from the mediator's viewpoint, is to get some idea on how far the parties are willing to go — to discover their bargaining limits. If the mediator is successful in this regard, he or she can use the information to assess the probability of an early agreement and then try to get the parties somewhat nearer to each other. This is sometimes a ticklish process, rendered impossible if the parties do not trust the mediator. The mediator will not generally disclose one party's total acceptable package to the other, because each side hopes to settle for something better. Rather, the mediator determines how far each will yield in a series of back-and-forth probes, requiring extreme patience and a strong sensitivity to the psychology of the situation. How he or she proceeds varies from case to case and from one meeting to another. It involves far more than acting as a messenger boy, mechanically conveying positions from one room to the other.

One mediator described the following situation as an example of the savoir faire and purposefulness with which a mediator should proceed.

> I had a case where the union had asked for a 15 percent increase in a one-year contract. Their spokesman told me he would go to 10, but not now — not until the company indicated some movement. The company was holding at 5, but said to me they would go to 7, if the union would come down a little. Both of the parties convinced me that they would go no further, and a strike seemed certain.
>
> In some cases, if I knew the parties well, I would tell them exactly what the other said. However, in this case I simply indicated to each bargaining team in separate meetings that there was some flexibility in the other's position, but I didn't know how much.
>
> Then I said to the union: "I'd like to see you get 10 percent or even 15, but I don't believe the company will go that high. In my opinion the most you can get is 7 or 8 percent. I may be mistaken, but if you hold to the 10 percent figure I think you'll have a strike."
>
> Then I went to the company and said: "If you hold to the 5 or 7 percent figure I can almost assure you that you'll have a strike. Now the decision is yours, and it's not for me to tell you how to spend your money, but in my opinion the settlement will eventually be 10 percent, and I think 10 percent might do it now. You might have to go as high as 13. If you want me to explore 7 percent I'll give it a try, because, as I've said, the union has indicated some flexibility. But I don't think 7 percent will get a settlement."

As the experienced mediator proceeds from separate sessions a keen sense of timing is necessary. A variety of devices are available as the occasion seems appropriate. However, if the mediator is convinced that the parties want a settlement and if it is clear that they are ready to move, the mediator will continue — finally bringing them together when he or she thinks the settlement is ready. Before then he or she may alternately plead, harangue, serve as an interested listener, make suggestions and, possibly, express his or her own opinions. On the other hand, the mediator may simply sit quietly and take notes the whole time, without saying a word — his or her mere presence providing impetus for the parties to talk.

Sometimes the mediator comes to know that the principal bargainers are shackled by their own bargaining teams, and finds some value in talking to them alone, apart from their negotiating teams. Perhaps the best known but least frequent mediation sessions have their climax in a hotel room with the two principal bargainers and the mediator hammering out final details in the wee hours of the morning with reporters hanging around outside waiting for the word: Is there a settlement or a strike?

The language of mediation is unique. It should be understood and appreciated by experienced bargainers, because sometimes this understanding is useful for their needs. In the example cited earlier, the mediator was saying to the employer that while the union was officially holding to 15 percent they would take 13. An experienced negotiator would immediately understand the language. He would also understand that the union would not present the proposal directly across the table because to do so would weaken their position. Suppose, for example, they came down to 13 percent and management promptly countered with 11. Having already conceded two percent, some of their members might have lowered their sights enough so that another two percent would not seem sufficient to warrant a strike.

Another illustration of the language of mediation was provided by the mediator in reference to the same example. As the strike deadline became imminent he called the sides together. The union still held to 15 percent, but the mediator knew they would go to 13. He also knew that the company was not ready to go that high. There was no point in separating them, because everyone knew how everyone else felt. So he made a suggestion: "Here's an idea. I suppose both of you will disagree with me but I'll try it out on you anyhow. Why not try out a longer term contract? Say 18 months — giving 7 percent now and 6 percent 18 months from now, so that the figure will come out to 13 percent?"

This was a risky move for a mediator to make, and it could have resulted in

Table 5–2
Summary of Settlements Stage for Contracts Covering 500 or More Employees in Canada, 1979–83

Stage at which settled	Year: 1979			
	Agreements	%	Employees	%
Direct Bargaining	246	43.9	567,060	50.5
Conciliation Officer	95	16.9	133,875	11.9
Conciliation Board	12	2.1	33,930	3.0
Post-Conciliation Bargaining	40	7.1	78,700	7.0
Mediation	44	7.8	60,280	5.4
Post-Mediation Bargaining	5	.9	5,405	.5
Arbitration	52	9.3	107,290	9.5
Work Stoppage	59	10.5	117,570	10.5
Bargaining after Work Stoppage	.3	.5	4,250	.4
Mediation after Work Stoppage	1	.2	3,660	.3
Arbitration after Work Stoppage	—	—	—	—
Legislation	4	.7	11,700	1.0
Other*	—	—	—	—
TOTAL	561	100	1,123,720	100

*Primarily represents agreements settled under government restraint programs

disaster if the parties did not respect and trust him. Furthermore, it could have caused the negotiating sessions to collapse if he made a slip in language. Suppose, for example, he said: "The union has told me they will settle for 13 percent, maybe even 10 percent, and I know the company can afford it!"

If the mediator has displayed a genuine desire to help, the parties might be receptive to a suggestion such as the one illustrated. However, an experienced negotiator should be wary of the possibility that such a suggestion could be made at the wrong time or by a mediator who did not enjoy the trust of both parties. In such an event the tactic could shatter whatever good had been accomplished so far. Thus negotiators should look out for the possibility, and if they fear that an ill-timed suggestion on settlement terms is forthcoming they should tell the mediator to hold back.

It is important to bear in mind that mediators have virtually no formal power. If they make a suggestion for terms of settlement or if they express their own viewpoints regarding the conduct of the parties these views carry no weight beyond the force of their own persuasive impact. Furthermore, mediators have no vested direct interest in the outcome of negotiations. The company and union must live together with the product of their agreement. Consequently the mediator's interest in helping to secure a settlement extends no farther than his or her pride in doing a job well. In some people this is considerable; in others it is negligible.

Year: 1980				Year: 1981			
Agreements	%	Employees	%	Agreements	%	Employees	%
251	45.9	482,325	39.9	199	41.5	300,080	34.1
79	14.4	113,300	9.4	87	18.2	138,085	15.7
8	1.5	43,065	3.6	5	1.0	25,160	2.9
27	4.9	46,090	3.8	32	6.7	72,305	8.2
65	11.9	134,415	11.1	35	7.3	80,295	9.1
7	1.3	4,450	.4	7	1.5	7,785	.9
42	7.7	124,975	10.3	43	8.8	92,115	10.5
47	8.6	191,900	15.9	70	14.6	156,000	17.7
17	3.1	58,905	4.9	1	.2	8,040	.9
3	.5	4,545	.4	—	—	—	—
1	.2	5,600	.5	—	—	—	—
—	—	—	—	—	—	—	—
—	—	—	—	—	—	—	—
547	100	1,209,520	100	479	100	879,865	100

Source: Labour Canada, *Collective Bargaining Review.* Ottawa: Minister of Supply and Services. Reproduced by permission of the Minister of Supply and Services Canada.

Table 5–2 (Continued)

Stage at which settled	Year: 1982			
	Agreements	%	Employees	%
Direct Bargaining	199	40.8	342,680	30.2
Conciliation Officer	59	12.1	163,490	14.4
Conciliation Board	10	2.0	30,665	2.7
Post-Conciliation Bargaining	28	5.7	88,265	7.8
Mediation	58	11.9	105,700	9.3
Post-Mediation Bargaining	6	1.2	5,405	.5
Arbitration	36	7.4	80,565	7.1
Work Stoppage	18	3.7	33,935	3.0
Bargaining after Work Stoppage	14	2.9	44,640	3.9
Mediation after Work Stoppage	—	—	—	—
Arbitration after Work Stoppage	—	—	—	—
Legislation	—	—	—	—
Other*	60	12.3	241,130	21.7
TOTAL	488	100	1,136,475	100

Settlement Stage

Table 5–2 indicates the stage at which negotiations involving negotiation units affecting over 500 employees were concluded in Canada for the years 1979–83. The largest number of negotiations were concluded by direct bargaining without third party intervention and without a strike. A strike was involved in only a relatively small number and percentage of negotiations, since where agreement is not reached directly, it is often achieved with third-party assistance.

Table 5–3 details strike and lockout activity in Canada for the years 1960–1982. Although strikes are frequently in the headlines, the percentage of working time lost due to strikes and lockouts is actually very small. The time lost through strikes and lockouts can be put into some perspective by viewing it in terms of days lost due to other causes. Twice as much working time is lost as a result of industrial accidents as is lost through strikes. The amount of working time lost through absenteeism is 10 times that lost through strikes.[55]

As was discussed in Chapter 1, Canada's relatively poor strike record in comparison to that in other countries is a function of the decentralized nature of bargaining here. Many key decisions made at the enterprise level in Canada are made centrally elsewhere. Those decisions are often made through collective bargaining, and they are not easy decisions to make. Given their nature, and keeping in mind the fact that the function of a strike or lockout is to compel a bargain, and only that, one can legitimately marvel that the process works as well as it does.

Any dissatisfaction with the negotiation process and the dispute resolution

Year: 1983				Total			
Agreements	%	Employees	%	Agreements	%	Employees	%
133	22.4	204,315	14.4	1,028	38.5	1,896,460	32.9
53	8.9	92,910	6.5	373	14.0	641,660	11.1
2	.3	1,365	.1	37	1.4	134,185	2.3
14	2.4	12,955	.9	141	5.3	298,265	5.2
36	6.1	60,405	4.2	238	8.9	441,095	7.6
4	.7	15,580	1.1	29	1.1	38,625	.7
16	2.7	32,475	2.3	189	7.1	437,420	7.6
38	6.4	98,245	6.9	232	8.7	597,650	10.4
—	—	—	—	35	1.3	115,835	2.0
—	—	—	—	4	.1	8,205	.1
—	—	—	—	1	.0	5,600	.1
—	—	—	—	4	.1	11,700	.2
299	50.1	903,230	63.5	359	13.4	1,144,360	19.8
595	100	1,421,660	100	2,670	100	5,771,060	100

processes attached thereto must be considered in terms of the alternatives available to the existing system.

The alternatives essentially are three. First is unilateral decision making. It reposes all power in the industrial relations field in one entity, with the employer or the state. The second is bi-lateral decision making. It at least precludes any one party from holding a dominating position. It, however, still eliminates an interested party: labour, management, or the public as represented by the government. The third is multilateral approach. It overcomes the deficiency of bilateral decision making and recognizes the interplay of market and institutional forces of supply and demand in the labour market, it features a high degree of employer determination, trade union participation, collective bargaining, and government involvement in a variety of capacities . . . Within industry, unions serve as countervailing power to management, and within the wider socioeconomic-political sphere, they function as potential agents for transformation in an increasingly pluralistic society.

Collective bargaining is the mechanism through which labour and management seek to accommodate their differences, frequently without strife, sometimes through it, and occasionally without success. As imperfect an instrument as it may be, there is no viable substitute in a free society. . . .[56]

Table 5-3
Strikes and Lockouts in Canada, 1960–1982

| Year | Number Beginning During Year | Strikes and Lockouts in Existence During Year | | Person-days Not Worked | |
		Number	Workers Involved	Person-days	% of Estimated Working Time
1960	268	274	49 408	738 700	0.06
1961	272	287	97 959	1 335 080	0.11
1962	290	311	74 332	1 417 900	0.11
1963	318	332	83 428	917 140	0.07
1964	327	343	100 535	1 580 550	0.11
1965	478	501	171 870	2 349 870	0.17
1966	582	617	411 459	5 178 170	0.34
1967	498	522	252 018	3 974 760	0.25
1968	559	582	223 562	5 082 732	0.32
1969	556	595	306 799	7 751 880	0.46
1970	503	542	261 706	6 539 560	0.39
1971	547	569	239 631	2 866 590	0.16
1972	556	598	706 474	7 753 530	0.43
1973	677	724	348 470	5 776 080	0.30
1974	1 173	1 218	580 912	9 221 890	0.46
1975	1 103	1 171	506 443	10 908 810	0.53
1976	921	039	1 570 940	11 609 890	0.55
1977	739	803	217 557	3 307 880	0.15
1978	1 004	1 058	401 688	7 392 820	0.34
1979	987	1 050	462 504	7 834 230	0.34
1980	952	1 028	441 025	8 975 390	0.38
1981	943	1 048	338 548	8 878 490	0.37
1982	608	677	444 302	5 795 420	0.25

Source: Labour Canada, *Strikes and Lockouts in Canada, 1982.* Ottawa: Minister of Supply and Services, 1983. Reproduced by permission of the Minister of Supply and Services Canada.

Notes

1. Labour Canada, Labour Data Branch, Provisions in Collective Agreements in Canada Covering 200 or more employees, April 1982. Ottawa: Minister of Supply and Services Canada, p. 2.

2. For a full discussion of "good faith" bargaining see: H. W. Arthurs, D. D. Carter and H. J. Glasbeek, *Labour Law and Industrial Relations in Canada.* Toronto: Butterworths, 1981, pp. 200–207.

3. In Prince Edward Island, a majority of employees in the bargaining unit must vote to approve such an arrangement. (Sec. 44, The Labour Relations Act.)

4. John P. Sanderson, *The Art of Collective Bargaining*. Toronto: Richard De Boo Limited, 1979, p. 12.

5. Sections 74–77.

6. Canada Labour Code, Part V, ss. 149–153; Manitoba Labour Relations Act, secs. 72–75; Saskatchewan, Trade Union Act, sec. 43.

7. John T. Dunlop, "The Industrial Relations System in Construction," in *The Structure of Collective Bargaining*, Arnold R. Weber, ed. New York: The Free Press of Glencoe, Inc., 1961, p. 179.

8. John C. Anderson, "The Structure of Collective Bargaining," in *Union-Management Relations in Canada*, John Anderson and Morley Gunderson, eds. Don Mills, Ontario: Addison-Wesley 1982, p. 179.

9. For a good discussion of this subject, see Arnold Weber, "Stability and Change in the Structure of Collective Bargaining," in *Challenges to Collective Bargaining*, Lloyd Ulman, ed. Englewood Cliffs, New Jersey: 1967.

10. Joseph B. Rose, *Public Policy, Bargaining Structure and the Construction Industry*. Toronto: Butterworths, 1980, pp. 3–4.

11. Ibid., pp. 74–78.

12. Joseph B. Rose, "Construction Labour Relations," in *Union-Management Relations in Canada*, John Anderson and Morley Gunderson, eds. Don Mills, Ontario: Addison-Wesley, 1982, p. 410.

13. British Columbia Railway and Canadian Association of Industrial, Mechanical and Allied Workers, et al. (1977) CLR 289.

14. Public Service Staff Relations Act, Sec. 26.

15. Public Service Labour Relations Act, Sec. 4.

16. Shirley B. Goldenberg, "Public-Sector Labor Relations in Canada," in *Public Sector Bargaining*, Benjamin Aaron, Joseph R. Grodin and James L. Stein, eds. Washington, D.C.: The Bureau of National Affairs, Inc., 1979, p. 273.

17. Jean Boivin, "The Public Sector," in *The Quebec I.R. System Presented to Non-Quebecers*, Proceedings of the 17th Annual Meeting, Canadian Industrial Relations Association, 1980, pp. 12–15.

18. In Ontario a strike is legal on the 17th day after the "no board" report was mailed, since the report is not deemed to be released until the second day after it was mailed.

19. Public Service Staff Relations Act, Secs. 2(u) and 36(l).

20. Public Service Labour Relations Act, Sec. 66.

21. Carl M. Stevens, "Is Compulsory Arbitration Compatible with Bargaining?" *Industrial Relations*, February, 1966, pp. 38–52.

22. For a further discussion of this topic see: S. A. Bellan, "Final Offer Selection: Two Canadian Case Studies and an American Digression," *Osgood Hall Law Journal*, Vol. 13, pp. 851–878; A. V. Subbarao, "Final Offer Selection vs. Last-Offer-By-Issue Systems of Arbitration," *Relations Industrielles/Industrial Relations*, Volume 33, No. 1, (1978), pp. 38–57.

23. Canada Labour Code, Part V (RSC 1970) Sec. 171.1; British Columbia Labour Code

(RSBC 1979) Secs. 70–72; Manitoba Labour Relations Act (SM. 1972) Sec. 75.1; Quebec Labour Code (RSQ 1977), Sec. 93.

24. For a description of early experience under the Canada Labour Code, see S. Muthuchedambaram, "Settlement of First Collective Agreement," *Relations Industrielles/Industrial Relations*, Volume 35, Number 3, (1980), pp. 387–409.

25. Herbert R. Northrup, *Compulsory Arbitration and Government Intervention in Labor Disputes*. Washington, D.C.: Labor Policy Association, Inc., 1966, p. 183.

26. Donald J. M. Brown, *Interest Arbitration*. Task Force on Labour Relations, Study No. 18. Ottawa: Privy Council Office, 1968, p. 26.

27. The Brotherhood of Railway Trainmen, *The Pros and Cons of Compulsory Arbitration*. Cleveland, Ohio: The Brotherhood of Railway Trainmen, 1965, p. 48.

28. Northrup, pp. 179–211.

29. Brown, p. 214.

30. Mark Thompson, "Evaluation of Interest Arbitration: The Case of British Columbia Teachers," in *Interest Arbitration*, Joseph M. Weiler, ed. Toronto: The Carswell Company Limited, 1981, pp. 79–97.

31. Joseph M. Weiler, "Interest Arbitration in British Columbia: The Essential Services Disputes Act," in Weiler, *Interest Arbitration*, pp. 99–131.

32. John Anderson, "Arbitration in the Federal Public Service," in Weiler, *Interest Arbitration*, pp. 43–77.

33. Richard E. Walton and Robert B. McKersie, *A Behavioral Theory of Labor Negotiations*. New York: McGraw-Hill Book Company, 1965.

34. See, for example: J. G. Cross, "A Theory of the Bargaining Process," *American Economic Review*, March, 1965; B. D. Mobry, "The Pure Theory of Bargaining," *Industrial and Labor Relations Review*, July 1965; J. Pen, "A General Theory of Bargaining," *American Economic Review*, March 1952; Carl M. Stevens, *Strategy and Collective Bargaining Legislation*. New York: McGraw-Hill Book Company, Inc., 1963; Oran R. Young, ed., *Bargaining: Formal Theories of Negotiations*. Urbana: University of Illinois Press, 1975; John M. Magenou and Sean G. Pruitt, "The Social Psychology of Bargaining: A Theoretical Synthesis," in G. M. Stephenson and J. C. Brotherson, *Industrial Relations: A Social Psychological Approach*. London: Wiley, 1978.

35. For a fuller discussion of this concept see: Howard Raiffa, *The Art and Science of Negotiation*. Cambridge, Massachusetts: Belknap Harvard University Press, 1982, pp. 44–65; and Walton and McKersie, pp. 11–57.

36. Benjamin M. Selekman, Sylvia Kopold Selekman and Stephen H. Fuller, *Problems in Labor Relations*. New York: McGraw Hill Book Company, Inc., 1958, p. 4.

37. Neil W. Chamberlain and James W. Kuhn, *Collective Bargaining*. New York: McGraw-Hill Book Company, 1965, pp. 170–71.

38. For further details on Boulwarism see: Herbert R. Northrup, *Boulwarism*. Ann Arbor: Bureau of Industrial Relations, Graduate School of Business Administration, University of Michigan, 1964; and Herbert R. Northrup, "The Case for Boulwarism," *Harvard Business Review*, September-October 1963, pp. 86–97. For a criticism of Boulwarism see: Benjamin M. Selekman, "Cynicism and Managerial Morality," *Harvard Business Review*, September-October 1958, pp. 61–70.

39. Yang Xishan, Larry F. Moore and Herb Magraff, "Behavioural Science Application in Vancouver Based Firms," *Relations Industrielles/Industrial Relations*, Vol. 38, Number 1, 1983, pp. 120–139; Ronald Belton and William Vincer, "The Joint Committee on Relationships at Ontario Hydro," *Proceedings*, Canadian Industrial Relations Association, 1980, pp. 503–507. For other examples, see James J. Healy, ed., *Creative Collective Bargaining*. Englewood Cliffs, New Jersey: Prentice-Hall, Inc., 1965, pp. 135–243.

40. "One Way to Avoid Strikes: Defuse the Confrontation Method," *The Financial Post*, November 8, 1975, p. 11.

41. Roger Fisher and William Ury, *"Getting To Yes"*. Boston: Houghton Mifflin Company, 1977.

42. Derek C. Bok and John T. Dunlop, *Labor and the American Community*. New York: Simon and Schuster, 1970, p. 226.

43. For a full description of this process, see Bruce Morse, *How to Negotiate the Labor Agreement*. Southfield, Michigan: Freuds Publishing Company, 1976; and Meyer S. Ryder, Charles Remus and Sanford Cohen, *Management Preparation for Collective Bargaining*. Homewood, Illinois: Dow Jones-Irwin, Inc., 1966.

44. Raiffa, p. 120.

45. John T. Dunlop and James J. Healy, *Collective Bargaining*, Rev. Edition. Homewood, Illinois: Richard D. Irwin, Inc., 1953, p. 56.

46. Ibid., pp. 62–63.

47. Thomas C. Schelling, *The Strategy of Conflict*. New York: Oxford University Press, 1963, p. 24.

48. Fred Charles Ikle, *How Nations Negotiate*. New York: Harper & Row, 1964, pp. 59–60.

49. Dunlop and Healy, p. 61.

50. Labour Code, R.S.Q. 1977, Sec. 109.1.

51. B.C. Labour Code (RSBC) Sec. 3(c) (d); Ontario Labour Relations Act, (RSO 1980) Sec. 71 a.

52. B.C. Labour Code, Sec. 1.

53. O.L.R.A. Sec. 71 (a) (2) (b).

54. British Columbia Ministry of Labour, *Guide to the B.C. Labour Code*, 1980, pp. 35–36.

55. For additional cost estimates on absenteeism see: Alexander Mikalachki and Jeffrey Gandz, *Managing Absenteeism*. London, Ontario: Research and Publication Divisions, School of Business Administration, The University of Western Ontario, 1982, pp. 1–2.

56. Task Force on Labour Relations. Ottawa: Privy Council Office, 1968, pp. 137–38.

MCDONALD CONTAINERS LTD. (A)

A. CHIEF NEGOTIATOR

Last August, Clive Armstrong, Manager of Industrial Relations of McDonald Containers Ltd., was on the verge of negotiating a new contract with Local 201 of the International Paper Products and Allied Enterprises Union of America (IPPU), the representative of the largest group of unionized employees of the St. Catharines, Ontario plant. The present contract was to expire on September 14. This would be the third time Armstrong had negotiated with this local.

Clive Armstrong had served as chief negotiator in all of McDonald's contract negotiations for the past six years. Still he felt fresh pangs of excitement as each negotiation approached. Dates for the first meetings had already been set. The initial one would take place August 12.

B. BACKGROUND

1. McDonald Containers

McDonald Containers was one of the largest producers of folding cartons and other packaging materials in Ontario. Sales had stabilized in the past few years at about $62 million, while profits had declined from a high of $2.5 million three years ago to $2.2 million last year. The decline in profits resulted from rising costs and increased competition.

The company had eight plants. The major products, folding cartons, were produced in six plants. There was some product overlap. Distance between plants made it economically unsound for one plant to absorb customer requirements for another, except in emergencies. Many of the company's packaging products were manufactured for the food industry. Of these, a large portion was for fluids, such as dairy products and soft drinks.

2. St. Catharines Division

The St. Catharines plant was McDonald's largest. It supplied over ten percent of the Niagara Peninsula market for containers in the food, cosmetic, and hardware businesses. Since it served the fluid industry in particular, sales rose in May and continued at a high level until the heat of summer subsided.

Workers at the St. Catharines plant were represented by three unions: the IPPU, the Niagara Carton Makers Union (NCM), and the Typesetters Union. The contract with the NCM would run until next April 30 and that with the Typesetters until next August 31. These were craft unions. The former represented thirty printers while the latter represented nine lithographers. The NCM contracts usually followed the pattern set by the IPPU.

The IPPU local bargaining unit included production, maintenance, quality control, material handling, and technical workers. The unit numbered 150, of whom 38 were female. The workforce swelled to about 175 during the summer sales and vacation peak. Students provided most of the temporary help. Since there was a union shop clause in the collective agreement, these students were required to pay dues.

Skills ranged from general labour to pressmen. Pressmen were highly skilled workers akin to printers in the NCM. Basic wages for the pressmen were $12.14 per hour. The lowest rate for general labour was $8.64 for males and $7.49 for females. The lower paid male workers were primarily material handlers and were located in each end of the production line. Most of the women in the IPPU were assemblers. About 90 percent of the workforce members, including all pressmen, were eligible for incentives. The incentive system was based on time standards established by use of stop watches. After observing and timing each operation, methods engineers prescribed a certain number of "standard hours," the time in which a so-called normal performer working at average skill and efficiency could perform the necessary job assigned to him. Workers who performed their jobs faster than the standard were paid a bonus. The bonus was a percentage of the negotiated base rate.

Up until four years ago, wages in the plant had been in line with other firms in the folding carton industry. Since then, wages had exceeded the industry average by about ten percent. However, they were below the average area rates by approximately five percent. Last summer, average wages at McDonald for all non-incentive hourly employees were a little over $8.30 per hour. Those on incentives averaged slightly over $9.10 per hour.

3. Union History

During World War II, a plant council of workers was formed in compliance with government wartime measures. After the war, the council continued as the representative of the workers and became affiliated with the International Pulp, Sulfite and Paperworkers Union. In the early 50s, the workers broke from the International and formed a local of the Box Employees' Union. The local was weak, non-militant, and poorly led. During this period, the foremen had complete control of their departments. There were no recorded grievances. In fact, the union held meetings occasionally to quash discontent. However, rank and file militancy rose until four years ago when the Box Employees' Union was decertified and the IPPU was certified in its place. IPPU appealed to the membership on a platform of rectifying the wrongs of the weak union. It promised economic benefits. Perhaps the most important reason for the Box Employees' Union demise was that it was working under a three-year agreement calling for small annual increases. During the term of that agreement, Canadian wages in general took off in spectacular fashion.

C. RECENT CONTRACTS

1. First Negotiation — Four Years Ago

Soon after the IPPU certification, Clive Armstrong met with George Sheehan, the union's international representative, to negotiate the first contract. The old Box Employees' contract was used as a starting point in the negotiations. Nevertheless, both men expected the negotiations to take a long time. Sheehan took a tough bargaining approach. Tension was frequent, and some conflicts arose. Armstrong was particularly upset when Sheehan informed the local newspaper of an upcoming strike vote. This caused customers of McDonald to make arrangements for alternative supply sources and gave rise to a strong rebuke by Armstrong.

After several weeks, the union applied for conciliation under provisions of the Ontario Labour Relations Act. After the first conciliation meeting, the company negotiators expressed concern about the apparent incompetency of the conciliator. He had led the company representatives to believe a settlement was near, but it soon became clear that he had badly underestimated the union's position. The company then requested another conciliator, and under his auspices, the parties came to an agreement. It was a two-year contract, calling for a 12 percent wage increase.

The administration of the new contract brought significant changes. In particular, the grievance rate rose to a steady stream, and the foremen had difficulty adapting. They had never before experienced challenges to their authority, but they were reluctant to seek advice or counsel of the industrial relations staff, a difficult thing to do after years of autocracy.

2. Second Contract — Two Years Ago

Negotiations for the second contract took a long time. The company started off by presenting its own proposals for changes in the contract before hearing union demands. Union bargainers scoffed at this procedure and tried to ignore the proposals. Later, as the parties discussed money, George Sheehan rejected attempts by Armstrong to make industry wage comparisons. Sheehan went so far as to say the identity of McDonald's competitors and their wage rates were irrelevant. He stated that area rates provided the only fair basis for comparison.

About the time the contract expired in mid-August, the union discovered that the company had been stockpiling finished cartons at a Toronto warehouse. Sheehan was quite upset, but his irritation was tempered by the fact that the inventory was small — about a week's supply. While no work action occurred, the union leaders threatened that the membership would refuse overtime. This threat was rendered ineffective when it became evident that workers would not go along.

Once again a conciliation officer was called in. After an 18-hour session, the sides finally reached agreement on a two-year contract in the early morning hours. The wage settlement was again an expensive one for the company. The increase was applied on a cents-per-hour basis and totalled about 16 percent.

D. RECENT DEVELOPMENTS

1. Environmental

Environmental developments were likely to have an important bearing on the current negotiations. First, there were significant economic trends: inflationary pressures were strong and wage settlements were high. At the same time, unemployment had risen to levels not experienced for a decade.

Locally, the labour market was active. Numerous plant closings and threats of closings had occurred in the Niagara Peninsula area in the past two years. For awhile in the spring there were threats of a brewery strike, but settlement occurred well before McDonald's negotiations started. Local strikes by civic employees were predicted in various Niagara Peninsula municipalities in August and September. In Brantford, Ontario, about 80 kilometres away, a manufacturer of hospital supplies had been struck by its employees who were seeking a 30 percent increase on a $4.50 base rate. When the company sought to bring in strike breakers from other communities, violence erupted leading to a court injunction and more than 60 arrests. The company threatened to close down its Canadian operations if the strike continued.

Another significant environmental development concerned women's rights. A recent amendment had been made to the equal pay statutes of the Employment Standards Act. Part V of this Act, Equal Pay For Equal Work, prohibited discrimination because of sex in employment conditions and hiring. It was interpreted as requiring equal wages for men and women doing substantially the same work; but since then companies and unions had been skirmishing about its meaning. Women's groups were putting pressure on the government to further expand the law to provide for equal pay for work of equal value.

2. Union Developments

In the two prior negotiations, the union seemed to lack cohesion. There had been frequent bickering among the local bargaining committee members and between the local committee members and George Sheehan, the union's international representative.

Last fall the union vice-president, Walter Stevens, resigned. Then, about three months later, an internal union uproar was caused when members came to believe that the union's executives had voted salary increases for themselves. The uproar eventually caused the union president, Julius Arthur, to resign. An international representative from the United States was called in to help smooth things over and set up an interim union executive.

Clive Armstrong was concerned that these conflicts would hinder settlement in the forthcoming negotiations. His fears seemed well-founded when the membership elected a bargaining committee before deciding on a new executive. Armstrong asked Walter Stevens, the chairman of the new bargaining committee, whether there would be a split between the executive and the bargainers. Stevens assured him that there would be no conflict, but it was hardly reassuring when Armstrong noted that none of the members of the bargaining committee were on the interim executive committee. There might be difficulties in getting union membership to ratify an agreement after it had been initialled by the bargainers.

3. Bargaining Committee

Armstrong described the members of the union bargaining committee:

George Sheehan—International representative for the IPPU in the Niagara

Peninsula area. Considered a strong man by members of the local. Very persuasive with membership. Fairly democratic at negotiations. Does not force members to keep the issues at hand, often lets them go on tangents. Knowledgeable in labour relations, literature, and law. Sometimes refers management to books and articles. In negotiations, actually chairs meetings for unions and serves as chief negotiator. Poised, plays roles effectively.

Walter Stevens — Chairman of committee. Former vice-president and department steward in the local. Late 30s. Over 20 years' service. Shipper. An average paying job. Appears to be personal friend of Sheehan's. Was active in having IPPU replace the previous union. Member of the two previous negotiating committees. Perhaps the best person to gauge feelings of the membership.

Alice Melvin — In her 30s. Eight years' service. Interested in female wages and benefits. Quiet at meetings. Apparently a behind-the-scenes disturber. A member of the union's founding executive. Former steward. A member of negotiating team two years ago.

Michael Newman — Diemaker lead hand. Fifteen years' service, early 30s. Not active in union before. Shy and not too talkative. An unknown quantity. First time on negotiating committee.

Harry Chelekian — Skilled, maintenance mechanic. Late 30s. Twelve years' service. Department steward. Concerned mainly about own area of work and himself. Talkative and overly emotional. Felt not to pull much weight with committee or members. First time on committee.

Jack Griffin — Early 30s, over seven years' service. Member of original IPPU executive. Former chief steward. Member of the previous two negotiating teams. Not active at meetings, not a key man.

In preparing their demands for the negotiations, the union bargaining committee held two general membership meetings. Armed with ideas from the members, they met to formulate their demands.

E. MANAGEMENT PREPARATIONS

In early March, Clive Armstrong and members of his department began serious preparations for the negotiations. They surveyed wages and benefits in the industry and area; they named their bargaining committee; and they developed management proposals for changes to the contract.

The naming of the bargaining committee was a formality. The same team had negotiated in the two previous contracts.

Clive Armstrong — Chairman and chief negotiator.

Daniel Burgess — Assistant to Armstrong. Responsible, along with the personnel manager to the St. Catharines plant, for pre-negotiation preparations.

John Curtis — General Manager, St. Catharines plant. He was accountable for the division's profits and had veto power over any agreement.

Frederick Lundberg — Personnel Manager, St. Catharines plant. Reported to Curtis.

William Cutts — Plant Superintendent, supervisor of the production foremen.

Ralph Reed — Manager Industrial Engineering.

John Yale — Manager of Production Planning and Material Handling.

As he did during the last negotiations two years ago, Armstrong made plans for management's proposals for contract changes to be presented at the start of negotiations. While the union had not greeted this tactic favourably, Armstrong believed it was important to give members of management an opportunity to make their viewpoints known before hearing union demands. After all, the first-line supervisors would be called on to administer the contract, and they should be made to feel that they influenced its formulation. Thus a series of meetings was held with foremen to secure their inputs. As a result, management prepared a 10-page proposal for changes in 32 separate contract provisions. These were condensed from significantly more proposals received from the foremen. If a foreman made a suggestion that was not incorporated into the final proposals, he was sought out and given the reasons for rejection of his suggestion.

Armstrong considered nine of the management proposals to be crucial. One of them would restrict the criteria for determining job assignments, in the event of a lay-off, to seniority and ability. The present contract contained an added factor — willingness by an employee to accept a lower classification of work. Some employees were unwilling to bump downward in the event of a lay-off and, because of this, they experienced difficulty when they filed for unemployment insurance. Armstrong believed the union would be receptive to removing the "willingness" criterion.

In the same vein, management was anxious to secure a contract rewording which would make "qualification" the sole criterion for filling temporary job classifications (ten working days or less). The existing contract called for a dual test: willingness and qualification.

Six of management's proposals concerned overtime distribution. They were also considered crucial. These would provide for sharing of overtime "as fairly and as reasonably as possible as circumstances permit." In addition, they would provide for sharing among all qualified employees.

One additional proposal was considered important in order to clear up past confusion. This regarded group insurance coverage for married female workers. The McDonald plan was designed with the expectation that husbands would cover their wives at their place of work. Consequently, married women working at McDonald were not enrolled for married coverage unless they made formal application. In such cases, the company would pay the premium for married coverage but deduct the difference between married and single premium costs on married coverage for married males. Family coverage was provided for widows and for divorced or legally separated female employees, provided they were not covered elsewhere.

Other items in management's list of proposals were considered by Armstrong to be window dressing. Mostly they dealt with improbable hypothetical situations. Nevertheless, they were included in order to pay tribute to those who put them forth. To some extent, they might serve as trading horses — items to be dropped in turn for the union's dropping one or more of their demands.

The union negotiators insisted on holding meetings at a neutral location. The Rendezvous Motel conference room was reserved for the first three meetings. Negotiations had been held there before. Armstrong felt it was important to have a comfortable place away from the plant, thus emphasizing the importance of the proceedings and, possibly, enhancing the bargainers' own feelings of importance.

1. BARGAINING STYLE AND STRATEGY

Armstrong would be chairman. He insisted that there be no visible disunity or bickering on the management team. As negotiations moved into the monetary stages, management would show no outward reaction to union demands. If caucuses were called to discuss offers, they would be held away from the presence of union negotiators.

Armstrong had a healthy respect for Sheehan's bargaining ability. He believed Sheehan represented the whole strength of the union team. False emotionalism or empty threats would not be effective tools for management to use against him.

When it came to talk money, Armstrong wanted to introduce wage comparisons from the packaging industry. He was concerned about getting McDonald's competitive situation across to the union bargainers, even if Sheehan himself displayed indifference. He expected that Sheehan would reject these comparisons and insist on making area comparisons. Most important, Armstrong would make no economic offer until all the union demands were on the table in such form that their economic value could be calculated and totalled.

Armstrong expected Sheehan to seek agreement on various union demands on a piecemeal basis. He would resist this tactic and would restrict the company's wage and fringe offer to one package. According to Armstrong:

> If you bargain item by item, you discover you have no money left when you come to wages. You have to do it in a package in order to cost it properly so you know what you're giving.

During the negotiations, Armstrong would provide no news releases for the press. Also the company would never communicate directly with the members of the union outside the bargaining room. Armstrong expected the union to apply for conciliation early. Nevertheless he would try to keep everyone at the bargaining table as long as possible before that happened.

2. ANTICIPATIONS

Armstrong did not know when the union would make its first concrete demands. He expected the first few meetings to focus solely on the language of the contract — not on money matters.

He did have an idea what the union's principal demands would be. He listed them:

1. Company to pay all premiums on medical insurance. At present, the company paid 75 percent of Ontario Hospital Insurance premiums and 100 percent of all other welfare benefits.
2. A major pension plan revision. Armstrong was not sure exactly what form this would take, but he expected to bargain over benefits. He would insist on bargaining only regarding costs to the company.
3. Severance pay, based on years of service.
4. No contracting-out clause.
5. Cost-of-living escalator.
6. Training plan to upgrade skills.
7. More vacation time and more holidays.

3. MONETARY OBJECTIVES

With negotiations about to start, Armstrong began to formulate his monetary objectives. This would be done in consultation with the Vice-President of Packaging. During the consultation, Armstrong would present his best guess regarding limits below which the union would strike and above which management should be willing to accept a strike.

Underlying all conversations about monetary limits was a deep concern over McDonald's long-term competitive situation in the industry. Thus, management was united in a desire to keep costs low. A budget had been set earlier in the year which included a 10 percent increase in labour cost for the whole year. Much of this was to cushion the increase called for under the existing contract; an average of 47 cents per hour effective last September 15.

Armstrong believed that an eight percent wage increase plus a one percent fringe settlement would be desirable. However, he doubted whether operating managers would be willing to hold these figures if faced with a strike. These questions would have to wait until the first meeting was over.

Items for Discussion

1. Comment on Armstrong's preparation for negotiations.
2. What do you believe should be management's bargaining objectives?
3. What would be your estimation of the limits below which the union would strike and above which management should be willing to accept a strike?
4. Identify the important elements of Armstrong's bargaining strategy. Appraise each of them.

McDONALD CONTAINERS LTD. (B)

NEGOTIATIONS BEGIN

On Thursday, August 12, the negotiations began at the Rendezvous Motel. As was traditional, the parties met at 9:00 a.m. and would remain at the bargaining table until about 5:00 p.m.

Sheehan (u): Well, who's paying for this?

Armstrong (co): The company has in the past, and we will continue to do so. But we aren't if we go to conciliation!

Members of bargaining teams chuckled. They were in a jovial mood. The contract would not expire for over a month (September 14). The chief negotiators handed out copies of their demands and proposals. The union submitted 35 demands: 12 with monetary implications. The proposals were skimmed quickly. (See Exhibit 1, for summary of union proposals.)

Armstrong (co): I notice that the union has not stated a specific wage demand. I remind you that this will be necessary before the company can seriously consider any monetary items. Let's divide your demands into non-monetary and monetary groups. We can start discussing the non-monetary ones. Then, after you clarify your wage demands, we can go on.

Sheehan (u): I agree to dividing them up. Oh, Clive, we would like to add to the wage demand. Could you write this in one of your sheets? Add "wage parity between male and female employees" to "subtantial wage increase."

Most of the morning was spent clarifying the meaning of the demands.

EXHIBIT 1

Summary of Union Proposals Submitted at First Meeting Between Local 201, IPPU and McDonald Containers Ltd.

A. CONTRACT CHANGES

1. Probationary employees
   — no summer rate for students
   — grievance possible on discharge and lay-off
   — rehiring according to service

2. Grievance
   — means any difference between union and company
   — lengthen filing period to 30 days and shorten reply by company to 3 days (the existing contract called for 15 days and 5 days)
   — possible to go to arbitration without going through grievance steps

3. Hiring
   — seniority criteria if qualified

4. Hours of work
   — 48-hours notice of shift change or time-and-a-half pay
   — new hours for two shift operations (the existing contract called for shifts from 7 a.m. until 4 p.m. and 4 p.m. until 12:30 a.m.)
   — some departmental and job changes

5. Local Issues
   — re-evaluate some job classifications
   — adjust some rates
   — coveralls for some workers
   — powerhouse: own union steward, one bulletin board, time-and-a-half on Saturday and double time on Sunday

6. Overtime
   — voluntary
   — list of overtime kept for calendar year

B. BENEFITS

1. Holidays and Vacations
   — add floating holiday at convenience of employee
   — increase number of weeks' vacation
   — add $25 per week vacation bonus
   — take vacation within year of anniversary date
   — leave granted for more categories of deaths among family members

2. Severance Pay
   — one week's pay per year service

3. Welfare
   — company to pay 100 percent of welfare package
   — add benefits — disability
   — life insurance — two times wages
   — sick benefits 60 percent wages for 52 weeks
   — semi-private hospital benefits
   — any future savings in premium for government welfare schemes goes to employees

4. Pension
   — improvement

5. Wages
   — substantial increase

6. Parity
   — equal female-male wages

At noon, each group had lunch separately and talked about its initial reactions.

Armstrong (co): Everything seems to be going all right.

Burgess (co): There aren't too many surprises except the one about opening the grievance process.

Armstrong (co): I wonder what Sheehan wants with that one. It could open up the process so that the union could grieve on everything from pollution to contracting out. I don't like it.

Burgess (co): They seem to be concerned about the rights of probationary employees.

Curtis (General Manager, St. Catharines Division): They really want to make probationary employees non-probationary. The supervisors won't go for that.

Armstrong (co): I didn't expect any female wage parity talk. I thought this was all squared away years ago.

Lundberg (Personnel Manager, St. Catharines Division): Maybe it was just an afterthought.

In the afternoon, the negotiators delved into the union proposals in more detail. The company proposals were left aside for the moment. However, when a union demand dealt with the same article of the contract that a company proposal did, Daniel Burgess brought it up. As a result, three company proposals were discussed as well.

Tentatively, the company and union agreed on two minor points—the number of shop stewards and the company proposal regarding procedure for allocating overtime. Then, the proposal for a change in the grievance process was considered.

Sheehan (u): By defining a grievance as any difference between the company and union, we can make the whole process more flexible.

Armstrong (co): What do you really want in doing this?

Sheehan (u): This will make our relationship less legalistic. We'll get used to solving more problems together.

Armstrong (co): It's unworkable. If we don't agree on some issues, who decides—an arbitrator? Wouldn't this change allow you to grieve anything from changing the position of the flag pole to contracting out?

Sheehan (u): Well, yes it would allow us to discuss questions of that sort. But we have nothing specific in mind.

Time elapsed. The parties agreed to continue to go over the union submission at the following meeting.

Armstrong gave his reactions to the first session:

> It started off pretty well. It seems as if the union is going to keep any bickering outside the meetings. The only disruptions concerned Harry Chelekian. He often gets off on a tangent and they try to quiet him down. This was expected. Everyone else is running true to form. George Sheehan and I are doing most of the talking.

> I presume Sheehan is going to play a waiting game. He comes on strong with theoretical talk at first, but not concrete wage demands. We will try to get through the union's non-monetary questions quickly. No reason to delay. We want to discuss our own demands. We'll agree to their requests if they are reasonable. I'll keep reminding Sheehan that he has to put a wage demand on the table before we can talk money. There is no pressure yet until we finish the discussion of the language of the contract.

> As for the non-monetary language changes, Dan Burgess is preparing a comparison of our proposal with theirs in cases when we both want to

change the same articles. He also will get comments from the people concerned regarding the language demands about department matters. This way we can refer to the demands more quickly and have an idea what it is really about. Dan is also costing the monetary demands where possible, mainly because we have no wage demand. This material will be necessary in a few weeks when we really get down to bargain money.

Items for Discussion:

1. Comment on first meeting. Is there significance to the fact that the initial dialogue concerned the union's demands?
2. Why does management insist on costing the monetary demands?
3. What position would you take regarding the various union proposals?
4. As chief company negotiator, how would you proceed the next day?

McDONALD CONTAINERS LTD. (C)

TWO MORE SESSIONS

The parties met again on Monday, August 16, and Wednesday, August 25. The company agreed to a number of minor changes in the contract and reached an understanding that health premium savings would be passed on to employees and/or the company in the event the government decided to discontinue premiums.

However, the company once again took a firm stand in refusing to pay welfare premiums for married women on the same basis as for married men. The union offered a minor compromise on this item, but Clive Armstrong stood firm. Armstrong also rejected the union's wish to have an impartial industrial engineer re-evaluate a number of job classifications which the union considered out of line.

The rest of the day was spent clarifying and discussing the company proposals. The union accepted some of the company proposals, including the desire to deny seniority rights to students. Other proposals were held for consideration at the next meeting.

On Wednesday August 25, the third meeting was held. Armstrong continued to direct bargainers' attention to company proposals. The union discussed these proposals with no objection. However, they felt many were uncalled-for and unnecessary. It was agreed to meet again the following Wednesday and Thursday to complete discussion of the non-monetary items.

REFLECTIONS

Clive Armstrong expressed pleasure with the progress so far. He was pleased that the union was seriously considering the company proposals.

One aspect of the meetings concerned Armstrong:

> I've been on the receiving end of some difficult questions from the union about some of these proposals we made. I figured they were important, because the foremen had submitted them. However, I'm finding that there is little defence for many of them. I have had to back down on a few, and I feel a little silly.

The next week, Armstrong had a meeting with his team about some of the questionable issues:

> I discovered, after all, that the supervisors weren't really concerned about some of these things I was supposed to argue in favour of. The foremen will probably just think I gave in but they are putting me in a bad position. I won't defend items which mainly arise out of hypothetical situations. I've learned something — next time we'll take a closer look at these proposals and find out just how important they really are. Now I'll have to withdraw them, but at least the foremen will know they have been discussed.

It was still too early to consider strike preparations. Armstrong anticipated reaching final agreement on as many proposals as possible. He was hoping Sheehan would make a monetary demand soon. He had been hounding him on this point and would continue to do so. He felt it was still early for the union to call for conciliation.

Items for Discussion

1. Why was Armstrong anxious for the union to make a specific monetary demand?
2. Evaluate Armstrong's comments regarding management's proposals which were apparently without defence.
3. Why do you believe Armstrong continued his opposition to payment of full welfare premiums for married women?

McDONALD CONTAINERS LTD. (D)

On Monday, August 30, the parties continued bargaining on language and non-monetary items.

The company presented a new proposal on the administration of vacations.

Pensions were brought up, and it was decided to have a life insurance company representative join the negotiators the following afternoon to answer questions and clarify technical points concerning various pension plans and their costs. Armstrong, while agreeing to invite an insurance representative to meet with the parties, emphasized that any costs from a new pension plan would be part of the package settlement and would be negotiated on a basis of cents-per-hour costs to the company, not on the basis of pension benefits to employees. He reiterated that no agreement could be reached on part of the economic package until the union made a full monetary proposal.

The union brought up female parity questions again. Armstrong said that costs arising from giving married females full married welfare benefits were part of the economic package. Regarding the issue of equal wages for male and female, the union claimed that some female jobs were more important than male ones. The management team tried to force the union to be more specific on this point. Sheehan said that equal pay was required by the Employment Standards Act, and the company was in violation. Armstrong suggested the parties obtain an official statement from the Ontario Labour Department on the matter.

Afterwards, Armstrong commented that he was pleased with the meeting's progress. He had hoped the union would comment on more company proposals, but he expected there would be progress in this regard the next day.

The married-women benefits question and wage parity issues had occupied considerable attention, but Armstrong was not willing to move on either issue and certainly would not give anything away at this stage without something in return. He felt Alice Melvin, in particular, was pushing the married benefits question. Her husband, a seasonal construction worker, received no benefits of this nature.

The following day was expected to be similar to Monday's session. Armstrong hoped more progress would be made to clear up the non-monetary items and to emphasize the need for a union wage demand.

Items for Discussion

1. Comment on management's continued refusal to discuss monetary items outside the context of a total economic package.
2. What position should management take regarding the question of female/male parity and married-women's rights to the same group insurance coverage as married men?

McDONALD CONTAINERS LTD. (E)

FIFTH MEETING
Conciliation Application

The following morning, Tuesday, August 31, Clive Armstrong and his fellow bargainers sat down once again across the table from George Sheehan and the union bargaining committee. Usually, the meetings opened with some hesitation, with either Armstrong or Sheehan reminding the group where they had left off the session before. Today was different. Sheehan cleared his throat and began.

Sheehan (u): In accordance with the company's request, the union will clarify its economic position. Any settlement must preserve the relationship in the wage and benefit package that exists with McDonald Containers and other industries in the St. Catharines area who employ the same number of employees.

Armstrong (co): That is totally unacceptable! You aren't being explicit enough as to what settlements you are referring to.

Sheehan (u): You are aware of the local settlements Clive; don't play dumb.

Armstrong (co): So, I'm dumb. Just give us a better idea of where you stand.

Sheehan (u): Just check the papers. We are not prepared to clarify our demands further.

Armstrong (co): We can't negotiate money until you do.

Sheehan (u): Well, I think it is also time to advise the company that the union will apply for conciliation at the conclusion of this meeting.

Armstrong (co): The company is opposed to your application at this time.

Sheehan (u): The union feels it is necessary to speed things up and get down to some serious bargaining.

Armstrong (co): Come on George, you're just trying to arm-lock the company. It isn't good to apply for conciliation when we have so many non-economic matters yet to decide. Moreover, you haven't even put a concrete wage demand on the table yet. The conciliator will probably just tell us to go back to the table ourselves.

Sheehan (u): We aren't trying to pressure the company at all—we just think it will speed our discussion up a bit. We will get a settlement without any pressure tactics. Also, there will be no negotiating this in the newspaper. I understand there was a little hard feeling about this before. We will reach a settlement on our own.

Armstrong (co): Let's go over as many items as possible and try to get the language questions out of the way.

Sheehan (u): Okay.

In the afternoon, two representatives from a local life insurance company joined the meeting and discussed the subject of pensions.

Sheehan (u): The union is interested in two possible pension plans. One would be a final earnings plan based on one tenth of one percent for the best five years of earnings, and the second would be a plan based on a monthly benefit based on years of service.

(The existing pension plan called for yearly payment of two percent of an employee's career coverage annual earnings times years of service, with employees contributing approximately one half the amount required to buy the plan. Only 50 percent of the employees were members of the plan.)

Stoneman (insurance co): Based on last year's payroll, the increase in cost to the company of the first plan you named would be about five percent of payroll.

Burgess (co): That works out to 55 cents per hour from my cost data.

Armstrong (co): The company position on this is that any Canada Pension Plan benefit must be integrated with any proposed plan. Secondly, the company will only negotiate from a cents-per-hour cost to the company. I would remind the union that comparable firms in the Niagara area have nothing similar to these plans. They are just too expensive.

Sheehan (u): We know they are costly, Clive, but there are cheaper ways of handling them. I have told the membership that there will probably be changes in the government pension plan within the next five years. We know it's costly, but the present plan is not really adequate.

Armstrong (co): It's part of the economic package.

Sheehan (u): Let's leave this for now and we'll get more information on it another time. We still have other business to discuss.

At this point, non-economic items were reviewed. The union withdrew many of their proposals, including extending time for filing a grievance, voluntary overtime, and longer notice for shift changes. Similarly, the company dropped about ten proposals. A few proposals were adopted. For example, students working in the summer would not obtain seniority rights.

The union held most of the remaining company proposals for further consideration. It was decided to meet again to clear up these items. The next session was set for Tuesday, September 7.

REFLECTIONS

The following day, Clive Armstrong discussed the August 31 meeting with his assistant, Daniel Burgess.

Armstrong: I was surprised that Sheehan mentioned conciliation, Dan. I really thought he would wait a week or so until some money was on the table.

Burgess: Sheehan was trying to lighten it though — he kept saying positive things about reaching a settlement.

Armstrong: That's right, Dan. I also recall him mentioning no publicity to the paper. I blasted him about that a few years ago and he made a point of bringing it up.

Burgess: Sheehan is softening a bit.

Armstrong: I think he realizes we're a pretty good outfit and doesn't want to rock the boat as hard as he has in the past.

Burgess: He does want a more harmonious relationship. But he has a monetary objective—and he wants to get it.

Armstrong: Right—and we don't know if he was bluffing about conciliation. We'll wait and see if we get the notice from the Labour Department. In fact, maybe Sheehan even called the papers right after the meeting. We don't know what he is doing.

Burgess: What issues are important at this stage, Clive?

Armstrong: The wage and benefit parity between male and female is the main one. Sheehan keeps talking about discrimination. You know as well as I do those jobs are not really comparable. Anyway, the cost of those demands is just too much.

Burgess: The pension situation is changing.

Armstrong: It looks like Sheehan is backing down on pensions. He's trying to convince their side that it isn't worth the money.

Burgess: You've been pretty non-committal so far, Clive.

Armstrong: I think I'll just wait on that one. I don't really know for sure, but I think Sheehan wants me to close the door on pensions.

Burgess: Sheehan can sell them without our help. The only guy who is really sharp is the new man — Newman.

Armstrong: He's got a head on his shoulders, but I don't know how much influence he has.

Burgess: Being shy and rather green as far as union affairs are concerned, he may not try to do much. Stevens still is close to Sheehan. He must be Sheehan's link to the membership.

Armstrong: Next meeting we'll try to clear up all the remaining non-monetary items and get final agreement. I dropped most of our poor proposals today.

Burgess: The only real issues are allocation of vacations and our desire to delete "willing" from the contract (which made the worker eligible for unemployment if he was laid off and unwilling to take a lesser-paying job). The main question we had about overtime allocation seems to be agreed to already.

Armstrong: In the afternoon, we can discuss wage comparisons. Maybe we can get more concrete demands out of Sheehan. I'll have the Vice President, Noel Ramsey, in to say a few words about our competitive position. This is the message we have to get across to the committee whether Sheehan listens or not.

Burgess: That's a step—we have to make them realize that our competitors in the Toronto area are well under our wage levels. By the way, I've finished that comparison on wages.

Armstrong: Good! I may even have copies made to give the union committee.

Burgess: What lies ahead — a strike vote after the conciliation meeting?

Armstrong: Probably. Remember, no publicity should get out to our customers or the newspapers.

Burgess: We meet with Mr. Kickoeffer (Executive Vice President) and Mr. Ramsey (Vice President — Packaging) on Friday about objectives for settlement and where we stand.

Armstrong: Right now my objectives for a settlement are coming down to eight percent in wages. Maybe I'm too optimistic — it's still too early.

Meeting with Vice Presidents

It was Friday, September 3. The following Tuesday, another bargaining session would be held. A week from then the contract would expire. Clive Armstrong sat down with his immediate superior, Executive Vice President William Kickhoeffer, and Noel Ramsey, Vice President of Packaging, to discuss the negotiations.

Armstrong reported that recent wage settlements in the area had been in the eight to ten percent range. However, he was concerned that his own superiors might be willing to go higher.

The executives expressed reluctance to dig in their toes and fight for a low settlement. They conceded that anything above 15 percent was out of the question, but there were indications that they would give in to 12 or even 15 percent settlement if faced with a strike. However, the men did not take a firm position in the matter; rather they decided to wait until the union put forth an initial demand before deciding on an economic limit.

The men decided to make a preliminary study of their situation should a strike be necessary. They did not want to stockpile. Staff personnel were assigned the task of discovering which major commodities could be produced at their other plants and in what quantities. They knew that there was little extra capacity elsewhere. There was some concern whether the unions in other plants would accept the work. It was hoped the study would be completed by September 10, the day when an executive meeting was scheduled to discuss the progress of the negotiations.

Items for Discussion

1. Evaluate Armstrong's assessment of the union's position regarding priority of demands. Do you share his belief that parity for women was most important and that Sheehan was backing down on pensions?
2. How should an appropriate economic package be determined?
3. Beyond what limits would you advise management to take a strike?
4. What, if any, preparations should be made for a strike?

McDONALD CONTAINERS LTD. (F)

SIXTH SESSION

On Tuesday, September 7, the bargaining resumed. Sheehan informed Armstrong that formal application had been made to the Ontario Labour Relations Board for conciliation. Mr. Noel Ramsey, Vice President, attended the session all day.

Daniel Burgess gave the union a list of tentative non-monetary agreements reached so far. Sheehan stated he was still not fully in accord with the changes in method of overtime allocation. He informed the company that another IPPU local had a workable arrangement which might resolve the difficulty and promised to distribute a copy of this agreement later in the day. Otherwise, he said the union felt the language changes were acceptable.

Some additional items concerning wage adjustments were discussed. Most were detailed, but minor, changes. Some tentative agreements were reached.

A representative from another life insurance company joined the meeting to answer some additional questions concerning pensions.

Sheehan (u): What would it cost to provide the present pension benefits to employees not presently enrolled in the plan?

Russell (insurance co): It would cost the company an additional $17,280.

Burgess (co): This, combined with the present cost of roughly $37,440, would make the total company contributions $54,720. This is 13.1 cents per hour.

Sheehan (u): Are the costs different between deposit administration and guaranteed annuity types?

Russell (insurance co): Both cost the same amount.

Armstrong (co): Remember, we won't negotiate benefits, just cost, George, and it will come off the wage settlement.

Sheehan (u): Well, we agree that the company must know what any plan will cost and that it should be fixed. We also know it will be part of the economic package and consequently would affect the wage increase. I think we should hold this matter.

Mr. Russell was excused at this point.

Sheehan (u): Clive, this guy is just selling life insurance. I recommend getting a third party, a consultant, in to advise us on the best way to spend our money.

Armstrong (co): It is probably the best thing to do if we want to change the pension plan, but I'm not paying for a consultant.

That afternoon, Armstrong reviewed the position of the St. Catharines plant in terms of industry wage rates and Niagara Peninsula area industrial wage rates.

Armstrong (co): Our divison's wage rates are substantially higher than our major competitors' in Toronto, even considering the fact that the major competitors have recently concluded union negotiations. We are below the Niagara area rates, but we can't compete effectively if we try to meet those rates. Mr. Ramsey, the Vice President of Packaging, can give a more detailed picture of our competitive position.

Ramsey (co): This division is experiencing severe competition in all sales areas. General sales lost so far this year, compared to last year, amount to approximately $1,500,000. This represents 18,000 hours of lost machine activity. Specialty rates are experiencing severe competition. American imports threaten the future growth of three of our most important product lines.

Sheehan (u): The union recognizes the problems the company is experiencing. However, your employees have a problem of their own, and they have their own responsibilities to meet. We expect a fair and reasonable settlement based on other settlements in the community. If this results in lost business and lay-offs of employees, it cannot be helped.

Discussion continued. Ramsey emphasized his figures with charts. The union bargaining committee sat quietly. Sheehan was more formal than usual, apparently out of respect for the presence of the Vice President.

As the meeting ended, one of the union bargaining committee members was overheard by Armstrong as he said to a colleague: "Well, it was the same old record over again. More crying."

Armstrong drove Ramsey home and dropped in for awhile to discuss the day's bargaining.

Armstrong: Well, I guess that's it until conciliation. No meeting is set. I'm fed up with having to remind them there's more business to get cleared up — we still have a lot of wage adjustment to talk about.

Ramsey: Sheehan is a bright negotiator, seems to have the committee in control.

Armstrong: Right, but he was formal today — trying to impress everyone.

Ramsey: Relations still seem to be good, no threats and flares of temper.

(Phone rings)

Ramsey: For you Clive — it's Fred Lundberg (Personnel Manager).

Armstrong: Hi, Fred. What's up?

Lundberg: Listen Clive, Walt Stevens grabbed me after the meeting. They want to meet again. They said next Tuesday the 14th, to clear outstanding non-monetary things.

Armstrong: I guess they need time to do their homework. Thanks.

Clive Armstrong left shortly thereafter. The next day, he reviewed what had transpired over the past day or two and began to plan for the next week:

> I guess we didn't really accomplish much out of the wage discussions — they think we're crying wolf. The quarterly report is coming out next month showing a profit decline — maybe it will emphasize our problems.

> I still want to get Sheehan to put something on the table — a real wage demand. So far he's trying to get us to agree to some side issues which involve money and then build on top of it. We can't fall into that trap.

We will have to outwait Sheehan. If we put some offer out before conciliation, that will be where we start to negotiate from. It is best to hold off — let Sheehan make a ridiculously high demand and then reply really low.

When it comes to fringes, we will have to watch not to give them their pick. Better fringes, especially vacations and holidays, will have to be applied elsewhere in the plant and may spread to other plants if we give them here. We can't go too much out of line.

Next week we'll have to meet with our own bargaining committee about the wage adjustments to decide where we stand. I can't try to defend something that just isn't defensible, as we did with some of the foremen's ideas.

On Monday, September 13, the day before the contract officially expired, Clive Armstrong received a copy of a request for conciliation filed by Sheehan on the 10th. A copy had been sent to him by Sheehan, but there was not yet an official notification from the Labour Department. Armstrong wondered whether the union had, in fact, made application.

In the afternoon, Armstrong met with the company's executive committee to relate negotiation progress. He informed the committee of data from recent newspaper clippings indicating the union had demanded increases of from 7.6 to 9.6 percent in wages. He expressed the belief that the union would settle for about nine percent, and he encouraged intensification of the study of available capacity in the case of a strike.

In the meeting, the executives arrived at a general set of goals — to settle between eight and ten percent total package. While Armstrong would try for a lower settlement, he knew he might have to accept something higher. The executives had not set an upper limit.

Armstrong reflected on what might happen, although he knew it would be close to a month before a legal strike could be held:

I'm not really pleased at the prospect of settling high. The company might be willing to take a short-term loss of profits in order to secure its competitive position in the long term. Yet we can't continue settling higher than our competitors indefinitely.

It's hard to tell at what point Sheehan would go on strike. He would have to know we were serious. He'll test us in case we're bluffing. If we threaten him, we will have to be willing to carry it through. If Sheehan knows we mean it, he might go to the membership and sell our best offer. But we have to be willing to risk it.

That afternoon, Armstrong was walking toward his office and met Michael Newman, a member of the bargaining committee. Both men stopped and said hello and talked briefly about the negotiations.

Armstrong: (co): These wage negotiations are quite confusing, with no one laying their cards on the table.

Newman (u): Right.

Armstrong (co): What would you do if you were me, Mike?

Newman (u): I don't know. You know Sheehan hasn't even told us what he thinks the wages should be.

Armstrong (co): Well how the hell is the company supposed to negotiate with you?

Items for Discussion

1. What is the significance of the union's apparent application for conciliation?
2. In apparently agreeing to discuss pension costs, has management strayed from its previously hard line regarding discussion of monetary items?
3. Comment on Ramsey's presence and presentation of financial information.
4. Is there significance to Armstrong's conversation with Newman?
5. What's the significance of the union's desire to meet on September 14?

McDONALD CONTAINERS LTD. (G)

FINAL MEETING BEFORE CONCILIATION

The next day, September 14, the company received official notice that the union had applied for conciliation. The contract's expiration date was midnight, but the law required that it continue in force until exhaustion of conciliation procedures. Similarly, a legal strike could not take place until conciliation procedures had been completed.

The union began the meeting by agreeing to the company proposal concerning allocation of vacations.

Then, they thrashed out the question of how to allocate overtime. George Sheehan put forth a compromise plan used by another firm: this, in spite of the fact that the union had tentatively agreed to the company proposal on overtime at the first meeting. The compromise would have required assignment and sharing among workers normally doing the work on the shift.

Armstrong (co): I don't disagree with the arrangement you propose, George. But it is going to take some time to get it implemented. We'll have to explain it to the foremen and make sure it is understood. It will probably be easier to solve it as we proposed.

Sheehan (u): Well, I disagree. Once you get it in, it will solve the overtime question once and for all.

Armstrong (co): Okay, it's agreed as long as we add that one stipulation we mentioned.

Chelekian (u): What about how I got cut out of overtime a few years ago. . . .

The discussion on overtime continued between Sheehan and Armstrong. Chelekian continued talking about a personal problem which had happened years ago. Ralph Reed made a sarcastic remark. Laughter broke out on both sides of the table until Chelekian flushed. He lost his temper and, for some reason, chose Dan Burgess as a target for venting his emotion.

Chelekian (u): Okay, Burgess. I'll get you. You're going to have grievances coming out your ears.

Stevens (u): Shut up, Harry!

Chelekian (u): You too Stevens; I'll deal with you at lunch.

A pause of stifled snickering and pursed lips lasted momentarily. Although such asides had been frequent regarding Chelekian, they had not reached such a peak of emotion before.

Sheehan (u): It's agreed then. I'd like to move on to other areas on which we can agree.

Both sides made further comments on other items which had not been settled.

Sheehan (u): We can't agree to delete the word "willing" regarding changing jobs because of lay-off.

Armstrong (co): If it's left in, the man cannot get unemployment insurance.

Sheehan (u): That doesn't matter—he should get it whether he is willing or not willing to take a poorer job when he's laid off. It's his choice. The unemployment people should only be concerned whether the man is working.

Armstrong (co): That's not how it works in reality.

Sheehan (u): It doesn't matter. We don't want it out of the contract. It would mean a man would have to take a lower classification job instead of taking a lay-off.

Armstrong (co): We have to tell the unemployment people he was unwilling to do so if it's still in the contract. It's to your advantage to take it out George.

No agreement was reached on this issue. The parties then agreed to some minor wage adjustments and language changes. Then the question of wage parity was brought up.

Sheehan (u): I have been mandated by my female constituents to reach wage and benefits parity between men and women. Thus the female rates have to be raised to the equivalent male rates. The Employment Standards Act says that all jobs of equivalent value have to be paid the same rate.

Armstrong (co): That's not true—we have the Act right here. It states that the criteria for establishing equal pay for equal work depends upon equal skills, effort, and responsibility. Not many female jobs are equal to the male jobs here.

Sheehan (u): It doesn't matter about the wording—I have a mandate. It's not a bargainable issue. We must have it.

Armstrong (co): To do this would cost about $87,400 or 21 cents per hour. I hope the men will understand that the women will get all the wage increases this year.

Sheehan (u): That's a consideration, but you have to do it anyway. The government will make you do it. It's not really a cost of this settlement.

Armstrong (co): Well, I've told you before—get the Department of Labour in here to look at the jobs. We won't have to raise them as you claim.

Sheehan (u): I don't want to get the government in. We don't want to get involved in legal process, Clive. We can work this out together.

Armstrong (co): It costs too much. The company can't afford it.

Ramsey (co): It will mean more lost sales, less work, and lay-offs.

Sheehan (u): The union is prepared to have the cost spread over the length of the contract. We want this. It is a policy of the International to eliminate wage differentials between male and female jobs. If this results in lost business and lost jobs, it is of no concern of the union.

The bargainers then turned to the question of married women's benefits.

Sheehan (u): We've been over this one before. It is another mandate issue.

Alice Melvin (u): It's unfair that I should not get married benefits the same as a man.

Armstrong (co): It costs too much.

Sheehan (u): How much?

Burgess (co): This demand to increase welfare coverage from single to married for married females would be $30,500.

Sheehan (u): Those figures are wrong.

After some discussion, the union conceded that Daniel Burgess's figures were correct.

A lunch break was held. Just as the company team left the room, Harry Chelekian accosted Walter Stevens. Their voices rose to shouts in the first outward display of temper among members of the union team.

In the afternoon, Clive Armstrong tried to get a more definite idea of the union's wage demands. For the first time, the voices of the bargainers on both sides were edged with tension and excitement.

Armstrong (co): Why can't you tell me what you want? Is it a big dark secret?

Sheehan (u): Why should I tell you?

Armstrong (co): How can we cost anything?

At this point, Clive Armstrong, his eyes alive, directed most of his remarks to the union bargaining committee, particularly Michael Newman, and not to the chief negotiator, George Sheehan.

Armstrong (co): I've got the Vice President here — he has a right to know. How can we do our costing — how can we negotiate with you unless we know your demands?

Sheehan (u): Okay. Would it make you happy if I said $2.10 over two years?

Armstrong (co): Yes. It's better than 2 bucks.

Sheehan (u) (pulling out a publication from his notes and plopping it on the table): This is a recent publication from the Economics and Research Branch of Labour Canada. This states that for the first quarter of the year, there was a 9.1 percent change in negotiated base rates. Does that give you an idea?

Armstrong (co): Is that your demand?

Sheehan (u): We aren't committed to anything — this figure represents federal increases, not area or provincial ones, which, as you know, are higher.

Armstrong (co): Like 9.6 percent or thereabouts?

The negotiations turned back to the female parity questions for the rest of the afternoon. As the negotiating session ended, George Sheehan made a closing comment:

Sheehan (u): As you know, we have applied for conciliation. The next meeting will be held with the officer. Our approach at conciliation will be not to tell the conciliation officer anything and to encourage him to hand down a no-board report so that we can enter serious negotiations afterwards. We will reach a satisfactory settlement on our own.

REFLECTIONS

Armstrong considered the September 14 meeting.

> I am quite pleased with the non-monetary agreements. The overtime settlement is really good. It's more than we wanted. It's good because it specifically outlines a method of allocating the overtime. The only agreement which may require some ironing out is the vacation scheme. But even that is okay.
>
> It would have been better if we could take "willing" out of the contract, but that's really to their advantage. I can't see why Sheehan disagreed with it. Originally, he asked me to take it out.
>
> The parity issue is becoming tough. However, I think Sheehan is bluffing about its importance. He just wants to be a champion to the International, because it is one of their policies. We can't afford it, and the men won't accept all the wages going to the women. Furthermore, Sheehan wouldn't have a leg to stand on if he did call the Labour Department in. I'm told there is a great deal of difference in almost all the jobs. I'm going to go into the plant in the next few days and do some of these jobs myself. I'll get a better idea of the differences, and maybe I'll stir something up.
>
> I was pleased that I got a more concrete wage demand out of Sheehan. I don't think he planned to put anything on the table at all. That chance meeting with Newman must have riled the committee up. They probably put some pressure on Sheehan to show himself. I'm sure he showed his hand before he wanted to.
>
> As far as that conciliation speech, I think he's joking. We'll settle it at conciliation.

The next day, September 15, the contract had expired. Nevertheless, its terms would be kept in force until there was either agreement on a new contract or a strike. On the 15th, Armstrong went into the plant and performed some of the female and male jobs in question. He became more certain of the company's position on this issue because of it. He was also intrigued by the reaction of the workers.

Female Worker: Why are doing this, Mr. Armstrong—you're not going to put men on our jobs are you?

Armstrong: No, I just want to see what the work is like after all the years I've been around here.

At a male work station, a worker asked a similar question: "You aren't going to put a girl on this job? You know they just couldn't handle it!"

Union Membership Meeting

On Sunday, September 19, the union membership met. Attendance was good. First, George Sheehan discussed the progress of negotiations and described some of the demands. He stated that while he felt the pension plan presently covering the employees was not adequate, an improvement in the plan would be extremely costly. There was no apparent reaction to this from the rank and file.

However, when Sheehan commented on the female wage parity issue, there was an uproar. Many men protested that the demands would help only women and take money out of the men's pockets. The argument continued for some time.

A strike vote was taken. It was passed by a huge majority. Then the membership voted in a new executive.

Alice Melvin, the female member of the bargaining committee, was elected president. The other members were newcomers. None of the old guard (not even Walter Stevens) were elected.

Clive Armstrong heard about the meeting through the grapevine. Some workers had come to him to complain about the parity issue, claiming they weren't in favour of it. Armstrong discovered that Alice Melvin had made remarks to employees at the meeting that she was not in favour of pushing the wage parity issue. Armstrong felt this reflected the females' fear that they would have to do male jobs if equal wages were paid. He thought his visit to the plant had had its effect.

Quarterly Report

The company's quarterly report was normally published on October 15 and sent to all employees. However, on Monday, September 20, there was an article in the *St. Catharines Times* speculating on the company's expected performance and reporting parts of an interview with McDonald's President. The President said there had been a dip in profits to $998,000 in the first two quarters of the year and that in the same period last year, profits were $1,097,000. However, he indicated that the third quarter of the current year would be somewhat improved over last year and that the full year would be only slightly below last year, barring unforeseen events.

Armstrong, on seeing the article said: "This makes us look a little silly. Ramsey and I have been telling them of our terrible situation, and now the President says we're looking pretty good."

ARMSTRONG RE-EVALUATES HIS SITUATION

Armstrong was still concerned about the effect of the President's statement:

> The whole thing is timing. When we start sawing off around six percent, it is going to matter who can wait it out longest. It will be tense, and I decided that I need a definite outside limit from the executive. As a result, we've beefed up the study we are doing. Only head office personnel are doing it. They are now figuring out if we can get competitors to supply some of our customers in case of a strike as well as using the extra capacity at our other plants. We are also finding out our fixed costs if there is a strike.

> We should have this information for the executive meeting the 24th of September. We've decided to consider the possibility of having to take a

strike. This may not be the year to get tough, but at least we're considering all the options. I'd like to set a total package limit of 10 percent a year.

We aren't going to make any of our moves obvious. We don't want to threaten the union — we may end up with a walkout. We just want to be prepared.

As chief negotiator, I feel much better about these negotiations with the union. My boss is trying to give me all the leverage he can. At the final meeting, I expect both the V.P.s (Kickhoeffer and Ramsey) will be there to show they're behind me all the way.

As far as the conciliation meeting is concerned, it's a little early to tell. I doubt if I'll make an offer for awhile. Hopefully, Sheehan will zero in on demands first. However, I expect to settle it with the conciliator. It may take a couple of meetings.

I'm not afraid of having a settlement overthrown by the membership unless we gave too little in wages to the men by agreeing to female parity. I doubt if this would happen. Sheehan must be concerned about the whole question. He must be feeling some pressure after that membership meeting.

Items for Discussion

1. Comment on Sheehan's apparent change in tactics.
   (a) His desire to retain the present wording regarding a laid-off employee's "willingness" to do a job.
   (b) His apparently premature statement regarding an economic package.
2. Comment on Armstrong's handling of the male/female parity issue. Sheehan claims this is not bargainable. What position would you take?
3. Do you share Armstrong's concern regarding the effect of the president's remarks?
4. What are prospects for settlement without a strike?
5. How do you account for the apparent difference in stated opinions regarding the conciliation process? Sheehan said he would be using it to set a deadline so that the parties could start bargaining. Armstrong said he expected to secure a settlement during conciliation.
6. Comment on the pros and cons of the Ontario law which requires that a contract must stay in force even after expiration unless parties have admitted to conciliation.

McDONALD CONTAINERS LTD. (H)

GOAL SETTING AND PREPARATION FOR CONCILIATION

On September 20, the Ontario Labour Relations Board notified the company and the union that Mr. John Crowley had been designated as conciliator and would meet with the parties on Wednesday, September 29, in accordance with Section 13 of the Labour Relations Act.

The Act required the conciliator to endeavour to effect a collective agreement and, within 14 days of his appointment, report the results to the Ministry of Labour. The 14-day period could be extended by agreement of the parties or by the Minister on advice of the conciliation officer that an agreement be made within a reasonable time. If the conciliation officer was unable to effect a settlement, he was required to report this fact to the Minister who then could take either of two steps: initiate procedures for formulation of a three-man conciliation board, or notify the parties that he did not deem it advisable to appoint a board.

In recent years, instances where conciliation boards were appointed under Section 16 of the Act were rare. Neither the company nor the union expected a board to be created in the McDonald case, so that failure to settle under auspicies of the conciliator would most likely result in the establishment of a strike deadline. According to the Act, a legal strike or lockout could commence 14 days after the Minister released a notice to the parties that he did not deem it advisable to appoint a conciliation board.

Clive Armstrong had experienced conciliation with Mr. John Crowley in connection with earlier negotiations at another plant. The experience was not good. Consequently, Armstrong did not have high expectations of a settlement as a result of the conciliation meeting and prepared himself and his bargaining committee for continuing negotiations after conciliation under the sceptre of a strike deadline.

Company Executive Meeting

On Wednesday, September 22, the top executives of McDonald Containers met to consider a then-secret study which had been prepared by the staff personnel at the head office. The study substantiated an already existing feeling that the company could not withstand a strike of more than one month. Other McDonald plants were operating at near capacity, and they were considered a poor source of alternate service to the St. Catharines plant customers. Competitors would willingly take up slack, but the risk of losing customers to those competitors in such a case was considered high. Thus the division made tentative arrangements (unknown to operating personnel in St. Catharines) that in the event of a strike, some key customers would be served by competitors who were located outside the St. Catharines market area. The added cost in freight charges would hopefully make the alternate suppliers unattractive for any long-term relationship, but acceptable for a month or so. Even with these elaborate arrangements, management feared that a strike of more than a month would result in a significant loss of business.

In the event of a strike, it would be necessary to lay off workers who were not members of IPPU. The company decided that welfare and insurance premiums would be continued for those employees. All these plans were made with utmost secrecy. Futhermore, no one in the company wanted or expected a strike. However, there were limits beyond which they were not willing to go. These were set tentatively at 10 percent per year in wages and fringes. If it became obvious that the union would hold firm for a settlement exceeding 10 percent, the company would "pull the plug" and activate strike plans.

CLIVE ARMSTRONG'S THOUGHTS

The rumour mill indicated to Armstrong that union membership was not willing to go on strike. However, originators of these rumours were considered apple polishers; so Armstrong greeted the information with skepticism. He did not feel that membership interest in the negotiations was meagre — that Alice Melvin's election as union president was a sign of apathy. Melvin had been the only serious candidate. Old-guard leaders had dropped from the scene, and younger people had not come to the fore to replace them. This apathy had been demonstrated a few days earlier when Walter Stevens, a member of the old guard and former union Vice President, contacted Daniel Burgess regarding a matter of contract administration. Stevens had no authority to do this, but the matter was pressing, and no one else took the reins.

Plans for Conciliation Meeting

Armstrong wanted to get a signed contract during the conciliation meetings, but he was apprehensive about the reaction of Sheehan to Crowley. During the negotiations of four years ago, a weak conciliator had been assigned. Sheehan promptly contacted the head of the conciliation service and arranged for a replacement — William Tunney. Tunney was able to win the confidence of both sides, and a settlement was reached in a single meeting.

Armstrong did not expect Sheehan to call for another conciliator this time. Rather, he expected that Sheehan would make a monetary appearance in order to establish a strike deadline; then he would negotiate. If Sheehan followed this tactic, Armstrong would make a token economic offer. Following this, Armstrong would look for a counterdemand. If there was no counterdemand, Armstrong would refuse to negotiate further and let the deadline move nearer, thus putting pressure on the union.

Armstrong believed Sheehan wanted a wage settlement between 8.1 and 9.6 percent. If the fringe demand was fairly low, the prospects for a less-than-10-percent settlement seemed good.

Armstrong believed that the company would gain most by waiting, and he hoped for settlement terms of less than 10 percent. He believed there was some chance that Sheehan would try to bargain privately—outside the presence of his bargaining committee. Armstrong would resist this, believing the waiting game would have the greatest impact if members of the shop committee felt responsible themselves for the consequences. Sheehan could maintain strength while waiting; shop committee members might not be able to.

Agreement on Non-monetary Items

On September 24 at 2:00 p.m. a meeting took place for the purpose of affixing signature to non-monetary agreements reached so far. Members of both bargaining committees were present. This supposedly left only the money items to be discussed.

Items for Discussion

1. Comment on the conciliation procedure under the Act. As a negotiator, how would this procedure influence your actions?
2. Comment on Armstrong's strategy. Under what conditions is a deadline useful in securing a settlement?
3. Comment on the company's strategy in planning for a possible strike. As a company negotiator, would you feel better or worse knowing that the contingency strike plans had been made?
4. Comment on the strategy of setting upper limits in advance on economic settlement terms. Do these unnecessarily hamper the negotiating team?

McDONALD CONTAINERS LTD. (I)

CONCILIATION, MEMORANDUM OF AGREEMENT AND RATIFICATION

Mr. John Crowley was appointed by the Ontario Labour Relations Board to meet with the parties as conciliator and attempt to effect a settlement. Crowley reserved a meeting room at St. Catharines' Thunderbird Inn and asked the parties to assemble at 10:30 a.m. on Wednesday, September 29.

The union and company bargaining teams arrived at the appointed hour. Mr. Crowley appeared approximately 45 minutes later, having called before to tell the parties that he'd been in an automobile accident. When he arrived, he indicated that he did not want the parties to meet together. So the company team departed to a room in the inn which they had reserved for themselves. Crowley then met with the union alone. This meeting lasted until shortly before noon.

At around noon, Crowley met with the company. He said he wanted to find out what their attitude was: whether they were there to get a settlement or not. Clive Armstrong stated the position taken by Sheehan earlier — that the reason he was going to conciliation was to set a deadline and get both sides negotiating. Armstrong then said: "If Mr. Sheehan has come to make an agreement, then we've come to make an agreement, but it's imperative that you find out from him what he did come here for."

Crowley (conciliator): Now look. Sheehan said you hadn't come up with any offer.

Armstrong (co): That's right!

Crowley (conciliator): Are you prepared to?

Armstrong (co): If you can determine whether Sheehan is here to make a deal or just go through these formalities, then we'll know where we stand.

Crowley said he would go back to Sheehan. The company negotiators then went to the dining room for lunch.

After lunch, the conciliator came back to the company negotiators and said that the union representatives were there to make a settlement if possible.

Armstrong (co): All right, give us some time and we'll make up a proposal.

Crowley had a list of items given to him by Sheehan which he said were still outstanding, and he gave this to Armstrong. There were 23, including all previous monetary demands and 5 non-monetary demands, the most important of which were:

1. Probationary employees shall have the right to grieve.
2. The union will have the right to grieve anything. (Sheehan had indicated earlier the kind of things he had in mind here. One such grievance might involve the company's right to discontinue an operation.)

About one hour later, at approximately 3:00 p.m., the company presented Crowley with a revised proposal on money items. The company offered to pay 100 percent of Ontario Health Insurance premiums. This was estimated to cost about $15,000 or 3.6 cents per hour. However, the company wanted to confine premium obligations for Ontario Health Insurance coverages to the existing maxima, so that in the event of premium increases, there would be no automatic requirement to pay the added amount. The company offered to replace the major medical plan with an improved plan under which the employee would pay the first $25 plus 10 percent of the remaining costs. The existing plan provided for single employees to pay the first $25 and those with families to pay the first $50. In addition, the existing plan required the employees to pay 20 percent of the added costs. This change would cost about 2 cents per hour.

Wages were tied in with increased vacation benefits and increased life insurance coverage as part of the two-year package. In the first year, there would be a 32-cents-per-hour wage increase. In the second year, there would be 28 cents coupled with four weeks' vacation for those with 15 years seniority (the existing contract called for four weeks after 16 years) and an offer to increase life insurance by $1000 for all people. The vacation and life insurance improvements were estimated to cost about 10 cents.

The conciliator took the company offer away with him and returned at 5:20 p.m. with a union counteroffer. The union offered to withdraw all non-monetary items. Regarding monetary items, they wanted the following:

1. Wages (per hour increases)

Effective Date	Males	Females
Date of Contract signing	.80	.90
One year later	.75	.85

2. Individual wage adjustments ranging from 10 to 30 cents in four job classifications.

3. Improved vacations as follows:

Year 1		Year 2	
Weeks	Seniority (years)	Weeks	Seniority
3	6	3	5
4	13	4	13
5	20	5	20

The union had withdrawn their earlier request for a $25 vacation bonus. The existing contract called for the following vacation schedule:

Years Service	Weeks Vacation
1	1
2	2
7	3
16	4
21	5

4. Holidays — one additional holiday to be taken at employee's discretion.
5. Premium for power house employees — $1 per hour for Sunday work. This was a reduction from the union's earlier demand for Sunday overtime rates for power house employees.
6. Insurance premium reduction — the union asked for a letter of intent indicating that any future reduction in Ontario Hospital or Health premiums would be paid to the employee as part of added wages.
7. Life insurance coverage — one and a half times the annual wage. The existing plan called for life insurance coverage of $5,000 for all females and between $5,000 and $10,000 for all male employees, the latter based on a graduated scale related to earnings.
8. Drug costs — complete coverage for drug costs after initial deductible amounts of $10 under single coverage and $20 under family coverage.
9. Increased weekly indemnity — sickness and accident benefits ($200 to $300 per week on a scale in accordance with wages) increased from 26 weeks to 52 weeks.
10. Breadwinner clause — family coverage for hospital and health insurance to married women on the same basis as for married men.
11. Pensions — monthly benefits equivalent to one percent of the average yearly earnings for the best five years of an employee's service, employees to contribute 50 percent of the cost.

The pension demand, estimated by the union to cost $60,000, caught company negotiators by surprise. Armstrong knew the estimated cost was low, because he had done some earlier figuring in anticipation of a demand for a non-contributory plan. At the time he discovered that contributory plans were more expensive than non-contributory plans, because they allowed for payment to those who separated from the plan before receiving benefits. Armstrong subsequently met with Sheehan and pointed this out. Sheehan said: "Yes, I know. I wanted to see if you were still awake!" This remark confirmed Armstrong's earlier belief that Sheehan was trying to give him a message: that he realized pensions were expensive and that union members were not going to pay for improved benefits. Consequently, he believed the issue was merely window dressing.

Company's Counteroffer

Early that evening, the company prepared a counteroffer and gave it to Mr. Crowley for conveyance to the union negotiators. It contained the following concessions:
1. Vacations — four weeks vacation after 14 years seniority.
2. Welfare — 100 percent payment for coverage under the Ontario Health Insurance Plan, with provision that premiums per month be spelled out, thereby averting the obligation to pay for increased premiums. The counteroffer did not include a limit on premiums for Ontario Health Services. So, by inference, this proviso was dropped.

3. Individual adjustments — the company agreed to increase the wage rate of the diemaker lead hand by ten cents, letting it be known that this was done to accommodate one of the members of the bargaining committee, Michael Newman, a diemaker lead hand who, according to Armstrong, was "obviously bargaining for himself." Armstrong told the conciliator that he believed the men who really deserved an increase were the diemakers, and if the negotiators were doing their job properly, they would have requested an increase for them, not for themselves. Armstrong asked the conciliator to convey this information to Sheehan.
4. Wages — effective on ratification:

Year 1	Males	Females
effective on ratification	.46	.48
Year 2		
one year after ratification	.43	.45

No further offer was made on other union demands. Regarding pension, Armstrong was convinced that if the company waited long enough, the demand would be dropped, because any form of increase would cut so deeply into wages that it would be distasteful.

Conciliator Calls Armstrong and Sheehan Together

At about 8:00 p.m. John Crowley, the conciliator, asked the two principal bargainers to meet in Crowley's room. When Armstrong arrived, he found Sheehan lying on one of the beds, looking sick. Sheehan said: "Clive, what'll we do? We're not getting any place!" Sheehan said he was having trouble with his own committee — that they needed to have at least $1.50 in wages over the two-year contract period. Sheehan said he believed the company was prepared to go as high as $1.60. Armstrong said $1.60 was too much.

Sheehan (u): Let's get down to brass tacks here. What do these things cost you? For example, one of the places we're really far apart on is vacations. The cost of vacations is important; what would it be?

Armstrong (co): Off the top of my head, I don't know.

Sheehan (u): What about the cost of female adjustments? We've got to bring these females' rates up. We're behind the community.

Sheehan conceded that pensions were too expensive but indicated the issue was still alive. Armstrong suggested consideration of a pension plan similar to the type adopted by the automobile industry — a certain benefit amount per month. The two men then considered the cost of such a plan and agreed that 24 cents per hour would buy benefits amounting to approximately $12.00 per month. With that, Sheehan seemed to lose interest.

Armstrong then agreed to calculate costs on the items still outstanding. He said it would take a couple of hours.

11:00 P.M.

At 11:00 p.m. Armstrong returned to the conciliator's room, with estimated costs for each of the union demands. Costs were stated in cents-per-hour equivalents. Excluding the demand for pensions, the total calculated costs were estimated by the company at 85.1 cents for the first year and 79.9 cents for the second year — a total of $1.65. Sheehan looked over the figures and attacked those ascribed to vacations, calculated by the company as 9 cents in the first year ($37,500 total) and 8 cents additional in the second year ($33,000). Sheehan said: "You don't replace men on vacation!" Armstrong explained that the company hired between 40 and 60 students each summer for this purpose, that he was not prepared to back off one nickel. He conceded that his figure was a maximum, but indicated the parties could stay for three weeks trying to arrive at the correct figure. Sheehan then attacked the company's figure for the "breadwinner" clause, stating that all women would not take advantage of it. This had been calculated at 4 cents per hour ($16,000).

Armstrong (co): What should (the figure) be?

Sheehan (u): We were just going through a list of all the women we have now, and it's not nearly that high.

Armstrong (co): Do you guarantee that they're going to be here for two years? All of them? The same people? The same status? None of them are going to get married?

At this point, Sheehan looked sicker than before.

Armstrong (co): Are you all right?

Sheehan (u): I'm just tired.

Armstrong (co): The total figure is $1.65, without pensions.

Sheehan (u): Is that out of the ball park?

Armstrong, then feeling strong, resorted to some propaganda, saying: "If you stick to this position, you'll find the company acting different than before."

Sheehan (u): What are you planning to do out there? Are you planning to close the place down?

Armstrong (co): No, we're not planning to, George, but we're not prepared to take a shellacking from you people every year, either!

According to Armstrong, the statement seemed to sink in — "the first time in all of these years!"

Sheehan (u): I want to go back and talk to my committee.

The conciliator, meanwhile, was exhibiting impatience — saying he had to get to Toronto for a meeting the next day. Sheehan, obviously irritated, said: "John, a poor excuse is better than none at all."

As Armstrong and Sheehan left the conciliator's room, Sheehan confided even more irritation with the conciliator, calling him a "damned liar" and saying that he didn't believe Crowley had an appointment the next day or that he'd had an automobile accident earlier in this day.

12:05 A.M.

Sheehan and Armstrong met again in the conciliator's room. At this point, the three men agreed that all bargaining was unofficial — that the official last offer would be made at the bargaining table.

Sheehan (u): How would you look at this, Clive?

And he put forth the following proposal:

Wages	*Males*	*Females*
Date of contract signing	70 cents	75 cents
One year later	60 cents	65 cents

Year 1		Year 2	
Weeks	Seniority (years)	Weeks	Seniority
3	6	3	6
4	14	4	14
5	21	5	21

Welfare
An extended health care plan.

100 percent paid by company, no limit on premium, with $10 (single) and $20 (family) deductible features.

semi-private hospital benefits.

Life Insurance
Increases of $3,000 per person.

Sheehan indicated the union still wanted the breadwinner clause but that pension demands had been dropped.

Crowley, the conciliator, then attempted to explain to Armstrong how the company could afford the proposed package. He said, "Your average rate is $9.02 an hour. You've already established that your limit is 10 percent a year. That's 90 cents in the first year. If you add 90 cents to $9.02 you get $9.92. So next year you can afford 99 cents. So we're talking over two years about an increase of $1.89."

Armstrong (co): Thanks for your advice.

Crowley (conciliator): On top of that there won't be any increases in Ontario Health premiums anyway. I've got a line to the Premier on that.

Armstrong (co): Mind your own business.

Crowley (conciliator): You're getting tired, Clive.

Armstrong (co): I'm tired of your political philosophies, John.

Sheehan then jumped on Crowley as well, with additional invectives. Then the two men looked at each other with smiles and Armstrong said, "I'll take this away and do some costing. It looks like we're moving in the right direction."

Crowley (conciliator): I'm not going to stay much longer. You'll have to work this out yourselves or have another meeting.

Sheehan (to Crowley): Listen, I've spent all day with that committee, and I've battered them into this thing. They're not going to get away now if I have to stay here all night—or all day tomorrow either. What do you think, Clive?

Armstrong (co): George, if I have to stay here 'til Saturday, this is not going to slip through our hands at this point. (It was early Thursday morning.)

Crowley (conciliator): How 'bout next week?

Sheehan (u): The hell with next week! Right now!

Armstrong went back to his committee then and told them he believed settlement was near.

1:30 A.M.

At 1:30, Armstrong returned to the conciliator's room with what he considered his final, unofficial offer. He said to Sheehan: "This is as far as we can go, George. We've stretched all the pennies."

Armstrong agreed to the union proposal on wages. On vacations Armstrong said the best he could do was four weeks after 14 years in Year One of the contract and three weeks after 6 years in Year Two. He agreed with the union proposals on welfare coverage and, regarding the breadwinner clause, Armstrong said:

We will pay married coverage for females as far as Ontario Health Services are concerned.

Sheehan (u): Bullshit! I want equal treatment for females. For you to throw that in at this time is bullshit!

Armstrong and Sheehan then left the room to go back to their committees. Outside, on the patio next to the swimming pool, Sheehan took his leave. Just then John Crowley came across the patio, briefcase in hand. It was obvious he was leaving.

Crowley (conciliator): Well, the only thing you're apart on now is the breadwinner clause. If you solve that, you've got an agreement.

Armstrong (co): Where are you going?

Crowley (conciliator): I'm going home.

Armstrong (co): Well then, leave me some carbon paper and your forms.

Crowley reached into his briefcase and withdrew the official forms on which parties normally record their memorandum of agreement. He seemed to do this reluctantly. Then he left.

Armstrong noticed a shadow next to the pool. It was Sheehan.

Sheehan (to Armstrong): You go ahead and write up the memorandum.

Armstrong (co): What about this breadwinner's clause?

Sheehan (u): I have a principle to uphold.

Sheehan then complained bitterly about the conciliator. While Crowley had left the official memorandum forms, he had not signed them. The signature carried no official weight, but it could be important to Sheehan when the time came to try to sell the package to union members. Sheehan told Armstrong he was going to write to the Labour Minister to complain.

Armstrong then went back to his committee to have a last hard look at the costs. Then, at about 3:00 a.m., he went to Sheehan, and in the company of Walter Stevens of the union team, Armstrong wrote up the memorandum of agreement. The only change from the union's last proposal involved the following wording for a "breadwinner's" clause:

It is understood that female employees are not entitled to 100 percent coverage where husband's employer is paying for comparable coverage.

So at 3:30 a.m. on Thursday, September 30, the parties had an agreement. On the following Monday, October 4, the union members ratified it by a vote of 124 to 4. Final costs were estimated by Clive Armstrong at 64.5 cents in the first year, equivalent to $269,000, an increase of slightly more than 8.8 percent. In the second year, the added costs would be 57.5 cents, roughly $239,000. The average increase for each of the two years was estimated as 7.7 percent.

Items for Discussion

1. Evaluate the role of the conciliator. Did he aid or hinder the agreement?
2. Trace the shifting balance of power between chief negotiators as the final bargaining sessions progressed.
3. Evaluate the tactics of the chief negotiators. How might they have been more effective?
4. Evaluate the terms of settlement.

ADDINGTON CHEMICAL COMPANY

"Bill, you wanted a strike — and you've got it!"

These words were spoken by Jim Redford, the President of Local 99 of the United Steelworkers of America, which represented the 500 production maintenance workers at the Port Colborne plant of Addington Chemical Company. The date was December 14, 1983, and the time approximately 11:00 a.m. With that statement, the union negotiating team walked out of the conference room at which negotiations had been taking place. The first strike was in 1947, shortly after the plant was organized by the Steelworkers. The last strike had been in 1978.

After the union representatives had left the room, Bill Murrill, the Plant Manager, to whom the union's last comment had been addressed, turned to Herb Howells, the Manager of Operations, and said, "Well, *I* didn't want a strike, but if we're going to have one, I hope we're ready."

Howells said, "We're as ready as we can be. I'm afraid it won't be a short one."

Bill Walton, the plant's Employer Relations Manager and chief negotiator, stood up and said, "I'm afraid I agree with Herb. Should we take over the operation?"

"Right now," said Howells, "Everyone should be ready. All it will take is a phone call, and I'd better make it now." Howells headed for his office.

When he reached his office, Howells issued the order for supervisory personnel, about 170 in number, to take over the operation of the plant. This was the first step in a plan to operate the plant in the face of a strike that had been under development for over a year. As it had traditionally done, the union had set 12 noon as the strike deadline. Howells knew that they would not walk out prior to that time, but he wished to have operations in the hands of management personnel prior to the strike deadline so that any last minute attempts by employees at sabotage could be avoided. The management personnel had reported to the plant that morning at 8:00 a.m. in preparation for the takeover. They had been told to come prepared to stay in the plant for two weeks.

Howells knew that it was the union's practice to begin a strike with a mass picketing and that nothing could enter or leave the plant in the face of that picketing. He knew that it would take the company from 10 to 14 days to get an injunction against the mass picketing and that until the injunction was obtained, entrance to and egress from the plant would not be possible, except by helicopter. A helicopter had been chartered and was on standby at the Hamilton Airport.

The Port Colborne plant of Addington Chemical was located on the outskirts of the city of that name on the shores of Lake Erie. The plant produced four different chemical products, in four different production operations. By-products from the production of its main product were used in the production of the three other products manufactured at the site. The plant area was large, with almost 500 acres within the chainlink fence that surrounded the area. In addition to the main plant area, there were three satellite locations. One was the pump-house and water treatment facility from which water from Lake Erie was purified and then pumped to the plant. The second area, not far from the pump-house, was the dock where bulk commodities were unloaded from lake tankers and sent to the plant on a conveyor system. Both of these locations were within sight of the plant, but separated from it by a highway. The third location was about 10 kilometres from the plant, and was an open-pit mine, where one of the basic raw materials for the chemical process was obtained. This site, known as the Vaughn Mine, was over 700 acres in size. The mineral obtained from the site was mined, crushed, and then delivered to the plant in large trucks. The company did not plan to operate the mine and the crusher during the strike, as approximately two months' worth of production requirements for the basic raw materials had been stored at the plant site. The stockpiling of this raw material had been underway for a year.

Security at the Vaughn site was a major concern of Howells, though. He knew that it would be difficult to protect the site from physical entrance, even with the expanded security force that the company had engaged. The large earth movers which were used to move the ore to the crusher and then to load the ore onto the trucks cost one million dollars each, and were inviting targets for anyone who wished to do malicious damage. The four large tires on each vehicle cost ten thousand dollars apiece, and they could easily be damaged by someone who was determined to do so.

Local management had developed a plan to use guard dogs to protect the site but top management at headquarters in Calgary was still sitting on the request to employ the dogs. Corporate management was concerned about the company image should such dogs be employed.

The strike plan which Howells was working from had been developed by a planning group composed of representatives from the distribution, purchasing, employee relations, and production departments at the plant. It was quite detailed and its basic budget of $600,000 had been approved by top management. Following this approval, purchase orders for each item needed had been written and were released according to the sequence laid out in the plan. Each item on the plan had been assigned to a manager as his responsibility. The plan prepared for 1983 was the fourth version of the strike plan. The first one was prepared in 1977 when the company had experienced its last strike. That strike lasted for three weeks.

Collective agreements at the Port Colborne plant were traditionally of two years' duration. October 31 had been the expiry date for these agreements for some years, although negotiations almost always dragged on until after Christmas. For example, the strike at the end of the 1977 agreement did not start until mid-January of 1978. Given the time of contract expiry, developing a plan to keep the plant running was extremely critical. The Port Colborne plant, like many other chemical operations, was not easy to shut down at all, and shutdown at the time when freezing temperatures could be expected would be extremely dangerous in that the freezing of liquids in any part of the operation could cause severe and perhaps irreparable damage to the production facilities. In many areas of the plant, the only heat available was that generated by the production process. If product was not being manufactured, no heat would be available, and as a consequence, pipes, valves, and production vessels might be subject to the effects of freezing. In brief, the company *had* to keep the facility operating — at least at minimum levels of production.

One of the plant's production operations *could* be shut down, and the company planned to do so in the event of a strike, although supervisory personnel would have to be on hand to ensure that the shut-down was done properly so as to prevent any damage to equipment. Also, portable heaters for this and the other parts of the plant had to be set up.

The strike plan was a very detailed document, outlining all the actions which had to be taken before the arrival of a strike deadline. The timing of these actions was stated in terms of the number of days prior to a strike deadline by which a particular action step had to be completed. For example, the rate of production during a strike had to be determined well in advance, so that appropriate levels of raw materials could be on site before the strike deadline. Several of the raw materials came by ship and were delivered at the company's dock. Because shipping on the Great Lakes was often suspended by the time that the strike deadline arrived, these raw materials were normally stored in sufficient quantity for the entire winter on company premises. Another requirement which was influenced by production rates was the storage of completed products. Since the company could not expect to have any rail traffic out of the plant for two weeks after a strike started, sufficient hopper cars needed to be in place prior to the strike deadline to hold two weeks' worth of production of the plant's principal product. Some of the plant's output was stored in large storage tanks on the plant site, and thus storage facilities did not have to be acquired for all products. Finally, stores for parts used in mechanical and electrical repair had to be in stock since they could not be easily obtained in the face of picket lines.

Howells knew that the last of the necessary hopper cars had been brought in the day before from St. Catharines, and that sufficient capacity for two weeks of production at projected levels was available. After two weeks, the company's ability to handle and ship its products was a function of the behaviour of the courts and the police.

Howells knew that the law was very clear in regard to picketing. Picket lines were not allowed to impede access to or exit from the plant, and that a court injunction against mass picketing which did so was routinely available, although such injunctions did take from ten to fourteen days to acquire. Once the injunction had been received, however, the key to continued operation of the plant would be the behaviour of the police. If they did not enforce the injunction, continued operation would be difficult. In discussions with the local police chief, prior to the arrival of the strike deadline, the company had been assured that the chief of police was prepared to enforce the law.

That had not been the case during the last strike in 1978. The behaviour of the police at that time had been one of the reasons why the strike had not continued beyond three weeks.

Basic police protection in the immediate area of the plant was the responsibility of the township in which the plant was located. The police force of the township consisted of a chief and three constables. In 1977–78, the police chief was close to retirement, and was apparently not interested in facing any confrontation situations. In order for him to deal with incidences of mass picketing, he had to call on reinforcements from the Ontario Provincial Police, from the town of Port Colborne and other towns, such as St. Catharines or even Hamilton. To do so, he simply had to request such assistance, saying that he could not control the situation. The chief apparently was unwilling to make such a declaration and thus was unwilling to seek help from any outside agencies. The three available constables were unable to control a situation in which there might be one or two hundred pickets at the plant, and thus entrance to and exit from the plant was effectively blocked by the union in 1978. In fact, when the company would advise the police chief that a delivery was expected or that a shipment was going to be attempted, the chief would call the union hall and tell the union that such a shipment or receipt of materials was anticipated and that he did not want any trouble. Such a message guaranteed that the union would have sufficient pickets on hand to stop the delivery or the shipment.

The basic strike issue in the 1977–78 dispute was a long-term disability plan. The union had been urging such a plan for the two prior negotiations and had put the company on notice that acquiring a plan, even if it was employee-paid, was a strike issue in 1977–78. The company had resisted such a move because such plans were not found in the chemical industry. However, at the time of the strike in 1978, a proposal for a company-wide L.T.D. plan was in the final development stages before going to the Board of Directors for approval. In the face of this, the company could not see any good reason to allow the strike to continue, particularly in the face of a situation where materials and personnel could not easily be gotten into or out of the plant.

Howells would have to wait two weeks to discover whether the new police chief meant what he said about enforcing the law, though. In the meantime, he had to ensure that the plant was operating, and that there was no sabotage to the production operations. The strike plan had ensured that everything necessary to keep the plant operating for two weeks was on hand. The company had adequate supplies of gasoline and diesel fuel stores so as to ensure that no fuel tanks would have to cross a picket line even after an injunction had been obtained. A bulldozer, a cherry-picker crane, and a snowmobile had been rented and were on the plant site. Several tractor-trailer rigs containing supplies for the personnel who would be operating the plant had been brought onto the site during the week preceding the strike deadline. Their supplies included coveralls, parkas, and boots in the appropriate sizes for the personnel who were expected to be on the strike. Employees had been instructed to bring clothing to wear under these items when they came to the plant that morning. Also in the tractor-trailers were towels and bedding as well as washers and dryers so that work and other clothing could be laundered. The vans also contained television sets, as well as video recorders and a supply of feature movie films. The pumphouse had similarly been stocked with the appropriate provisions, although on a smaller scale.

A caterer and a crew of eight cooks had been engaged. They were in the plant prior to the strike deadline. The plant did not normally operate a hot food service, relying instead on vending machines, and thus stoves and refrigerators as well as cooking implements had also been set up. Refrigerator trucks with enough food for two weeks were also on the site. House trailers had been set up to provide sleeping accommodation and lounge facilities for the management personnel who would be operating the plant on twelve-hour shifts.

Howells believed that if management was to operate the plant for any length of time, it was necessary to ensure that the personnel operating the plant "feel good about what they are doing," and that what he called the "creature comforts" were well looked after. These were: 1) good food, 2) clean, dry clothes of company issue, 3) a good bed, and 4) adequate shower and sanitary facilities. An attempt by management to operate a plant at a company that Howells worked for earlier in his career had failed, he believed, largely because the company had not made adequate preparations for the comfort of the supervisory personnel who would be operating the plant. He was determined that that would not happen this year at Addington.

Background to the Dispute

The company had taken a different approach to the negotiations which began in October, 1983, than it had in prior years. This was the result of several factors. One of the factors was economic. For the first time in anyone's memory, a combination of reduced economic activity and price cutting by competition had created a situation where the company had decided that it had to face up to production inefficiencies that were a consequence of earlier management decisions.

The production inefficiencies had been in place for some time, stemming from the time when the plant was essentially a branch plant operation, run out of another company operation in Buffalo, New York. At that time, in the early sixties, it was believed that a newer production technology would make the plant obsolete. Until that technology became available, the company's main goal was to keep the plant running. A plant manager had been imported who was told to provide continuing operation at any cost. Subsequently, a combination of the failure of the new technology to produce the production efficiencies expected and new developments in the existing technology had meant that the Port Colborne plant was economically viable for the foreseeable future. A new local management team had been put in place and the branch plant status terminated. However, a number of inefficiencies remained, some of which the company was attempting to clear up.

A further source of difficulty with the Port Colborne operation was in the nature of its location and the international union which represented its employees. The company's operation was the only major chemical facility in the area, which was dominated by the steel-making operations of Dofasco and Stelco. The dominant union in the area was the United Steelworkers. Other chemical operations generally were organized by other unions such as the Energy and Chemical Workers Union, which did not have the steel industry and heavy manufacturing industry orientation of the Steelworkers. The Steelworkers often appeared to have expectations about wages and benefits that the company officials believed were unrealistic in terms of the chemical industry.

In 1983, given very tough economic times, many employers had set out to acquire changes in work rules and other concessions from their unions. Prior to the start of the 1983 negotiations at Addington Chemical, the Steelworkers had announced that they would not agree to any concessions. Throughout the period of negotiations employees could be seen in the plant wearing a badge stating "No Concessions."

The company did not intend to seek major concessions in work rules, but they were determined not to agree to any union demands which might reduce manufacturing efficiency. They also hoped to achieve some savings in the operation of the cost of living agreement (COLA) in the contract. The company desired to change the method of payment of cost of living allowance from a weekly to a quarterly basis, and not to fold the cost of living adjustment into base rates during the term of the agreement.

The company had made the local union and its negotiating committee aware of the financial difficulties which the plant was experiencing. As a part of a presentation made in Ottawa relating to dumping charges that the company was filing against some of its offshore competitors, a complete and detailed financial picture of the operation of the plant was made available to the union. The union was informed that for the first time in its history, the plant was not operating at a profit; that overall, company sales were down by 12 percent, profits were down by 65 percent (to their lowest point in 5 years); and that return on investment had decreased by 50 percent in 1983.

The company was also determined to have negotiations concluded at a time reasonably close to the expiration of the collective agreement, and not to have them drag out until January or later. It believed that the union and employees would be less willing to face a strike prior to Christmas and the paid holidays associated with the holiday season, than they would be in mid-January. The union had been informed of the company's desire in this regard. As one management participant said, "We were not going to play the game of controlled concessions or prolonged giveaway."

Negotiations began in early October. The union had submitted a list of three hundred demands, two hundred of which related to contract language changes and another hundred of which related to either grievances which had been settled by arbitration or which were still pending. The company announced that it was absolutely determined not to make any concessions on matters that had already been settled in its favour via the grievance arbitration process. By early November, the union proposals had been examined in bargaining meetings and the company had agreed to only four items involving changes in contract language. The company informed the union that it was not prepared to make any more concessions on union non-economic items.

In its initial proposal, the company proposed a three-year contract with no wage increase and no cost of living payments. By early December, the company had moved to a proposal of a two-year agreement with no wage increase in the first year and 25 cents in the second year. (The average base wage rates in the plant were $12.29 per hour under the old agreement.) It proposed that the cost of living agreement continued as it had in the past except for quarterly rather than weekly payments. The $1.74 currently paid as a cost-of-living allowance under the old agreement would not be folded into base rates as it had in the past, but would continue to be paid as a separate amount for each hour worked for the duration of the new agreement. A few minor improvements in benefits, including changes in pension benefit calculations, life insurance (from $24,000 to $25,000), sickness and accident insurance benefits (from $255 to $265 per week), and the meal allowance for overtime work (breakfast from $5 to $5.50; dinner to $7 from $6.50) were also included. It was this offer that the union rejected on December 14.

The company's position in negotiation was also a function of the fact that Addington employees were the highest paid in the immediate area, with benefits that management believed were the equal of any available. After the strike started, the company came to believe that the strike was as much a result of the changes made in their pattern on bargaining as any other factor. The union did not take the final offer to the membership, having secured a strike mandate in a vote several weeks before the strike deadline. Company officials found this somewhat surprising, since they had attempted to make clear to the union that the company's ability to increase wages and benefits was severely limited. They could only assume that the decision to call a strike without presenting the executive's and the bargaining team's dissatisfaction with the nature of the company's final offer to the employees was mainly a function of the union executive's and the bargaining team's dissatisfaction with the nature of the negotiation process in 1983.

Some time before the strike deadline, the company had sent a letter to all employees outlining the difficulties that the plant was experiencing and suggesting that a large settlement was simply not possible this year. In retrospect, company officials were not satisfied with the tone of the letter, nor its timing, since it seemed to further alienate the union bargaining committee by giving the appearance that the company was attempting to negotiate directly with the union bargaining committee.

The Strike Begins

Company managers took over the operation of the plant without any incident. No attempts to sabotage any of the equipment were discovered. The employees left the plant in an orderly fashion at the noon strike deadline, and set up picket lines. Picketing at all entrances involved large numbers of individuals, and the company applied for an injunction to limit the number of pickets at each gate. The company had increased its normal plant security force from eight to twenty-four. Plant security was an operation that was normally contracted out and an increase in the number of guards was not difficult to achieve. Shortly after the strike began, entry into the Vaughn Mine area was detected but no damage to equipment resulted. These incidents were described as pranks rather than any attempt at malicious damage. The security service reported to Mr. Murrill, the

Plant Manager, that they could not guarantee the security of the mine area. A request for the utilization of guard dogs was again sent to company headquarters in Calgary, which — with some misgivings and trepidation on headquarters' part — was granted. Guard dogs were put into place at the mine area, and no further entry was attempted. The company's fears about negative publicity resulting from the use of guard dogs did not materialize.

As the strike continued, and prior to the receipt of the injunction, some additional personnel were brought into the plant by helicopter. These individuals were from the company's headquarters in Calgary as well as some from another company plant in Sarnia, Ontario. Although the number varied somewhat during the term of the strike, not more than 30 individuals were brought in from the other company locations. Fifteen members of the 40-person salaried bargaining unit at the plant were kept on, doing their normal work. The others were laid off for the duration of the strike. In addition to the security force, personnel from sub-contractors who worked on cleaning and some maintenance work in the plant had been brought in prior to the strike and would be expected to stay in place until injunctive relief was obtained. Only two individuals who did not normally work in the plant in some capacity were brought in by the company. These were a diesel mechanic and an instrument technician/repairman. The skills represented by these two individuals were not available in the management workforce at the plant or in management ranks outside the plant. These were the only two "scabs" employed by the company, although the union, on a number of occasions, accused the company of engaging more. The plant nurse was also on regular attendance. She was one individual who had no difficulty in getting through the picket line. Company officials speculated that this was due, in part, to the fact that picketers knew that they might be visiting her later, at a time when she had a hypodermic in her hands. During the strike, the nurse had few demands made on her normal services, and ended up spending most of her time working in the quality control laboratory.

Twelve days after the strike started, the company received an injunction prohibiting mass picketing and limiting the number of pickets at each gate to six. The local police were informed that the company intended to move personnel in and out of the plant in order to begin two regular twelve-hour daily shift operations of the facility. At the time that the first movement out of the plant was attempted, the union set up a mass picket line of 150 to 200 employees. The township police arrived along with eleven Ontario Provincial Police cruisers and two paddy wagons from the St. Catharines' police force filled with officers equipped for riot duty. The picket line was peacefully dispersed, and after that time, there were no major incidents at the plant gates. Shipments were made, and personnel entered and left the plant without any difficulty except for the catcalls of the pickets. Prior to a shift change, the company's security force swept the road area in front of the plant, frequently gathering up several buckets worth of nails in the process. Other than this, the company experienced no difficulty from the picket line. The local police were present for shift changes and for movement of materials in and out of the plant. The company provided them with notice of the latter.

During the strike, attempts were made to shut off the electrical supply to the plant by short-circuiting the power lines. Company officials heard that one attempt to throw a chain across the line resulted in blindness to an employee that lasted for three hours. These attempts did not cause any severe disruption. The company was prepared for any major disruption in electrical power, though, because portable generators and diesel operated pumps had been acquired and hooked up prior to the strike. These generators were one of the more expensive items in the company strike plan, costing $30,000 to $40,000 each to rent. Such generators were needed at each of the locations.

The company had taken care to have these pumps and generators hooked up by outside contractors. During the 1978 strike, the company discovered that a diesel pump installed at the pump-house by the company's own maintenance personnel had been connected in a way that made it impossible for it to function at all.

As had been the case in 1978, the telephone line out of the plant was cut, despite the fact that at the company's urging, that line had been covered with a steel sheath by telephone company personnel prior to the strike deadline. The telephone repair crews repaired the broken line several times, before informing the union that the costs of any subsequent repair would be billed to the union. Following that, the telephone lines remained open.

The existence of communication in and out of the plant was something that company officials viewed as critical during the strike. They knew that it was particularly crucial during the first two weeks of a strike, when management employees would not be able to leave the plant. Being able to communicate with their families during this period was important, and company officials took care to insure that they were able to do so. This involved having helicopter service available for emergency entrance and exit from the plant if necessary.

In manning the plant during the strike, the company attempted to insure that jobs which required a great deal of physical effort were manned at the level that they normally were, while jobs requiring lighter physical effort, such as those in the boiler house, were manned at approximately 75 percent of the normal level. As the management personnel gained experience with running the plant, they began to discover that some tasks, particularly maintenance tasks, could be accomplished with much lower levels of personnel and much less time than they had come to expect. For example, when the production operation which had been shut down initially was started up in mid-January (due to customer demand), part of that start-up operation, which normally took three pipefitters, was accomplished by a process operator and a "janitor" who happened to walk by at an appropriate time. (This incident also illustrated the *esprit de corps* that management personnel were developing as the strike went on, and the fact that everyone seemed willing to help out when necessary.) Another example of discovered inefficiency involved a shot-filled coupling which needed to be changed at fairly regular intervals. This operation normally was scheduled for six to eight hours of work time and involved two skilled hourly maintenance people. The first time that one of the managers attempted to make the change, he discovered that it did require two people to complete the job, but the changeover was accomplished in only two hours. The second change was done in 1.25 hours, and by the end of the strike, the change operation was being completed in half an hour.

The amount of work done by the management personnel operating the plant was reflected in the amount of food consumed. The caterer had estimated that he would need to serve 1.5 times a normal portion. At the beginning of the strike, worker replacements were consuming three times the normal portions of food. By the end of the strike, this had fallen to 1.7 times the normal portion. The company had instructed the caterer to provide the best food that he could. Steak was available on demand at any time. Also included on the menus were crab legs, shrimp, scallops, roast beef, and roast pork. The food was extremely well prepared, which may have also accounted for the sizes of portions consumed.

The caterer served wine with the Christmas dinner that was served at the plant, but other than this, no alcoholic beverages were made available by the company. No objection was made, however, to light drinking after an individual's shift had been completed. A beer after work in the lounge was okay, but anything heavier would probably have been frowned upon, although company officials were not aware of any instance of alcoholic consumption that went beyond a beer or two after work.

One of the things that Howells thought was critical and took steps to insure was good communication. In general, company officials believed it was easier to communicate with individuals when only two shifts were operating as opposed to the normal four. A newsletter was produced, providing data on levels of production as well as the status of negotiations. It also contained anecdotes about the operation of the plant. In addition, a variety of newspapers was made available on a daily basis.

One of the things that Howells was careful to communicate carefully was the company's pay policy. He discovered that some of the individuals who had been brought in from other company locations expected to get their regular salary, plus an operator's salary, plus overtime, and that when they discovered they were not making that amount they tended to get upset. The company had an "on strike" pay policy, which Howells took care to communicate after this discovery. The policy provided for working 12 hours per day, seven days a week. Individuals were paid for 13 hours work per day. Work over eight hours was paid at 1.5 times the regular hourly rate. The hourly rate assigned to individuals was done by taking their regular salary and dividing by 2,080 hours. If this produced an hourly rate which was less than that assigned to the job that they were working on, they were given the higher hourly rate. The operation of the salary policy produced a situation where individuals actually worked 84 hours per week but received 123 hours' pay. Thus, the staff who worked in the plant during the strike received almost three times their normal salary during the time the strike was on (assuming that they worked a normal 40 to 42 hours work week).

The Strike Ends

The union had its first general meeting after the strike began on February 5. This was billed as an information meeting, one at which the company's final offer was presented to the membership for the first time. The membership's response to the offer was heated. According to company officials, the typical response was, "You mean to tell me I've been on strike for seven weeks and that's all you've got for me? I'm staying on strike!" A motion was made to vote on the company's final offer, and the final result was a ballot in which 63 percent of those voting voted against accepting the offer. After this meeting, negotiations resumed, but the company made no changes in its final offer.

Two weeks later, the offer was again put to a vote. It was defeated by a vote of 54 to 46 percent. One of the factors which company officials believe influenced the second vote was the fact that the stockpile of the basic raw material used in the production process was visibly shrinking and at current production rates, would be exhausted within about two weeks.

At this point, company officials were faced with the alternatives of either trying to settle the strike or attempting to open and operate the mine and crusher. With the assurances of the police that protection would be provided for the trucks carrying the ore to the plant from the mine, the company decided to attempt to operate the mine facility. On February 24, management personnel began operating the mine equipment and the crusher, and the first convoy of trucks moved from the mine to the plant, preceded and followed by police cruisers. With the opening of the mine, the company had an infinite supply of the basic raw material needed to operate the plant.

Negotiations continued for two more weeks. The company agreed to sweeten its final offer by allowing COLA payments to be folded into base rates on the last day of a two-year contract, which would expire October 31, 1985. With this modification, the membership voted on March 11 to accept the company's proposal. The vote was 67 percent in favour and 33 percent against. On March 13, normal operations resumed, and the 12-week strike was over.

Aftermath

From the company's point of view, the strike had provided several valuable lessons. Most supervision in the plant had not come up through the ranks but had been hired directly into supervisory positions. Operating the plant provided them with an opportunity for "hands on" experience for the first time. They could understand how hard jobs were to do and how much time they should take to do. Company officials thought that this provided supervision with a great deal more self-confidence. Bargaining unit employees seemed to have more confidence in management as well. As one manager put it, "Before the strike they really didn't think we could operate the plant. Well, we showed them."

Company management adopted a rule that if a particular maintenance task had been done by production workers during the strike, it stayed a production job after the strike, and did not return to the jurisdiction of the maintenance department. One dramatic consequence of management experience during the strike was that shortly after the strike ended, the hourly workforce was reduced by 50 individuals. Thirty-five were laid off and another 15 positions were eliminated through attrition.

The company had also achieved some minor relief on work rules as a result of negotiations. For example, maintenance employees called in for overtime on the night shift would no longer be taken into town for breakfast, but would have their breakfast brought into the plant as was the case with production workers. Also, maintenance workers in the quarry would drive their own cars into the mine/crusher site and no longer be given a ride in a company vehicle driven by a special driver.

Company officials believed that it would be some time before the union engaged in another strike. They believed that they had demonstrated conclusively that management personnel could operate the plant in the face of a strike. Although many individuals were physically tired by the time the strike ended, the general belief of plant management was that operations could have continued for some time beyond the point at which the strike was ended without serious difficulty.

JONES AND SMART, LTD. (A)

AN UNAUTHORIZED REFUSAL TO WORK

It was six o'clock in the morning when the phone rang. Frank Gagliardi, Chairman of the Shop Committee for Lodge 331 of the International Association of Machinists (IAM),[1] was having his second cup of coffee before starting for work. Frank's union represented all production and maintenance employees at Jones and Smart, Ltd. Starting time at the company was 7:00 a.m. and phone calls around six were not uncommon, but somehow Frank resented the ringing that morning. It was still dark outside and raining. It was September 1 — a morning that Frank Gagliardi would not soon forget.

Frank answered the phone wearily. It was Chris Walker, Labour Relations Manager of the plant. Walker told Frank that there was a picket line at the main gate and asked him to come in to the plant as soon as possible. Gagliardi said that he would be right down. He washed, dressed, finished his coffee, and started for the plant.

Both Chris Walker and Frank Gagliardi had been expecting a walkout by timekeepers, schedulers, and expeditors after negotiations between the company and the union representing those people had collapsed the day before. So Walker's call was no surprise.

The striking workers, 17 in all, were represented by Local 12 of the Office Employees Union (OEU). The same group had walked out once before, on June 5, and the production and maintenance employees had refused to cross the picket line. Frank Gagliardi was the elected leader of these production and maintenance employees, 425 in number, and he agreed that their action of June 5 had been a technical violation of the wording of his union's collective bargaining agreement with the company. The OEU employees had returned to work on June 6, and the company had taken no disciplinary action against any of its employees for their actions. However, on June 5, company representatives had made it clear that they did not feel the IAM leaders had fulfilled their contractual responsibilities to get the employees in to work.

Several meetings had taken place after June 5, and the company had reiterated its position — claiming that the wording of the contract placed a high degree of responsibility on IAM leaders.

While Frank Gagliardi was driving to work he reviewed the incidents since June 5, bearing in mind Section 8B of the IAM Contract.

---

[1]Lodge 331 of the International Association of Machinists (IAM) was one of three union entities representing several IAM-organized firms in the area. Officers of the Amalgamated Lodges (President, Financial and Recording Secretary, etc.) were not employees of Jones and Smart. Nor did these men play an active part in the plant's bargaining relationship. Frank Gagliardi, for all practical purposes, was the ranking IAM representative at Jones and Smart.

Section 8B, *No Cessation of Work*   There shall be no unauthorized strike or lockout during the term of this Agreement. Should any unauthorized strike occur at any time or times, the Local and International Union officials will meet with the Company as soon as possible and will take appropriate action to end such strike, including (without limitation) public renunciation of such unauthorized strike, instructions to employees to return to work, and the posting of such notice as shall be agreed upon by the Company and the Union. The Union further agrees that in the event of an unauthorized strike, the Company may take such disciplinary action as it deems appropriate against those workers who take part in such unauthorized strike. The Union reserves the right to question such disciplinary action through the Grievance Procedure. For the purpose of this Agreement, the term 'strike' shall include any strike, cessation of work, slowdown, picketing or other organized interference with production.

As long as the Union complies with the above provision, the Company agrees not to bring any legal action for damages against the Union for breach of this Section.

Those workers who were picketing were not in violation of any contract, because their union had no contract with the company and conciliation procedures under the Labour Relations Act had been exhausted. The OEU had been recognized on March 15 of that year and representatives had been bargaining, off and on, with the company since then. One of the items of contention was the company's insistence that a "No Cessation of Work" clause, similar to Section 8B of the IAM agreement, be included in the new contract. This clause differed from most no-strike provisions by placing significantly greater responsibility on union leaders, and the OEU wanted no part of it. This issue, plus wages, union security, and several other contractual matters, were responsible for the walk-out on June 5 and for the stalemate of August 31.

Production and maintenance employees were under contract — their representatives having signed a two-year agreement which ran to June 30 of next year. Thus, if IAM members refused to cross the picket line, they would violate the "No Cessation" provision, and would subject themselves to disciplinary action.

JUNE 5 WALKOUT

At 6:10 a.m. the OEU, dissatisfied with the progress of contract negotiations, set up a picket line led by area representative John Machin. Machin was not an employee of Jones and Smart, but all the other pickets, never more than 15 in number, were. Frank Gagliardi arrived at the plant that day at about 6:35, 20 minutes earlier than usual, following a call from Mr. Walker. Some of the production and maintenance employees had already arrived and were milling around in the parking lot, across the street from the main gate.

After parking his car, Gagliardi walked across the street to a guardhouse next to the main gate, where he met Mr. Walker and Mr. Herbert Parsons, Personnel Manager of Jones and Smart. Parsons was Walker's superior. Mr. Walker had just come from the guardhouse, where he had delivered an announcement over the public address system which could be heard across the street. Walker said that the IAM was not on strike — that there was work for everyone who wanted to come in.

Frank Gagliardi gave the following account of his June 5 meeting with Parsons and Walker, and his actions after that.

> Mr. Parsons asked me, what are we going to do. I said, "Well, I am going to go out and inform those people that they have to cross the picket line." I said, "Do you have any suggestions?" He just shrugged.
>
> After that, I would say there were about 75 to 100 of our people gathered in a group across the street and I went over and read them the contract clause stating that there would be no unauthorized walkout during the term of the agreement, and I told them that they had to comply with this clause.
>
> By then some of the other members of the shop committee showed up. I think there were three or four who were there. We got together and I told them to set about to acquaint these people that we had a contract to comply with, that there would be no support of any picket line.

At about 7 o'clock Mr. Carter Cook, Grand Lodge Representative of the IAM, arrived at the plant. Mr. Cook, not an employee of Jones and Smart, had been called by Mr. Parsons at 6:30. He conferred with Gagliardi and the committee-men — then went over to talk with Mr. Parsons.

Meanwhile, members of the IAM shop committee talked to employees, who were still reluctant to cross the picket line. Three members did cross the line, giving rise to a slight altercation — described by Gagliardi:

> The way they started to go through the picket line was that one man in particular whom I remember was Sam Johnson, he had like a running start, and as he came up to the line he was met by three pickets. Mr. Johnson took a swing at one, and they started swinging at him. Then one man came from behind and hit him on the head a few times. The other two people, I didn't really get a chance to notice what happened, but I know that they were met with violence, because one in particular let out a yell, and I found out later he had been jabbed with a straight pin or safety pin or something, a sharp instrument.

The day shift employees listened to their committeemen and then to repeated urgings of Mr. Walker over the public address system. Walker then asked Gagliardi to take over the public address microphone and urge his members to go to work. Gagliardi did that, saying: "The IAM is not on strike and the IAM should come to work." Nevertheless, only three production and maintenance men crossed the line that day, and by 8:15 most of the 345 first shift employees had started heading for home.

Mr. Gagliardi then proposed a meeting with the company to discuss actions to get the people back to work. At 8:30 he, Cook, and the first shift members of the IAM shop committee entered the plant. Mr. Cook asked Mr. Machin, representative of the OEU, to take the pickets away from the employment office gate so that the five IAM men could get by. Mr. Machin agreed. There were four police-men nearby, watching with interest as the men entered. Normally there were several policemen in the area directing traffic, but this day they stayed longer than usual, and they were joined by their superintendent.

The meeting was held in the plant personnel office. Mr. Parsons and Mr. Cook composed a notice, several copies of which were posted on the fence around the plant shortly before noon.

> In accordance with an article in the labour agreement between Jones and Smart Ltd. and Lodge 331, the members of the union are contractually obligated to refrain from work stoppages during the term of said Agreement.
> The International Association of Machinists and Lodge 331 hereby instruct all Jones and Smart Employees who are members of Lodge 331 to report for work as quickly as possible.

In addition, arrangements were made to place an advertisement in the local newspaper, *The Spectator*. The paper, published in the afternoon, had an 11:00 a.m. deadline, and the ad was not prepared in time. So it did not appear until the following day, June 6. It was paid for by the company but submitted with union approval.

THE INTERNATIONAL ASSOCIATION
OF MACHINISTS
LODGE 331 JONES AND SMART UNIT

> In accordance with an article in the Labour agreement between Jones and Smart, Ltd. and Lodge 331 the members of the union are contractually obligated to refrain from work stoppages during the term of said agreement.
> The International Association of Machinists and Lodge 331 hereby instructs all Jones and Smart employees to report for work as quickly as possible.

Carter C. Cook
Grand Lodge Representative

In addition, radio and TV time for spot announcements was purchased to convey the same message. Finally, during the meeting, Messrs. Parsons and Cook signed the following stipulation:

> It is hereby stipulated and agreed that no disciplinary action of any kind shall be taken against any member of Lodge 331 employed at Jones and Smart, Ltd. because of refusal to cross picket lines established at the plant gates on June 5.

The second shift employees started arriving in the parking lot about 3:00 p.m. on June 5. Frank Gagliardi and his committeemen circulated among them and told them what their responsibility was. None of the 80 second shift employees, scheduled to start work at 3:30, crossed the picket line. According to Gagliardi: "Once they saw the picket line, they just wouldn't have anything to do with it." That evening the following telegram was sent by Mr. Parsons to Mr. Cook:

> The unauthorized strike at Jones and Smart Plant has not been stopped. Action by the International Association of Machinists has not been sufficient to meet IAM obligations under no strike clause in present agreement between Jones and Smart, Ltd. and International Associa-

tion of Machinists. No effort was made by IAM officers or leaders to cause second shift workers to report for work and cross picket lines set up by OEU. No aggressive action or violence occurred to cause hesitation on IAM strikers' part. We expect effective efforts from union officers and leaders immediately. If such action is not forthcoming promptly we intend to proceed with procedures under labour agreement and law.

JUNE 6

On June 6, the OEU workers reported to their jobs, and negotiations resumed. There were 31 production and maintenance employees absent that day. Only 18 had been absent on June 2, the work day preceding the picketing.

The company called a meeting of union committeemen. Gagliardi was not able to attend. However, the three first shift committeemen, Larry Costello, James Kitching and Neil Crone, were there, and they later reported to Gagliardi. Mr. Parsons told the committeemen that the union had not fulfilled its obligation under the contract. In the event of a future stoppage, Parsons said, he expected the committeemen to report for work and enter the plant. Furthermore, Parsons said, the union leaders were obligated to lead other employees through any established picket line. He said, "We expect you, as committeemen, to carry employees through the picket line on your shoulders."

JUNE 30, FRIDAY

The company and IAM representatives had a policy meeting to discuss matters of general interest. All the union committeemen attended. Mr. Parsons stated that negotiations with OEU were not going well and that the union might set up another picket line. Parsons reviewed what he considered "appropriate action" by the union leaders. In addition, he told the committeemen that if there was a similar incident where IAM employees refused to cross a picket line, the company would put 100 names in a hat and pick 10 arbitrarily for discharge.

Frank Gagliardi asked Mr. Parsons what he considered "appropriate action." According to Gagliardi the following conversation ensued.

> He (Parsons) said he would expect us to do everything possible, including carrying people on our back through the picket lines. Naturally, he said, he would want us to come through the picket line too. At that point I asked him, "Well, we can't possibly act as employees and committeemen at the same time. If you want us to report for work and go through the picket line and go to our jobs, we are willing to do that. If you want us to stay outside the plant and urge the people to go to work, we will do that. We can't do both."

I asked him then point blank, "Now, do you want me to go in as an employee or do you want me to stay out and tell these people that they have to go to work?" And he says, "Well, we want you to do both." I said, "Which do you want me to do first?" He just shrugged. He said, "I don't know."

AUGUST 29, TUESDAY

The following letter was sent to Frank Gagliardi by John Machin, Representative of OEU.

TO ALL MEMBERS OF LODGE 331

Greetings:

We of the Office Employees Union are taking this opportunity to give you an up-to-date report of the difficulty we are having in attempting to negotiate a contract with Jones and Smart. Because of the many rumours which have been circulated attendant to these negotiations, and because our problems are the same as those which will confront your group in the near future, we feel you should be completely informed as to all the issues in the event we are forced by the company to take strike action in the near future. Following are some of the terms Jones and Smart wants us to agree to:

(1) No wage increase. Management wants its supervisors to have discretionary authority to hand out merit increases to those whom it feels are deserving.

(2) Management only wants to give our Union ONE HOUR per week on company time to investigate grievances!

(3) Management wants us to sign an impossible no-strike clause—one which would make it mandatory for us to cross YOUR picket line in the event your group had a strike.

(4) They want us to sign a clause to the effect that our Union will not aid or assist any of our members who may want to appeal an arbitration decision through the courts.

(5) They want the unilateral right to change the hours of work. If we agreed to this we would also be agreeing that we could not grieve a drastic change in starting and stopping times.

(6) They want to regulate seniority to a minor role in lay-offs, transfers and promotions. Only after skills, abilities, capabilities and dependability are measured by management will seniority be a considered factor.

Throughout all of our meetings the Jones and Smart management has taken the attitude that they must have "discretionary" rights and, to that extent, they are trying to get us to agree to a contract which would give our members nothing more than second class representation and protection. We are not trying to force management to agree to impossible terms. We only want what is fair to both parties. We believe that our position is substantially just and we are willing to place the unresolved issues before any arbitrator in the country for review.

Fraternally,
Office Employees Union

Soon after receipt of this letter Frank Gagliardi received a call from Mr. Parsons. Parsons asked Frank to call a membership meeting, to explain the company's position and to warn members against any repetition of the June 5 events. Gagliardi immediately scheduled a meeting for the next day, Wednesday, August 30, and circulated the following notice.

ATTENTION: UNION MEMBERS

There will be a very important meeting Wednesday, August 30, at Simeone's Restaurant. An international representative will be on hand to answer all your questions on matters which concern all of us.

Time: 2:00 p.m. Night Shift
      3:15 p.m. Day Shift

F. Gagliardi
Chairman
Shop Comm.

According to Frank Gagliardi, 40 to 50 members attended the 2:00 p.m. meeting for the night shift; close to 200 attended the day shift meeting. Gagliardi said he felt these had been good turnouts in view of the late notice. Following is his account of the meetings:

> The company had asked me to call the meeting and they had handed me a list of proposals that the office employees had given them. They explained that the office employees were asking for certain seniority clauses, conditions of work, that they couldn't possibly give them, and the company explained to me what they thought the office employees were entitled to and what they weren't entitled to and explained to me how it had taken the IAM so many years, twenty years, to get some of the benefits that the office employees wanted in one year. One thing, for example, the union shop.
>
> All I did actually at the meeting was to explain the company's position on these things, and also what the OEU was asking for in terms of fringe benefits and seniority clauses and things like that.
>
> I read Machin's letter to them. After I was finished with that, I told the people that we could neither support nor condone any picket line or strike by the OEU and that if any member did, in fact, not cross the picket line, that he would be subject to any disciplinary action the company might mete out.
>
> I told the people too about the company's suggestion that if any member did not, in fact, come to work, that they would put 100 to 200 names in a hat and draw out a certain number and discharge or discipline that number that they did draw out. Of course the members already knew about that idea anyway.

Machin, area representative of the OEU, appeared at the meeting of the day shift employees and asked if he could speak. Following is Gagliardi's report of what transpired.

> There was a question of whether it would be proper or not for Mr. Machin to speak. The membership seemed to want to hear him, so we let him speak.
>
> After he spoke on the counter proposals by the company, I pointed out to the membership that we could not support any picket line or any strike by the OEU. I asked Mr. Machin if this was not true, and he said, "That's right." He said, "Contractually, you cannot support us in any strike."

The meeting on August 30 was not a regular Local Lodge meeting. It was strictly an informative meeting. No minutes were taken, and no votes were taken. Frank Gagliardi said he knew, however, that if Machin set up another picket line most IAM employees would not cross. He had heard Carter Cook express his philosophy, and he believed most of the members subscribed to it — that "neither he, nor his father before him, would ever cross a picket line set up by any union."

The next night at approximately 9:00 p.m., negotiations with the OEU broke down.

AUGUST 31

The OEU prepared a notice to be distributed to Jones and Smart employees the next day. A copy was delivered to Frank Gagliardi's home.

NOTICE
TO ALL JONES AND SMART EMPLOYEES
WE ARE ON STRIKE!

This strike is not of our making. We offered to submit all unresolved issues to arbitration and this offer was refused by Jones and Smart.

Why did Jones and Smart refuse to arbitrate? The answer is simple. The know perfectly well that any arbitrator in the country would reject out of hand some of their ridiculous proposals! The management of Jones and Smart is bound and determined to force us to sign an agreement which would be a joke. Not only that — but — they would then attempt to force these clauses on Lodge 331 during your next negotiations.

It appears that they are using us as a testing ground for their negotiations with your group next summer.

We ask all of you, as individual workers, not to cross our picket line. We are fighting for the right not to have to cross your picket line if you have to conduct one in the future. Our fight is your fight. We must support one another if we are to achieve better wages and working conditions. The IAM and the office employees are currently fighting together on the picket line against Briggs Motors in Toronto. We have fought with you side by side. In each of these instances we have won joint victories. It can be done here!

GET TOGETHER!   STAY TOGETHER!   WIN TOGETHER!

P.S. REMEMBER — THERE IS ABSOLUTELY NO PROVINCIAL OR FEDERAL LAW WHICH CAN COMPEL YOU TO CROSS A PICKET LINE! THIS IS A FACT WHICH ANY LAWYER WILL GIVE YOU!

Frank Gagliardi was in a dilemma as he drove to work that rainy Friday morning, September 1. His relations with the company had usually been cordial, but formal. He knew the company expected his committee to lead the IAM employees through the picket lines, but he sincerely doubted whether anyone would follow.

Those who had entered the plant on June 5 had since been given the silent treatment. To add to the problems, Sam Johnson, the man who led two other members through the line on June 5, had been made a foreman two weeks after the incident — a fact that sat uneasily with many IAM members.

The IAM had never been on strike against Jones and Smart since Gagliardi had been a committeeman. He had participated in an unauthorized walkout two years earlier, which resulted in the suspension of the shop committee chairman, but he had not been fully aware of the circumstances then.

As he approached the plant, Frank Gagliardi observed ten to twelve pickets moving in front of the three entryways to the plant. Some were carrying umbrellas. Others were carrying placards. A policeman was directing traffic. Another policeman stood near the main gate and parted the pickets as automobiles driven by supervisors entered the property. A few office workers, not represented by any union, were seen entering the main gate on foot; walking past the pickets, without any evidence of trouble. Gagliardi noticed that the parking lot was about half full — normal for this time of the day — but he did not see any IAM members attempting to enter the plant. Most of those who had arrived were sitting in their cars in the lot. It looked like the OEU, at 17-member union, had successfully convinced the production and maintenance employees that they should not cross the picket line.

JONES AND SMART, LTD. (B)

THE POWER OF A PICKET LINE

Frank Gagliardi was Chairman of the Shop Committee for Lodge 331 of the International Association of Machinists (IAM). The Union had 425 members — the production and maintenance employees at Jones and Smart, Ltd. Jones and Smart engaged in machining and assembling of hydraulic pumps, motors, and control devices. Relations between the company and union could be characterized as being at the containment level—each party expecting the other to abide by strict wording of the collective bargaining agreement. Grievances were frequent.

Frank Gagliardi had been called on the telephone at 6:00 a.m. on Friday, September 1, by Christopher Walker, Jones and Smart's Labour Relations Manager, who told Frank that a picket line had been set up by the Office Employees Union (OEU), a 17-member organization recognized last March 15 as bargaining agent for timekeepers, schedulers, and expeditors.

Mr. Walker also called the other three IAM committeemen who worked on the day shift: Larry Costello, John Kitching, and Neil Crone. Mr. Herbert Parsons, Jones and Smart's Personnel Manager, called Mr. Carter Cook, Grand Lodge Representative of the IAM. All the men started for the plant at about 6:15 a.m. It was a cold, rainy morning. Following is Cook's version:

> Well, about six o'clock in the morning I received a call from Herb Parsons, and he said "Your friend has done it again." I asked Herb what he meant, and he said, "There is a picket line up — led by your friend John Machin."[1]
>
> I said, "I will be right up."
>
> I immediately got dressed and got in the car and came up to the picket line. Machin started over toward me, and I told him, "Get the hell away from me. Don't you know my telephone number?" He said, "Well, it would have been three o'clock in the morning." I said, "I don't care what time it was. You should have called me."
>
> With that, I met with Frank Gagliardi. About the same time Herb Parsons came over. We had a short conversation. Herb asked me what we could do to get this thing settled. I said, "Well, the first thing we have got to do is get the picket line removed." And I said, "The best way to do that, in my estimation, is to sit down and negotiate fairly with the office workers."

Frank Gagliardi came over from the parking lot where he reported quite a few of the men had begun to gather. He said, "Come on, fellows, let's go." One of them asked Gagliardi where he was going. Gagliardi said, "I am going to work. Let's go." When he got to the picket line he met committeemen Jim Kitching

---

[1] John Machin was the Area Representative of the Office Employees Union (OEU). Machin did not work for Jones and Smart.

and Neil Crone, and three of the OEU pickets came over. According to Gagliardi this is what happened:

> As I got to the picket line these three pickets came up to me and told me to stay away unless I wanted to get hurt. One of these in particular told me he would jab me in the teeth if I made any attempt to get across.
>
> One of the pickets was carrying an umbrella. The other two had sticks with signs on them: placards.
>
> I walked over to Mr. Machin and asked him if he would withdraw his picket line. He said, "You're crazy. I will never take it down." I said, "Well, if you don't withdraw it, we will have to find some other means of getting it down for you." He told me, "I don't care what you do. You people won't cross the picket line."

Then Gagliardi, Crone, and Kitching crossed to the parking lot where they were joined by Larry Costello, the fourth shop committeeman on the day shift. Gagliardi got the people to form a group, about 75 people. He told them he didn't want the same situation that happened before, that they should cross the picket line and go to work. One of the men said, "Let the company file a grievance if they don't like it. We have been filing plenty of them." Then Gagliardi told them that this was not a matter on which a grievance could be filed — that they were required to honour the contract and cross the picket line and go to work. Gagliardi said, "Don't forget, the company can take disciplinary action against you like they said they would. So if you don't cross, there may be some discipline." And another person in the group yelled out, "Let them file a grievance if they don't like it."

Meanwhile, several Jones and Smart foremen were attempting to convince employees that they should enter the plant. The foremen were equally unsuccessful. Mr. Walker asked some of the foremen what reasons employees gave for not crossing the picket line. Walker reported as follows:

> Some of them said they didn't want to get their heads bashed in. Some of them said, "We don't want to be called scabs." Some of them said, "We went in the last time and we've been blacklisted; we're being given the silent treatment."

Mr. Walker stated that one foreman reported to him that he overheard Frank Gagliardi say to an employee, "Go to work, but don't cross the picket line."

Several employees tried to cross the picket line, but decided against it when they encountered threats. Here is the story of Richard Stone, one of these employees:

> I arrived about 20 minutes to 7:00, and I went over and parked my car. I walked across the street up to the picket line. There was a policeman there and there were some foremen in the gatehouse.
>
> Mr. Machin took an umbrella — an unopened umbrella — and poked it at me, in a violent sort of way. Once he hit me in the stomach with it—not hard. I didn't say anything to the policeman. He saw it, I'm certain. I turned around after two or three times and walked across the street again.

Larry Costello, first shift committeeman, reported as follows:

> I got to work about 6:30. A few other committeemen were there. Two of us proceeded up to the picket line. Erik Lawson and Harry Couchon[2] came over to me and threatened me bodily. They said, "You better get out of here or else." So they shoved me and I went back.

Meanwhile, Mr. Walker obtained a bullhorn, a battery-operated, portable loudspeaker, and while the union leaders were talking to their members, Walker used the bullhorn to broadcast the following message:

> The IAM is not on strike. There is work for all. Come to work. All gates are open.

Walker's broadcasts were repeated over and over — later Plant Superintendent Eugene Dressler took over the bullhorn, relaying essentially the same message. The OEU pickets greeted the bullhorn with hoots and hollers — trying to drown it out.

At about 7 o'clock a Volkswagen panel truck owned by a local radio station arrived at the scene. The newscaster, named Robert Clemente, talked to Frank Gagliardi and Carter Cook. Later in the morning the following news item appeared over the radio.

> Although instructed by their union officials to report for work this morning at the Jones and Smart plant, members at Local 331 of the International Association of Machinists did not cross the picket lines set up at the factory by the striking members of the Office Employees Union.

Shortly after 7 o'clock, when it was apparent that the IAM employees had not been convinced that they should enter the plant, Mr. Parsons came over to where Gagliardi and Cook were standing and said to Cook, "Get these people in to work. If you don't you are going to get hit with a suit." Mr. Walker joined the group and asked whether the committeemen were going to go to work. Mr. Cook turned to Walker and said: "What are doing here, you smart college kid — go on back to your law books."[3]

Parsons and Walker then turned around and started to walk away, and Gagliardi said, "Herb, what about our meeting?" Parsons turned again and said, "This will constitute our meeting under the contract."[4]

[2]Members of OEU employees of Jones and Smart.

[3]Mr. Walker was a young man, age 27, who had graduated from McGill University Law School three years ago. He went to work for Jones and Smart that same month as Labour Relations Manager, reporting to Mr. Parsons. Mr. Walker and Mr. Cook were never on friendly terms. In Walker's words: "We seem to rub each other the wrong way, and we usually have — it ends up with words."

[4]Under the "No Cessation of Work" provision in the contract a meeting between the company and the union was required in the event of any unauthorized strike, in order to take appropriate action to end the strike. See Jones and Smart (A) for the exact wording of the provision.

Gagliardi turned to Carter Cook and said, "Well, I guess we had better spread out and try to get these people in there." Cook said, "Yes, I guess you had better do that, and I will see what I can do to get Machin to take his picket line down." Following is Gagliardi's version of what transpired during the next 30 minutes.

> So we went through the parking lot — three of the committeemen and myself. The lot was emptying out pretty fast. There was a group of maybe ten people who were standing on the side. I told them to cross the picket line and go to work, and they just laughed at me. I went from car to car, and I told the rest of the committee, "Get as many cars as you can, and tell these people that they can't go home, they have to go through the picket line to work."
>
> As we were doing it, the people that were driving away were making a few remarks, like one man made a remark—I said, "Where are you going?" He said, "I am going home." I said, "For Christ's sake, you have to go to work." He said, "Go shove it. You go to work!"
>
> By 7:00 only about one-third of the cars were left. We went up to each individual car and talked to the employees there.

At about 9:15 Mr. Cook, Mr. Crone, and Mr. Gagliardi left the parking lot and went to Charley's Kitchen, nearby, for a cup of coffee. They were joined by the other committeemen, Mr. Kitching and Mr. Costello, and proceeded to Simeone's Restaurant, where they thought some of the members might have gone. Simeone's was the scene of many union gatherings — a place used regularly for business meetings and social events.

Soon thereafter Mr. Machin came in to the restaurant. Frank Gagliardi and Cook talked with Machin and urged him to withdraw the picket line.

Cook: I don't see what the hell you've got to gain by picketing.

Machin: Well, maybe the company will meet with us and maybe grant our demands.

Cook: As far as we are concerned, what you should do is go back and negotiate and remove your picket line so our people can get to work.

Machin: As long as the people are honouring the picket line, I can't see it.

Cook: Would you be willing to take it down Tuesday morning?[5]

Machin: Well I can't promise you, but I will get my committee together and try to talk them into removing the line and to negotiate with the company without involving you.

At about 10 o'clock, after talking to several of the IAM members at Simeone's, the union committeemen and Mr. Cook went home. All of them were soaking wet from being out in the rain most of the morning, and they wanted to change clothes.

Mr. Walker had been phoning all the committeemen asking them to come to the plant and make phone calls to each of the employees urging them to come to work. When Frank Gagliardi got home — about 10:30 — the phone was ringing.

---

[5]The following Monday, September 4, was Labour Day—No work was scheduled that day at Jones and Smart.

According to Gagliardi:

Walker was on the wire. He told me that all the other committee members were coming down to the plant to make phone calls. I said, "I will have to check. I don't think this is a requirement under the contract, that we have to make phone calls." Furthermore, I didn't think it could do any good.

He said, "Are you refusing to make phone calls?" I said, "No, I am not refusing to make phone calls. I will check with Carter Cook to find out whether this is one of our requirements."

And he asked me the same question then, "Well then you are refusing to come down." Then I got a little perturbed, and I said, "I don't give a goddam if you have a tape recorder on the wire. I am not refusing to come down and make phone calls. I am going to check with my Grand Lodge Representative, and I will let you know."

Then I called Carter but I couldn't get in touch with him. So I went down to the plant at about 11:30. When I got there the whole committee was there: Mr. Crone, Mr. Kitching — even the second shift men, Di Paola and Horton.[6]

I asked them if the company had called them, and they said, "Yes," that they weren't sure why. I said, "Walker told me that you were going to make phone calls. What's going on?"

They said, "We didn't say that. All we said was that we would come down. He didn't say we would make phone calls." So I said, "Well, we had better go in and find out what the hell is going on." So we went up to the picket line. Then Mr. Machin met us and told me again, he says, "Frank, you had better not try and cross this line or I will shove this umbrella in your teeth."

So we started toward the office gate. There were not any pickets down there, but Machin sent two men down there right away. I said, "Look, we have to meet with the company. Why don't you just step aside and let us by?"

He said, "You are not going anywhere." This is when Mr. Petrocelli[7] called out and said, "Are you going to work Frank?" And he started laughing. I said, "Sure Dick, if you will bust it open for me, I will go to work."

Then I said to him, "Call Mr. Parsons and tell him to come out. We can't get by."

We stood near the picket line waiting, and Mr. Petrocelli reached out of the guardhouse window with his camera and told me to smile. I gave one of the pickets, Mr. Richards, a playful bump and said, "Here's something for your camera!"

Then I said, "We had better get the hell away from here. All these people want to do is photograph us."

We went across the street. Then Mr. Parsons and Mr. Walker came out. There was a short conversation. Mr. Parsons said, "We want you to come in and make phone calls to the first and second shift." I said, "Well, Herb, I don't know whether we are actually supposed to make these phone calls under our contract." I said, "Why don't you wait?"

[6]Alfred Di Paola and Joseph Horton were IAM Shop Committeemen who worked on the second shift. They had not been present earlier in the morning.

[7]Richard Petrocelli, first shift foreman, was sitting in the guardhouse. He had a motion picture camera.

He said, "We have got it set up for it." I said, "We can't possibly contact everybody in the whole bargaining unit, because they don't all have phones. Also, we don't believe that you want us in there to make phone calls actually." To me this was an excuse to get us by the pickets.

I told Parsons we had tried to get by the pickets, but Machin wouldn't let us by.

Mr. Cook, having been called by Mr. Parsons, arrived on the scene. Cook told Mr. Parsons he did not believe the committeemen were required to make phone calls. Cook said, "Herb, I don't believe we could get anybody to come to work, especially if they thought we were inside the plant. Besides," said Cook, "there is a telephone down at the union hall that can be used if we want to call employees."

Mr. Parsons then gave Cook drafts of newspaper and radio ads which he had prepared. He said he expected Cook to take whatever steps were necessary to put them on the air and in the newspaper. Both drafts were identical:

> Lodge 331 is not on strike at Jones and Smart. All International Association of Machinists employees have a contractual duty as members and individuals to report for work and enter the plant for work.
>
> Therefore, the International Association of Machinists and Lodge 331 orders all Jones and Smart employees to report for work and enter the plant to work at the beginning of their next shift.
>
> As Union Officers and Official International Representatives of the IAM we cannot condone or support any action by the Office Employees Union which prevents members of the IAM from working.
>
> This announcement is authorized by Carter H. Cook—IAM Grand Lodge Representative, Frank Gagliardi, James Kitching, Neil Crone, Larry Costello, Alfred Di Paola, and Joseph Horton—Jones and Smart IAM union representatives.

Mr. Cook put the drafts in his pocket but took no steps until that evening to have ads placed. He said he thought he could do more good trying to get people back to work by staying on the scene.

There was no further conversation regarding phone calls, and the union committeemen never did enter the plant that day — Friday, September 1.

There was a further conversation, reported by Mr. Gagliardi as follows:

> Mr. Walker then asked us to come to work. He said, "Are you going to report for work?" I said, "I am here to report for work." He said, "Why don't you cross the picket line?"
>
> "I already tried to cross the picket line," I said. "Would you guarantee me free access to the plant?" He said, "We don't have to do that. Just go right through the picket line." I said, "If you will guarantee me free access to the plant, I am more than willing to come to work."
>
> Then Carter Cook said to me, "You shouldn't even be here. You have got a bad knee." I said, "I know that. Regardless of that, I will go to work if you will provide me with free access to the plant."

The committeemen claimed that they did secure a guarantee from Mr. Parsons that any damage to employees' property would be paid for by the company.

However, Parsons refused when he was asked to put the guarantee in writing. The committee was concerned about automobile damage, because during the June 5 picketing one employee's car was immobilized. All four tires were flattened.

At about noon Mr. Gagliardi and Mr. Cook went to the union hall where they met with the IAM committeemen. They asked the committeemen to report back to the plant around 2:30 to talk with the second shift employees as they arrived. Gagliardi and Cook discussed their next move—Cook concentrating on trying to get the picket line removed. Frank Gagliardi said that while he and Cook were in the union hall he received several phone calls.

> We were getting calls from the press. The Canadian Press called and they asked us what happened. I told them that the office union was out on strike, and that some of our people were supporting the picket line, or wouldn't cross the picket line. He asked me if the IAM was on strike, and I told him no, that we were not on strike, that our contract didn't expire until June 30 of next year. He asked me if anybody had crossed the picket line and I said, "No, not that I know of." Then he said, "Well what is going to happen now?" I said, "Well we are going to try to get the people back."
>
> I had another conversation with a C.P. representative and I had another conversation that day with a man from some television station. I think it was CHCH. They all called the union office.

According to Mr. Gagliardi, he and Cook agreed to put spot announcements on the radio and to run the ad Mr. Parsons had prepared. They jointly agreed that the best way to get the people to work would be to have the picket line withdrawn. So Cook resumed efforts to contact the District Director of the OEU. He was not successful.

At 2:30 p.m. Gagliardi, Cook, and the committeemen returned to the plant. There were between 10 and 12 pickets, about the same number as in the morning. Three policemen were present, one directing traffic and two between the picket line and the main gate, near the guardhouse. Supervisory personnel, delivery trucks, and a few non-union office workers were entering and leaving the gate without any trouble. The rain had subsided a bit, and about 50 employees of the second shift were in the parking lot.

Between 2:30 and 3:30 there was a repetition of the 7:00 a.m. events. The committee members circulated among the employees urging them to go to work; the foremen did the same. No second shift employees attempted to enter the plant. There were a few instances where union leaders and company representatives nearly clashed that afternoon. Mr. Cook stated that if the foremen had stayed away the union leaders might have been more successful. Following is an account of Frank McAllister, second shift foreman, who was circulating in the parking lot.

> I tried to talk one of my employees, Don Freitag, into coming to work. I said, "What do you say Don, let's go to work, there is a lot of work inside and you are actually not on strike. We would like to have you come in and get some of it cleaned up."

He said he would like to, but he didn't want to get his car smashed up. He said he had a large investment there in his new automobile and, therefore, he didn't think he had better go in to work.

Within a few minutes I saw another one of my men, Fred Dullaney. He was standing beside his car. And I asked him if he would come to work—that we had a lot of work to get cleaned up.

"Well," he said, "I don't want to get hurt. I'm afraid to go in. I don't want to get my family involved in this thing."

While I was standing trying to talk with Dullaney, Mr. Cook—I learned his name later—came down. He was walking through the lot shouting, "Who is this balloonhead?" So, I tried to ignore it, pretending I didn't realize that he was addressing me. He was looking around saying, "Who is this balloonhead?"

Finally, I turned to him. I said, "Are you referring to me?" He said, "Yes." I said, "Well, I'm not a balloonhead." So he said, "What are you going to do about it?" So I said, "I don't think I'm going to do anything about it, but I'm not a balloonhead." Then he said, "What are you, a strike breaker?" I said, "No, I'm not a strike breaker." So he said, "What are you doing down here?" I said, "Well, I'm down here to try to convince my men to come in to work. They are not on strike as far as I know, and their position is in the plant at this time working. And I've got plenty of work for them to do."

So at this point he said, "What about those poor kids on the picket line there? They got to eat, you know." "Well," I said, "As far as I'm concerned, you may be thinking of them, but you're not thinking of six hundred other men who also have to eat and whose families are looking for their week's pay this week. It's your obligation, in my estimation, to advise them to go to work." He said, "Who says so?" I said, "You have a contract and you are supposed to adhere to it." I said, "I'm not in the same category to try to get them back to work as you are." He said to me, "What contract?" I said, "Well, you have a contract." He said, "Oh that's two years ago." I said, "Well, it's still valid, so, therefore, I feel that you should be helping to enforce it."

So he reiterated with the same thing, "You are a balloonhead." He repeated, "You are a balloonhead." And he finally came right up close to me as if he was agitating a fight. And I said to him, "Look if you are provoking me so I should take a swing at you, you are crazy." At this time, apparently, we had raised our voices and a few people had gathered and two policemen came down.

The policemen walked up as if to break up the discussion, and at that time I felt he became a little more arrogant. And I said to him. "These policemen are here to protect me as well as you." I said, "Let's drop the whole thing." The policeman said, "Let's break it up fellows; let's not get into any discussion because it can lead to trouble." Then we broke it up.

We started to walk away. At this time Chris Walker and Herb Parsons, who were a few paces away, came down. Walker started to say something and Cook said, "Why don't you go back to your law books — you smart punk?" So I said, "This is no place for me," and I got out of there, and I walked over and back to the guardhouse.

Shortly before 3:30—the time the night shift usually started work—a newsboy appeared at the plant gate with the afternoon edition of *The Spectator*. Page one carried the following story.

OFFICE LOCAL STRIKES AT JONES AND SMART, LTD.

Production Halted as Workers Refuse To Cross Lines

Approximately 15 newly-organized factory office workers at Jones and Smart, Ltd. plant went on strike this morning over a contract-negotiating stalemate, and caused production by 500 workers to be halted.

First-shift members of the International Association of Machinists, bargaining agent for production employees, honoured the picket lines of the Office Workers Union, turning back at the factory gates when they saw the office employees' picket signs.

Orderly Picketing

Police Superintendent Thomas Bone headed a large detail of police at the plant gates, but picketing was orderly and no incidents resulted.

The strikers are all men employed as time-keepers, schedulers and expeditors in the factory. Office workers in the administrative offices are not involved.

Today was the second time in less than three months that the Office Workers Union, which won bargaining rights in an election in April, caused production to be stopped. A one-day strike took place June 5.

The union reported contract negotiations broke down Wednesday night, with many issues, including wages, union security, and contractual clauses remaining unsettled.

Although it was indicated when negotiations broke down that a strike would be called, the union apparently gave no advance notification of a strike date, and today's picket lines came as a surprise to most people who reported for work at the plant.

Reports No Progress

John Machin, area representative of the striking union, said no progress was made in the union's first quest for a contract at the plant.

The union representative said a last-minute effort to avert a strike was made by the union through a proposal to submit the contract dispute to an arbitrator, with the choice of an arbitrator left to the company.

Management made no statement on the strike or on the work stoppage by the IAM members but indicated it would have a report later in the day.

When the office workers set up picket lines last June 5, and production workers honoured them, the IAM issued an order to its members to go back to work. They were told that under a no-strike clause in their contract they were contractually obligated to refrain from a work stoppage during the term of the agreement.

There was no statement from the IAM today. There were reports an IAM representative arrived on the scene, but that IAM members continued to turn back and go home when they saw the pickets.

Picketing started shortly before 6:00 a.m. and continued all morning.

In the late afternoon Carter Cook called Herbert Parsons and told him that the IAM was publicly going to denounce the strike and instruct its people to report for work. He told Parsons that arrangements had been made for radio spot announcements. He read the proposed announcements to Parsons over the phone, and they were broadcast, exactly as written, on two of the local radio stations. This announcement also appeared in *The Spectator* on Saturday, the 2nd.

NOTICE

Early in the evening of September 1, Messrs. Cook and Gagliardi dispatched the following telegram to Mr. Parsons:

International Association of Machinists disavows any participation in the strike called by the Office Employees Union and instructs the members to report for work on Tuesday, September 5, on their regular scheduled shifts.

In addition to the ad placed by the IAM, *The Spectator* carried the following front page article on Saturday, September 2.

Saturday, September 2

STRUCK-PLANT MACHINISTS TOLD TO WORK

**Union Disavows Any Link to
Jones and Smart
Office Help Walkout**

Officials of the International Association of Machinists last night instructed their members to return to work Monday at Jones and Smart, Ltd., Hamilton plant, which was successfully shut down yesterday by a strike of Office Workers Union.

Some 500 production workers, members of the IAM, refused on both shifts yesterday to cross the picket line manned by pickets from the 15-member officer workers local organized in March. It is the second strike by the office workers union since then.

IAM officials last night, however, disavowed ''any participation in the strike called by the Office Employees Union and instructed its members to report for work on Tuesday, September 5, after the Labour Day holiday, on their regular scheduled shifts.''

Office Workers Union spokesmen said the production workers went back home at the sight of the pickets, despite company efforts, via a hand loudspeaker, to persuade the production workers to enter the plant and take up their jobs.

The company said it planned to bring court action against officials of the machinists union for damages resulting from loss of production. The IAM contract with the company contains a no-strike clause.

Office Workers Union spokesmen said the

company has been attempting to get the same kind of clause into their contract, and that this is one of the issues over which negotiations broke down Wednesday after seven meetings.

The strikers said the Teamsters Union is also honouring their picket lines.

Police Superintendent Thomas Bone headed a large detail of police at the plant gates, but picketing was orderly and no incidents resulted.

The strikers are all men, employed as timekeepers, schedulers and expediters in the factory. Office workers in the administrative offices are not involved.

Questions

Mr. Parsons and Mr. Walker stayed at the plant until nearly 9 o'clock Friday night. They considered many questions:

1. What kind of discipline, if any, should be handed out to the IAM people?*
2. Should some sort of random discipline be used, such as drawing ten names from a hat?
3. What should be done about negotiations with the OEU?
4. What is the likelihood that the OEU will continue picketing the next work day?
5. Will the disavowal by the IAM be effective in getting production and maintenance employees back to work?
6. What effect should the *Discharge Without Just Cause* provision of the contract have on their decisions? The provision is reproduced below.

Discharge With Just Cause   *Provision from Collective Bargaining Agreement*

The company agrees that it will not discharge any regular employee except for just cause.
However, if a discharge becomes subject to the grievance procedure and his discharge is found to be unjust, the employee shall be restored to his former position and status and shall receive retroactive pay in full to the date of said discharge.

Mr. Gagliardi and Mr. Cook were considering the following questions on Friday night, September 1.

1. What, if anything, should they do between now and Tuesday morning?
2. What action should they take if the picket line is formed on Tuesday, the 5th?
3. What are the long range implications of the September 1 incidents? For example, should the union seek a revision of the *No Cessation of Work* provision in the contract.

*Two years earlier the Shop Committee Chairman of Jones and Smart was suspended for six months for leading a walkout in violation of the contract. The case went to arbitration and the arbitration reduced the penalty to four months. In his opinion, the arbitrator stated, "any Union Leader who exercises his leadership role to foster or encourage a walkout in violation of the agreement must be subjected to severe or even extreme penalties."

6
THE GRIEVANCE CHALLENGE

The process of negotiating collective agreements provides the basic framework for the "web of rules" that is the output of the industrial relations system. However, the day-to-day *administration* of the collective agreement is the process that really puts flesh on the bones provided by the collective agreement. In this sense, the most important aspect of industrial relations involves the process of living with, administering, managing under the collective agreement. The agreement itself may be a masterpiece of legal rhetoric, but it is little more than an impotent sheaf of paper except for the day-to-day actions of the parties who are covered by its provisions.

The collective agreement is essentially administered by management, subject to challenge from the union. The nature of both management action and union challenge is quite variable. For example, in taking any action that is governed by the terms of the contract, such as discipline, lay-off, or job assignment, management may simply take the action and wait for a union response. Management may also consult the union in advance of the action or simply notify the union in advance, even where such action is not required by the agreement.

On the other hand, the union's response to management action can range from acquiescence to a verbal comment or complaint, a written grievance, or the use of pressure tactics such as a wildcat strike or a slowdown, even though such tactics are illegal. The manner in which the parties administer the collective agreement is very much a function of their relationship. A containment-aggression type of relationship is, by definition, legalistic and likely to involve a high grievance rate and frequent recourse to arbitration, while in a cooperative relationship there would be few, if any, formal grievances, and recourse to arbitration would be a rare occurrence.

Thus, in practice, there is a great deal of variation in the rate with which management decisions are challenged by grievances. (The grievance rate is usually expressed in grievances per 100 or 1,000 employees per year.) There are differences in the grievance rate between industries, companies, plants within the same company, departments within the same plant, shifts in the same department, and even, over time, within the same shift in the same department. Variations in the grievance rate are a function of many factors, including the nature of the work, union and management policy, and, most importantly, union and management leadership.[1]

The cases which follow provide a number of concrete examples of grievance procedures. In general, grievance procedures have a number of steps to them, with the number of steps varying from contract to contract. Most procedures begin with an informal, oral first step between the aggrieved employee or employees and the first level of supervision. The informal nature of the process at this level makes distinguishing complaints and grievances extremely difficult. Technically, a grievance is an allegation that the contract has been violated. Such a distinction is not particularly useful, since in a very basic sense, the grievance procedure is a communication process which serves to inform management of problems in the workplace.

At some point in the procedure, the grievance is reduced to writing, and at this time the section of the agreement which has been violated is usually spelled out. The contract usually specifies time limits within which each step of the procedure must be completed. Contracts often provide for an expedited grievance procedure for certain types of grievances, most often those involving discipline or discharge. Time limits and expedited procedures are designed to provide for a speedy resolution of the problem which exists. Speedy resolution is important in the face of potential employee hardship; it also reduces the size of retroactive costs (e.g., back pay in a discharge case) for management. Although discussions are held at every step of the procedure, once a grievance has been put in writing, all management responses and union appeals to further steps in the procedure are written.

The extent to which the contractually-outlined grievance procedures are actually followed depends on the relationship between the parties. Time limits may be waived, issues may be considered even though not reduced to writing, settlement may be made on a "once only" basis, etc. Very often special efforts will be made to settle a grievance before it reaches arbitration, often after a grievance has reached that step and a hearing has been scheduled. This is so common that many arbitrators have a cancellation fee for hearings scheduled but not held.

Grievances can be filed by individual employees, groups of employees, or by the union in what are called policy grievances. Policy grievances are grievances which are general in nature over situations which affect or which may affect a number of employees.[2] Grievances can also be filed by management. The union and management have final say in the disposition of grievances. The collective agreement is between the management and the union, acting as the agent for employees. Thus, for example, it is the union, and not the individual employee, which decides to take a case to arbitration or not to take a case to arbitration.

ARBITRATION

As was discussed in Chapter 5, virtually all Canadian jurisdictions forbid strikes during the term of a collective agreement and require that all disputes over the application, interpretation, or administration of the collective agreement be submitted to arbitration if they are not settled in the prior steps of the grievance procedure. This type of arbitration is known as "rights" arbitration, and is the final step in the grievance procedure in virtually all Canadian labour-management agreements.

While the grievance procedure prior to arbitration is often informal and does not always follow the established procedures, once a dispute reaches arbitration, the process becomes formal and legalistic. Arbitration is a judicial function, with the role of arbitration paralleling ". . . that of a court in attempting to formulate a legal answer to the issues raised by the parties or posed by all the relevant facts."[3] In all jurisdictions, arbitrators' awards are enforceable as if they were an award of a court.

Forms of Arbitration

BOARD VERSUS SINGLE ARBITRATOR

In Canadian industrial relations practice, particularly the private sector, arbitration is most frequently conducted by boards of arbitration. In the public sector, legislation most often calls for the use of single arbitrators. In the United States a single arbitrator is used in the great majority of cases.

Arbitration boards are generally tripartite, and usually only one member, the chairman, is a true neutral. The practice is for the parties each to select a representative to the board. The union and management representatives then select a neutral chairman, although the parties themselves can also select the chairman. Where the parties cannot agree on a chairman, or a single arbitrator, provision is usually made for the Minister of Labour or Labour Relations Board to appoint one. Most contracts provide that the decision of the board shall be a majority decision, except that where there is no majority the decision of the chairman shall govern. Some contracts provide only for a majority decision, however. (In the U.S., where grievance arbitration is not required by law, almost all contracts still provide for it.)

The advantages to the parties of using a board as opposed to a single arbitrator lie in the ability of the partisan members to provide technical or other advice to the neutral. The use of a board also permits the mediation of contract disputes rather than strict arbitration.

Disadvantages cited in the use of an arbitration board relate primarily to the time delays involved in selecting a panel and in hearing and deciding a case. The partisan nature of the parties' representatives may mean a complete and time-consuming rehash of the proceedings during the board's deliberations. Some chairmen make deliberations only a formality and then retire to write a decision which is submitted to the other members. In these situations, the partisan members are obviously superfluous. Where a majority report is required, the chairman's job is made even more difficult, and chairmen sometimes find that they have to compromise their own best judgement to secure a majority vote. Delays in the procedure increase the cost of arbitration, and the presence of the partisan members alone represents an additional cost for the parties. (The parties' nominees to arbitration boards may serve without pay, particularly when they are from other companies or unions. However, nominees may also be professionals such as lawyers, and as such are remunerated for their services.)

AD HOC ARBITRATORS VERSUS PERMANENT UMPIRES

Different arbitration board chairmen or single arbitrators can be selected for each case sent to arbitration, or the parties can select a permanent arbitrator, often called an umpire. The permanent umpire is selected for a given period of time, such as the duration of the contract, or simply to serve at the pleasure of the parties. Normally he is paid a retainer fee. Ad hoc arbitrators are used far more frequently than permanent umpires.

The advantages of having a permanent umpire include the fact that time need not be wasted in selecting an arbitrator. The permanent umpire becomes familiar with the provisions of the parties' agreement, their day-to-day relationship, their personalities, and their customary practices. Where a large number of disputes is likely to arise, a permanent umpire offers the parties a cost advantage. Finally, the parties come to know how he is likely to rule on an issue and adjust their behaviour accordingly.

On the other hand, finding an individual who both parties believe in and who will continue to be acceptable to them is no easy task. Once the parties have selected a permanent umpire there is some danger that they will resort to his services too quickly, before really attempting to reach agreement themselves. The parties may decide to make the umpire earn his retainer, which must be paid regardless of whether his services are used. Finally, there may be a tendency on the part of a permanent umpire to "split" awards—some for the union, some for the company, without due regard for the merits of the cases. Of course, in such a circumstance, the umpire would not be fulfilling his function and the parties would be wise to eliminate the use of his services. In any event, the services of a permanent umpire are useful only as long as he has the complete confidence of the parties.

Companies and unions can secure many of the advantages of having a permanent umpire simply by continuing to use an *ad hoc* arbitrator, as long as his services are satisfactory. By using ad hoc arbitrators the parties can bring special skills, such as industrial engineering, to bear on particular cases.

Even though the parties may not be dissatisfied with a particular ad hoc arbitrator, either or both of them may feel precluded from using his services again for political reasons, particularly in the face of an adverse arbitral decision. In using many different arbitrators, the parties are subjecting themselves to the greatest drawback to the use of the *ad hoc* arbitrators. This is the lack of knowledge on the part of the arbitrator of the circumstances of the parties. Also, a series of ad hoc arbitrators may well provide conflicting rulings on similar issues, leaving the parties with few useful clues to appropriate future action.

EXPEDITED ARBITRATION

Section 45 of the Ontario Labour Relations Act, provides for an expedited arbitration process on application of either party to a collective agreement. The section was added to the act because of complaints from unions about the lengthy delays involved in the conventional arbitration process. Under this section, once the grievance procedure set out prior to arbitration has been exhausted or 30 days after a grievance has been filed (14 days in the case of a discharge grievance), the Minister of Labour will appoint a single arbitrator upon application by either party. The arbitrator must hold a hearing within 21 days. If the parties agree, the arbitrator may make an oral award followed by written reasons for the award. Under this section, the Minister may appoint a settlement officer to attempt to mediate an agreement rather than an arbitrator.[4]

Extensive use has been made of this provision in Ontario, in part fulfilling the prophecy made when the provision was enacted, that unions would use the expedited procedure more as a way to avoid the political problems attendant in refusing to take a case to arbitration than to obtain quick justice.

The use of expedited arbitration on a voluntary basis can be found in the U.S. steel industry, and in Canada, under the agreement between the International Nickel Company and the United Steelworkers, as well as in the B.C. longshore industry. In these situations, grievances are submitted to the informal, expedited procedure by mutual consent of the parties. Decisions are frequently oral, and are not precedent setting. The parties also continue to use the regular arbitration procedure for more important issues.

The Arbitration Hearing

Once the arbitrator or arbitration board is selected, the stage is set for the actual arbitration hearing.

Although judicial in nature, arbitration is more informal than a court proceeding and can be a friendly procedure. Even though it is of an informal nature, the arbitration proceeding must provide for a full and fair hearing of the issue, and in order to ensure "natural justice" (and to prevent the judicial vacation of the award on procedural grounds) the following procedures must be met:
1. All interested parties must receive notice of the time and place of the hearing and must have an opportunity to attend.
2. The parties must be permitted to introduce evidence, without unreasonable restrictions.
3. The parties must be permitted to fully cross-examine adverse witnesses.
4. The parties must be allowed to make concluding oral arguments.
5. If they so desire, the parties must be allowed to file post-hearing written briefs.[5]

These requirements are reflected in the normal order of procedure in an arbitration hearing. After introductions, the arbitration hearing normally proceeds as follows:

1. Opening statement by the moving party, followed by a similar statement from the other side.
2. Presentation of evidence, witnesses and arguments by the moving party.
3. Cross-examination by the other party.
4. Presentation of evidence, witnesses and arguments by the defending party.
5. Cross-examination by the moving party.
6. Summation by both parties, usually following the same order as in the opening statements.[6]

MOVING PARTY AND BURDEN OF PROOF

The moving party is the party which has initiated the arbitration action. This is almost always the union, and the general rule is that the moving party presents its case first. The order of presentation is a function of the fact that the side which bears the burden of proof or has the onus of proving their case presents its case first, and in grievance arbitration, the union bears the burden of proof, except in discharge cases.[7]

The doctrine of burden of proof ". . . is that where the evidence is exactly balanced . . . between the proponent and opponent of a proposition, the proponent, or the one who advanced the proposition has failed to prove it."[8] In terms of a grievance arbitration, the party which has advanced the grievance would be considered the proponent and would thus have the burden of proof. Normally, this would be the union. However, most arbitrators have held that the employer bears the burden of proof in discipline cases. The burden of proof in arbitration cases is generally not the criminal standard of "beyond reasonable doubt," but the civil standard of balance of probabilities.[9] Thus the principle of burden of proof in arbitration cases comes into play only when the evidence presented by both sides is equal. The evidence is so rarely equal that an arbitrator is seldom required to decide a case solely on the basis of burden of proof. In order to be assured of winning a case, however, the proponent must be sure that his evidence is greater than his opponent's. If the evidence is of equal weight, then the proponent cannot be sustained by an arbitrator.

Some arbitrators have applied a more stringent standard than the civil standard, in discharge cases or discipline cases which involve a criminal act, a standard which moves toward the criminal standard. The rationale used is that discharge is an extreme penalty and such action requires a higher degree of proof. However, most arbitrators still use the civil standard of proof for discipline and discharge cases.[10]

THE ISSUE

The arbitrator's job is to make a decision in regard to the dispute between the parties. At some point in the arbitration proceeding, a clear statement of the issue (or question) to be resolved by the arbitrator must emerge, e.g., "Was John

Doe discharged for just cause?" Clearly, an arbitrator cannot make a decision until he knows just what he is being asked to decide. Also, as will be discussed later, an arbitrator's decision which goes beyond the bounds of the question submitted to him can be overturned by a court. Thus, arbitrators are careful to have a clear statement of the issue before them.

Sometimes the parties will meet prior to the arbitration and agree to a statement of the issue. This is called a stipulation of the issue. The stipulated issue is given to the arbitrator prior to or at the beginning of the hearing. At the same time the parties may provide the arbitrator with a statement of the remedy sought, the contract, and any facts which are not in dispute. They may also provide him with a statement of his authority, which is different from that contained in the contract (or when no such statement exists in the contract), as well as any statement as to how they prefer the procedural details of the hearing to be handled. Taken together, this package is called a submission to the arbitrator.

More frequently, though, the issue will emerge in the course of the hearing. The grievance statement, as processed through the grievance procedure, may serve as a statement of the issue. At other times the arbitrator may simply pinpoint the issue during the hearing and ask the parties if they agree that this is the issue he is to decide. If an arbitrator cannot get the parties to agree to a statement of the issue he may refuse to hear the case[11] or adjourn the proceedings.[12] On the other hand, he may continue to hear the case and as part of his decision provide a statement of the issue in dispute.

Arbitrability

The fact that an issue has been considered in the grievance procedure does not necessarily mean that it can be taken to arbitration or be considered by an arbitrator under the terms of the contract. That is, all grievances are not necessarily arbitrable.

Collective agreements usually put some restrictions on the types of issues that may be arbitrated. Most clauses restrict arbitration to disputes over the application, interpretation, administration, or violation of the contract. While this might seem sufficiently broad to cover any possible grievance, in practice this is not necessarily so.

Strictly defined, a grievance is a charge that the contract has been violated. However, complaints of a general nature may find their way into the grievance procedure. Many managements are anxious to have any employee gripe or complaint aired, and in practice the words "complaint" and "grievance" are used interchangeably. However, in order to be arbitrable, a complaint must be a *bona fide* grievance — a charge that the contract has been violated.

Another situation which may affect an arbitrator's jurisdiction to hear a case is one where the time limits specified in the contract have not been followed. If appeals have not been logged, nor replies received in a timely fashion, the argument may be made that the grievance has been abandoned and thus the arbitrator or arbitration board does not have jurisdiction to hear it. (The Ontario and British Columbia labour relations legislation gives arbitrators the right to hear untimely grievances in certain circumstances.)[13]

Who decides whether a dispute is arbitrable? In both Canada and the United States, this question is generally left to the arbitrator to decide. If one party refuses to permit arbitration, the other party may ask a court to order arbitration. In the United States, the Supreme Court has established that courts must order arbitration, unless there is an absolutely clear exclusionary contract provision. If there is any doubt as to whether a case is arbitrable, it is to be decided in favour of arbitration.[14] In most Canadian jurisdictions, legislation requires that arbitrability be determined by an arbitrator, and the courts have generally enforced this legislative dictate. A later section on judicial review will further discuss the relationship between arbitration and the courts.

Thus, a company faced with a union demand for the arbitration of an issue which the company believed to be nonarbitrable, could not refuse to schedule and attend an arbitration hearing on the issue. If the company did refuse, it would be ordered to arbitration by a court of law. In the arbitration hearing, the company would first have to argue that the issue was not arbitrable, and the arbitrator would first have to decide the issue of arbitrability. This would take place as a "mini-hearing" before the actual case was heard. If the arbitrator decided the issue was arbitrable, the arbitrator would then proceed to hear and decide the case. If the arbitrator decided that the issue was not arbitrable, the proceeding would stop at that point.

OTHER PROCEDURAL MATTERS

Depending on the preferences of the parties and the arbitrator, witnesses may be sworn and a transcript of the hearing taken. The arbitrator has the power to exclude witnesses (except for the parties directly concerned). That is, the arbitrator may require them to leave the hearing room during the testimony of other witnesses. This is done to preserve "purity of testimony," and at the request of the parties. If the arbitrator finds it necessary, he may visit the plant in order to see the physical site involved in the dispute. This is called "taking a view." This may not be done without both parties being present or having the opportunity to attend. The arbitrator may call or cross-examine witnesses or he may ask for specific evidence. In doing so, arbitrators generally try to tread a fine line between gaining a complete understanding of the case and appearing to present a case for one side or the other. Arbitrators generally have the power to subpoena witnesses or evidence if the parties refuse to provide these voluntarily.

RULES OF EVIDENCE

Arbitrators are not required to adhere to the legal rules of evidence. Arbitrators generally allow great leeway in the admission of testimony and other evidence. This is because arbitrators usually want to give the parties as much opportunity as possible to present their cases as they see fit. Also, on some occasions, arbitrators' decisions have been overturned by the courts because the arbitrator refused to admit evidence of some sort.

Thus arbitrators may admit hearsay evidence or allegations without proof. (Many arbitrators, though, will sustain objections about the introduction of this kind of testimony.) However, the admission of evidence does not necessarily mean the arbitrator must act on it. Usually the arbitrator will admit all evidence "for what it is worth." In the case of hearsay, this is not much.

In general, the overriding principle used by arbitrators in accepting and evaluating evidence is called the "best evidence" rule. This rule is expressed well in this citation:

> This Board, of course, is permitted to entertain testimony which would not be considered evidence in a court of law, but nevertheless arbitrators should be careful to apply the best evidence rule wherever possible, and the best evidence is, of course, testimony given by witnesses who saw the events which are described or made the statements attributed to them.[15]

Arbitrators may make a decision on the basis of purely circumstantial evidence, although they will generally refuse to accept improperly or illegally obtained evidence, or confessions which were obtained under duress. Arbitrators have treated the failure of a grievant, or others with a knowledge of the situation, to testify at a hearing, as leading to the inference that their testimony would be damaging to the grievant.

Despite the fact that evidence is freely admitted in an arbitration case, both parties can and do object during the hearing to the evidence offered by the other party. Objections that the evidence is hearsay, or is immaterial, irrelevant, or incompetent may not get the evidence removed from the record, but will serve to remind the arbitrator of the weight which should be given that evidence in considering the record of the hearing.

One rule of evidence that must clearly be followed by arbitrators is that they must not hear evidence from any source except in the presence of both parties. The operation of a tripartite arbitration board is open to this sort of error. As Curtis says:

> . . . it may afford a party an excellent opportunity for reaching the ear of the arbitrator without approaching him directly. A party ordinarily expects its nominee to make its position clear and to point up its arguments so that the chairman will give them the weight they are expected to carry. Occasionally a nominee is called upon to present evidence, which, for some reason the party does not want to produce at the hearing. Clearly the chairman who accepts evidence through such a channel is acting improperly. The party that attempts to present evidence in such a way is also acting improperly, besides risking whatever merits its case may possess.[16]

Having heard the case, the arbitrator must proceed to make a decision. He can make his decision only on the evidence placed before him by the parties. The evidence presented in arbitration cases is sometimes contradictory. The arbitrator must sift through the testimony to reach the best conclusion he can as to the facts. Determination of the weight, the relevance and the authenticity of the evidence is part of the arbitrator's task in reaching a decision.

Arbitrators' decisions are not made in a complete vacuum, however. Standards for arbitral decisions exist in both precedent (the findings of other arbitrators) and in general rules of contract interpretation. These standards are of use to arbitrators in deciding a case, and to the parties in arguing a case.

Precedent

Precedent does not have the force in arbitration that it has in civil or criminal law. Precedent in arbitration can be differentiated into two types: authoritative and persuasive. Authoritative precedents are those which must or should be followed whether the arbitrator agrees with them or not. Arbitrators are not under any obligation to follow persuasive precedents, but may take them into consideration, giving them as much weight as their intrinsic merit will allow.[17]

Examples of authoritative precedents are those set by a permanent umpire or board chairman. One of the major purposes of such an arrangement would be voided if precedent were not followed. Decisions by ad hoc arbitrators involving the interpretation of a specific contract provision between a company and a union will generally not be reversed by another arbitrator, unless, perhaps, he feels strongly that that decision was wrong.[18] Thus, an interpretation given to a clause in a particular agreement by an arbitrator will stand until the agreement is changed.

The extent to which persuasive precedent affects an arbitrator really depends on the arbitrator. Some arbitrators rely heavily on precedents cited by the parties, while others do not. In nearly all cases, the arbitrator will consider the precedents cited, and the parties should take care to make sure that the cases they cite are germane to the one at hand, lest the arbitrator be negatively influenced by the citing of irrelevant material. Also, reading precedent is time-consuming for the arbitrator and can increase the costs of arbitration. However, precedent can be useful to arbitrators, and it is worthwhile for the parties to seek out other cases similar to their own, if only to discover what arguments arbitrators find most cogent.

Precedent in arbitration cases can be found in several sources. Canadian cases are summarized in *Labour Arbitration Cases*, published by the Canadian Law Book Company (Toronto) in cooperation with the Central Ontario Industrial Relations Institute. U.S. citations can be found in *Labor Arbitration Reports* published by the Bureau of National Affairs, Incorporated and *Labor Arbitration Awards* published by Commerce Clearing House, Incorporated.

Principles of Contract Interpretation

The core of the arbitrator's job is the interpretation of the collective agreement. Certain standards exist to help him do this. These have been developed through arbitration precedents and the common law of contracts. While these standards are not absolute, they can be a useful guide to preparing arbitration cases and also in deciding whether to take cases to arbitration.

First of all, arbitrators will not interpret a contract in such a way that the application of the clause would result in an unlawful act. Similarly, where necessary, arbitrators will look at the rulings of administrative tribunals such as the Labour Relations Board and the decisions of courts (particularly the highest courts) for guidance in interpretation. Arbitrators will also interpret an agreement so that the application will not result in harsh or absurd results.

AMBIGUITY

The very existence of a claim for arbitration is an indication that the parties disagree over the interpretation of the agreement, that is, certain alleged ambiguities exist in the contract. However, the arguments that the contract language is ambiguous must be plausible. A mere claim that it is ambiguous is not enough, and if the words are plain and clear, the clear meaning will be applied by the arbitrator.

Even though contracts have become increasingly detailed over the years, they still contain much ambiguity. Frequently, contracts are ambiguous because the parties believe that they cannot spell out in detail all the language which might be necessary. Discipline is a primary example of this type of situation. Most contracts specify that management shall discipline only for "just cause." Such a phrase is clearly ambiguous and deliberately so, to provide the parties with a reasonable amount of flexibility in the face of the impossibility of spelling out penalties for every conceivable disciplinary situation which might arise during the term of an agreement. Sometimes the parties provide ambiguous language in the contract because they cannot agree to more specific language. At other times, the language is not seen as ambiguous until the parties attempt to apply it to a specific situation. In any event, all agreements have some ambiguities; if this were not so, there would be little need for arbitration.

The primary rule to be observed in the interpretation of collective agreements is that the intent of the parties in drafting the agreement must be preserved. Thus where ambiguities exist, the arbitrator may examine the precontract negotiations to help determine what the clause meant to the parties at the time the agreement was signed. Where ambiguity cannot be resolved in any other way, it will be resolved by interpreting the contract language against the interpretation proposed by the party who drafted it during negotiations. Arbitrators will also look at the contract as a whole in order to ascertain the intent of the parties with regard to a specific section. A clause would not be interpreted so as to nullify or modify another part of the agreement. However, where a contract has specific language covering the issue in dispute, that language will prevail over general language which only deals with the issue by inference.[19]

Probably the most important standard used by arbitrators in interpreting ambiguous contract language is past practice. If the parties have consistently and repeatedly behaved in a manner that gives ambiguous language a specific meaning, then the agreement will be interpreted in light of that behaviour.[20] For example, suppose a contract has a statement which reads: "The Company shall continue to make reasonable provisions for the safety and health of its employees." Assume also that the company always provided gloves for occupants of particular jobs. In all probability, the company could not now require employees to purchase gloves for this job. Most, if not all, arbitrators would rule that the past practice of supplying the gloves free of charge, in the absence of any other evidence, gives meaning to the words, "make reasonable provisions."

However, past practice only governs in the face of ambiguous language. Clear language prevails over past practice.[21] Thus, if the contract provides for one thing and the parties have in practice followed another course, the contract language will prevail if a dispute occurs.

Past Practice Where the Contract is Silent

Where contract language is ambiguous, arbitrators will rely on the past practice of the parties to help determine what the language means. But what about situations where there is no contract language covering the issue, but a practice exists? Does the existence of a practice constitute an implied agreement, precluding its change during the term of an agreement? This question goes to the heart of the most contentious issue in arbitration. It relates to management's ability to make changes during the term of an agreement in the absence of explicit contractual restrictions.

"RESERVED RIGHTS" THEORY

Managements have generally argued that prior to collective bargaining they had unilateral control over wages, hours, and all other conditions of employment. This unilateral control, or "management right," still exists except where specifically limited by the collective agreement. Thus, where the contract is silent about an issue, such as the "right" to subcontract out work, management has the right to take unilateral action. A past practice, unless specifically mentioned in the contract, is not binding on management and may be withdrawn at any time.

"STATUS QUO" THEORY

Some contracts have clauses which are designed to insure continuance of established practices. Even where such clauses do not exist, unions have argued that the "status quo" at the beginning of the agreement, modified by practices that have been accepted during the agreement, should be maintained until the parties agree otherwise. Thus any practices which exist at the beginning of an agreement must remain in force during the term of the agreement, unless the parties agree to a change. Following this theory, management does not have the right to make unilateral changes in wages, hours, or conditions of employment during the term of an agreement, even if the contract is silent on the matter.

In general, most Canadian arbitrators have followed the "reserved rights" theory. However, some arbitrators and court decisions have held that there must be a clear statement of the management's right to act in an area in the management's rights clause in the collective agreement, or the arbitrator or arbitration board may look at the entire contract to judge the appropriateness of the management action or view that action in terms of its fairness.[22]

Some of the most contentious cases regarding management rights have involved the contracting out of work normally done by bargaining unit members. In general, Canadian arbitrators have refused to limit the employer's rights to do so, except where the contract has an express prohibition against doing so. Some arbitrators have required that subcontracting be done in good faith and for valid business reasons.[23]

Another area of interest is the ability of management to increase wages *above* the levels prescribed in the collective agreement, either directly or by the unilateral imposition of an incentive scheme. Arbitral decisions in this area are mixed, and this area is sometimes seen as one exception to the general rule that the collective agreement may not be unilaterally changed by either party.[24]

In summary, then, the general drift of Canadian arbitration decisions would permit management to introduce change mid-contract where there is no prohibitive language. However, that right has been restricted, on occasion, by tests of reasonableness, fairness, good faith, compelling business interests, and the intent of the contract as a whole. As a consequence, management rights cannot, by any means, be considered to be unfettered.

Judicial Review

As was mentioned above, the awards of arbitrators and arbitration boards are enforceable as if they were an award of the court. Under some circumstances, arbitration awards are reviewable by the courts if one party disagrees with the award and appeals the decision. Some of these appeals have been made all the way to the Supreme Court of Canada.[25]

There are four grounds on which arbitration awards can be appealed and for which the courts will set aside (vacate or quash in legal terminology) arbitration awards. These are:
1. Denial of natural justice.
2. Exceeding the jurisdiction of the arbitrator.
3. Bias or fraud.
4. Error of law on the face of the award.[26]

A denial of natural justice would occur if the hearing was not a fair hearing for both parties. A jurisdictional error would occur if the arbitrator failed to answer the question submitted to him, or if the arbitrator amended or altered the contract.[27] Boards or arbitrators could also be found to have exceeded their jurisdiction if they heard a grievance that was not timely, or if they had not been selected in the manner set out in the collective agreement. Given the nature of their task, board chairmen and single arbitrators are supposed to be impartial and any evidence of bias or fraud or venality on their part would be grounds for setting aside their award.

The concept of error on the face of the award is a little more complex than the other concepts discussed above. In general, this type of error would be found to exist if the arbitrator interpreted a contract in a way that the court found the language of the contract could not reasonably bear.[28] Such an error could also be found where an arbitrator used hearsay testimony to reach a decision in the face of direct testimony. It could also occur, for example, where the arbitrator declared contract language to be ambiguous and a court believed the language was clear and unambiguous.[29]

In one sense, the concept of error of law on the face of the award can be used by the courts to reverse arbitral decisions that the magistrate disagrees with. However, this is rarely the case, and the courts will generally only reverse an arbitration decision where they believe it is clearly wrong or absolutely unreasonable.[30] Thus, although arbitration decisions are reviewable by the courts, the grounds for that review are relatively narrow. Such a review is time-consuming and costly, and anyone contemplating such an appeal should consider this as well as the fact such appeals, particularly when done by management may well reduce the long-run attractiveness of the grievance procedure as a dispute-settling mechanism. As we shall see in the section on pressure tactics later in the chapter, and in the Great Lakes Iron and Steel case, the available alternatives to the grievance procedure are not particularly attractive.

SELECTED ISSUES IN CONTRACT ADMINISTRATION

Collective agreements in Canada exhibit great scope and variety. The decisions of arbitrators and boards of arbitration which interpret those agreements fill volumes. Every agreement is unique, and since the starting point for the administration of the collective agreement is the language of the agreement itself, every situation can be said to have its own special issues and problems. The issues discussed here and in the cases which follow this chapter are typical, but our selection cannot pretend to be all-encompassing. Our purpose is to develop an appreciation for the overriding importance of skillful administration in forming and developing a mature industrial relations climate. This is a job for all managers, not just for industrial relations managers alone. The development of skill and understanding in the subjects dealt with here should have transfer value in understanding and dealing with the host of industrial relations issues which practising managers meet every day.

DISCIPLINE

Many labour agreements provide management with the exclusive right to establish rules and regulations to govern the conduct of employees, and most agreements give management the right to discipline employees for "just cause." Unions generally reserve the right to challenge discipline actions through the grievance procedure. If rules and regulations are well known, non-discriminatory and administered in a fair, unbiased manner, the disciplinary actions based on them will most likely be upheld by an arbitrator.

Work rules cover a wide variety of topics, ranging from hours of work to production output expected, and from dress, to conduct, to attendance. They are justified most often by the need to maintain order, consistency, and efficiency in the organization.

Unions are generally reluctant to participate in the formation of rules and regulations; rather, they prefer to police their administration—challenging their efficacy in specific cases. It is easier and potentially less embarrassing for unions to challenge a rule or regulation formulated by management alone than one in which the union played a part in framing.

Disciplinary programs should be designed for the purpose of correcting behaviour, not simply for punishment. For this reason, discipline is frequently progressive; that is, penalties become increasingly severe as violations of rules are repeated. The first violation might bring a verbal warning, the second a written warning, the third a three-day suspension, and the fourth discharge. Penalties also are likely to vary with the seriousness of the offence. Tardiness might result in verbal warning, while smoking in an area where hydrogen gas is present might result in immediate discharge. Penalties are generally limited to verbal and written warnings, suspension and discharge, although, in some cases, demotion and deprivation of seniority rights have been used, and accepted as appropriate by arbitrators.[31]

In any disciplinary program, it is impossible to anticipate all possible actions that might call for discipline. That is why the all-encompassing expression "just cause" is contained in most collective bargaining agreements. Managements governed by a "just cause" provision are repeatedly called on to exercise judgement in cases of misconduct, whether or not the misconduct was covered by a specific rule or regulation, and their judgement is subject to challenge by the union.

Discipline cases are the subject of more arbitration cases than any other type. As a result, there is more industrial jurisprudence on this subject than on any other.[32] The decisions of arbitrations can, and indeed must, provide useful guidelines for the administration of discipline.

In considering grievances over discipline, arbitrators generally must answer two questions:
1. Did the offence for which discipline is being imposed occur?
2. If so, does the penalty imposed by the company seem appropriate?

Thus, management must first be able to prove that the alleged offence actually occurred. Having done this, management must be able to demonstrate that the penalty imposed for the offence is appropriate. In doing so, the following considerations come into play:

1. Where a *rule* or *work standard* is being applied, management must show that: It was known to the employee. It was reasonably related to safe, orderly, efficient operations. Training to meet a standard was adequate.
2. Rules and standards must have been applied consistently. The penalized employee must have the worst record. All violations must have been treated in the same manner, all other considerations being equal.
3. An employee must have had reason to believe a penalty would follow a given offence. The employee must have been told the potential consequences of particular acts; should have been warned in writing, and should have received a final warning.
4. The prior record of the employee must have been taken into account.
5. The seriousness of the offence should have been considered.
6. The length of service of the employee should also have been considered.
7. Other considerations which should be taken into account include: Was the offence an isolated incident in the employee's employment history? Was the employee's behaviour, in whole or in part, provoked by actions of company

management? Was the offence committed on the spur of the moment as a result of a momentary aberration, due to strong personal impulses, or was the offence premeditated? Does the penalty imposed have the effect of creating a special economic hardship for the grievant in the light of his particular circumstances? Does the employee have rehabilitative potential?

Culminating Incident

Very simply, the doctrine of culminating incident says that a severe penalty (usually discharge) may be appropriate for an offence for which such a penalty might not usually be applied, *given the past poor record of the employee.*

To invoke the culminating incident doctrine, the company must prove: (1) that the final incident actually took place; (2) that it is an offence for which some sort of discipline would normally be applied; and (3) that the employee had been notified and warned about the unsatisfactory elements in his or her work record. Very often a "final" warning of impending discharge is required. Some arbitrators have held that for the work record to be introduced in the arbitration hearing, it must be mentioned in the discharge letter or notice.

Section 61.5 of the Canada Labour Code provides statutory "just cause" protection against discharge for all non-unionized non-management personnel with more than 12 months service in the federal jurisdiction. Under this section, an individual who has been discharged may make a complaint to the minister, who will appoint an inspector to investigate and attempt to mediate a settlement. If the investigator is unsuccessful in resolving a dispute, the minister may appoint an adjudicator who will hear the case just as an arbitrator would, and apply the same standards.[33]

Non-Disciplinary Discipline

A special kind of situation occurs when an employee is unable to do his or her assigned work for reasons beyond the employee's control, such as illness, alcoholism, or the effect of aging. Such situations are difficult to administer, since the situation is not the employee's fault, yet results in losses of various kinds to the employer, who is also not at fault. In general, arbitrators have held that some of these losses must be borne by the employer. After a certain point, however, transfer, demotion, or even discharge is possible. In such situations, management must demonstrate:

1. That it, as the employer, is having its legitimate interests compromised by the continuing presence of the employee at work or in a particular job.
2. That the condition giving rise to the management action is outside the control of the employee, and is a continuous, recurring, or intermittent condition.
3. That it is unlikely to be corrected in the near future, or that
4. Even if the employee can return to work (or the job held), he or she cannot be reasonably expected to do so without endangering himself or herself, other employees, or the employer or the property thereof.
5. That there has been some culminating or final incident.
6. That the deficiencies of the employee's performance and their impact on operations have been discussed with the employee.

7. That management has acted fairly and equitably without discrimination.
8. Where discharge is involved, that there is no job to which the employee is entitled, under the collective agreement, that the employee can perform.

In their search for appropriate, meaningful penalties short of discharge, many managements have applied disciplinary suspensions without pay for serious misconduct. This kind of action causes employees to experience some loss of earnings and, according to its advocates, causes some reassessment by the employee of the conduct giving rise to the suspension. However, in recent years, disciplinary suspensions have been used less and less, and appropriately worded disciplinary warnings have taken their place. Sometimes employees are given time off *with pay* to consider the seriousness of their actions and the fact that they are placing their employment in jeopardy.[34] There are two reasons why this is done. Firstly, the company may be depriving itself of an important skill — thus sacrificing productivity and know-how in order to establish its right to impose discipline — a foolish, wasteful action. Secondly, there are an increasing number of employees who play the rules and regulations game to the hilt — committing violations just frequently enough or seriously enough to warrant a suspension but not so seriously as to cause a discharge. In this way, they can get some much-desired time off while not sacrificing the job itself.

One principle in the administration of discipline can be stated unequivocally. If an infraction occurs which might require discipline, management should always, without exception, investigate with extreme care, away from the immediate "heat" of the circumstances, before prescribing final punishment. The annals of industrial relations practice are replete with instances where managements, acting in haste and without adequate information, took inappropriate action, sometimes against innocent employees, with consequences that soured their industrial relations system for several years to come. The burden is on management to administer justice in the workplace fairly, consistently, and without prejudice.

Seniority

Seniority is a concept based on the philosophy that longer-service employees should have greater protection than those with less service. There are two basic types of seniority: benefit seniority and competitive status seniority.

Benefit Seniority

Under benefit seniority, the level of wage or fringe benefit received by an employee is related to his length of service. The length of vacations is frequently tied to years of service: two weeks after one year's service, three weeks after five years' service, four weeks after fifteen years' service, five weeks after twenty years' service. Severance pay is generally related to the length of the employee's service, as is the amount of pension benefits: e.g., $15.00 per month per year of service. Benefit levels under group insurance plans are sometimes related to seniority, as is eligibility for profit sharing or other bonus arrangements. Sometimes wage levels are related to accumulated employment time or, on the other hand, to length of service in a particular job category.

Competitive Status Seniority

Competitive status seniority is used where length of service determines an employee's status vis-a-vis other employees. Competitive status seniority is used in lay-offs and recalls, promotions, transfers, work assignments, shift preference, the allocation of days off, and vacation times. Employees with the longest continuous service are usually the last to be laid off, and the first to be recalled. They are also given priorities in promotion and transfer, and have their choice of work assignment, work shift, and vacation time.

The concept of seniority has been accepted in many walks of life as an equitable, objective decision-making criterion. In union management relationships, the concept has existed since the earliest collective agreements were signed. Generally, there has been little controversy regarding benefit seniority, but the area of competitive status seniority has been the source of considerable controversy, especially as it relates to promotions, job assignments, and lay-offs. While unions and managements agree that length of service is an important factor in determining these matters, they often tangle when seniority versus ability arguments arise. Most managements seek to place greatest weight on ability in making such decisions while most unions place prime emphasis on seniority.

Usually these issues are dealt with in collective agreements by way of complex contingent language. In practice, there are many types of seniority-ability provisions in agreements. The four types listed below serve to illustrate the range of such provisions:

1. Promotions will be made solely on the basis of seniority.
2. The most senior applicant shall be promoted, provided he has sufficient ability to do the job after a reasonable training or break-in period.
3. Where skill, ability and physical fitness are relatively equal, seniority shall govern.
4. Promotions shall be made on the basis of skill, ability, and physical fitness, to be determined solely by the employer.

Clauses like (1) and (4) are rare. Employers are generally unwilling to accept seniority as the sole criterion for the promotion of employees. Employees, through their unions, are generally unwilling to give the employer unilateral control over promotions. The result of these two conflicting viewpoints is usually a contract clause like (2) or (3).

Clause (2) provides that as long as the senior person can perform the job satisfactorily, he or she is entitled to it, even if other applicants have greater ability. Under clause (3), the applicant with the greatest ability would presumably get the promotion, even if he or she had less seniority than other applicants. Only where the ability of applicants is equal would seniority provide the decision criterion.

Regardless of the type of clause found in the agreement, certain administration problems are likely to arise in promotion situations: How is "ability to do the job" to be defined? When does an employee have the ability to do the job and when does he or she not? What does "relatively equal" mean? Sometimes clauses that are written do not specify the relative weights to be given to seniority or ability. For example, "Promotions shall be based on ability, seniority, skill, physical fitness."

There are certain guidelines to the resolution of seniority versus ability issues. These guidelines have been developed through the experience of unions and management with these problems and through the decisions of arbitrators.

Some of the criteria for judging ability are the following: proficiency test, experience on the job, education, production data, performance ratings, age, personality traits, and absence, tardiness, and discipline records. While the acceptability of these criteria varies according to their exact nature (particularly in arbitration), it is important from a managerial point of view to develop fair, reasonable, appropriate, and consistent standards and apply them in an unbiased manner. Where such standards have been applied without union challenge for a number of years, arbitrators have been reluctant to allow them to be discarded.

In all promotion cases, the onus is on the grieving employee to prove that he or she has the requisite skill or ability required under the contract. In grievances under clause (2) type provisions, the grievant merely must prove that he or she can perform the job satisfactorily and then the onus shifts to the employer to justify the decision made. Under clause (3) type provisions, the burden of proof borne by the grieving employee is much more onerous.[35]

Seniority in Lay-offs and Recalls

In the absence of clear differences in ability, it is generally accepted that the most senior employees should have greatest job security. In most situations, this means they are the last to be laid off and the first to be recalled.

Controversies often arise concerning the right to bump during reductions in force. In situations where plant-wide seniority prevails, and where senior employees can displace junior employees in other classifications of work, there may be long chains of "bumps" set off by a single lay-off. Because of the tremendous administrative problems involved in any chain bumping situation, managements tend to favour seniority systems which provide for exercise of bumping rights on a restricted basis — within a department and within a classification, if possible. Unions, on the other hand, tend to favour plant-wide bumping rights, unrestricted by differences in classifications, even if it means expenditure of time and efficiency in training replacements.

The result of these divergent views is frequently some sort of compromise. In some situations, plant-wide seniority is workable; in others, department seniority is best. Frequently, several departments with similar operations are grouped together, and labour "pools" created, through which new employees enter the plant workforce and into which senior employees displaced from their department can "bump," displacing the most junior employees. The possible variations are almost endless, but the job of developing an appropriate lay-off and recall system is a major item on the bargaining agenda of most unions and managements.

The main administrative problem with lay-offs and recalls is in keeping good records of seniority dates and then taking the appropriate action based on those records. Depending upon the system in use, an employee may have four different seniority dates; date of hire (plant seniority), date of entry into the department (department seniority), date of job acquisition (job seniority), and the date from which various benefits are calculated (benefit seniority).

PRODUCTION STANDARDS AND INCENTIVES

Production standards have many forms. All of them are designed to provide a fix on probable output and to provide a benchmark against which individual performances can be compared. Sometimes rates of pay are tied directly to production standards in the form of piecework incentives. More often, they are tied indirectly to the standards; those workers who consistently attain or exceed standards are rewarded more often with raises in pay and promotions than those who do not.

If production standards are set consistently and updated whenever changes in methods of operation are incorporated, they are useful devices for predicting costs, for scheduling production, and for locating workers who are ill-suited to the jobs to which they have been assigned. In the latter respect, a good standards program can help supervisors determine where additional training and instruction should take place and, occasionally, can help determine where replacements are needed.

In instances where production standards are tied directly to earnings by way of an incentive plan, there is far more concern by workers and their representatives about the derivation of the standards. Usually standards themselves are subject to a grievance, provided there is challenge registered within a reasonable time after they have been set. And since many standards are subject, in part, to subjective assessments by a methods engineer, long and bitter battles are sometimes fought over the question of the methods engineer's judgement in assigning a few thousandths of a second as an expected time for doing a job. Naturally, in an incentive plan, the workers benefit from standards which provide them plenty of time to do a job, because any improvement they can make in actual performance to shorten that time will result in direct additions to their pocketbooks.

In collective agreements covering situations where incentive systems are in operation, there are usually clauses which protect workers against capricious and frequent changes in standards. A typical clause providing such protection is the following:

> Present incentive rates are not to be changed unless there has been a significant change in methods, tools, material, design or production conditions.

Such clauses are designed to protect workers from arbitrary "rate cutting" where a standard has been improperly set or where an individual worker has managed to develop his own production short cuts that allow for production (and incentive earnings) at above-standard levels.

Some managements, in an effort to cut costs, try to make minor changes in method or design in order to achieve a restudy of a job and thus change the standard. Where such attempts occur, and even where changes in methods, tools, materials, or design are legitimate, another question arises: Were the changes significant enough to warrant a restudy of the job and a change in the standard? This question is often the subject of a grievance.

When a restudy is done, there is often a question of whether the new rate is fair. On changed jobs, the question of fairness is usually related to the employee's earnings levels before the change was made. If the employee does not have the same earnings opportunities under the new standard that he had under the old, he will understandably feel that his pay has been unreasonably cut.

Demoralized Incentive Plans

Where jobs are not restudied as a consequence of minor changes in method, material, or design, there is a tendency for incentive rates to become out of line over time. Usually, in such cases, earnings have gradually crept up as well. Thus old jobs are likely to have higher earnings than new jobs. Often, workers assigned to nearly identical jobs adjacent to each other find that the earning opportunities for one are far better than those for the other, giving rise to complaints, grievances, and demands to make the opportunities alike. Neither companies nor union leaders are readily able to cope with such complaints, and the grievance machinery sometimes gets bogged down with cases that are extremely difficult to solve. When this occurs, and when there is general agreement that incentive earnings are unrelated to effort, the system is said to be "demoralized."

Demoralized incentive systems are intolerable for both unions and companies. From the union's standpoint, they represent a split in the ranks between those who have jobs with attractive opportunities to make money and those who do not. From the company's viewpoint, they often indicate higher-than-normal labour costs. In some instances, the costs have been so high that companies have been forced to shut their doors. More often, however, a demoralized system has given rise to a contract demand for complete revision or abolishment of the system. Such a demand is always accompanied by a high price tag, because when an incentive plan is discontinued or revised, the unions usually want a guarantee that past earnings levels will be maintained.

HOURS OF WORK

The eight-hour workday and 40-hour workweek, with fixed starting and quitting times Monday through Friday, are generally thought to be the standard pattern of employment. However, many organizations operate on quite different patterns. Some production facilities, for example, operate around the clock: 7 days a week, 365 days a year. Workers sometimes have starting and quitting times which vary from one week to the next. In some operations, like stevedoring, the hours are dependent on the availability of work. In others, for instance banks and supermarkets, the hours are largely determined by customer convenience. In some companies, the employees work four days a week, ten to twelve hours each day, then take off the next three days. In still others, there are no fixed starting and quitting times; rather, the worker himself decides what hours he will work, constrained only by company expectations that he will put in a stated number of hours each week and will accommodate his schedule to others who may be dependent on his presence at certain times.

Most collective agreements contain a section titled "Hours of Work." Often, this spells out the starting and quitting times for all categories of employees covered by the agreement. Where more than one shift operates, the agreement will also indicate whether employees will remain on one shift or rotate from one to the other. In most situations, it is considered more desirable to work one shift than another; consequently premium payments are specified as inducements for those assigned to less desirable shifts. Sometimes a lesser number of hours is prescribed for these shifts either as a substitute for, or in addition to, monetary inducements. Changes in a work schedule after it is posted often call for premium pay. In general, in the absence of provisions to the contrary, management has wide latitude in scheduling work, including adding shifts, moving to continuous operations, changing the hours of shifts, and changing the shifts to which employees are assigned.[36]

Overtime

Most jurisdictions in the United States and Canada prescribe limits in working time beyond which workers must receive premium pay. Similarly, premium pay is required in most jurisdictions for work performed on Sundays and holidays. Some jurisdictions prohibit work on these days.

In most collective bargaining agreements, there are provisions calling for premium pay for overtime work that are normally more liberal than those required by law. The subject of overtime is one of the most frequently debated subjects between companies and unions. Until recently, unions expressed a consistent interest in maximizing the opportunities for overtime pay, and employees were generally eager to fatten their pocketbooks with time and a half or double time pay for additional hours worked. As a result, elaborate arrangements were worked out between many companies and unions to insure equitable distribution of overtime work. In some companies, for example, it is necessary to post lists of employees each week, with the number of overtime hours indicated next to each name. When work in a given category is available on overtime, the employee with the least number of hours who is qualified for the job must be asked first whether he or she wants to work. If the overtime opportunity is refused, the individual is charged with the hours offered, but is not paid. The next employee with the least number of hours is then asked to accept the overtime. This process is repeated, with appropriate clerical adjustments being made to the lists, until a full complement of workers is secured.

The allocation of overtime work gives rise to many complaints. Sometimes, for example, a worker is skipped over in order to secure a person who is better qualified for the work. This then gives rise to claims for penalty pay. Most arrangements give some leeway to management to skip over workers in special circumstances, but many bitter battles are waged to be sure that overtime work is handled in a fair manner.

An issue of relatively recent vintage concerns the compulsory nature of overtime. Some contracts require employees to perform overtime work at management's bidding, provided they are given adequate notice. In other company-union situations, there is no such requirement stated in the contract, and in those situations, arbitrators have generally ruled that such overtime work is compulsory. However, at times, arbitrators have placed restrictions on the amount of overtime that can be required. This means that an employee who refuses such work without good reason can be penalized for unexcused absence. Repeated refusals could lead to discipline and, possibly, discharge.

In recent years, many unions have fought to eliminate or limit the use of compulsory overtime. The use of extensive overtime by companies when some employees are laid off has been particularly contentious. From a management point of view, it is difficult to efficiently manage almost any operation without the use of some overtime. Management's ability to retain some flexibility in the use of overtime and in the scheduling of work in general is likely to be a function of how reasonably and fairly such scheduling is done.

JOB CLASSIFICATION AND JOB ASSIGNMENT

Job classification is the process by which various jobs are grouped for the purpose of compensation. Those jobs which are of a similar nature or content are placed in the same classification and assigned the same wage or salary range.

In some firms, the respective classifications are determined by a process known as job evaluation. There are many different plans for job evaluation. Some involve simple ranking of jobs; others involve sophisticated factor analysis.

Where a union is present, the nature of the evaluation plan is often negotiated, and the actual evaluation is frequently a joint process. The initial issues are: 1) What factors are to be measured? 2) What are people going to be paid for? Once these factors — called compensable factors — are determined, a second issue must be addressed: What shall the relative weights of these factors be?

One of the best known job evaluation systems is the Cooperative Wage Study (CWS) which was developed by the United Steel Workers of America in cooperation with 86 steel firms in the United States in the late 1940s. Now, after numerous revisions, the CWS plan is used in many industries throughout North America. Twelve Factors are used to determine the proper evaluation of a job. Each of them is weighted in accordance with the chart below.[37]

Factors	Weight	Job Requirement Measured
1. Pre-Employment training	1.0	The mentality required to absorb training and exercise judgement for the satisfactory performance of the job.
2. Employment training and experience	4.0	The time required to learn how to do the job, producing work of acceptable quality and of sufficient quantity to justify continued employment.
3. Mental Skill	3.5	The mental ability, job knowledge, judgement and ingenuity required to visualize, reason through and plan the details of a job without recourse to supervision.
4. Manual Skill	2.0	The physical or muscular ability and dexterity required in performing a given job, including the use of tools, machines and equipment.

Factors	Weight	Job Requirement Measured
5. Responsibility for materials	10.0	The obligation imposed either by authority or by the inherent nature of the job to prevent loss through damage to materials. Both the care required and the probable monetary loss are considered.
6. Responsibility for tools and equipment	4.0	The obligation imposed on the workman for attention and care to prevent damage to tools and equipment with which he is usually working or which come under his control. Both the care and the probable cost of damage at any one time are considered.
7. Responsibility for operations	6.5	The obligation imposed on the workman for utilizing capacity of equipment or process by maintenance of pace and machine speeds. This includes planning, instructing and directing the work of others.
8. Responsibility for safety of others	2.0	The degree of care required by the nature of the job and the surroundings in which it is performed, to avoid or prevent injuries to other persons.
9. Mental effort	2.5	The mental or visual concentration and attention required by the job for the performance of work at normal pace. Select that level which best describes the average degree of muscular exertion required throughout the turn.
10. Physical Effort	2.5	The muscular exertion required by the job when the employee is performing at a normal pace.
11. Surroundings	3.0	The general conditions under which the work is performed, other than hazards, and the extent to which these conditions make the job disagreeable.
12. Hazarads	2.0	The probability and severity of injuries to which the workman is exposed, assuming that the workman is exercising reasonable care in observing safety regulations.

Each of the factors is broken down into degrees which are used to indicate the extent to which the factor is present in any particular job. The following is an example of how one of these factors, physical effort, is broken down.[38]

Factor 10, Physical Effort

Consider the muscular exertion required by the job when the employee is performing at a normal pace. Select that level which best describes the average degree of muscular exertion required throughout the shift.

Code	Job Requirements	Numerical Classification
A	Minimum physical exertion. Perform very light work such as sitting or standing for purposes of observations, and such work as very light assembly and adjustment. Plan and direct work. Weigh and record.	Base

Code	Job Requirements	Numerical Classification
B	Light physical exertion. Use light hand tools and handle fairly light materials manually. Operate crane-type controls, light valves. Operate truck or tractor. Sweep, clean up. Shovel light material.	0.3
C	Moderate physical exertion. Handle medium-weight materials. Use a variety of medium-sized hand tools for performing tradesman's work. Climb and work from ladders. Operate heavy controls and valves. Use light sledge.	0.8
D	Heavy physical exertion. Use heavy tools and handle heavy materials manually. Shovel heavy material. Use pick, heavy bars. Operate heavy pneumatic tools.	1.5
E	Extreme physical effort. Extremely heavy lifting, pushing or pulling.	2.5

In installing a new system, once the jobs are evaluated, jobs with similar (but not necessarily exact) point totals are grouped into job classifications. Finally, wage rates are assigned to each classification. At the Steel Company of Canada, for example, jobs are grouped into 28 job classes, with about a fifteen-cent-per-hour wage difference between each classification.

Administrative Problems

Once a job evaluation plan has been installed, administrative problems are likely to be encountered in two types of situations, one involving a new or changed job and one involving technological change.

With new jobs, the issue is the evaluation of the job and its classification. Since the process is subjective, there is room for disagreement. Since the classification influences the rate of pay for a job with perhaps a ten or more cent-per-hour difference between one classification and another (and this over the life span of the job), there is an incentive for the employee and the union to attempt to place the job in the highest possible classification. There is a similar incentive for management in the opposite direction. Both parties face the constraint of keeping the classification and pay of new jobs more or less in line with that of existing jobs.

Changes in existing jobs create similar problems. When changes are made, the issue becomes: have enough duties been added or subtracted to merit a change in the classification? Under most systems, minor changes should not result in a change of classification; but when are changes to be considered major and when minor? Naturally employees can be expected to resist a downward classification, simply because of its impact on earnings.

Aside from minor changes in jobs, changes in technology can create real problems under a job evaluation system. Problems occur when changes created by technological change are such that the factors used in the existing system cannot provide for the maintenance of earnings levels which existed prior to the change. For example, suppose a manufacturing process is automated so that all the machine operator has to do now is push a button, instead of making complicated adjustments to the machine. The level of skill required of the machine operator has obviously declined. In a plan where the factor of skill has a relatively large weight in the job evaluation system, the job could be expected to be reclassified at a lower level, and the employee would be faced with a wage cut. Under circumstances like these, the parties are frequently under pressure to change the plan so that earnings opportunities can be maintained.

Job Assignment

The process by which individuals are placed in various job classifications is called job assignment. In the absence of restrictions in the contract, management has the right to change work assignments, job content, manning requirements, and the nature of classifications, in order to create new classifications, abolish classifications, or to determine the line of progression.[39] In a more general sense, management, again in the absence of restrictive provisions in the collective agreement, has the right to increase or decrease the size of the workforce, shut down departments, set up new ones, and to move work from one department to another, or even from one plant to another.[40]

One recurring class of problems in union situations has to do with the assignment of "bargaining unit work" to individuals, such as supervisors or clerical personnel, who are not in the bargaining unit. When such disputes have reached arbitration, the determination of what constitutes bargaining unit work has been made on a case-by-case basis. In the absence of restrictive provisions, even where work is found to be work normally done by members of the bargaining unit, management may assign such work to individuals outside the bargaining unit as long as such work does not become a significant part of that individual's duties.[41]

UNION PRESSURE TACTICS

Sometimes union members consider grievance procedures and arbitration too cumbersome and too time consuming to satisfy their immediate needs. Sometimes they want to apply pressure to gain a bargaining advantage during negotiations for a new contract. And sometimes workers, acting without direction from their union leaders, wish to express their dissatisfaction with the way matters are being handled by their own leaders. In either of these instances, they are likely to resort to pressure tactics.

The strike is the most familiar pressure tactic. However, there are many others—some legal, some not—all calculated to demonstrate dissatisfaction and to achieve a goal that is not considered achievable through normal bargaining or grievance procedures.

Most often pressure tactics take the form of work slowdowns, wildcat strikes, picketing, or sabotage. Usually, they are short-lived and difficult to cope with, even though most collective agreements call for stiff disciplinary penalties for those who engage in such tactics.

Work Slowdowns and Wildcat Strikes

Work slowdowns are most effective in operations calling for on-time performance or tight scheduling. One variation of work slowdown is "work-to-rule." Here workers do exactly what they are told — nothing more — and observe all precautions, whether or not the precautions are warranted. At one time, Montreal transit workers engaged in work-to-rule tactics during negotiations with that city. Bus drivers made sure that all fares were collected, all change given out and all passengers seated before moving the bus. Furthermore, they used special care to move across intersections only on full green lights when no pedestrians were crossing, and they were careful to avoid cutting off other vehicles. The result: buses were running far behind schedule, throwing the system into considerable confusion.

Work-to-rule tactics are virtually impossible to cope with because no one is violating rules. Furthermore, it is difficult, if not impossible, to locate the leaders who initiate the practice. Frequently, union negotiations and union officers are not directly responsible; rather, they share concern with management for ending conditions that gave rise to the practice.

Sometimes slowdown tactics are crude and more obvious than work-to-rule tactics. Most familiar are deliberate slowdowns that often accompany the installation of new incentive rates. Automobile parts producers with incentive rates have experienced this phenomenon each time a new model change is instituted. The objective, of course, is to maximize the increments in the rate so that when incentive efforts are applied, the earning opportunities will be greatest. Typically, the go-slow phenomenon lasts about a month during each year. During this time, a great number of rate grievances are filed, and battles are waged between union leaders, methods engineers, and management representatives over a few hundredths or thousandths of a second in the assigned incentive rates: with the unions wanting more, methods engineers less, and management wanting to get production rolling.

Most obvious among slowdown tactics are those which are blatantly announced and led by worker representatives in order to satisfy an immediate need. Often these are full-fledged illegal strikes, called "wildcats." The causes of wildcats vary considerably, from alleged safety hazards to a management decision to implement a new work practice, or from contracting out work to securing the reinstatement of a suspended or discharged employee. Such tactics are usually barred by law or by the contract itself and can be dealt with through the application of discipline. However, if large numbers of workers are doing the same thing, discipline may be impractical.

Under most legislation, slowdowns, work-to-rule, and wildcat strikes are illegal, and violators can be fined for participation in such tactics. However, doing so requires management to seek consent to prosecute from the Labour Relations Board, and then to attempt to convince a magistrate to impose fines. The procedure is so cumbersome that it is rarely used except as a threat. In Ontario and British Columbia, the Board has the power to order an end to an illegal strike or lockout, and such an order has the effect of a court order, with anyone failing to follow such an order subject to penalties for being in contempt of court.

Also, unions (but not employees) are liable for damages suffered as a result of a wildcat strike, where the union can be found accountable for such a strike. Because unions are not legal entities in most jurisdictions and cannot be sued for damages in a court of law, management must use the grievance procedure to acquire damages. The grievance is filed against the union for violating the no-strike provision of the collective agreement. The right of a company to do so was established in a decision by the Supreme Court of Canada in a case involving the Polymer Company and The Oil, Chemical and Atomic Workers Union.[42]

Sabotage

Sabotage takes many forms. It is the most insidious of all pressure tactics because it can be accomplished by a single person and is often impossible to track down. One of the more subtle forms of sabotage was experienced a few years ago by a major U.S. international air carrier in a dispute with luggage handlers. In order to demonstrate their power, the handlers — perhaps just one or two — switched baggage tags at John F. Kennedy Airport in New York, causing near frenzy among passengers as they landed in Rome or Paris and discovered that their baggage had gone on to Athens or Beirut.

Other forms of pressure tactics include study sessions, wherein workers take a few hours or a day off to hold a meeting with the obvious intention of calling attention to their demands or grievances. Policemen and firemen have sometimes exercised a form of pressure called "the blue flu." This tactic involves mass absenteeism caused by an imaginary illness, calculated to call attention to the workers' particular demands.

Merchant seamen have a familiar tactic called the "bed bug" routine. If they have a grievance and do not get satisfaction in its resolution, they sometimes call the Coast Guard, claiming there are beg bugs in the laundry. It is obligatory for the Coast Guard to conduct a search in response to such claims, unless it knows them to be spurious. Usually, on searching, the Coast Guard finds a bed bug or two placed in the laundry by one of the seamen. Meanwhile, the vessel has been delayed several hours or days during the investigation.

Such is the nature of pressure tactics — innovative sometimes in their conception but commonplace in their purpose. The potential for their use should serve as a reminder to management of the need for efficient, fair, and effective administration of the collective bargaining agreement, and for a constructive relationship with the union.

Notes

1. For a full discussion see: David A. Peach and E. Robert Livernash, *Grievance Initiation and Resolution: A Study in Basic Steel.* Boston: Graduate School of Business Administration, Harvard University, 1974.

2. Earl E. Palmer, *Collective Agreement Arbitration In Canada*. Toronto: Butterworths, 1983, p. 175.

3. Ibid. p. 3.

4. The B.C. Labour Relations Board has, under Section 96 of the B.C. Labour Code, the capacity to appoint a settlement officer or an arbitrator, but the B.C. provision is not an expedited arbitration procedure, and the parties may contractually exempt themselves from this provision of the act.

5. Clarence M. Updegroff, *Arbitration and Labor Relations*, Washington, D.C.: The Bureau of National Affairs, Inc., 1970, pp. 244–5.

6. American Arbitration Association, *Labor Arbitration*. New York: American Arbitration Association, 1966, pp. 16–17. For a more complete discussion, including tactical considerations, see: John P. Sanderson, *Labour Arbitrations and All That*. Toronto: Richard De Boo Limited, 1976, pp. 45–92.

7. Donald J. M. Brown and David M. Beatty, *Canadian Labour Arbitration*. Agincourt, Ontario: Canada Law Book Limited, 1977, p. 106.

8. Updegroff, p. 252.

9. Brown and Beatty, pp. 110–111.

10. Palmer, pp. 268–271.

11. C. H. Curtis, *Labour Arbitration Procedures*. Kingston, Ontario: Department of Industrial Relations, Queen's University, 1957, p. 51.

12. Palmer, p. 33.

13. Ontario Labour Relations Act, Sec. 44(6); British Columbia Labour Code, Sec. 98(e). For a discussion of the timeliness issue, see Palmer, pp. 195–202.

14. This basic rule, and the definitive statement on arbitrability and the courts' role in the arbitration process, is found in a simultaneously issued set of opinions called "The Trilogy": United Steelworkers of America v. American Manufacturing Company, (1960), 363 U.S. 564; United Steelworkers of America v. Enterprise Wheel and Car Corporation, (1960), 363 U.S. 593; and United Steelworkers of America v. Warrior and Gulf Navigation Company, (1960), 363 U.S. 574; and also in a later decision: John Wiley and Sons Incorporated v. Livingston, President of District 65, Retail Wholesale and Department Store Union, (1964), 376 U.S. 543.

15. 12 L.A.C. 1980 (Reville, 1961).

16. Curtis, p. 67.

17. Frank Elkouri and Edna Elkouri, *How Arbitration Works*, Third Edition. Washington, D.C.: BNA Incorporated, 1974, pp. 373–375.

18. Brown and Beatty, pp. 13–15.

19. Palmer, pp. 130–131.

20. Brown and Beatty, pp. 130–132.

21. Paul Prasow and Edward Peters, *Arbitration and Collective Bargaining*. New York: McGraw-Hill Book Company, 1970, p. 59.

22. Palmer, pp. 589–595.

23. Palmer, pp. 446–455.

24. Palmer, pp. 115–116.

25. In B.C., some appeals were heard by the Labour Relations Board. See Sec. 108 of the B.C. Labour Code.

26. Sanderson, p. 124.

27. Brown and Beatty, p. 29.

28. Sanderson, p. 127.

29. Brown and Beatty, p. 33.

30. Ibid.

31. Palmer, pp. 251–259.

32. For an interesting and readable summary of these cases, see Bruce Young, *At the Point of Discharge*. Toronto: Canada Labour Views Co. Limited, 1978, and *State of Suspension*. Toronto: Canada Labour Views Limited, 1980.

33. S. Muthuchidambaram, "Adjudication of Unjust Dismissal Complaints from the Unorganized Sector under the Canada Labour Code: A Legislative Background and an Analysis of Selected Cases," *Proceedings*, 18th Annual Meeting, Canadian Industrial Relations Association, 1981, pp. 535–570.

34. See for example, John Huberman, "Discipline Without Punishment", *Harvard Business Review*, Vol. 42, No. 4 (July-August, 1964), p. 62. See also Bruce Young, *State of Suspension*, pp. 4–10.

35. Brown and Beatty, pp. 260–262.

36. Ibid., pp. 208–209.

37. D. H. Everest, "Steel Industry Plan," *Handbook of Wage and Salary Administration*, Milton L. Rock, Editor-in-Chief. New York: McGraw-Hill Book Company, 1972, pp. 2–72.

38. Ibid., p. 73.

39. Palmer, pp. 479–980.

40. Ibid., pp. 469–470.

41. Brown and Beatty, pp. 183–184.

42. 33 D.L.R. (2nd) 124 (S.C.C.).

ALEXANDER BERT, LTD.

On the morning of September 8, 1983, two separate letters arrived on the desk of Mr. Frank Hall, Director of Personnel for Alexander Bert, Ltd. The first was a grievance resulting from an employee termination. The second letter enclosed a medical report and doctor's comments from the hospital to which this discharged employee had been sent.

Mr. Hall reviewed the new information and wondered whether the decision to terminate Mrs. F. Thorenson would hold in arbitration.

THE EVENTS OF AUGUST 31

The discharge notice and subsequent grievance arose out of incidents at the Alexander Bert, Ltd. plant in Chatham, Ontario on August 31, 1983. At 7:30 on the morning in question, Mr. Steven Rolfe, foreman in one of the machine shops, became concerned about one of his employees, Mrs. Freida Thorenson. He described her as behaving "as though someone was sticking pins in her. She was twitching and jumping around, chewing something violently." He further explained that he had observed Mrs. Thorenson in a similar state before.

Out of concern for her safety, Mr. Rolfe changed Mrs. Thorenson's work, along with two other women, to that of racking in the plating shop.[1]

He took this action at about 8:00 a.m. About 15 minutes later, he noticed a number of employees standing back from the operation, staring at Mrs. Thorenson. He said,

> She was behaving very irregular. She was still chewing violently; she was moving around all over the place, with very exaggerated body movements — jerking. She was also fumbling with some parts; she dropped one part.

Mr. Rolfe was unsure of what to do about the situation, so he sought more expert advice in the person of Mr. Frank Hall, the personnel manager. He was instructed by Hall to accompany Thorenson to the first aid office. This he did, and he left her there, not to see her again until 11:00 a.m. Mr. Hall came to the first aid office around 8:30 and found Mrs. Thorenson lying on the bed, but with both legs on the floor. She was perspiring heavily, and when asked what was happening, she spoke very rapidly making it very difficult to make out what she was saying. Hall said:

> She went on and on for five or ten minutes, telling about her emotional problems at home; she said her nerves were bad. She was talking about someone who had been hurt in the back of a truck some time ago. She said she had taken some nerve pills, but she had not had any drug at that time. Speed was one of the drugs she mentioned, but not at that time.

The company nurse, Mrs. Margorie McMahan, was there at the time and suggested that Mrs. Thorenson rest for awhile. Mrs. McMahan said she would look

---

[1]The term racking referred to the placement of lightweight plated metal sheets into wooden racks for storage and later shipment. It was simple, not dangerous manual work.

in on her occasionally and that she would promptly summon a doctor if she believed it was necessary.

Hall left Mrs. Thorenson and returned about 12:15 to find her sleeping. He woke her and accompanied her to Mrs. McMahan's office, adjoining the first aid room, to use the telephone to call her husband. Hall said her body movements were still very exaggerated and that her eyes were "flashing around."

Miss Janice Nelson, secretary to the personnel manager, stayed with Mrs. Thorenson for the morning. She gave a similar description of Thorenson's actions. She said that Mrs. Thorenson was chewing something quite violently; she had difficulty sitting still — crossing and uncrossing her legs. According to Nelson, Mrs. Thorenson was constantly looking at her fingers, at times digging under one nail with the nail of another finger. Miss Nelson reported seeing a skin rash on Mrs. Thorenson's hands. She said that Thorenson would not look at her, and for the most part, talked and hummed to herself. In answer to a question, she did not give a complete answer; she used disjointed words. It was necessary to repeat questions three or four times before she would reply. Miss Nelson, like Hall, described the woman as perspiring profusely.

Meanwhile, Mr. Hall had arranged for Mrs. Thorenson to see Dr. Arthur Hodgson, the company's doctor, at 3:00 p.m. at the Chatham General Hospital.

Dr. Hodgson filed the following report:

> Mrs. Thorenson's doctor is Richard Gilman, an assistant professor in the Department of Community Medicine, with a small, private practice. Dr. Gilman told me that he had seen Mrs. Thorenson on August 13, when she complained of a skin problem due to crystals of methedrine coming out of her skin, and that there were insects crawling under her skin. Dr. Gilman prescribed a tranquilizer, describing the phenomenon described by Thorenson as 'hallucinations.'

Dr. Hodgson stated that when Mrs. Thorenson arrived at the hospital on August 31, she was very distraught, was hallucinating, and appeared to be in a psychotic condition. He described the skin condition on her hands and said the area under her fingernails appeared to have been "dug at" by her fingers or possibly a sharp instrument. Her hallucinations took the form of insects crawling under her skin and snakes crawling on her face. Dr. Hodgson said that all of these symptoms strongly suggested that Mrs. Thorenson had been taking drugs, "most likely methedrine or speed." He stated that to reach the point of hallucinations from "speed" required prolonged, heavy use, that a single dose would not give that result. He further remarked that it was unlikely that the excessive perspiration was caused by methedrine, but that with street purchases of the drug, one could not be certain of what other drugs or substances might be included in the mixture.

After examining Mrs. Thorenson and performing some tests, Dr. Hodgson determined she was under the influence of methedrine and decided to have her admitted to the hospital under the care of her personal physician. His report continued:

Dr. Gilman said, 'She was not medically fit for anything.' He believed that she should 'remain in the hospital for at least a week and then enter a rehabilitation centre for drug users.' Mrs. Thorenson agreed to undergo the treatment. Mrs. Thorenson said that she had been taking drugs off and on for about a month prior to August 31, but that she had not taken drugs of any kind on August 31. She attributed her condition to emotional disturbances at home; her husband had been unemployed for over a year. She admitted taking methedrine early in the morning on the day prior to August 31, but said she felt no ill effects from it. She said she had obtained the drug that day from a friend, who earlier had procured it for himself by prescription from a doctor. Mrs. Thorenson claimed to have two witnesses who could be called upon to testify that she had not acted abnormally on August 31.

MRS. THORENSON IS DISCHARGED

On Friday, September 3, 1983, Mr. Hall met with Steven Rolfe, the machine shop foreman. Together, they reviewed the events of August 31 and the report filed by Dr. Hodgson.

The discharge notice issued by the company on September 3, 1983, read:

On Tuesday, August 31, 1983, you reported for work under the influence of unprescribed drugs. This is a direct violation of item 2 of the established plant rules and regulations, clearly posted on the main bulletin board in the plant.

You are hereby informed that your employment with this company has been terminated for:
a) Being under the influence of unprescribed drugs;
b) Medical unfitness.
The termination is effective Friday, September 3, 1983.

The posted rule to which reference was made is shown in Exhibit I.

EXHIBIT I

PERTINENT SECTIONS OF PLANT RULES AND REGULATIONS

Any employee committing any of the following acts shall be disciplined by reprimand, suspension or dismissal depending upon the seriousness of the offence and the past record of the employee. . .

(2) Reporting for work or being present on company property under the influence of alcohol or unprescribed drugs or bringing alcoholic beverages or unprescribed drugs on the premises.

THE EVENTS THAT FOLLOWED

On September 8, 1983, Mrs. Freida Thorenson filed this grievance with Mr. Frank Hall.

I was given a leave of absence on Tuesday, August 31, 1983, at which time I went to the hospital because I was sick. On Friday, September 3, 1983, I received a telegram from the company stating I was dismissed. Action requested by me is that I be reinstated in the company to my former position, without any loss of seniority, and that I be paid for all straight time and all overtime hours which I might have worked but lost because of the action taken by the company.

The other letter, addressed to Dr. Hodgson from Dr. Gilman, advised that Mrs. F. Thorenson had discharged herself from the hospital on September 4, 1983. Dr. Gilman could offer no explanation or opinion why this had happened, but enclosed a copy of the hospital's patient history (see Exhibit II).

EXHIBIT II

CHATHAM GENERAL HOSPITAL
CAPSULE PATIENT HISTORY

Name: Thorenson, Freida M. (Mrs.)
Date Admitted: August 31, 1983
Time: 3:15 p.m.
*Assignment:*W3 R 211
Physician: Richard Gilman, M.D.
Intern: John Hotchkiss
History: Patient incoherent,-no history taken.

August 31, 1983

	3:15	4:00	5:00	6:00	7:00
Pulse	120	110	80	72	72
B.P.	230/180	225/170	200/150	180/110	180/100

Symptoms: Incoherent, lacks muscular control, eyes — no focus.

Patient said she took Methedrine approx. 1:00 a.m. 30th. Tests confirm presence of drug — methedrine — in blood.

Treatment: Intravenous — sugar solution. 2 15 mg. diazepam.

Gilman: September 1, 1983 — Patient satisfactory. 7:00 a.m. off intravenous. Administer diazepam as needed.
September 4, 1983 — 2:15 p.m. Patient discharged self.

After reviewing all the information he had accumulated to date, Mr. Hall decided to talk to the witnesses that Dr. Gilman had referred to in his early comments.

Mr. Irving Dahlke had been with Alexander Bert, Ltd. for 12 years. Hall knew that Dahlke was a close friend of Mrs. Thorenson, both on the job and socially. Mr. Dahlke stated that he had worked with the grievant on the day in question (August 31) and had seen nothing unusual in Mrs. Thorenson's behaviour. Dahlke also offered information on Mrs. Thorenson's personal life.

Mr. Homer Edmonds had also worked with the grievant on the day in question (August 31). He stated that there was nothing unusual in Mrs. Thorenson's behaviour, and further that the foreman, Mr. Rolfe, had always shown a dislike for Mrs. Thorenson.

Mr. Edmonds said he did not know Mrs. Thorenson particularly well, having been transferred to this section of the plant three months prior to the incident. Company records showed that Edmonds had been transferred as a result of a disagreement with a foreman in the Shipping Department. He was described by management as a very militant union member with an obvious mistrust for management and supervisory personnel. Edmonds' personnel record is attached as Exhibit III.

EXHIBIT III

SUMMARY PERSONNEL RECORD OF MR. HOMER EDMONDS

Name: Edmonds, Homer H.
Marital Status: Single
Age: 25
Dependents: 0
Number of years' service: 3
Absenteeism: Warned for tardiness, May 1982. No problems since that time.

Promotion Record: Started as Labourer. Promoted to Materials Handler (forklift) in Shipping Department July 1981. Transferred to Machine Shop A as Materials Handler in May 1983.

Attitude: Transferred in May of 1983 after heated verbal exchange including the use of profanity, with Foreman Burke in Shipping Department. The May incident was the culmination of a series of minor incidents. Does not respond well to authority. Distrusts and dislikes supervision in general. Militant unionist.

Discipline Required: Oral warning — Tardiness, May 1982
Oral warning — Abusive language, December, 1982.
Written warning — May 1983, Abusive language and insubordination.
Transferred out of Shipping Department.

Mr. Hall then began to compile certain information about Mrs. Thorenson's personal life — some he was aware of previously and some he had gathered from Mr. Dahlke.

During childhood, an unhappy home life led her to seek solace in the streets. She became involved with a "fast crowd" and was married at the age of fifteen. Within less than a year, the marriage broke up leaving her with a child. She gave the child up for adoption.

Fortune smiled on the teenager for awhile when she became involved with and married James Thorenson. He was 28 years old, ten years her senior, and was a maturing influence on her. Everything appeared to be going well. A year later, she gave birth to a child, Martha. The child developed a grave illness forcing Mrs. Thorenson to return to work in order to pay for some exorbitant medical bills. The child has never recovered, thus requiring periodic hospitalization and expensive medications.

At the time Jim Thorenson married, he was gainfully employed as a heavy equipment operator. Unfortunately, four years later he injured his back, thus rendering him unfit for this occupation. When he recovered, he obtained employment in a factory, but was dismissed when it was learned that he had lied on his application when asked about his medical history. His subsequent attempts to gain employment were frustrated by either his medical history or the fact that he had been fired previously for having given a false statement regarding his medical history. The jobs he held thereafter were of a temporary nature.

With additional time on his hands, Jim Thorenson spent it drinking. The drinking became a real problem for both himself and Mrs. Thorenson. There were incidents of his having violently attacked others, including Mrs. Thorenson. At the time of Mrs. Thorenson's dismissal, he had not been employed for more than a year. Two doctors had recommended that he submit to treatment for alcoholism, but he had refused.

Mrs. Thorenson sought comfort in the form of tranquilizers. In the beginning, doctors prescribed these for her, but finally refused unless she submit to psychiatric help. She said that she could not for fear of losing her job. The legitimate channel closed to her, Mrs. Thorenson obtained drugs illegally. She admitted to one of her friends that she was afraid to use the "street drugs" because she couldn't be sure of what they contained, but that she had no choice. She had suffered ill effects from these drugs and seen a doctor in hopes that he would prescribe something for her nerves. He had not done so. (Mrs. Thorenson's personnel record is attached as Exhibit IV.)

EXHIBIT IV

SUMMARY PERSONNEL RECORD OF MRS. FREIDA THORENSON

Name: Thorenson, Freida M.
Marital Status: Married
Age: 27
Dependents: One female child, age 8
Number of years' service: 7

Absenteeism: Not absent for illness in past two years. Has been absent to care for daughter's illness on a number of occasions. Warned of implications of such behaviour and has not taken time off in past year.

Promotion Record: Has advanced from Job Class 1 through Job Class 5 in better than average time.

Attitude: Generally very good, but in past year and a half has been described as "moody" and "troubled" while on the job. She has explained this behaviour as due to "personal problems" and that she would try not to bring them to work in the future. Foreman Steven Rolfe has complained that this employee has a tendency to daydream while working, thus endangering herself and others. He further reported an instance when she arrived at work ill — that she staggered as if to faint and then she perspired profusely. This department instructed Mr. Rolfe to bring the employee to the first aid office if a like situation occurs in the future.

Discipline Required: There is no record of disciplinary action having been taken against this employee for any cause.

While this was the first disciplinary action taken at Alexander Bert, Ltd. for alleged drug use, managers in the area were becoming increasingly concerned that the drug problem would eventually surpass the problem of alcoholism among factory employees. Mr. Hall had clipped an article from a business publication that addressed the drug abuse problem. This article is summarized in Exhibit V.

EXHIBIT V

The New York Chamber of Commerce recently released the U.S. business community's first thorough study of the drug problem in the business world.

According to the study, drugs have become a 'startling . . . ominously growing problem' in the business world. Thomas K. Stainback, executive vice-president of the Chamber, said that business leaders with whom he had spoken said the problem had not been at all serious two years ago, but has become a serious threat.

The Chamber's report was based on a study it commissioned from the Research Institute of America, which investigated 80 companies with major operations in New York City. Here are the major findings.

—Majority of the companies expect drug abuse to triple among their employees this year.

—Only five of the 50 companies reported no use of drugs on their premises. All five were small firms with low turnover.

—Turnover due to dismissal of employee drug abusers cost one company $200,000 in 1979. Absenteeism, poor work performance, higher insurance rates, were among the costs related to employee drug abuse.

—The business community has yet to agree on a clear and consistent policy for dealing with employee drug abusers. Although many firms have strict policies of immediate dismissals of users, other companies admit that there may soon be too many users to permit the application of so severe a policy.

—The companies surveyed found no greater incidence of drug abuse at the lower end of the employee ladder. Contrary to all indications of greater drug abuse by lower income groups, top level executives had as high a rate of drug use as the lowest paid employees.

—Identification of drug abusers has proved costly and far from 100 per cent effective. Urinalysis is the only identification technique available, and each test costs $55 to $75.

The study warned that it has become unrealistic for any company to believe it can somehow skirt the risk of "bringing drug abusers, narcotic addicts, and pushers into companies. Drugs have become an integral part of the university scene, it warned; and hiring university graduates must inevitably mean hiring of drug abusers."

Mr. Hall then called in Paul Martin, president of Local 1212 of the United Auto Workers, the representative of Alexander Bert workers. Martin said the company had been too severe in their discipline. No one had previously been disciplined for drug abuse, but he cited three cases wherein the company had discharged employees for suspected alcohol intoxication. Three of the four employees involved in these cases were reinstated as a result of arbitration hearings. Mr. Martin cited Mrs. Thorenson's flawless work record over the seven years she had served the company as further evidence of injustice. He stated:

> The company suggests that Mrs. Thorenson wantonly disregarded its rules and regulations. This is incomprehensible, given her desperate personal situation. She could not afford to lose her job. If, as the company contends, she was under the influence of some drug, then I submit that it was involuntary. Involuntary ingestion of a drug cannot be separated from the contraction of measles. It is only when the inflicted person refuses treatment, can we condemn them. Mrs. Thorenson did submit to treatment. Management has acted irresponsibly; no arbitrator will let it pass.

Hall then reviewed the arbitrators' decisions that Martin had made reference to (Exhibit VI). He also re-examined the provisions in the collective agreement that covered discharge procedure (Exhibit VII). He wondered if he had made the correct decision to discharge Mrs. Thorenson. Or should the employee be reinstated without loss of seniority and back pay?

EXHIBIT VI

ARBITRATORS' DECISIONS ON PRIOR CASES OF DISCHARGE UNDER THE COMPANY'S ITEM 2 OF THE PLANT RULES AND REGULATIONS

Case #1: Discharge for drinking, reduced by the board of arbitration to a suspension

Two employees were discharged for drinking on the premises when the company was requested by one of the employees to grant time off to appear in court as the result of an accident. This request for time off was about one week after the incident. Both employees signed statements that they had been drinking on the job, and that each had consumed a 12-ounce bottle of whiskey.

An arbitration board made up of Messrs. George Hanratty, Douglas Rosenbloom, and Brian Milton handed down the following decision:

> It would appear from the evidence that there was nothing out of the ordinary in the grievors' work performance on the night in question. There was no evidence or complaint from the foreman or other employees; all the work was done adequately and there was no damage to the equipment. The company introduced evidence of its rules and regulations under the Industrial Safety Act, which prohibits buying or consuming alcohol on the premises. There was no question that the employees knew of the rule. In fact, one of the grievors, when asked, directly admitted he did.
>
> The union testified that employees had not always been discharged when caught drinking in the plant, and gave one specific incident.
>
> The two company supervisors called to rebut this evidence, in effect, supported it instead.
>
> The Board indicated that in any ordinary case, the facts could well justify discharge. However, the character of these two offenders was sufficiently distinctive to cause the Board to reassess the judgement of the company. Each employee had approximately 22 years of seniority and both were in their early 50s. The loss to these employees could never be replaced in the working expectancy which remains for them. The problems of their age, coupled with their record as employees whose discharge was for drinking on the job, would make their ability to compete in the job market almost impossible.
>
> The employees had a completely spotless record for their terms of employment with the exception of one who had been sent home once for reporting to work after drinking, in 1966. It appeared to the Board that the company in the past had exercised discretion in looking at all the facts of the situation and the offender before imposing discharge. Perhaps in response to a drinking problem they felt was growing more serious, the company had decided to discharge all such offenders automatically. We do not believe this to be an unreasonable step, but we believe it would have been somewhat more just and equitable for them to give the employees, including the grievors, fair warning that discharge would be automatic for an offence of this nature. Hence the Board ordered the grievors reinstated in the belief that they have this power under the terms of the contract. The Board further determined that the penalty imposed should be different than the accidental time lapse between the discharge and the date of the arbitrator's award and imposed a four-month suspension.

Case #2: Discharge for intoxication and damage to property of other employees

An employee with 17 years of seniority was discharged for intoxication. When he left the premises at the finish of his shift, he proceeded to drive his vehicle from the parking lot and collided with the sales manager's car, causing $165.00

damage. Then he backed into another employee's car causing $200.00 damage, and the latter car was forced into a third car causing additional damage. The sales manager testified that when he saw the grievor driving off the property, that he chased him, caught him, and found that the grievor was intoxicated. He had all the symptoms: he was glassy-eyed, his speech was impaired, he was unsteady on his feet, and stumbled when he walked. The police were called and he was arrested and charged with impaired driving, but the charge was dismissed.

The arbitrator, S. A. Dunster, would not consider evidence introduced by the company which indicated the breathalyzer test had found an alcoholic content of 2.7 percent, in that the officer who took the test was not present at the hearing. The arbitrator did, however, conclude that in his opinion, the grievor was in an advanced stage of intoxication. Applying the principles of probability, it appeared reasonable to conclude that the grievor had been drinking on the job. The arbitrator noted that seven months prior to this incident, the grievor, having been intoxicated on company property, had been given a warning that a second offence would lead to instant dismissal. Discharge upheld.

Comment

Dealing with the evidence of the witness regarding the grievor's condition, the arbitrator made reference to a previous arbitration case involving Consolidated Truck Lines, 4LAC966, where this appeared:

> In the courts of this province, laymen need not be qualified as experts giving opinion evidence as to whether or not another person is intoxicated. The clinical manifestations or apparent symptoms with the odour of liquor and lacking any other explanation for them, they permit as a reasonable conclusion that such a person is under the influence of alcohol. So Chief Justice Robertson of the Supreme Court of Ontario has held.

Case #3: Employee discharged for consuming alcohol on company property reinstated with two-week suspension

Company rules provided that the following was a disciplinable offence: "possessing or drinking any alcoholic beverage on company premises at any time or working under the influence of alcohol." The grievor was seen by his foreman going to a coat rack where he extracted a "mickey" and proceeded to pour some of the contents of it into a container, presumably to drink from it. Another foreman was called to witness the act. When the witness arrived, the grievor was standing in front of the shipping department. Under questioning, the grievor admitted that the jacket and bottle were his.

The arbitrator, Mr. Daniel Kheel, said that on the day in question, the grievor was "in possession"; the sole question was whether he was consuming from the bottle. The grievor admitted ownership, but denied consuming—but as a cup of coca-cola with alcohol in it was found, bottled and produced at the hearing, a good many factors led the arbitrator to the opinion that the grievor had consumed some of the contents of this bottle. However, bearing in mind that the employee had served the company for many years without blemish with only one verbal warning about drinking, the arbitrator felt that in discipline there should be a graduated increase in penalties — a four stage procedure, and he could not therefore agree to accept the same degree of seriousness as the company had placed on the act. Added to this was the admission by the company witness that aside from the problem in question, the grievor was a good worker and in relation to lateness and absenteeism, had a very good record. Consequently, it was the arbitrator's view that the grievor should be reinstated to his employment, just cause for discharge not having been proven. A two-week suspension was prescribed with back pay ordered for his absence in excess of the suspension.

EXHIBIT VII

RELEVANT CONTRACT PROVISIONS

Article 2 — Reservations to Management

7.01 A claim by an employee that he has been unjustly discharged or suspended from his employment shall be treated as a grievance if a written statement of such grievance is signed by such an employee and lodged, beginning at Step 3, within four (4) working days after the employee has been notified of such discharge or suspension.

7.02 Such special grievance may be settled by confirming the management's action of dismissing or suspending the employee or by reinstating the employee with full compensation for time lost, or by any other arrangement which is just and equitable in the opinion of the conferring parties or in the opinion of the Arbitration Board.

7.03 In the event of a discharge or suspension, a Union Committee man shall be present wherever possible, and in all cases the Plant Chairman shall be notified immediately thereafter.

7.04 To ensure continuous and successful operation of the Plant, it may be necessary to exercise discipline at any time.

    (a) Any action taken by management with respect to the issuing of suspensions or warnings must be done within three (3) working days of the Company's knowledge of such offence.

    (b) Should such action taken by management affect the employee's active employment with the Company, it shall be taken in the presence of a member of the Union Committee, wherever possible, and in all cases the Plant Chairman shall be notified immediately thereafter.

    (c) Where the Company issues a warning in writing, it shall be on standard form supplied by the company. This form shall be in three copies and shall be signed by the foreman or supervisor. One copy shall be retained by the employee's Shop Steward, one copy shall be retained by the employee, and the third copy shall be signed by the Shop Steward and retained by the foreman or supervisor to acknowledge receipt of the warning.

7.05 Such written warnings or suspensions shall remain on the employee's record until the employee has accumulated a continuous period of twelve (12) clear months without further warnings of suspensions. In such an event, the employee's record shall be cleared.

THE APEX CASE

The Railroad Products Division of R. G. Budd Company manufactured galvanized steel grated walkways for freight cars and diesel locomotives and sold them exclusively to the Apex Railroad Products Company in the United States. Aside from adjustments needed to accommodate differences in width and length, the various walkway sections were manufactured in the same manner. Steel sheets were sheared and notched by a press to produce strips ranging in height from 2 to 2½ inches, in thickness from $\frac{3}{16}$ to $\frac{5}{16}$ of an inch, and in length from 1½ to 4 feet. One edge of each strip was flat; the other had scallops designed for firm footing. The strips — called beam bars — were fitted in criss-cross fashions with somewhat heavier, non-scalloped crossbars. The bars were nested in preformed notches cut on both bars at three-inch intervals. A press forced the bars together, and the galvanizing operation — following straightening and grinding — served to weld them sufficiently for the purpose they would serve.

The key operations in production of walkways were called "assemble and press." These had been essentially unchanged for the past 24 years. "Assemble and press" involved two men. Each man worked on one side of an assembly table, with the tables placed on two sides of a large ram press. When the assembly of a section was completed, one of the operators pushed a button to move his table underneath the press. Then he pressed another button to activate the press — forcing the bars together via the notches — and a third button to move the table from under the press so that the assembled walkway could be removed from the jig. Work was then begun on a new assembly. The controls of the assembly tables were wired so that it was impossible for the tables on opposite sides of the press to be activated at the same time.

Operators on the assembly tables were instructed by their foremen to activate each of the three buttons only after the prior operation was completed. Thus, the button to lower and raise the press was to be pushed only after the assembly table had moved in under the press and had stopped. Times, in fractions of a minute, were assigned to the three button-pushing operations as follows: table in — .155; press — .080; table out — .130. Industrial engineers recorded those times based on stop-watch observations. The total time for the three operations was .365 minutes.

Soon after the assemble-and-press operation was inaugurated, the operators modified the prescribed technique to activate the press, starting the downward action of the ram while the assembly table was moving into position under the ram. A highly skilled operator could time the action so that the press ram made contact with the grating just as the table came into full position. Then, just before the pressing had been completed, the button initiating the "table-out" action was activated. Thus, the table began to move from under the press at about the instant that the ram was released. As a result of their skill in exercising these short-timing techniques, some operators were able to reduce the total time for the combined three elements to as low as .250 minutes. Consequently, earnings on the assemble-and-press operation were extremely favourable. First shift operators during the past year realized earnings averaging $16.10 per hour, 44 percent over normal; second shift earnings were $15.96 per hour, 42½ percent over normal; and third shift earnings were $14.00, 25 percent over normal. Third shift earnings under the synchronized method were considerably below those of the first two shifts, because the third shift operated only two or three months, cumulatively, in each year, and operators on assemble-and-press had little time to become accustomed to the job before facing lay-offs. Time study policy at R. G. Budd was informally acknowledged to allow 30 percent earning opportunity on all jobs. Consequently a 30 percent factor was added into all machine-controlled operations where operators were not able to exercise skill and effort.

The synchronized method of assemble-and-press was observed and acknowledged by supervisors in the shop and by the industrial engineers. No one discouraged it or attempted to change it. This was a favourite job in the division — one with steady employment characteristics, less than average difficulty in performance, and high earnings. The only time the synchronized method caused trouble was when an operator failed to time the buttons correctly, so that the press ram reached the bottom of its stroke before the assembly table was in position. Sometimes this resulted in considerable damage to the table, but most often it simply caused spoilage of the walkway section to be pressed. Repair bills caused by damage from improper synchronization of the press averaged $11,250 each year for the past ten years. Repairs to the press and table of such damage resulted in an average of four days' down time each year. Because of this, foremen in the division always instructed new operators to activate the three buttons as prescribed by the original time study.

The Suggestion System

Approximately one-and-a-half years ago, R. G. Budd Company initiated a suggestion plan designed to tap the ideas of all employees for improvements that would save the company money. It was an attractive plan — providing 25 percent of the first year's estimated savings to the originator of the successful idea. All employees were eligible to make suggestions, except that eligibility did not extend to those whose suggestions could be considered within their direct area of responsibility. The Industrial Relations Director, for example, could not receive an award for a suggestion to change the wording of a collective agreement which he had responsibility to negotiate. Eligibility for awards under the suggestion plan was decided upon by a committee of three — headed by the Industrial Relations Director. Whenever in doubt, the committee decided questions of eligibility in favour of the person making the suggestion — thus endeavouring to preserve the attractiveness of the suggestion system.

Last June 5 the committee received a suggestion from Mr. Philip Evans, industrial engineer assigned to the Railroad Products Division. It was a scheme for rewiring the electrical circuits for the assembly tables and press so that a foolproof synchronized operation would result. Under Mr. Evans's suggestion, the assembly operator would push only one button — not three. When the assembly table reached a predetermined spot, the press would be automatically activated so that the ram would meet the assembled grating at the precise moment the assembly table stopped. Then, as soon as the ram released from the grating, the assembly table would move automatically back into place. Using the new system, pointed out Mr. Evans, the company would save on the costs of damage caused by improper synchronization of the three buttons, would raise production of inexperienced operators, and, most important, would save the high incentive wages which served to make assemble-and-press such an attractive job through the years.

The suggestion committee turned over Mr. Evans's suggestion to Mr. Harry Bateman, an industrial engineer whose job it was to investigate and determine the feasibility of cost savings ideas that were submitted. Mr. Bateman consulted with Mr. Edward Artz, Superintendent of the Railroad Products Division, and the two men lost little time in recommending that the suggestion be adopted. The total cost of rewiring the tables and press was estimated at $2,100. The total savings in repairs caused by improper synchronization of the buttons were estimated at $11,250 per year, and the savings on wages were estimated at $1,400 per year. This latter figure was, at best, a rough estimate, because neither Bateman nor Artz could know exactly how much in wages would be saved as a result of the change. Clearly the attractiveness of the job would diminish, and the company, through the years, had benefitted from the skill of assemblers staying on the job year after year. Mr. Artz observed that time used by moving assembly tables — under and out from the press — and by activating the press itself constituted less than $1/12$ of the job. Each of the two tables was activated every four minutes, on the average, with the press coming down every two minutes. Since the total time allowed for activating the table and press was slightly over $1/3$ of a minutes (.365), the men were occupied in manual assembly for approximately $11/12$ of their time — time unaffected by this change.

The Grievance

"If the division could save on repair costs alone, the suggestion is worth adopting," said Mr. Artz. Consequently he assigned an electrician to rewire the activating mechanisms of the tables and press, and on Monday, June 15, the new system went into effect. Mr. Evans timed the tables and press that day and assigned .260 minutes — a reduction of .105 minutes from the previously assigned time. The operators immediately filed a grievance claiming an illegal rate cut. "We've been running this job through our own skill at .250 minutes," pointed out one operator. "Now you make an 'improvement'—adding .01 to the actual time and you want to cut our rate. This is outrageous."

Mr. Joseph Majda, Contact Board representative of the union, was summoned to the division and, after talking with the operators, went to see Messrs. Evans and Artz. Mr. Majda pointed to Section 12 of the Time Study Policy of the Collective Bargaining Agreement. He said that by changing the rate, the company was in violation of this section:

Section 12. Established standards and rates will remain in effect for the life of the contract unless there is a change in methods, procedures, feeds, speeds, dies, machines, jigs, fixtures, products or materials which tend to increase or decrease production. In these cases, a restudy will be made and only those elements affected by the change will be adjusted. If it appears on examination that the resulting rate is clearly out of line, a conference will be called between the Contact Board representatives for the area and management to review the factors involved in the rate to determine the best procedure for adjusting the rate.

The above procedure for changing standards is based on the principle that where proper standards exist, any changes will permit the same earning opportunity as existed under the original standard.

Section 12, in its present form, had been adopted by the company and union 11 years ago. It had been the subject of repeated grievances since then — the union consistently claiming that any change of rate that reduced earnings on a job was a violation. Company representatives, on the other hand, were inconsistent in their interpretation of the section. Some agreed with the union. Others contended that earning opportunities referred to a "normal" worker expending "normal" effort on a job he could do well under the prescribed method. Such a worker, they said, should earn 100 percent of the assigned rate. In their support these company people pointed to Section 8 of the Collective Agreement's Time Study Policy.

Section 8. One hundred (100) percent shall be considered normal. The levelled time shall reflect the performance of the average worker working efficiently at a job he can do well, working at normal effort under the prescribed methods to produce the production standard (yield) under the conditions.

Other company representatives argued that Section 12 was designed to prevent wholesale rate cutting — that rates could be changed only when bona fide methods changes occurred: this, even though both company and union agreed the rate was out of line because of sloppy time-study practices, or lucrative because operators had devised effective short cuts. Until the Apex Case arose in June this latter view had prevailed. Section 12 had never been challenged in arbitration.

Upon receiving his report from Mr. Bateman, the Industrial Relations Director had to consider three questions — all three of which were related.
1. Should a suggestion award be tendered to Mr. Philip Evans?
2. If an award to Mr. Evans is made, what should be its amount?
3. Should the incentive rate on the assemble-and-press operation be reduced as a result of the rewiring?

BEAVAIR

Beavair is the only Canadian airline serving Florida tourist trade from the Toronto area, an especially lucrative business during the peak tourist season from Christmas time until late April. In November the Florida traffic, typically, is light, especially on Mondays. It was on a Monday that Captain Donald Hower's regular flight was cancelled. As a result, Captain Hower filed a grievance on behalf of the flight's entire crew, asking for round-trip pay.

Captain Hower's crew was based in Toronto. The crew members were scheduled daily to work Flight 604 from Toronto, departing at 11:00 a.m. and flying nonstop to Miami, and Flight 615 from Miami to Toronto, departing Miami at 5:30 p.m. Both Flights 604 and 605 used DC-9 jets, with a capacity for 94 people.

On November 9, a Monday, two DC-9 flights were scheduled by Beavair from Toronto to Miami, departing in the morning. Flight 602 was scheduled for a 9:30 a.m. departure, with an intermediate stop in Tampa. The other one was Flight 604 — Captain Hower's flight. The DC-9s assigned were Aircraft No. 728, assigned to Flight 602, and Aircraft No. 722, assigned to Flight 604.

Both aircraft — 728 and 722 — experienced minor technical difficulties on November 9, causing the mechanical department to notify the flight coordinator that Aircraft No. 728, assigned to Flight 602, would not arrive at the starting gate until 10:00 a.m., one-half hour after the scheduled departure time. Aircraft No. 722, assigned to Flight 604, would be at the gate at 11:00 a.m. As a result of this knowledge, the flight coordinator decided to delay the departure of Flight 602 until 10:30 and Flight 604 until 11:30.

Shortly before 10:00 a.m., the flight coordinator received new information from the maintenance department that Aircraft No. 728 would be further delayed because of a nose wheel steering problem and would not arrive at the gate until 12 noon. Aircraft No. 722 had been cleared for departure and would arrive at the gate at 10:30, one-half hour earlier than the maintenance department had previously estimated. The flight coordinator thereupon assigned Aircraft No. 722 to Flight 602 with a revised starting time of 11:00 a.m. He cancelled Flight 604 because of "mechanical problems and late operation." All passengers booked on the two flights were accommodated on Flight 602, which departed at 11 o'clock with 90 passengers, 42 of whom departed the plane in Tampa. Forty-eight went on to Miami.

The decision to cancel Flight 604 caused cancellation of Flight 611, scheduled to depart from Miami bound for Toronto at 3:15, using the turn-around aircraft. Flight 611 had been assigned to a Miami-based crew, headed by Captain Garrett Hodges. Captain Hodges' crew had a Toronto-to-Miami return flight scheduled at 10:00 p.m. — Flight 616. All passengers who had reserved space on Flight 611 were accommodated on other flights.

The cancellation of Flights 604, Toronto to Miami, and 611, Miami to Toronto, left the crew scheduling department with two crews: Captain Hower's crew in Toronto with its southbound Flight 604 cancelled and northbound Flight 615 from Miami operating, and Captain Hodges's crew in Miami with northbound

Flight 611 cancelled but southbound Flight 616 operating. Crew scheduling decided to assign Captain Hodges's crew to Flight 615 from Miami to Toronto, returning to Miami on their regular flight, Flight 616 at 10:00 p.m. Captain Hower's crew was cancelled for the day.

Upon learning of the cancellation, Captain Hower requested permission for his crew to deadhead[1] to Miami on nonstop Flight 600 scheduled to depart from Toronto at 1:35 p.m. Flight 600, using a DC-8 aircraft, would have arrived in Miami at 4:20, in sufficient time to enable Captain Hower's crew to fly its scheduled return trip on Flight 615, provided Flight 600 operated on time. According to company regulations crews were required to report to their assigned flight one hour before scheduled departure time. Consequently, a slight delay could have caused Hower's crew to miss its required report-in time: 4:30. This fact, plus the availability of Captain Hodges's crew in Miami, caused crew scheduling to deny Captain Hower's request. Hower chose not to pursue the request further, knowing that the Canadian Airline Pilots Association (CALPA), of which he was a member, had gone on record repeatedly as being opposed to deadheading.

At about 10:30 a.m., after Flight 604 had been cancelled and his request to deadhead on Flight 600 had been refused, Captain Hower was asked to taxi Aircraft No. 728 to see if it was fit. He did this and then reported to the maintenance department that the craft was airworthy. This was at approximately 11:00 a.m. With this knowledge, Captain Hower filed for pay for his entire crew, consisting of himself, a copilot, a flight engineer, and three cabin attendants. He cited Section 8, paragraph 5 of the Airline Pilots Association contract—a section copied in the various contracts covering all other crew members. It is quoted as follows:

A (crew member) who is removed from his regular bid trip or trips at company request shall be paid and credited on a trips missed basis not less than he would have earned had he not been so removed. A (crew member) will not be considered to be removed at company request when his trip or trips are cancelled due to a mechanical failure or weather.

Captain Hower looked upon this as a clear case where the airline had consolidated four flights into two because of lack of traffic. Although mechanical failures might have delayed the departure of Flights 602 and 604 on November 9, they were not, in Captain Hower's opinion, responsible for cancellation of either flight. In support of his position Captain Hower pointed out that Flight 602 was delayed for one-and-one-half hours, and it eventually left at the time originally scheduled for Flight 604, 11:00 a.m. The aircraft assigned to Flight 602 was ready to go at 11:00 and, if traffic had been sufficient, it is reasonable to assume the company would have reassigned the craft to Flight 604.

Captain Hower acknowledged that it was the company's right and that it was good business to consolidate flights when possible. November 9 was a Monday, a

---

[1] *Deadhead* is a term used to describe travel by a non-working aircraft crew to reach their assigned flights or to return to home base after completion of assigned flight.

day when traffic was unusually slow. The company, without doubt, saved considerable money by cancelling Flights 604 and 611. "Payment of the crew," observed Captain Hower, "would be 'peanuts' when compared to the amount saved." The total amount claimed for the five crew members was $1,523,50. In further support of this claim Captain Hower pointed to three earlier cases where flights had been cancelled for better load considerations, and crew members who were affected had been paid for the unworked flights. In none of those cases had mechanical failures been involved. There were no instances on record where mechanical failures had caused cancellation of flights and where crew members subsequently filed for pay.

Terrence Crosby, Vice President of Operations for Beavair, considered Captain Hower's claim, but he was disposed to reject it. Mr. Crosby looked upon this as a mechanical situation that was met in an intelligent fashion by the flight coordinator after considering reports from the maintenance department and the reservations department. Mr. Crosby said he was satisfied that mechanical problems were, in part, responsible for the decision to consolidate Flights 602 and 604 and to cancel Flight 611. "If we pay Hower's crew," said Crosby, "it will set a precedent that will require paying whenever a flight is cancelled for any reason." Crosby wondered whether Aircraft No. 728's apparent availability at 11:00 a.m. would weigh heavily in an arbitrator's mind so that Section 8, paragraph 5 of the contract would be interpreted in Captain Hower's favour. He wondered, in addition, whether the denial of Captain Hower's request to deadhead would be influential inasmuch as Hower's scheduled return flight — Flight 615 — had not been cancelled. The collective agreement provided for deadheading if space were available in order for crews to reach assigned departures, and Flight 600, the potential flight for deadheading, had departed that day with only 41 persons aboard (its capacity was 133). In addition, Flight 600 had departed and arrived on time.

Crew members were compensated for deadheading at one-half their regular rates of pay. In checking with the flight coordinator, Mr. Crosby was informed that Aircraft No. 728 had been cleared at 11:00 a.m. and could have been readied for departure by 12 noon.

BUCKLIN CORPORATION

Bucklin Corporation was a large integrated sand, gravel, and construction company which employed 150 permanent employees and up to another 300 temporary employees during the peak summer months. The company operated several gravel pits, including crushers and asphalt plants, throughout Vancouver Island and the lower mainland of British Columbia. The company's sand and gravel business was reasonably steady through the winter; the company operated its asphalt plants and auxiliary mobile equipment primarily during the summer months as it successfully bid on government road construction and paving contracts.

Bucklin's largest pit operation was located in the central Vancouver Island area. At this site, the company maintained a large fleet of mobile equipment, including front-end loaders, dump trucks, bulldozers, paving machines, rollers, and graders. At the Mid-Island Pit there was a large, well-equipped maintenance shop situated on the perimeter of the pit; next to the shop was an equipment "marshalling" yard and a small, fenced power substation which serviced the maintenance shop and the crusher and asphalt plants which were located elsewhere in the pit area. Exhibit I is an organization chart for the Mid-Island Pit.

EXHIBIT I

ORGANIZATION CHART FOR MID-ISLAND PIT

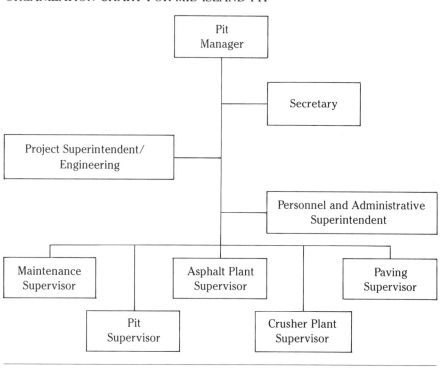

The maintenance shop was under the supervision of Joe Lateko. The maintenance shop day-shift crew comprised six mechanics, four welders, one pipefitter, and three electricians. In addition, there were three apprentices, two mechanical and one electrical, and six service employees (i.e., labourers, oilers, tiremen, etc.). The crusher operated on two shifts 8:00 a.m.–4:30 p.m. and 4:30 p.m.–1:00 a.m. There was only a skeleton crew of one mechanic, one welder, and one electrician on the second shift to provide troubleshooting and "patch" repair services for the crusher and the mobile equipment which serviced the crusher. The two most junior journeymen in each trade rotated on the shift work each week. Apprentices were not included in the rotation until the fourth and final year of their apprenticeship.

One of the key factors in profitability for the company was the efficacy of the maintenance function. If machines were down, customer orders were missed and delays developed in the progress of contract work. The delays were particularly troublesome because there were usually penalty clauses for them in paving contracts. Also, a substantial portion of revenues was often withheld until project completion. The road building and paving season was limited by weather. If delays were encountered and a season was shortened by weather, the company could find itself in a cash squeeze while waiting through the winter for an opportunity to resume the project in the spring.

Bucklin had found itself in this unenviable situation three years ago on a major government contract. The company was fortunate enough to negotiate half the outstanding amount as an advance on the basis of unusually poor weather conditions throughout the summer. Without that advance, the company would have come very close to bankruptcy. However, the company also recognized that many of the delays were caused by problems in their Mid-Island maintenance shop. There had been a continual series of labour disturbances that year, including sit-down strikes and "work-to-rule" disputes. Productivity and work quality had been poor. Equipment had often broken down "on the road" with problems which should have been detected and corrected as part of the regular preventative maintenance service routines.

As these unscheduled maintenance problems developed, more of the maintenance resources had to be devoted to getting the disabled machines back in order which, in turn, caused a growing backlog of preventative maintenance routines. This, in turn, generated still more unscheduled maintenance problems. By the end of that summer, the shop was in turmoil; the machine operators and drivers were critical of the maintenance crew because their income was influenced by the amount of material hauled and mileage paved; and the company missed its scheduled completion date. The maintenance supervisor was fired the same winter. His replacement, Joe Lateko's immediate predecessor, had been able to avoid serious labour disturbances. While there had still been problems with overall productivity in the shop, there had been no wildcat strikes or other labour disruptions during his two-year tenure.

Bucklin was a unionized contractor; the employees were members of the International Rock and Quarry Workers Union (IRQWU) Local 33. Negotiations were currently underway for a new collective agreement. The expiry date of the existing collective agreement was June 1, approximately six weeks away. Bargaining was conducted on a company-wide basis but the contingent from the Mid-Island Pit traditionally dominated the proceeding. Selected provisions from the current collective agreement are contained in Exhibit II.

EXHIBIT II

SELECTED RELEVANT PROVISIONS
FROM THE COLLECTIVE AGREEMENT

ARTICLE 4
No Strikes — No Lockouts
4.01 (a) — The Union agrees that neither the Union nor its officers, nor its members, shall in any way authorize, encourage or participate in any strike, work stoppage, walkout, slow-down, or any act of a similar nature which would interfere with, limit, or impede production during the term of this Agreement.

(b) — The Company agrees that there shall be no discrimination against any employee by reason of his legitimate activities as a member of the Union.

4.02 — In case any of the aforementioned acts restricting or eliminating production should occur in violation of the above, the Company shall have the right to discharge or discipline any or all the employees taking part in such act or acts, providing, however, that any such action by the Company shall be subject to the grievance procedure if any employee believes he has been discharged or disciplined unjustly.

4.03 — The Company agrees that there shall be no lockout of employees during the term of the Agreement.

ARTICLE 7
Discharge and Discipline
7.01 — If it is alleged that an employee has been discharged without just cause, the grievance shall start at Step 3 and if it is alleged that an employee has been suspended without just cause, the grievance shall start at Step 2 of the grievance procedure, within five (5) working days. The disciplined or suspended employee shall be given the opportunity of seeing a Steward of Union President before he is required to leave the premises.

7.02 — If it is agreed or decided at any stage of the grievance procedure, except arbitration, that an employee has been suspended or discharged without just cause, the Company shall reinstate him in his job without loss of seniority. A reinstated employee is to be paid his wages at his regular hourly rate, including shift premiums, for the time lost, limited to a maximum of the employee's regular numbers of hours per week, less amounts earned during the time lost.

7.03 — Where an arbitrator has been selected to determine a question respecting an alleged unjust discharge or suspension, he shall have power and jurisdiction to:
(1) uphold the discharge or suspension OR
(2) vary the penalty OR
(3) substitute a different penalty OR
(4) direct reinstatement.
and in cases (2), (3) and (4), may in addition order the Company to pay the employee full or

partial compensation (less any amounts of money earned by the aggrieved employee during any time lost) in accordance with his regular hourly rate, including shift premiums. It is understood, however, that if an employee is reinstated, he shall retain his full seniority.

7.04 — All warning slips and reprimand slips shall be considered as a form of discipline and shall be subject to the provisions of the grievance procedure. A copy of each disciplinary slip shall be sent to the Union.

ARTICLE 8
Officers, Committees and Stewards

8.01 — The Union may choose up to a maximum of one (1) Steward from each shift in each Department and a Grievance Committee of not more than three (3) members, all of whom must have completed their probationary period.

8.02 — The Union shall notify the Company in writing of the names of all Officers, Committeemen and Stewards and members of the Grievance Committee and of any changes in the same. The Company shall post the names and titles of first line supervisors.

8.03 — The Union Officers, Grievance Committeemen and Stewards shall notify their supervisors and they shall arrange a mutually satisfactory time to leave their work to attend to their duties as outlined in this Agreement. They shall be paid their regular hourly rate, as defined in Article 19, Section 19.13, for the hours that they were scheduled to work if they attend meetings called by the Company, which are held during their regular working hours.

8.04 — The functions of Stewards and Grievance Committeemen are to consider, investigate and attempt to settle grievances. If, in the course of investigating a grievance, a Steward or Committeeman enters a department or section of the operation other than that of their authorized work place, or if it involves the investigation of the condition of equipment, they must notify the responsible member of the supervision and they shall arrange a mutually satisfactory time for such investigation. Such time during working hours is normally without loss of pay. A supervisor shall accompany the Steward or Committeeman to the place where the investigation is to be carried out. It is understood that the Steward or Committeeman, upon reaching the place where the investigation is to occur, shall have the opportunity of consulting privately with the employees concerned. Requests for time off will be kept to a reasonable level and such time off will not be unreasonably withheld.

ARTICLE 11
Safety and Health

11.01 (a) — The Company and the Union, realizing the benefits to be derived from a safe and healthy place of employment, agree that they and all employees, Union Stewards and Officers, and the supervisors at all levels, shall cooperate to the fullest extent to promote safe work practices, health conditions and the enforcement of safety rules.

(b) — It shall be the duty of every employee to report immediately, in writing, to his supervisor, any alleged unsafe working conditions. Any concern regarding general safety conditions is to be reported in a similar manner.

Two weeks ago, the shop steward in the Mid-Island Pit asphalt plant had been suspended for one day for "abusive and threatening language" to his supervisor. All of the employees in the Mid-Island Pit, including the maintenance shop, had walked out for one day to serve the suspension in "sympathy" with the shop steward. The union filed a grievance and also filed an unfair labour practice with the B.C. Labour Relations Board alleging harassment and discrimination of union officials. Both the grievance and the unfair labour practice were still pending and would likely not be resolved for at least six months.

Joe Lateko had recently been appointed as supervisor of the Mid-Island maintenance shop. He had been with the company for six years as a maintenance supervisor in a smaller operation. He had been in his new job, at Mid-Island, for three months and believed he had a well experienced, qualified crew.

When he first arrived, he had assembled his crew and discussed his goals and had expressed his hope that they could work cooperatively and harmoniously together. He had also invited his crew to feel free to discuss work and personal problems with him and promised to invite their participation in resolving departmental problems. The employees appeared to be receptive and this had resulted in what Lateko thought was an immediate improvement in maintenance morale and work quality.

Through regular meetings with his employees, Joe had achieved some limited successes with his group in generating a minor design modification on the paving machines which was estimated to save approximately $12,000 per year in maintenance costs. He was also currently reviewing two suggested warehouse procedural changes which arose in a recent crew meeting. The potential savings of these two suggestions was up to $8000 per year in wasted mechanical time waiting for parts at the warehouse counter. Joe thought this was a good start, but was anxious to generate more enthusiasm and momentum in these crew discussions on productivity and cost savings.

Despite some encouraging achievements, a few things were troubling Joe. Over the past three months, following his initial crew meeting, Brent King, the maintenance shop steward, who was also on the union negotiating team and Pit Grievance Committee, had come into his office privately on two occasions to complain about one of the mechanical apprentices in the shop. Brent was a journeyman mechanic. The apprentice, Darlene Miter, was nearing the completion of her first year as an apprentice. Brent told Joe that Darlene wasn't pulling her weight, that she was generally disrupting the crew. Joe had observed that Darlene was a little aggressive, but he had not seen or been told of any poor work on her part.

Brent had also indicated on these occasions in Joe's office that he was pleased to hear Joe talk about cooperation because, as shop steward, he felt he could be helpful to Joe in keeping things on an "even keel." Brent indicated that Joe's immediate predecessor had been practical and sensible and had often sought Brent's advice and assistance in dealing with crew "personnel" problems. Brent had also indicated that Joe's immediate predecessor had been open-minded with respect to allowing time off for union business. He had pretty well left it up to Brent's discretion in allowing appropriate time off. Brent said that he thought it was a sensible arrangement in view of the substantially reduced labour problems in the department. Brent indicated to Joe that the supervisor who had been in charge of the shop three or four years earlier had been a real "hard nose" and had gone out of his way to make up rules and enforce them. The result had been many unnecessary squabbles. Brent said that same supervisor had felt it was particularly important to limit Brent's time away on union business.

During these discussions, Joe had not committed himself as to what approach he might take with Brent. He was still trying to get a "feel" for his new department and had been particularly busy with revising the maintenance planning schedule, which was needed as a result of a large government contract which Bucklin had recently won near Nanaimo. He had just completed the planning schedules the previous week.

Brent King was a large, powerfully built individual. He had been born and raised in the area. In high school and for several years after he had been well known in local rugby circles for his hard, aggressive play. He still was active in the executive of the local rugby association. Joe found Brent abrasive and was suspicious of his motives in offering his assistance to help keep things on an "even keel." Brent was the type of person that one would prefer to have as an ally because he was physically intimidating. Joe did not like Brent and did not see him as particularly clever. He had not made up his mind as to how he was going to handle Brent, though.

King had requested time off, with pay, on the previous two Friday afternoons for union business and Joe had approved these requests. Brent had explained that he needed the time to research some literature as part of a number of ongoing grievance investigations.

Joe, in the last three months, had experienced one grievance which was a result of a written warning (second level of discipline) given to a tireman for repeated lateness. The grievance was currently at third stage (Pit Manager) where Joe expected his decision to be upheld. A verbal warning to the tireman followed by the written warning, which was being grieved, were the only two formal disciplinary situations which Joe had initiated while at the Mid-Island Pit.

Two operating supervisors had complimented Joe during conversations over the past month. They both commented that things apparently had improved in the maintenance department since Joe's arrival. Both had warned, however, that Brent King was a real troublemaker with a short fuse, and that he had one "helluva" high opinion of himself and his importance around here. One of them said, "We should have fired him three years ago for stirring up that mess in the shop." Another one added, "Most guys in the shop think he is an ass, but they don't have the nerve to tell him where to go." One supervisor had commented that while Joe's immediate predecessor had been able to keep the lid on labour problems, Brent King in his opinion had been getting away with 'murder' with his requests for time off for union business, especially on Fridays. He commented that it was demoralizing to his operating crews to see it happen.

A week ago, one supervisor had told Joe that at the union's special general meeting which was called a week or so earlier to talk about the suspension of the asphalt plant shop steward, the only one to stand up and argue against walking out to support the steward was Darlene Miter. She apparently had "given them hell," and had been especially tough with Brent King.

Joe knew that Brent's son, Ron, had applied and had been unsuccessful on the job posting for the apprenticeship competition that Darlene had won. Joe had heard through the grapevine that Brent had been upset enough when his son hadn't won, but that to be beaten by a woman was apparently even more upsetting to him.

APRIL 18 INCIDENT

When he reported for work on the morning of April 19, Joe Lateko was immediately told of an incident that had occurred early in the previous afternoon shift. A front-end loader had smashed into a power pole as the loader was turning to leave the marshalling yard at the start of the shift. The operator had received a minor concussion and bruised ribs; the machine incurred approximately $20,000 damage. While the accident was not disastrous, the potential was alarming. The cause of the accident was brake failure due to a punctured brakeline. The machine had been down for the entire day shift for scheduled preventative maintenance servicing. A visual inspection of the brakeline and testing the brake cylinder were part of the scheduled routine. It was clear, from the timing of the accident, that the problem should have been detected and corrected during the previous day-shift work. Joe interviewed the two people responsible for the loader's maintenance work on the previous day, Brent King and Darlene Miter.

Brent King's recollection of the events was as follows:

> I was given the maintenance work order for the loader about 10:00 a.m. and was told by my supervisor that Darlene would be available about 11:00 a.m. to help out. It was a major overhaul, so I started work immediately. About 11:30 a.m., Darlene came over and said she was ready for work. I asked her what had taken so long because we were in a hurry. She told me to 'mind my own business'; that she 'didn't report' to me. I told her that if she didn't start doing a little more around here, she wouldn't be 'reporting' to anyone. I gave her a number of things to do, one of which included the visual check of the brakeline and checking out the cylinder. About 4:15 she came to me and said she was finished with everything and was going to the washroom. I asked her specifically about the brakes and she repeated that everything had been done. When I finished my work at 4:25, I signed the work order as being complete. I think she has really messed up this time and it could have been a serious situation. It is about time she took things seriously around here.

Darlene Miter's recollection of the events was as follows:

> About 11:30 a.m. I went over to Brent to help him work on the loader. I had been working on the paving machine with another mechanic on a rush job to get it ready for the new government contract. It took a little longer than we expected. When I got over to the loader, Brent was agitated about something. He gave me hell for being late and told me I had put him in a 'bind' to get the job finished by the end of the day. He told me a number of

things to do but never mentioned the brakes. I worked hard for the rest of the shift. I finished everything by about 4:15 or 4:20 and went over to Brent, who was still busy, to tell him I was done and that I was going to the washroom. He muttered something, sort of under his breath, about women and washrooms. I told him I had finished everything he had given me and I walked away. I am sure he didn't say anything about brakes or brake cylinders. He has it in for me and is trying to cover up his mistakes by blaming them on me.

Exhibit III presents a summary of the Personnel Records of the two employees.

EXHIBIT III

SUMMARIES OF EMPLOYEE RECORDS

A. *BRENT KING:*
  — Age 42, Married
  — Education — Grade 12
  — Seniority — 18 years (10 as a journeyman mechanic)
  — Safety — two minor accidents; the last one was four years ago resulting in two days' lost time due to a cut finger.
  — Attendance — no record of A.W.O.L.'s.
             — good attendance, averaging less than four days per year absence due to illness.
             — uses union leave-of-absence provisions extensively averaging almost ½ shift/week over the past two years.
  — General Comments
      — Has been a union shop steward for 7 years and a union grievance committeeman for four years.
      — An adequate tradesman.
      — Discipline — 1 day suspension (8 months ago) by a relief supervisor for insubordination.
             — 5 day suspension (3 years ago) for inattention and lack of cooperation which resulted in a major overhaul having to be redone.
             — 3 day suspension (3½ years ago) for abusive language to a supervisor.
             — 1 day suspension (4 years ago) for abusive language to a supervisor.

B. *DARLENE MITER:*
  — Age 24, Single
  — Education — 1 year University in Math and Physics
  — Seniority — 3 years
  — Safety — no accidents
  — Attendance — no record of A.W.O.L.'s.
             — good attendance, averaging 3 days per year absence due to illness.
  — Selected as apprentice 1 year ago
      — ranked highest, among applicants, in pre-selection aptitude tests.
  — General Comments
      — Has had a number of heated arguments with other employees in

maintenance shop since her selection as apprentice, but discussions have always abruptly stopped when supervisor approached.
— Has been a good worker both as a labourer (2 years) and since
— her apprenticeship selection.
— Discipline — Verbal warning (6 months ago) for frequency of leaving job to go to the washroom.

ASSIGNMENT OF WORK

Work assignment in the maintenance shop followed a work order system which was generally initiated by the maintenance supervisor, in this case, Joe Lateko. Work cards were submitted to the supervisor by both operators and tradesmen as problems were identified. Joe would summarize and allocate jobs to his employees in writing on a daily basis. Safety priority jobs could be initiated by anyone depending on their urgency; they were usually filed through the supervisor and immediately passed on, by the supervisor, to the appropriate tradesmen. They were written on a red work card. If the supervisor was not present, then the senior tradesman in the shop allocated the "red card work" and left a note for the supervisor regarding the assignment for record purposes and follow up. As employees reported at the start of each shift, the work orders were usually in their personal "slots" to be picked up. Joe was responsible for work scheduling including maintenance routines and unscheduled breakdown repairs. Following the completion of a job (work order) the journeyman assigned to the job signed the bottom as complete and included an estimated number of man-hours devoted to the job. The cards were then returned to the supervisor's office. Joe used these man-hour figures to assist him in planning future work.

Journeymen, when working with apprentices, had always informally been considered like a "lead hand," although they had never been officially vested with formal organizational authority. Each journeyman had a different style of distributing work to apprentices. Some would issue written instructions, others verbal instructions, others would jointly determine with the apprentice, based on the supervisor's work orders, a reasonable way to split up the work.

No one could recall a situation where a journeyman and apprentice openly disagreed regarding accountability on a particular assignment. In the past, when a journeyman and apprentice were involved in a poor performance situation, the two employees had always, voluntarily, accepted mutual responsibility. The allocation of discipline, in such situations, had always been based on the supervisor's judgement. Often, but not always, the journeyman received a more severe penalty. No one could recall, however, a similar case which had so directly resulted in a serious accident.

The Pit Manager and the Personnel Manager were both away from the work site on April 19. Lateko decided not to take any action regarding the incident the previous day, until he had discussed the situation with the Pit Manager on April 20. He wished to have a recommendation ready for that meeting, however, and wondered what course of action he should suggest.

CANWEST LIFE ASSURANCE COMPANY

"What a perfect summer day!" thought John Parkin, the General Manager of Canwest Life Assurance Company, as he approached the company's General Office in Winnipeg, Manitoba. Parkin was returning from a service club luncheon meeting. As he turned the corner to approach the entrance to the parking lot, he was thinking that if his 2:00 p.m. meeting didn't last too long, he might be able to get nine holes of golf in before dinner.

Thoughts of teeing off quickly vanished when he saw the picket line in front of the massive building. Twenty-five or thirty people, including several small children, were parading in front of the building. Most of them carried signs and they seemed to be handing out leaflets. One sign said: "Canwest Fires Unjustly," another said, "YOU may be next," while a third read, "CPL supports Sandy Walker."

"Who are those people out there?" Parkin asked as he entered his office, responding, in part, to his secretary's apprehensive look.

"Mr. Fraser said they weren't our employees," she responded.

"Well it's a damn good thing," Parkin said. "That clerical union is enough trouble as it is. That still doesn't answer my question, though. Who are they and what do they want?"

"Mr. Fraser said that he'd be available if you wanted to see him about this," the secretary said somewhat defensively.

"Get him up here," Parkin ordered. "I'll call him right away," Miss McKellar replied. "Oh, a reporter from the newspaper called asking about a statement regarding the demonstration."

"How can I make a statement when I don't know what the hell's going on?" Parkin said as he marched into his office.

"Well I have his number if you want to call him back. I think they had a photographer from the paper taking pictures," Miss McKellar said.

"Oh, God," said Parkin to no one in particular.

About five minutes later, Michael Fraser, the company's Director of Employee Relations, entered Parkin's office. He was accompanied by Jane Hughes, the Director of Data Processing.

"Come in. Sit down. Explain this mess to me," Parkin said.

"Don't get too excited, John," replied Fraser. "None of those people are our employees. They're all friends of Sandy Walker from the Canadian Party of Labour and the 'Unwed Mothers' Day Care League' or whatever crackpot group she's a member of."

"Who is Sandy Walker?" Parkin demanded.

"She used to work in Data Processing," Jane Hughes responded. "She was fired last Thursday, the 21st."

"By you?" Parkin asked.

"By me," Hughes replied.

"Well, give me all the facts," Parkin said.

"Sandy Walker has worked here for three years. She was employed in May three years ago following her graduation from the University of Manitoba," Hughes began. "She had worked in our Brandon district office for the previous three summers. Despite the fact that her supervisors there recommended that she *not* be offered permanent employment, she was recommended by the university employment people in Employee Relations for a job as a supervisor trainee in Customer Relations following university," she continued, fixing a hard glance at Mike Fraser.

"All we did was recommend," Fraser interjected. "The Manager who hired Sandy said she did a good job in Customer Relations," Fraser said. "It wasn't until she was transferred to Data Processing that we began to have trouble with her."

"Why was she transferred?" Parkin asked.

"I believe it was a development move," Jane Hughes said.

"It was," said Fraser. "She had progressed nicely in Customer Relations and had received good performance reviews. We decided that after two years there she should gain experience in other aspects of the business. She seemed happy for the opportunity at the time."

"Well, she only stayed happy for about two weeks," Jane Hughes said. "When she came into Data Processing, we started out in the conventional manner, with two weeks of data entry work so that she would be familiar with that particular job. After that, she was supposed to begin a brief training program so that she could supervise and help train the data entry operators. This was on April 18th of this year. On the day that she was to begin her training, she told me that she didn't want to take the training, that she was no longer interested in being a manager at Canwest. She said that she could not ask the poor working girls to work the way we expected them to. I told her that this seemed like a rash decision on her part and that she ought to think about it for another day.

"I interviewed her the next day," Hughes continued, "and she was determined to assume a non-management job — to continue as a data processing operator. I told her that I would consider her request. The next day, I again talked with Sandy. She had not changed her mind. She said that she might consider a transfer to secretarial work in the Sales Department, and I helped her fill out a request for transfer form. I told her there was no guarantee that she would have a job in Sales — that it would depend on an opening being available — and her being acceptable to the manager involved. I said that I would investigate the possibility of her remaining in Data Processing as an operator, and that until we had things straightened out, she could continue to work in that capacity.

"In the course of that conversation," Jane Hughes said, "Sandy used several phrases that seemed radical-sounding, so I decided to do some checking into her background. I found that she was very active in such groups as the Pro-Abortion League, The Transcendental Meditation Society, Day Care Centres for Working Mothers, The Communist Party, and the CPL. Sandy is a Sociology graduate from the U. of M. She majored in Social and Political Thought, so everything that's happened is not really surprising.

"Anyhow, as you well remember, Mike," Jane said, looking at Fraser, "I suggested that, since Sandy had been hired as a manager and since I rather suspected her motives for wanting to be a clerical worker, her services be terminated.

The proposal was turned down by the Employee Relations Department."

"Now just a minute, Jane," Fraser said. "There was no way that we could have followed that suggestion. The woman had been a good employee for two years. Her record clearly indicates that she was an above-average employee. How could we turn down a perfectly legitimate request, even if it was a little unusual, on the basis of your suspicions?"

"Well, my suspicions were correct, weren't they?" Jane Hughes countered. "Just look outside at the pickets."

"I think they're gone," Fraser said. "They've got their picture in the paper, and now that they've got what they wanted, they've quit. Did you see the leaflets they were handing out?" Fraser handed two pieces of paper across the desk to Parkin. (The handouts are reproduced as Exhibits I and II on pages 303 and 304.)

"The shorter one was handed out at the door this morning," Hughes said, "while the longer one was handed out by Sandy and others on the picket line."

"Was this girl marching?" Parkin asked.

"She was leading the parade!" Fraser said.

"What's this business about a petition and harassment, Jane," said Parkin, reading the leaflet.

"Well, let me tell you about the rest of her career with us," Hughes said. "Employee Relations made the decision not to follow my recommendation to terminate Sandy the week of April 25th. All this time she continued to work as a data entry operator. It took Accounting and Employee Relations another month to come up with a pay rate for her, taking into account her summer work and her service as a manager. She continued to be paid at the manager's rate until May 23rd. She had no complaints when she got her new rate, even though she took a sizeable cut in pay.

"All of this time we continued to train her as a data entry operator. On April 28th, May 25th and June 23rd, her immediate supervisor, Helen Andrews, conducted in-depth reviews of her performance with her. Sandy was told that she was not meeting productivity, quality, or incorrect data reporting standards. All of this is documented, and additional training was provided as a result of these discussions. Her productivity was only 80 percent of what we expect from experienced operators and she was making far too many errors.

"On July 6th, Sandy circulated a petition among the other key punch operators opposing the office practice of notifying a supervisor before trading with another operator when doing Schedule 7 processing. This is a very repetitive and boring type of work that we try to spread around among the operators and also watch to see that it doesn't get done in place of other work which is more important.

"I called Sandy into my office the next day. I told her that we didn't need petitions or group pressure to bring about change in the operation. I explained to her that the practice was a long-standing one and why we believed we needed to involve the supervisor in the scheduling or trading of Schedule 7 work. I suggested that it might be best to get the facts before getting so many people involved. Sandy said that no change would occur without group pressure. She said she could see nothing wrong with the petition. I suggested to her that unless her attitude and performance improved, we could not retain her in data processing.

"Sandy asked what the possibilities were of transferring into another department. I sent her to the Employment Office, but apparently there were no openings available at that time.

"Shortly afterward, she filed a grievance through the union, complaining about the practice against which she had circulated the petition. On July 18th, I had a meeting with Mary Phillips, the Local President and Grievance Committee Chairman, about the grievance. In the course of this discussion, I told Mary we were quite concerned about Sandy's performance and might have to take disciplinary action. On that same day, Sandy's supervisor, Helen Andrews, did a check on Sandy's work and discovered a large number of errors. She told Sandy, again, that the quantity and quality of her work were unacceptable.

"Last Thursday, July 21st, Helen again took a check on Sandy's work. Her volume had increased, but her error rate had also gone up. Helen again told her that her work was unsatisfactory. Helen also spoke to the Union Steward saying that she couldn't seem to get through to Sandy but had to somehow in order to get improvement. The Steward simply said, 'Good luck!'

"Helen then came to me and I decided to talk to Sandy myself. I decided that we should give her a final warning and two weeks to improve to a satisfactory level or lose her job.

"When Sandy came in I began to discuss her record with her, but she absolutely refused to hear anything I had to say. She said she didn't believe there was anything wrong with her performance, that her work was fine. I explained that her work was far below standard in terms of quantity and quality, and that individuals who had been on the job for a shorter time than she had had better performance levels. She refused to believe that and insisted on seeing the records. I told her the records were confidential and this only made her more insistent that there was no need for her to improve her performance.

"I could see that the interview was not getting anywhere, that she was just not accepting what I had to say about her work. I couldn't see that a final warning and two weeks to improve was going to be at all effective, so I discharged her."

"And then she showed up today with her friends," said Parkin. "Has she filed a grievance?"

"Not yet," Fraser said. "I'd guess she wanted to have her little demonstration first. She has fourteen days to file a grievance, and under the circumstances, I'd guess the Union will be interested in pushing it."

Parkin agreed with Fraser's assessment. The union, the Association of Clerical and Technical Employees (ACTE), had been certified for three years. While it had not been really militant, it had not passed up any opportunities to demonstrate its worth to employees.

"Well, when we get the grievance, we've got trouble," Fraser said.

"Why's that?" Parkin asked. "After what happened today, I can't see taking her back."

"Under the contract,*" said Fraser, "we're required to give the union advance

*The specific clause referred to here is reproduced on page 305.

notice of any disciplinary action and we didn't in this case, did we Jane? When did you notify the union about the discharge?"

"I told the Steward on Friday afternoon," Hughes said.

"Also, the discharge was not preceeded by any final warning. Sandy Walker was just discharged. She was never told she was going to lose her job. She was never given any time off as an indication of how serious the situation was. I think we'd have real trouble getting this discharge to stand up in arbitration."

"Well grievances are your business, Mike, and you'll have to handle it. I must say that this whole situation has not been handled very well, though," said Parkin.

They were interrupted by a knock on the door. It was Parkin's secretary.

"The newspaper reporter is on the phone again. He says that if we want to have any comment from us in the story that will appear tomorrow, he needs a statement from you now," she said.

EXHIBIT I

Canwest Life Fires Unjustly!

July 21st, Sandy Walker, a data processing operator, was fired.
Why?
Canwest Life says she's making too many errors, they can't afford to
 keep her on any more.
This is untrue.
What is the <u>real</u> reason?
The real reason is she's being made a scapegoat, a scapegoat for
 filling out an ordinary grievance form.
July 6th, Sandy and some other data processing operators signed a
 petition against Canwest's new procedure of having to call the
 supervisor before trading Schedule 7 processing. They didn't
 think they should have to call the supervisor. They never had
 to before.
The harrassment began:
   1. Sandy was called in alone to the boss' office. She was told
      she must "be very unhappy working in the office as an operator."
   2. They threatened fo fire her!
   3. They told Sandy to improve the amount of data she processed
      in shift. (This she did.)
      - July 11th, Sandy filed an individual legitimate grievance
      under working conditions concerning having to call the
      supervisor before trading Schedule 7 processing.
Harrassment increases:
   4. Every shift since July 6th, her work has been checked.
   5. July 18th, manager emphasized improve speed and accuracy.
      After, the manager emphasized improve speed and accuracy.
      (This she did.)
   6. July 21st, a supervisor sat in with her and observed her
      work. (All the while, every day, her work was being checked.)
      Several errors during observation. Constructive discussion
      with supervisor after.
   7. 2:30 p.m., FIRED!
Filing the grievance was the real reason they harrassed Sandy. Filing
the grievance is the real reason they fired her. The observations at
the same time weren't to help her, they were to catch her!

Canwest Life has tried to isolate one person, Sandy, who dared to
fight back. It could be your turn next.

Sandy wants her job back. We must all fight for that and an end
to all Canwest's harrassment of its employees.

EXHIBIT II

C A N W E S T L I F E F I R E S U N J U S T L Y - - - P R O T E S T M A R C H !

July 21st, Sandy Walker, a data processing operator was fired.
Sandy has worked for Canwest Life for 3 years.

She's being made a scapegoat, a scapegoat for union activities.

She filed a grievance on Monday, July 11th -- fired on the 21st!
This is a threat to all of us. It could be your turn next.

We can file grievances. We do not have to keep smiling to keep
our jobs.

An injury to one is an injury to all. It's our common concern
and our strength is in numbers.

Sandy wants her job back. We must all stand for that and an
end to Canwest Life's harrassment of its employees.

JOIN THE PROTEST MARCH TODAY, 12 NOON, IN FRONT OF CANWEST LIFE
750 MAIN STREET.

I T ' S A F I G H T F O R Y O U R O W N J O B S E C U R I T Y

EXHIBIT III

COLLECTIVE AGREEMENT PROVISIONS

ARTICLE 7
Notification to Union Representatives.

The Company agrees to advise a Union Representative of the employee concerned, in advance, when an employee with service of six (6) months or more is demoted for disciplinary reasons, dismissed, suspended, or given final warning.

When the Company finds it necessary to take immediate action in any of the above circumstances, the Company shall advise a Union Representative of the employee concerned immediately after the employee has been advised.

GREAT NORTHERN TELEPHONE COMPANY LIMITED

"Mr. Harper is here to see you," said Ralph McGraw's secretary.

"Send him right in," McGraw replied. McGraw was the Industrial Relations Manager for Great Northern Telephone Company Limited. Bill Harper was the company's District Manager in Century, Ontario, a town of about 175,000 people located in the south-central part of the province. Harper was reponsible for all telephone installation and repair in the district which was centred around the city of Century. Harper had come to brief McGraw on a grievance filed by the Canadian Telephone Workers' Union, which represented all of the company's employees involved in the construction, installation, maintenance, and repair of telephone facilities, both in customer and company locations. The grievance involved the discharge of a young employee named Jim Hall for misappropriation of company funds.

After the usual preliminaries, Harper and McGraw turned their attention to the case at hand.

McGraw: Well, Bill, let's get down to business. I have a meeting scheduled with the union on this grievance next week, and I'd like to make sure I've got all the facts for that meeting.

Harper: Well, I'll tell you Ralph, I thought at first that this case was really cut and dried. But the more I think about it, the more I wonder whether we could potentially be in trouble on this one. When I denied the grievance at the second step of the procedure, I was reasonably confident that I was doing the right thing. However, the more I think about it, I'm not so sure.

McGraw: Why don't you first just lay out the events as they happened and then we can talk about some of the ramifications.

Harper: OK. The employee involved, Jim Hall, is 24 years old. He worked for us for fifteen months. All of his time with the company had been spent working as a coin telephone repairman. His work has always been good, and has been good since day one. He did well during his training program and has continued to do well since he started working on his own.

But, on October 19th, he was caught in a security audit of a pay phone that he was sent to repair. The audit was a standard one, conducted by an internal auditor and a representative from the security department. The telephone in question was located near the entrance of a shopping mall. An out-of-service condition was created on the telephone, and $5.15 in marked coins were deposited in the coin chute of the telephone. As you know, coins which have been collected into the collection box of the telephone are not capable of being reached by a repairman. Only coins which have been caught in the telephone mechanism can be reached and collected by a repairman. The auditor and the security representative taped a hand-written out-of-order sign over the coin slot on the phone and then reported the condition to the repair service office. They kept the telephone under constant surveillance until the repairman arrived. The coins which were placed in the machine had been marked with a fluorescent dye.

The repairman, Hall, arrived at the scene about 10:30 a.m. He pulled his repair truck up to the curb, right next to the entrance, went in, checked the phone to see that it was indeed out of order, went back and moved his truck into a parking spot about 75 feet away from the entrance, returned to the mall, and then proceeded to repair the telephone. The repair job involved a check on a terminal at one end of the shopping mall. He had to return to his truck to get a ladder to check the terminal. There was a second coin telephone right next to the one that was out of order, and Hall used it to call the test centre to get a test line and tone. After repairing the telephone, Hall went back to his truck and started the motor. At this time, he was approached by the auditor, who showed him his credentials, and asked him to turn off his engine and wait while the security man checked the telephone. The auditor entered the cab of the truck from the other side and waited for a signal from the security man. At this point, the stories begin to differ.

According to the auditor, the minute he got into the truck, Hall reached into his coat pocket and grabbed a plastic bag of coins, threw them at the auditor and said 'Here.' He also emptied his pockets of coins and gave them to the auditor. He also said, 'I hope you'll forget that I turned on my engine.' Hall now claims that nothing like this happened.

After examining the pay phone, the security man ascertained that the marked coins were neither in the collection box nor in the coin chute. The three men then returned to the repair centre, where a check of the coins Hall had in his possession in the truck indicated that they were the marked coins which had been placed in the telephone. Hall was indefinitely suspended by his foreman, Andy McMillan, pending further investigation.

The next day, McMillan, as he's supposed to do, checked with one of your industrial relations people to see what the usual practice is in cases of this type. Apparently, the answer he got was that where a senior employee was involved, the typical disciplinary penalty was a two-week suspension. There were at least three prior cases like this which had involved senior people with, say, 15 years' service. Where such an incident involved a junior employee, the employee had, in the past, been dismissed. There have been several cases involving the discharge of short-service employees.

By the way, I don't know whether you know or not, but the job of coin telephone repairman is one that we either start new employees out on or one which we give to older, more senior employees to handle when they become physically unable to handle conventional repair work. Thus, it's unlikely that you're ever going to find an employee in this kind of situation with a medium amount of seniority. They either have got a lot of seniority or very little.

Anyhow, with this information in hand, McMillan, in consultation with me, decided to discharge Hall. He was sent a letter which I have here for you which said he had been discharged for misappropriation of company funds. The union was also notified. The following day, the union submitted the grievance. The grievance alleges that there was not just cause for dismissal, as required under the Agreement.

McGraw: OK. Have we got documentation to show that the foreman had covered the company's code of conduct with the employee?*

*The company had a printed code of conduct which covered company rules and regulations regarding the safeguarding of communications, the responsibility of handling company funds and company property, as well as proper conduct on the job. Each employee was given a copy and the contents were discussed with each employee by his supervisor every year.

Harper: Yes. Here is the sheet signed by both the employee and the foreman, indicating that they had reviewed the contents of the code. It was signed in December of last year.

McGraw: How about any training programs?

Harper: Hall took the coin telephone course in May of this year. In that course, the procedure for handling any coins found in the process of repairing a telephone is completely covered. The foreman, McMillan, says that he again covered the procedure for handling coins with Hall when he went with him on two occasions following the actual training course. The training course specifically covers the auditing/security procedure so all employees know that they may be subject to this kind of check. They also know that they can lose their jobs if an audit uncovers the misappropriation of funds.

McGraw: There's no way that Hall can claim ignorance of the proper procedures then?

Harper: Hell, no. The training program is designed to ensure that everyone knows very clearly that the repairman is to record the amount of money found in the mechanism on the repair ticket and if it is not possible to redeposit it in the machine in which it was found, it is to be *immediately* deposited in another phone, and that the test centre is to listen as the coins are deposited to record the amount of the deposit. They know they can be disciplined for failing to follow this procedure.

Now, there was a phone right next to the one that he was working on which was operating because he called the test centre from it, into which he could have deposited the coins that he found. He absolutely did not do so. In fact, the failure to deposit the coins in the prescribed way is fully conceded by both Hall and the union. In fact, they will even allow that he should be subject to some discipline as a result of the failure to follow the prescribed routines. However, what they're really claiming is that he shouldn't be discharged because we cannot prove misappropriation, and that, in fact, misappropriation was not intended.

McGraw: How's that?

Harper: Let me tell you what Hall's story is now. Hall says that in the process of removing the housing from the out-of-service telephone, he somehow hit the coin relay which caused the money in the phone to reject. He says he put the money on the shelf. Then, he says, because there were people around in the mall when he had to go back to the truck, he took the money with him. He then says that because there were children in the vicinity of the truck, he decided not to leave the money out on the console of the truck but to put it in the pocket of his jacket.

McGraw: He doesn't deny that he had the money in his jacket, then?

Harper: No. But he says that he only put it there because he was afraid one of the children might be tempted to break into the truck to get it.

McGraw: But after he had completed the repair job, he returned to his truck and started it up as if to leave.

Harper: That's right. But he says that he was about to record the amount of money on the repair ticket before depositing it and that he was going to drive the truck closer to the door and put the money in the telephone as required.

McGraw: Had he filled out a repair form when the auditor approached him?

Harper: No. However, he had started up his truck when the auditor approached him. I just don't think that if he were simply going to fill out the repair ticket, he would have started the truck. The trouble is that he's got a *plausible* story. It may not sound completely good, but it's possible that he could have returned the money. The auditing team followed *their* procedures to the letter. However, the procedure as it is set out calls for the repairman to be stopped before he leaves the scene.

McGraw: Well, I'm not at all surprised we've got the grievance. The union really pushed hard in the last negotiations to have us discontinue this kind of auditing procedure. They said it was demeaning. Even though we refused to concede in negotiations, I'm certain that they haven't lost their interest in this subject.

Harper: Well, they were very heated about the whole thing in the second step grievance meeting. They say that misappropriation is not proven and that it wasn't intended. They say that Hall had not left the vicinity of the coin telephone and indeed intended to deposit the money before he did leave. They say he wouldn't have kept the $4.15 segregated in his jacket if he had intended to take it. He would have just put it in his pocket. Hall now claims that he was 'shook up' by the auditor when he approached him and that all he intended to do when he showed the auditor the money in his jacket was to show that the money was indeed separate. He knew that the situation looked bad even though he really did not intend to take the money.

McGraw: Well, I see what you mean about having second thoughts about this case. I'm convinced that given the union's opposition to these auditing procedures, they'll take the thing to arbitration. I suppose that Hall's a reasonably popular employee?

Harper: Yes. The union played that song in the second step hearing too. They claimed that he's not only well-liked but his work record is exemplary. And that's quite true.

McGraw: Well, given the fact that he's got a good record, even though he doesn't have much seniority, and that it's *possible* he could have intended to deposit the money and was stopped before he could do so, it is really quite possible that an arbitrator could order him to be reinstated with some kind of suspension.

   Now, our policy on misappropriation cases has been pretty clear. Where an employee has a fair amount of seniority and a good record, we have let it go with a suspension as penalty, at least for the first occurrence of an offence. Where employees have had low seniority, though, we have discharged. Misappropriation of funds, or of equipment, or even of working time, has been something that we have been historically very tough on. But it seems to me that we might consider changing our policy on this voluntarily because if an arbitrator decides to reinstate Hall, it would mean that our policy *has* been changed, whether we like it or not.

   I also think we'd better get together with the auditing people to see whether the audit procedures can be improved. They always claim that their audit procedures are airtight. But after this case, I'm not so sure.

Harper: I checked with the auditing people before I gave the union an answer at the second step. They really don't see what they can do to change the procedure. They also seem to think that granting the grievance would put the procedure in jeopardy for the future.

McGraw: I can see that. But if an arbitrator says that we haven't adequately proved intent here, the procedure will be ruined anyhow.

Harper: Let me tell you one other thing that I've thought about since I denied the grievance. You know, we have a policy of hiring people who have served time in prison — of trying to rehabilitate people with criminal records. Here we've got a young fellow who has given every indication of being an excellent employee and we don't seem to be willing to take a chance with some kind of rehabilitation for him. I wonder if that's really consistent.

McGraw: Hmmm. That's an interesting point. Well, I'll give all of this some thought before I meet with the union next week and talk to some other people, including the auditors as well. We'll have to make a decision one way or the other pretty soon. Thanks for your time, Bill. I'll be back in touch with you before I make a formal reply to the union.

JOHN HEMSTEAD & SONS LTD.

John Hemstead & Sons Ltd. manufactured several varieties of string, rope, and twine. Four years ago the company closed its baler twine plant in Springhill, Nova Scotia, and moved all operations to Halifax. As a result, about 225 new jobs were created at the Halifax plant, and baler twine came to constitute about 50 percent of the plant's total production.

Baler twine was sold through a small number of large-volume distributors, and it was common practice in the industry to make sales commitments in the late summer of each year for delivery the following year. Last July Hemstead salesmen committed the company to delivery of 22 million pounds of twine in the next 12 months. Based on an estimated average production of 28,000 pounds per shift, the Production Manager, Mr. Jason McCleod, anticipated that delivery obligations could be met by running three shifts, each forty hours per week. This would put production operations at or near capacity for five days a week.

It was not long before the company gave signs of failure to meet expectations, producing only 1.2 million pounds of baler twine in the month of August. Thus, in September, the company, at Mr. McCleod's insistence, changed its schedule — requiring 44 hours per week on the first and second shifts and 47 hours per week on the third shift. Mr. McCleod calculated the new schedule on the assumption that most of the production employees would willingly work the overtime hours. However, the overtime work was on a voluntary basis, as it had always been in the past.

By September 29, Mr. McCleod was dismayed to discover only 1.23 million pounds of twine had been turned out in the first three weeks of the month — below the rate needed to meet sales commitments. This was because many more workers than expected had elected not to work on Saturdays. On the first Saturday in September, 15 percent of the production workers were absent. On the second Saturday the figure was also 15 percent and on the third it was 12 percent. While accurate production figures were not in for the fourth week, Mr. McCleod received word on the 29th, a Friday, that more than 16 percent of the production workers had indicated to their foremen that they did not intend to work the next day, September 30. Thus, Mr. McCleod decided to institute compulsory overtime effective the following week. He posted the following notice next to time clocks in each department.

NOTICE

It is expected, and indeed required, that all employees work each day during the work week. Effective Saturday, October 7, scheduled overtime work will be compulsory.

Many departments are now working a 5½-day scheduled work week. Check your bulletin board or ask your foreman for the presently scheduled hours of work in your department.

To insure the security of your job, it is extremely important to maintain a good attendance record.

The following Monday, Mr. McCleod learned that 16.5 percent of the productive workforce had been absent the previous Saturday. Production for the day had been 48,000 pounds for 15 work hours. As a result, Mr. McCleod had a meeting with the production foremen on Monday morning. He said that effective the following Saturday the regular procedure for unexcused absences — used for normal workdays — would apply to overtime work. Under this procedure employees absent without good reason received an oral warning for the first offence, then for succeeding offences a written warning and a three-day suspension. In the event of four such absences, the employee was discharged.

On November 6, Mr. Frederick Thompson, who had been absent for the fourth successive Saturday on the 4th, was discharged. His only reason for the absences was that he did not feel like working.

Mr. Thompson had received an oral warning following his absence on Saturday, October 14, a written warning for his absence on October 21, and a three-day suspension, October 30, October 31, and November 1, for his absence on October 28. On the Monday following each of the absences he indicated that he felt 40 hours of work in a week was sufficient and that the company, under the labour agreement, had no right to insist on more.

This was the first instance where the company's unexcused absence procedure had been used in respect to refusals to work overtime. The procedure had been in existence for nearly twelve years and had never been seriously challenged by the union. In its years of existence, two discharges and seven suspensions had been levied for excess unexcused absences.

The following day, November 7, Mr. Thompson filed the following grievance:

> I feel that I have worked my normal 40 hours under the terms of the
> contract and have been unjustly discharged. I request pay for three
> days of suspension and for time lost as a result of my unjust discharge.

Mr. Thompson was represented by Local 12 of the Textile Workers Union of America (TWUA). Mr. George O'Toole, General Secretary of the local, indicated that Thompson's was a test case — that more than 200 members of the local had received warnings for Saturday absences in the last month and that all of them, if necessary, were likely to stay out on subsequent Saturdays to preserve the workers' belief that overtime never was and never should be made compulsory. According to Mr. O'Toole, the union never assented to a change in hours, and the labour contract expressly forbade a unilateral change.

Prior to holding a grievance meeting to discuss the Thompson case, Mr. McCleod met with Mr. O'Toole to show him the production figures and to demonstrate the need for overtime work. "I can't help it if your salesmen committed you to do more work than you can handle," said O'Toole. "We signed a contract to work 40 hours per week — no more, no less. And we've reaffirmed time and again during negotiations that overtime work, when available, is voluntary. If you want to reopen the contract, just say so, and I'll approach the membership. But I'll warn you — a reopening on this issue will reopen it on other issues as well."

Mr. O'Toole pointed out to Mr. McCleod that other alternatives were open to him. He said there were about 150 union members in the area without work and a fairly large unemployed population in Halifax which could be hired to augment the existing workforce. As another alternative, Mr. O'Toole suggested that Hemstead could schedule eight hours instead of four for those who wished to work Saturdays. In this way the needed production could be attained with a reduced workforce. As another, Sunday work could be scheduled. Since the contract called for double time pay on Sundays, this might attract a significant additional number of people.

Mr. McCleod rejected all three of Mr. O'Toole's suggestions, pointing out that the nature of the production operations was such that maximum efficiency was obtained only when all or nearly all workers were present. Machine operations predominated at Hemstead. With the increased production schedule, the plant operated at or near capacity during the week. To add more employees would be impossible. "More hours on Saturday or overtime on Sunday is out of the question," said Mr. McCleod, "because of the great expenses involved." Mr. McCleod had figures to show that efficiency dropped by nearly 20 percent during overtime hours worked in September.

Mr. McCleod said employees were obligated to work the overtime if the company required it.

While honestly feeling his position was right, Mr. McCleod wondered what he should do. On the one hand, it seemed clear to him that the union would not move from its position and that within a few weeks many more employees, in addition to Mr. Frederick Thompson, would face suspensions, and possibly discharge, if they continued to refuse Saturday work. This could involve some loyal, long-service employees. On the other hand, promises had been made to customers and Mr. McCleod felt he needed to assert, once and for all, the right of the company to require overtime work.

Pertinent Contract Clauses

ARTICLE I.
Management
It is recognized that the employer has the responsibility of operating the business and of promoting and maintaining its welfare; it is agreed that it is to the interest of employees, as well as stockholders, that the welfare of the business be promoted and maintained. It is further agreed that the employer must be free to exercise its best judgement along such lines, among others, as increasing or decreasing operations; removing or installing machinery or equipment, or changing its nature; the regulation of the quality and quantity of production; the relieving of employees from duty because of lack of work; the employment, laying off or re-employment and transfer of employees; maintaining discipline and efficiency of employees; the demotion, promotion or discharge of employees for cause as efficient operation of the plant shall, in the opinion of the employer, require; provided that the exercise of such functions by the employer shall be in conformity with the provisions of this contract.

ARTICLE II.
A. Hours
The pay week shall begin and end at midnight Sunday night. The regular hours of work per shift shall be eight (8) hours per day and forty (40) hours per week from

Monday through Friday, inclusive, except that in those departments where the full forty (40) hours are not regularly scheduled from Monday through Friday, the regular hours of work may be less than eight (8) hours per day from Monday through Friday and as many hours on Saturday as are necessary to make forty (40) hours.

ARTICLE II.
B. Schedule of Hours

A schedule of the hours of work for each shift and each group of employees, and establishing a work week, shall be prepared immediately by employer and delivered to the local union. The union will be advised of any proposed change in schedule of hours, before adoption. Any dissatisfaction with a change in schedule of hours adopted by the employer shall be handled as outlined in Article IV, the grievance procedure of this agreement.

ARTICLE II.
C. Overtime

1. All employees shall be paid one and one-half (1½) their regular rates of pay for work performed in excess of eight (8) hours per day or forty (40) hours per week.
2. All employees, except firemen and engineers whose regular work week includes Sunday work, shall receive twice the regular rates of pay for work performed on Sunday.
3. Work performed on Saturday shall be paid for at the rate of one and one-half (1½) times the employee's regular rate of pay, except in the following cases:
   (a) Those hours worked on Saturday as part of the regular schedule by employees in any one of the departments referred to in the exception of Section (A) above.
   (b) Those hours worked on Saturday by the third shift as part of its regularly scheduled work week of 40 hours.
   (c) Where the work is performed by engineers and firemen whose regularly scheduled work week includes Saturday work.
4. Engineers and firemen shall be paid one and one-half (1½) times the regular rates of pay for work performed on the sixth day, and twice the regular rates of pay for work performed on the seventh day, in their regularly scheduled work week.

ARTICLE IV.
Grievance Procedure

Step 1. Should any employee feel that he has been unjustly treated, he or his union representative, or both, may discuss the problem with his foreman in an attempt to adjust the matter promptly.

Step 2. Problems not settled in Step 1 may be appealed to the Production Manager. They shall be discussed, if appealed, within seven (7) working days of the appeal. The Production Manager shall answer in writing within seven (7) working days of the meeting.

Step 3. Problems not settled in Steps 1 or 2 may be appealed to a Board of Arbitration. In event of such an appeal each party shall choose one (1) representative who, in turn, shall select a third impartial member. Failing to agree on an impartial member, the two (2) above-mentioned representatives shall select an impartial member from a panel of seven (7) arbitrators furnished by the Department of Labour. The impartial member shall be selected by the company representative and the union representative, each alternately striking a name from the list until only one name remains. . . The Board of Arbitration shall render a decision on the grievance within the scope of this Contract, and under no circumstances shall it modify or change this Contract. The decision of the Board shall be final and binding on both parties.

In considering the chances of success if he submitted the overtime issue to arbitration, Mr. McCleod went back over notes he had collected from negotiations in past years. Article II, in its present form, had been written first 22 years ago and had existed in the same form ever since. During those 22 years no employee had been forced to work overtime, although there were many instances when overtime work was performed. Until now, sufficient numbers of workers had been willing to work overtime, when needed, so it had been unnecessary to compel the employees to work more than 40 hours.

Mr. McCleod, himself, had joined the company 24 years ago, but he had not participated in negotiations until seven years later. However, there were notes in his files written by Mr. Caleb Shepard, now deceased. Mr. Shepard had been a member of the management negotiating team during the early years. The notes collected by Mr. Shepard in negotiations of 22 years ago indicated that the company's intent, in agreeing to Article II, was to give the company a right to compel overtime. On the other hand, Mr. George Franko, chief negotiator for TWUA at the time, also kept notes — shown to Mr. McCleod by Mr. O'Toole. They indicated that Mr. Franko, at the time, intended that Article II would provide for voluntary overtime work and that a company proposal for phraseology that would require overtime at the company's discretion was turned down.

Apparently the issue did not arise again until a grievance meeting that took place six years later. At that time the union had made a request to Mr. McCleod that maintenance workers should be permitted to work overtime whenever operating employees worked. The grievance was rejected by Mr. McCleod at the time, arguing that the company was not required to provide overtime work for maintenance men, that mere existence of the need for production work on overtime did not automatically call for maintenance support. The decision was not appealed.

Mr. O'Toole had taken notes on the grievance. These indicated that Mr. McCleod and other management representatives had argued that parallel rights were involved — that management did not have to provide overtime and, in turn, the employees did not have to work overtime. The union's notes contained a quote reading as follows:

Mr. Jacks (company Personnel Manager) stated that the union could not force the management to work any employees over forty (40) hours per week, and management, similarly, could not force any employee to work over 40 hours.

Neither Mr. McCleod nor Mr. Jacks could recall Jacks' having made such a statement but neither did they rule out the possibility.

Thirteen years ago (three years after the grievance) both the company and the union addressed themselves in contract negotiations to the specific issue of whether an employee could be compelled to work overtime. Mr. McCleod's notes read as follows:

> Mr. O'Toole (chief TWUA negotiator) brought up the question of overtime — saying that foremen sometimes discriminated between one group of workers and another regarding overtime — that workers felt overtime was not compulsory. Mr. George Franko (member of the TWUA team) then commented that one group of men had been asked to work, with the idea that they had to work, whether or not they wanted to. Mr. Jacks (company Personnel Manager) then asked what use is an employee if we can't get him to work when we need him. Mr. Jacks added that we try to avoid overtime, because it is expensive, but he asked whether a worker whom we asked to work overtime and refuses is worth as much as one who says yes. Mr. Franko didn't answer the question but he referred to cases where a man doesn't feel like working for reasons of health, the foreman won't require him to work, but he wants some evidence he is ill.
>
> Mr. O'Toole pointed out the collective agreement spelled out a regular schedule of hours and said that when a man does that regular schedule he fulfills his obligations. The union objected to foremen going to individual workers to get them to work overtime and making veiled threats if they refused.

In the negotiations of 13 years ago both company and union agreed that in administering overtime a worker should be given two days' notice, if possible, in the event weekend overtime was scheduled, and that an attempt would be made to equalize overtime hours within each worker classification. Anyone who refused overtime work, the parties agreed, would be charged with the hours, as if they were worked, in calculating equal distribution. Then, several days later, the parties returned to the matter of compulsory versus voluntary overtime. Mr. McCleod's notes disclosed the following:

> Mr. Franko then raised another point — that a foreman should not say to a man, "Work or suffer the consequences," if a man has a reasonable excuse. Mr. Jacks replied that if a man explains his reasons to the foreman, there should be no problem.
>
> Mr. Lanning (TWUA Steward and member of the negotiating team) asked whether under the contract the men are compelled to work. Mr. Jacks replied with a question asking if his previous reply to Mr. Franko sounded like compulsion. Mr. Lanning then said that his men wanted to know if they refused to work just because they didn't want to, would they be compelled to work. Mr. O'Toole then interrupted — asking if we could get something in writing — that the union wanted to end griping caused by foremen who ask a worker to work along with veiled threats, "If you don't you'll have to suffer the consequences."
>
> Mr. Dick Lanning commented that men had not been asked for a reason when they declined overtime work — that the foreman just went on to the next man. He added that practically everyone wants overtime.
>
> Mr. Franko then said, "It's not compulsory for people to work if they are not feeling right or have other plans." Mr. Franko said the union

would advise workers to cooperate, but then men want to feel they're free — without any threats.

Mr. McCleod pointed out that in the past 90 percent of those who had been asked, worked. There could be a problem if 25 percent refused and 15 percent gave no reason. Mr. Franko admitted that this might present a problem but said management could not invoke a penalty under the agreement if a man refused to work.

Mr. McCleod said the company wanted men to work overtime when there is overtime work to do — that no one had been fired for refusing to work — yet. (Everyone agreed on this matter.)

Mr. McCleod said these negotiations were the first time he had heard of threats being used by foremen to compel overtime — that there would be none of that in the future. Mr. Jacks added his comment — that naturally we can't compel anyone to work, and this is the first he had heard of any threat.

Mr. McCleod was not sure whether notes from past negotiations were relevant to the issue at hand, because the issue of compulsory overtime had never presented itself in day-to-day operations. He wondered whether he should approach the union representatives and ask for an agreement. To do so would be tantamount to admitting his own doubts about whether management could compel overtime under the existing contract. Also, it would risk opening other provisions of the contract to renegotiation. The existing agreement still had almost two years to run, but Mr. McCleod was aware of dissatisfaction within the union because leaders had settled for a wage increase in negotiations one year ago giving a 5.2 percent a year increase for the next three years. Other firms in the area were signing this year for 7 percent and more.

Mr. McCleod felt reasonably certain he could win a case if it were brought to arbitration; but the time, expense, and potential damage to existing relationships all deterred him from that course of action.

MacINTOSH METAL COMPANY

Harry Brown, Industrial Relations Manager for MacIntosh Metal Company, was reviewing two signed statements that were on his desk. The statements were from two employees, Arnie Tiddle and Jack Bell, who had been discharged two weeks before. The statements read as follows:

Statement of Jack Bell

I, Jack Bell, hereby make the following voluntary statement regarding what took place in the plant on the 4–12 shift on May 16th.

I was working the 4–12 shift on Friday, 16th of May at No. 1 furnace. About 9:00 p.m. I went down to No. 2 furnace and Arnie Tiddle offered me a drink. I accepted. He had a mickey of whiskey. Between then and shortly after the 10:00 p.m. rest period, Arnie and I had consumed his bottle of whiskey. I took his empty bottle, went out to my car on the parking lot, partially filled his bottle with Walker's Special Old Rye Whiskey from a bottle I had in my car and brought the part bottle back into the plant. I went to and from the parking lot by way of the Casting Department. The part bottle of rye was put in Arnie's locker. I had one small drink out of the bottle just when I brought it in. I went back to my own area and before we quit the shift I went back over to No. 2 furnace area, and Arnie said, "It is all gone."

Arnie and I left the plant together and went to my car where we each had one drink from my bottle which I had in the car. Arnie then left to go to his car, and I drove home. I knew nothing of Arnie's accident until the next Tuesday night when Arnie came over and told me. As far as I can recall, this is the whole story, and it is the truth.

Statement of Arnie Tiddle

I, Arnie Tiddle, hereby make the following voluntary statement regarding what took place in the plant on the night of Friday, the 16th of May.

I was working the 4–12 shift on Friday, 16th May, at No. 2 furnace. When I came in on shift I brought with me a mickey of Golden Wedding Rye Whiskey. I put the bottle in my locker in the furnace area. I didn't touch this bottle until after the 8:00 p.m. rest period. I had a drink out of the bottle first. Then Jack Bell came over. Nobody called him. I offered him a drink. Jack and I consumed that bottle. There was no one else drinking with us. Shortly after the 10:00 p.m. rest period, Jack Bell took my empty bottle out to his car on the parking lot, partially filled it with whiskey, brought it back to the furnace area and put it in my locker. Between then and the end of the shift we finished that bottle.

Before leaving the plant we arranged to meet at Jack's car on the parking lot, and we each had one drink out of his bottle in the car. As far as I know Jack drove off the lot first. I eventually drove off the lot and turned south on MacKenzie Avenue. I had an accident at the intersection of McKenzie Avenue and Cedar Hill Road. I hit a light standard at that point. This accident happened about 12:15 a.m. I was arrested by the City Police and spent the night in jail and was released on bail about 10:00 a.m. that same morning.

That was the first time that I ever brought any liquor into this plant, and if I ever get back, it will be the last time.
This statement has been read over to me, and it is the truth.

The company had learned of this drinking incident about one week after it had occurred when Arnie Tiddle approached his foreman to inform him that he needed time off to appear in court. When the foreman asked why he had to be in court, Arnie explained about the car accident and the impaired driving charge. The foreman, realizing what shift Arnie had worked on the day of the accident, reported this to Mr. Bill Johnson, the Works Manager. The Works Manager then called Arnie into his office and later Jack Bell, where he got the complete story as it appeared in the signed statements from the two employees. Mr. Johnson suspended the two men and then two days later, sent them each their discharge papers along with the following letter:

I have given careful consideration to views presented by the union about the severity of the penalty imposed on you for the admitted act of bringing liquor into the plant in violation of plant regulations. I have also reviewed all other aspects of the case.

We have always been aware of the serious hazard to other employees which an act of this kind presents. It could well be a matter of life and death. That is the reason we have made such an act cause for discharge, and have consistently applied this policy.

I regret that you deliberately decided to expose your fellow employees to this hazard and thereby exposed yourself to the established penalty. However, I cannot agree that the penalty is too severe because to modify it would indicate a lessening of our concern for the seriousness of the offence, and that is simply not the case.

Yours very truly,

(signed) Bill Johnson
Works Manager

The two employees filed a grievance over the discharge, and Mr. Brown was preparing for a third step grievance meeting with the union. The meeting was due to start in a few minutes.

MacIntosh Metal Company was a small metal fabricating company. The plant where this incident took place was situated in Metro Toronto where metals such as titanium and magnesium and other special alloys were processed for use in high technology industries such as aircraft and aerospace construction. The plant produced metal sheet, tubing, extrusions, and other fabricated metal parts. The plant employed approximately 150 production employees. The customers demanded high precision products, manufactured to extremely close tolerances, and thus the plant was highly mechanized with expensive machinery. The metal products which the company manufactured were somewhat expensive.

The management and union had developed a very good working relationship and had experienced no strikes for many years. The nature of the relationship was reflected in the low grievance and arbitration rate that had existed over the past few years.

At the plant, the company was aware of a drinking problem that existed, especially during the summer and near Christmas. At these times liquor and beer bottles sometimes were found during clean-up, but it was difficult to catch offenders. The company was very concerned about this problem due to the high precision production required, the expensive machinery and product, and the safety of the workforce.

The union, The International Association of Machinists and Aerospace Workers (IAM), Lodge 174, had a fine record of concern for its members. It had been established in the company for 26 years and enjoyed strong support from its constituents. The union preferred to settle disputes as quickly as possible on the production floor, where they arose. However, they did not compromise their beliefs on employee welfare or fairness to employees, and would go to arbitration if they believed justice was not being done.

Mr. Brown left his office to go to the meeting in the conference room. Present at the meeting were:

For the union: Claude Weston, President of Lodge 174
                    John Sacks, Vice President of Lodge 174
For the company: Harry Brown, Industrial Relations Manager
                    Bill Johnson, Works Manager

Harry Brown (co): Good day, gentlemen. I wish this meeting could have been called for more pleasant reasons, however, I guess we should get right to the problem. I trust you all have copies or have seen copies of these documents. (He showed them the two signed statements from the grievants, and Mr. Johnson's discharge letter. The all nodded their agreement.) Well, then, where should we start? Maybe you, Claude, could state the union's position.

Claude Weston (u): Thank you, Harry. The union position is quite simple: we think you're being far, far too hard on these guys. You would not even have known about it if Arnie hadn't explained why he needed to go to court; there was absolutely nothing wrong with their performance the night they were drinking, no damage to the equipment or the product, no injuries, all their charts were correctly marked, no complaints from other employees or the foremen.

Bill Johnson (co): Aw c'mon, Claude, you know that isn't the point at all. The two men, by their admission, were drinking on the job. It wasn't just a casual sip, which is serious in its own right, but they consumed a bottle and a half of rye during the last half of the shift. Then Arnie went out and hit a telephone pole and was charged with impaired driving. I shouldn't have to remind you that the equipment they're working with is worth $200,000 and those bundles they're lifting into the furnace are worth $1,000 to $3,000 each. You can imagine what our customers would do if they thought we allowed men in an impaired condition to try to meet their specifications! This has got to be a high precision operation! Besides, lifting those bundles in and out of the furnace could be a dangerous job to both the machine operators and other employees. It's not fair to our men to have guys drunk in the plant.

John Sacks (u): We're not arguing whether the two men were guilty of a crime. They themselves admit that! What we're arguing is the severity of punishment. The men had no basis for knowing that they would be discharged for drinking on the job. There aren't any rules posted in the plant about drinking.

Harry Brown (co): You're not seriously trying to say the men didn't know they would be disciplined if caught, John! 'No drinking on the job' is such a basic rule, especially in a plant. Nobody has to have it individually explained to them that it is dangerous and wrong to be impaired while operating machinery!

John Sacks (u): Well the rules aren't published and nobody came up and told them. You're just assuming they should know. Anyway, let's assume they did know it was wrong; they had no way of knowing they would be discharged. You say, Bill, in your letter, that it is established policy to discharge offending employees. That's not quite right either. Remember Dick Moorehouse, three years ago? He was caught drinking just before the Christmas holidays, and the company let him off with a week's suspension, not a discharge.

Bill Johnson (co): That case was different than this one. He had one drink, just before he left the plant on Christmas eve. You know full well that men have been discharged for drinking, and we feel this case is at least as serious as those discharge cases. Remember, these two men were impaired; Arnie was even charged with impairment by the police and found guilty in a court of law!

John Sacks (u): You've had some pretty strong suspicions that men have been drinking and not done anything.

Harry Brown (co): Where we've had *evidence*, we've discharged.

Claude Weston (u): Still, though, Harry, discharge is not established as an *automatic* penalty for drinking on the job. Take a look at Tiddle's and Bell's records: Both have more than twenty years seniority; both have been described by their foremen as good, responsible workers; Arnie has a spotless record and Jack, except for being sent home three years ago for reporting to work after drinking, has a perfect record too. These guys are in their early 50s and by discharging them now you not only make them lose all their seniority and seniority benefits, but seriously hinder two good men's chances of getting other jobs. At their age they'll have a tough time competing in the job market, plus they'll have the stigma attached, and always following them around, that they were fired for drinking on the job. If you discharge them you'll seriously jeopardize their chances of supporting their families! And for what? One mistake against more than twenty years of loyal service. We feel they should have built up a little bit of good behaviour capital on which to draw a little consideration.

Harry Brown (co): True, the two men, for the most part, have been very good employees, but the fact still remains: They were drunk on the job and that is a very serious crime. You know, as well as I do, that the company has rules against drinking and the Industrial Safety Act has regulations. Here, look at them.

He handed the other 3 members of the meeting copies of the company rules and Industrial Safety Regulations which read:

Company Rules
(2) No person is allowed on Company property while under the influence of alcohol and no alcoholic beverages are permitted on the property at any time.

Industrial Safety Regulations
7.(1) Every employer who is in charge of a factory shall ensure that no person whose faculties are impaired by alcohol or a drug or who has in his possession any alcohol remains in the factory.

(2) No person whose faculties are impaired by alcohol or a drug or has in his possession any alcohol or drug shall enter or remain in any factory.

Harry Brown (co): In our opinion drinking on the job is a serious enough offence that it can be cause for discharge, even on the first offence! We don't feel that we have to individually inform each employee that it is wrong to drink on the job because it is such an elementary principle that no one can plead ignorance. Furthermore, we feel we are entirely within our rights to discharge these men, and I quote from our contract:

Section III — Management Rigths
3.01 Nothing in this agreement shall be interpreted as limiting the Company in the exercise of all the rights, powers, authority and regular and customary functions of Management and without limiting the generality of the foregoing these rights shall include . . . the right to suspend, discharge or otherwise discipline employees for cause subject to the right of any employee to lodge a grievance in the manner and to the extent herein provided.

I am very sorry that this incident has taken place, and that it involved these two men. But the company just cannot afford, either economically or morally, to have men in an impaired state operating heavy equipment at risk to other employees' well being, and company machinery and products. We feel that if the discharge is not maintained, employees will feel they have the right to get drunk at least once on the job without fear of discharge. We can't operate under those conditions.

Claude Weston (u): We appreciate your concern, Harry, and your responsibilities. But the fact still remains that the men did not know or expect discharge as a punishment. Also, in view of your past practice with regards to drinking and your recently increased concern for the drinking problem in the plant, we feel you are unfairly trying to make an example of these two men in order to establish a clear policy. We don't think these men deserve that kind of treatment, and we don't think this is the way to go about establishing a new policy, at their expense. These men deserve consideration because of their seniority, age, and good service.

Questions:

1. If you were Harry Brown, what would you do next? What are the implications of your action?
2. Evaluate the case as if you were an arbitrator. What decision would you give?

PERSONAL PAPER COMPANY

"Three days' premium pay for six days worked is outrageous!" declared John Simmons, the Industrial Relations Manager for Personal Paper Company. "Gentlemen, let's be reasonable. It's ludicrous to make that kind of claim!"

Mr. Simmons was in the midst of a meeting with representatives of the International Woodworkers of America, Local 391, who were pressing for remuneration for six employees arising from a recent grievance at the company plant in McBride, British Columbia. This was the third step in the grievance procedure; if no settlement could be reached, the company and the union would be forced to go to arbitration.

The company, based in Vancouver, was a large pulp, paper, and paper products manufacturer which supplied companies in Canada, Britain, and the United States. Personal Paper Company had recently engaged in an extensive plant modernization program in order to help maintain its competitive position in the international market. The program included the purchasing of new, very complex, and expensive machinery. The company had been considering the possibility of changing its operating hours from three shifts per day, five days per week, to seven-day swing shifts, in order to more fully utilize its costly new equipment.

The union, however, had long been opposed to any kind of changes which might disrupt its members' private lives. A main plank in their platform had been to insist on compensation for inconvenience and disruptions. In negotiations the year before, the union had adamantly refused a company request to introduce round-the-clock operations through the use of swing shifts.

The grievance confronting the committee during this meeting was filed by six employees from the Bleaching Department. It read as follows:

Grievance Statement

We the undersigned worked an overtime shift Sunday, July 15, 4–12 shift. We were requested by our Foreman, Mr. Jack Wheatly, to report for work Monday and Tuesday, July 16 and July 17, and changed to the 4–12 shift on Wednesday, July 18.

We received 1½ pay for Sunday, July 15, and also 1½ pay for changing to the 4–12 shift on Wednesday, July 18.

Under the terms of the current collective agreement, we feel we are entitled to 1½ pay for Monday, July 16.

Present at the meeting are:

For the union: Bob Latum, President for Local
                Ted Barner, Business Manager
For the company: John Simmons, Industrial Relations Manager
                Alf Reimer, Personnel Manager

Bob Latum (u): Cool down, John. We're not trying to be unreasonable. We feel that the men who filed this grievance have a legitimate point, and we feel they're entitled to premium pay for the Monday shift. Let's review once more what happened. Alf, have you got the company's documentation of the events in question?

Alf Reimer: (co): Yes Bob, I have them here with me. The six employees who filed the grievance were working the 8 to 4 shift during the week of Monday July 9, to Friday, July 13. According to our usual shift rotation, the following week, Monday, July 16, to Friday, July 20, they would have normally worked the 4 to 12 shift. However, due to a few production delays and some other circumstances, Jack Wheatley, the foreman of the Bleaching Department, on Thursday, July 12, asked the six employees who filed this grievance if they would work overtime on Sunday, July 15 from 4 to 12, and also to report on Monday, July 16, and Tuesday, July 17, to the 8 to 4 shift instead of the 4 to 12 shift. The six employees agreed at that time to work during the requested times. They worked as they had agreed and the company paid them time and one-half for Sunday, July 15 and time and one-half for Wednesday, July 18 because Wednesday they returned to their regular shift. Is there any disagreement concerning this account of events?

Ted Barner (u): No, Alf. That's our understanding of the actual events too. Our disagreement, then, appears to be solely on the interpretation of the relevant contract clauses. Our point of view is the following. Consider the clause:

9.01 Work Week The normal work week for each employee shall be five (5) consecutive days of eight (8) hours per day within the period 8:00 a.m. Monday to 8:00 a.m. Saturday.

9.02 Work on Sunday All Sunday work, except for emergency reasons or occupations where continuous preparatory or clean-up attention is necessary, will be considered voluntary, it being understood that Company policy is to eliminate Sunday work. If an employee commits himself to Sunday overtime to meet production commitments, Sunday will no longer be considered as voluntary for the employee concerned.

12.03 Irregular Shift Changes An employee shall be paid time and one-half for the first assigned shift worked under the following circumstances:
(a) if, after leaving the plant at the end of his regular work week, he is requested to change his shift for the coming week;
(b) if he is requested to change his shift after the beginning of his scheduled work week;
(c) if he returns to his regular shift after the beginning of his scheduled work week;
(d) if he misses the first shift of his regular work schedule as a result of the irregular shift change.

As you recall, Jack Wheatly, the foreman, asked the men to work on Sunday, July 15 and they agreed to it. Therefore, by the last sentence in clause 9.02, after agreeing to work, Sunday was no longer a voluntary shift. Sunday, then, was actually the first day of these employees' scheduled work week. Remember the Olson Award from the arbitration we had last year over a similar kind of incident? Mr. Olson, the arbitrator, ruled, and I quote:

> Although section 9.01 of the collective agreement excludes Sunday from part of the *normal work week*, the effect of the last sentence of Section 9.02 is to make Sunday work, when accepted by the employee, non voluntary. The Board agrees with the Union's suggestion that an employee who agreed to work Sunday and did not appear for work, could validly be disciplined by the company. Since Sunday work, when accepted, becomes non voluntary, it must be considered to be part of the employee's work week and since the employee, once he agrees to work Sunday, is therefore scheduled and obligated to work Sunday, the Sunday shift must be considered to be part of the employee's scheduled work week. Again, since Sunday is normally considered to be the beginning of the week, an employee who works Sunday must be considered to have begun his scheduled work week. Thus, in the present case, the grievor's (and in this regard the Board accepts the Union's submission that Section 12.03 is personal

to each employee) scheduled work week commenced on Sunday November 23rd. Since the grievor worked 4:00 p.m. to 12.00 a.m. on Sunday and then returned to his regular shift, i.e., 8:00 a.m. to 4:00 p.m., on Monday, November 24th, his shift changes fell within the literal wording of Section 12.03 (c).

Therefore, in our opinion, there can be no doubt that Sunday July 15, was the first shift of the six employees' scheduled work week. Further, we all agree that the regular shift for the week would ordinarily be 4 to 12. However, the men reported to work, upon request by their foreman, at 8:00 on Monday, July 16, and Tuesday, July 17. Therefore the effective change in their shift occurred on Monday, July 16, which is after July 15 which was the first shift in their scheduled work week. Thus, by applying 12.03 (b) literally it is clear that the men are entitled to time and one-half for Monday July 16. In other words, Monday must be treated in a similar manner as in the Olson award. The spirit of that award is to compensate for the dislocation of a person's working hours during a week.

John Simmons (co): Hold on a second, Ted!
It appears to me that you are misunderstanding 12.03 (b) and the Olson award. In 12.03 (b) the word "after" does not refer to the timing of the shift change but rather, the timing of the request to change the shift. As the Olson award points out, Sunday was the first shift of the six employees' scheduled work week, and as we have all agreed, this scheduled work week was established on Thursday July 12, well in advance of the first shift. The basic concern in this issue is that an employee will be compensated for irregular shift changes. However, once the employee's scheduled work week is clearly established for him, he is then able to plan his activities around this schedule without disruption. Thus, in our opinion, by applying the literal translation of 12.03 (b), the employees are not entitled to premium pay for Monday July 16. Further, the Olson award deals with the application of 12.03 (c) which is not in dispute in this case. The regular shift in the present case is 4–12 which was returned to by the employees on Wednesday, and for which they were compensated appropriately. However, in the Olson award, the regular shift was 8–4 which was returned to by the employee in that case, on Monday and for which he was subsequently reimbursed. Therefore, although the actual hours involved in the Olson award are the same, namely 4–12 shift Sunday and 8–4 shift Monday, the circumstances around these hours are entirely different. Due to these different circumstances and due to the application of 12.03 (c) in the Olson award instead of 12.03 (b) which is the clause in question here, the Olson award cannot possibly be considered as a precedent for this case.

Alf Reimer (co): It seems we've reached an impasse, gentlemen. Why don't we have a short recess to recollect our thoughts. Let's reconvene in a half hour. Hopefully someone can shed a new light on the subject at that time.

John Simmons mulled over arguments on the meeting in his office as he waited for the meeting to reconvene. In the past, the company and the union had developed a very good working relationship. The company took great pride in its record of concern for employee welfare. Yet, he had pressures from above voicing concern for greater utilization of the new, expensive machinery. He was worried about the possible outcome of an arbitration hearing in view of the previous decision involving these same contract sections just a year ago. It appeared that the union was willing to push this grievance to arbitration unless he formulated a suitable solution.

PORT ERIE HYDRO

On April 27, 1984, Brian Rowe received notice that, effective the following June 15, his employment with the Hydroelectric Commission of Port Erie would be terminated. Following that he would receive two weeks vacation pay, and his name would be removed from the roles on June 29. He had been discharged.

The discharge notice, sent by mail to Rowe's home, had been signed by Mr. S. W. Schofield, the Commission's General Manager. In the notice Mr. Schofield stated the reasons for termination as follows:

> . . . unsatisfactory performance of your work, your inability to learn and your poor attitude on the job.

The next day, April 30, Rowe went looking for his union representative, Ken Tripp. Mr. Tripp was President of Local 1175 of the International Brotherhood of Electrical Workers and had held that office for the past ten years. Local 1175 represented all employees of the Commission except those working in offices or carrying titles of foreman, supervisor, or above. Rowe had been a member in good standing since 60 days following his initial employment by the Commission on January 12, 1980.

Tripp told Rowe that as a matter of policy the union always filed a formal grievance in the event of discharge action and said that he would do that within five days. Then he asked Rowe to give him all the facts, favourable or not, that he could about himself, his work history, and events which he believed might have caused the discharge action. Following his talk with Rowe, Tripp made an appointment with Mr. Schofield to learn what he could from him. Then he planned to meet with the union's grievance committee to decide what action to take. Following are the facts which Mr. Tripp believed were most vital in deciding how to proceed.

THE FACTS

Brian Rowe had been employed by the Commission on January 12, 1980, as a Storeman Learner 3 at an hourly rate of $8.00. On March 30, 1980, he was promoted to the position of Storeman Learner 2 and on April 13 to Storeman Learner 1. On August 1 of the same year he was advanced to the position of Storeman Improver 3, a so-called permanent staff classification carrying with it the removal of probationary status and obligatory membership in Local 1175. On November 30, 1980, he was promoted to Storeman Improver 2.

Assignments to various classifications and progressions through the classifications were governed by Section 42 of the Collective Agreement. This section had been in existence at least since 1965 when Tripp became an officer of the union, and probably much longer.

Section 42. The Basic Pay Scale shall be operated and interpreted as follows:

   a) each employee shall be given:
     i) a trade classification,

ii) an appointment, and

iii) a grading . . .

b) In each appointment there are one or more gradings, indicated 3, 2, or 1.

c) In the case of Learner Appointments 3, 2, and 1, progression is considered at the end of three (3) months. Also the Commission may act to shorten the normal progression period.

d) In the case of the Improver and Junior appointments, the progression is considered at the end of six (6) months.

e) In the case of Journeymen and Senior Appointments progression is to be considered at the end of one (1) year.

f) To move from one grade or appointment to the next requires that the employee have the necessary qualities, ability, and knowledge, and has been recommended to the management by the foremen and superintendents of the departments concerned. The employee is to be given a copy of the recommendation.

Until Rowe's case came to his attention, Mr. Tripp had never experienced problems with Section 42. Rowe was the only person in his memory who had failed to progress at or near the prescribed time periods. In talking with Mr. Schofield the two could recall only one instance of a man being held back even one time period.

While most individuals progressed as Section 42 would indicate, the union leaders were regularly made aware that management considered such progression to be discretionary with themselves, not automatic. It was based on recommendation of the foreman or department head, and as a matter of procedure confidential rating sheets and rating charts were completed by individual foremen at the time employees were considered for progression.

According to Mr. Schofield it was Rowe's failure to progress in a normal fashion which led to his discharge. "If people can't go to the top," said Schofield, "we don't want them."

Following his tenure as a Storeman Improver 2 Rowe was transferred at his own request to the position of Lineman Improver 3 on October 11, 1981. For four months prior to the transfer he worked as a Lineman Learner at his Storeman Improver 2's rate $7.50. When the transfer became official he received the assigned rate for a Lineman Improver 3 — $10.00. All this manoeuvering prior to the change in classification was illegal according to the contract but was not at issue now, and Tripp chose not to pursue it. The matter of contention now, and the reason for discharge, was that Brian Rowe had retained his position as a Lineman Improver 3 since then — more than 2½ years. During that time Section 42 would have required his consideration for advancement five times. And here lay the crux of the problem.

The Commission was small, employing only 238 people. The union had long shared the belief with Commission management that employees should advance through the various categories, to develop flexibility in work assignments and increase their earnings. Ideally everyone would eventually attain journeyman or senior status. In fact the union had committed itself by virtue of Section 12 of the Collective Agreement to help develop the ability of employees.

Section 12. The Commission Management will recognize three (3) representatives of a Shop Committee set up by the union which will pay particular attention to:

a) Developing, assisting and instructing junior employees in the proper carrying out of their duties;

b) advising Commission management in regard to abilities and attainments of employees when such information is desirable.

The shop committee had never played an active role as suggested by Section 12. Indeed, until the Rowe case, there was no apparent need for union assistance in helping develop employees, because everyone had advanced without undue delay.

Both Schofield and Rowe were in agreement that Rowe's failure to advance had been caused by a weakness in performing overhead work. All representatives of union and management acknowledged that overhead work was essential to a lineman's package of skills, but there was disagreement on whether Rowe was very anxious to develop overhead skills. In fact, he had given indications that he was content to remain as a Lineman Learner 3 indefinitely.

There was nothing in the contract which said that failure to advance through the various appointments was grounds for discharge, but on the other hand Rowe's continued presence as an Improver 3 could block other, more ambitious workers from the opportunity to obtain much-needed experience to move through the classifications. For this reason it could set an undesirable precedent of mediocrity among members of the workforce. Tripp, long an employee of the Commission and a journeyman lineman himself, appreciated that the Commission needed people who would rise above mediocrity. There were many ambitious young people seeking employment, and opportunities should be made available for some of the more highly qualified.

Yet, on the other hand, Rowe probably had a case. No one had warned him that his deficiencies on overhead work might cost him his job, and furthermore there was evidence that management had not given him much opportunity to perform overhead. In fact, Rowe said that for at least 24 months of his approximately-30-month tenure as an Improver 3 he had been assigned to work on the ground, including considerable time driving a "Go Devil" (service truck) and performing storeman's work, work that was not directly associated with a lineman's job. No one in management challenged those estimates.

While they were not spelled out in writing, the duties of a lineman were clear. A Lineman Improver was expected to do any kind of construction, maintenance and repair work on electric lines carrying up to 600 volts. This included underground work and pole work, and it consisted primarily of the ability to string wire and make joints. Climbing ability was considered essential, as was the ability to work well in cooperation with other linemen. While management and union representatives generally agreed that it was important for linemen to develop skills so that they could pass through the grades, no one was able to describe with precision the differences between grades 3, 2, and 1. According to Mr. Jason Conlin, the Commission's Line Superintendent, progression depended on subjective judgement by management. Grades, according to Conlin, were largely intended as devices for compensation.

In investigating the case, Mr. Tripp was able to uncover only three rating

sheets for Rowe. The first, dated April 3, 1982, contained a statement by Foreman Michael Barlow as follows:

> I recommend that this man (Rowe) stay at the above classification and
> appointment (Lineman Improver 3) until a little more effort is put into
> learning the fundamentals of line work. Brian's climbing is improving
> but he is very timid and awkward while on a pole, since he has spent so
> much time driving a "Go Devil" (this has been corrected). I think a more
> accurate report may be made in six months.

Mr. Barlow had been Rowe's direct supervisor since February 1, slightly over
two months prior to the date of the rating sheet. He had worked prior to that as
a Journeyman Lineman on maintenance and repair teams to which Rowe had
been assigned and had registered complaints on more than one occasion with
Mr. Conlin about Rowe's lack of flexibility and general uncooperativeness.

Mr. Barlow remained as Rowe's supervisor until December of 1982, about ten
months in all. Tripp went to see Barlow following his conversation with Schofield,
and Barlow said that in his opinion Rowe "didn't seem to have much ability,"
that he "didn't know his left hand from his right and was shy on the pole."

Mr. Barlow said he did not believe Rowe would improve as a lineman, and for
that reason he assigned him most often to storework and driving the "Go Devil"
— "jobs that needed doing and that he was most qualified to do." Barlow estimated that Rowe had been on overhead work, climbing poles and restringing
wire, for part of every day for approximately two weeks under his supervision.

A second rating sheet regarding Rowe was dated October 2, 1982, and it too
was signed by Barlow.

> Brian is progressing favourably on underground work (splicing, etc.,)
> but I cannot truthfully recommend him to Improver 2 until he adapts
> himself more handily to the mechanical aspects of overhead line work.

A note was appended to the bottom of the rating sheet and signed by Mr. Peter
Dobbyn, the Commission's Chief Engineer.

> On the basis of the above statement by Mr. Barlow, the attached rating
> sheet and my own personal observations concerning the attitude of this
> employee I recommend that he receive no progression at this time.

The third rating sheet on Mr. Rowe was dated April 1, 1983, and signed by
Foreman Gerald Lawson. Rowe had worked under Lawson since December of
1982. According to Lawson's rating sheet:

> There is not much I can do to recommend Brian Rowe in the Lineman's
> classification. Since being with me he has been a truck driver. I have
> had him climb occasionally doing secondary work, also he has done
> some secondary U.G. (underground).

Foreman Ralph Crump appended the following note:

> When speaking to Brian Rowe last fall about not doing well at line work
> he informed me that he did not care to climb poles. This man will not
> make a lineman.

A third note on the bottom of the same form was signed by Jack McCafferty, Chief Engineer:

No recommendation for appointment to higher classification.

Mr. Tripp went to see Mr. Lawson and learned that Rowe had climbed poles on only two occasions while working for him. Tripp asked Lawson whether Rowe himself had ever shown initiative by asking for more opportunity to work overhead. Lawson said he had not and added, "I don't think he was too keen to climb poles."

Mr. Lawson said he believed it would take a person from one week to one month to develop competence in climbing poles and a similar period to learn the work needed at the top of the pole. He agreed with Tripp that if a man climbed only once a week the learning process would be slowed but said it was not necessary to climb once a day.

In his investigation, Ken Tripp uncovered some additional company work records. These showed that Rowe had been assigned to the "Go Devil" for 276 hours between July 30, 1982, and November 2, 1983. According to Tripp's calculations this amounted to slightly more than 11 percent of the total time available during this period, allowing for vacations and holidays.

Tripp thought it was curious that Rowe had never apparently raised a grievance or complaint about his failure to advance. When he asked Rowe about this Rowe said he had complained to Mr. Barlow about his frequent assignment to the "Go Devil," to underground work and even to stores work. Once when he raised a complaint, stating that truck driving and stores work was not part of his job description, Barlow commented about Rowe's "surly" attitude. After that Rowe decided not to complain further. He said he was not a complainer by nature and that he did not wish to jeopardize his employment or advancement possibilities by being disagreeable — that a new car, a mortgage, and three kids made him somewhat less prone to complain than he might have been if his obligations were not so great.

During his tenure as a Lineman Improver Rowe applied twice for an opening with the Commission as a meter mechanic. He was rejected on both occasions. First he was rejected in favour of a student on summer vacation. The commission and union were then negotiating a new collective agreement, and a rate had not yet been agreed upon for the job. The student worked on the job for about five months, then quit to go back to school, at which time Rowe applied again. This time he was told that he lacked one of the necessary qualifications: a grade 12 education. Rowe complained then, saying that he had received a certificate of equivalent education competence from the Canadian Armed Forces, where he had served for two years before being hired by the Commission. Rowe pointed out that the same certificate had been accepted by the Commission as evidence of grade 12 when he initially applied for work. When the Personnel Director said he would check Rowe's claim, Rowe dropped his request, explaining later to Ken Tripp that he feared discrimination if he pursued it. As it turned out the meter mechanic's rate of pay was set at 25 cents an hour above the rate

Rowe was then receiving as an Improver 3 and 12½ cents above the rate of a Lineman Improver 2.

While Rowe never received a formal indication beyond the rating sheets that his work as an Improver 3 was unsatisfactory or that failure to advance could lead to dismissal, he acknowledged that Mr. Conlin had talked to him on three or four occasions about his failure to progress, indicating that he needed to develop greater competence on overhead work. On one of these occasions Rowe apparently said to Conlin, "To be truthful I don't care if I ever climb another pole for five years." Conlin interpreted this to mean that Rowe lacked desire; Rowe said it was an expression of his own frustration in being unable to receive opportunities for climbing. He said that in making the remark, "I meant that I wasn't getting advanced." It was at about the same time that he applied for the meter mechanic's job, "because I was reasonably convinced I had no future as a lineman."

On one occasion, during the summer of 1983, Rowe took matters into his own hands. He asked Walt Manley, a Lineman Journeyman, to work with him on a weekend instructing him on pole climbing. Manley spent six hours doing that and said that he saw considerable improvement. He said to Tripp that he could give Rowe the training he needed to become competent if Rowe wanted him to, but indicated that he believed it would take from nine months to a year to develop sufficient overhead experience to advance from an Improver 3 to an Improver 2.

Tripp's Analysis

After talking at length with various company representatives and with Brian Rowe himself, Ken Tripp was convinced that discharge action against Rowe was unwarranted. Apparently the discharge had been for Rowe's failure to advance, and nothing in the contract or past practice between the parties had indicated this was a cause for discipline or discharge. Furthermore no one had warned Rowe that his failure to advance could lead to discharge.

Mr. Schofield had told Tripp that the discharge was for poor performance as a Lineman Improver 3, in addition to his failure to advance.

In Tripp's opinion this position was unconvincing. If Rowe was performing so poorly as an Improver 3 why had he been kept on the job for two and one-half years? When he asked Schofield this question Schofield remarked: "If anything, we allowed him to continue too long. Are you going to crucify us for that?"

In considering what action to take, Tripp felt that three contract provisions were relevant, aside from Sections 12 and 42 already cited. These were the Appeal Against Dismissal Section, the Arbitration Section, and the Management Rights Section.

Section 11.   Appeal Against Dismissal. Any employee desiring to appeal against dismissal must do so in writing to the Grievance Committee not later than five (5) days from the date of dismissal. The Grievance Committee shall notify the Commission Management in writing of the appeal within five (5) days. After receipt of such letter the Commission

Management shall write the Recording Secretary of the union, giving reasons for dismissal. In case of reinstatement, the employee shall be paid in full for all time lost unless otherwise provided in the final settlement by the Grievance Committee or the Arbitration Board.

Section 8. Arbitration. Responsibility to the citizens is the mutual responsibility of both the Commission and the employees and requires that any disputes be adjusted and settled in an orderly manner without interruption of the service to the citizens. Therefore, both parties agree that if any differences occur, during the effective period of this Agreement, which cannot be settled by the usual grievance procedure, such differences will be settled by arbitration as provided in the Ontario Labour Relations Act.

The Board of Arbitration shall not have any power to alter or change any of the provisions of this Agreement or to substitute any new provision for any existing provisions, or to give any decision inconsistent with the terms and provisions of this Agreement.

Section 13. Management Rights. The union acknowledges that it is the exclusive function of the Commission to:

a) maintain order, discipline and efficiency;
b) hire, discharge, lay off, classify, direct, transfer, promote, demote, and suspend or otherwise discipline employees; and
c) generally manage the activities or work in which the Commission is engaged and, without restricting the generality of the foregoing, to determine the work to be performed, the methods and schedules of performance, etc.
d) The Commission agrees that these functions will be exercised in a manner consistent with the provisions of this Agreement, and a claim that the Commission has exercised any of these rights in a manner inconsistent with any of the provisions of this agreement may be the subject of a grievance.

The grievance procedures, Section 9 of the contract, provided for three steps prior to arbitration. All steps required notice in writing stating the nature of the grievance and citing the relevant sections of the contract which were allegedly violated. All required written responses from the management. It was necessary to file a first-step grievance within five days after facts giving rise to the grievance were made known, and five additional days were provided for written responses from management following the respective grievance meetings. First-step grievances were to be presented to the direct supervisor involved in the action. The second step provided for determination by the relevant superintendent, the third for determination by the General Manager. In the case of dismissals it was normal procedure to appeal directly to the General manager, bypassing the first two steps because, as a matter of practice, the General Manager always was involved personally in the taking of discharge action.

In his conversations with Mr. Schofield, the General Manager, Ken Tripp encountered a technical, legalistic argument by Schofield which made him feel uneasy. Schofield claimed that an arbitration board would not have authority under the collective agreement to determine just cause for discharge. He pointed to Sections 13 and 11 of the contract as his authority. According to Schofield, Section 13 gave the Commission certain exclusive rights, including the right to discipline and discharge. Section 11, according to Schofield, gave the Arbitration Board a right to review cases of dismissal but not to apply a "just cause" test. He argued that the Board's power was limited to a review of the fact of dismissal, to satisfy itself that the Commission had some cause for what it did — that the right to discipline or discharge was unqualified by "cause" or "just cause."

In discussing these technicalities with Mr. Schofield, Tripp was referred by Schofield to a 1977 case involving the Ainsworth Electric Company and Local 105 of the International Brotherhood of Electrical Workers (IBEW). Tripp looked up the case and made the following findings.

The Ainsworth, IBEW collective agreement provided that:

> The Company has exclusive rights to the following privileges, except where they are specifically modified or denied by clause or terms embodied in this Agreement. Without restricting the generality of the foregoing sentence or the jurisdiction rights of Local 105, the exclusive rights of the Company include the following: To hire, displace, discharge members of working forces.

The Arbitration Board, using a prior decision by Arthur Harris in its support, ruled the Board had no jurisdiction to rule on just cause for a dismissal.

The Board stated that the Ainsworth management rights clause was, in its opinion, even more restricting than the clause considered by arbitrator Harris. Quoting from the opinion:

> It may well be that where a management rights clause does not contain any provision for dismissal for just cause, that in common law an action may be maintained for unjust dismissal and that a court might well conclude that a dismissal would be actionable unless just cause or proper notice were present. Still this Board in view of the wording of the collective agreement does not consider it proper to import such words into the agreement to clothe the board with jurisdiction to hear the grievance.

In the contract dealt with by Arthur Harris a management rights clause was involved which contained no just cause criterion. The final sentence of the clause stated: "These rights shall not be used in violation of the specific terms of this agreement nor to discriminate against any employee." Harris said it would require a "decided wrench of the language" to attribute the meaning "unfair" or "unjust" to the word "discriminate." Consequently he concluded the collective agreement gave him no jurisdiction to make a binding decision. Then, interestingly, Harris gave his views on the merits anyway saying, "Lacking jurisdiction, my finding can have only the force that the company may wish to give it as a matter of moral compulsion."

All this discussion on arbitrability made it clear to Tripp that the Commission would most likely fight to uphold the discharge even as far as arbitration. Since Schofield himself had written the discharge letter there was not much likelihood of winning Rowe's reinstatement in the third-step grievance meeting.

Ken Tripp was reasonably convinced that the Rowe case would have to be appealed to arbitration. He had explored a compromise with various company representatives which would open the way for Rowe to move to another occupation, but the ways were barred because there were no immediate prospects for openings for which Rowe might be qualified. Furthermore, it was the Commission's policy to promote from below wherever possible in each classification, starting with a Learner. A few occupations, such as meter mechanic, required immediate qualification without a prior Learner appointment, but with the unemployment situation as it was the prospects of a highly qualified person being available for any of these occupations were extremely high. Consequently Tripp would have to fight Rowe's discharge on its merits.

In the first instance he would have to exercise care to word the grievance properly. Then he would have to develop arguments on the issue of arbitrability, because if an arbitration board was prevented from ruling on the merits Tripp believed, all would be lost. Assuming he could get around the arbitrability issue, Tripp felt reasonably confident he could win the case on its merits. He believed the company would fight hardest in upholding their contention that inability to advance is cause for discharge. However, the Commission might also try to show that Brian Rowe was incompetent as a Lineman Improver 3, a possible cause for discharge in itself.

R. G. WILLIAMSON COMPANY LIMITED

The Weapons Division of R. G. Williamson Company produced swords, épées, and sabres used in the sport of fencing and by various theatrical and motion picture groups as props and garnishments for "period" costumes. About 45 production workers were employed in the division.

The final operations in the production of these weapons involved straightening, grinding, straightening again, then inspection. A team of four men worked on these operations. Each member of the team received an hourly rate based on his classification and, in addition, received a group incentive bonus for each weapon turned out. The first straightening operation was performed on a mechanical straightening press, operated by a man classified as "Straightener B." From the press the section went to a grinder operator who removed small burrs. Also he produced a high lustre and semi-sharpness to the blades. Following grinding the weapon went to a Straightener A who, working with an inspector, provided the final touches with an assortment of mallets, hammers, and a small hand press. The inspector placed the weapon in a jig, made several measurements, and applied the final polishing touches with a buffer. While tolerances were not severe, it was essential that the weapons used for fencing comply with requirements of the various amateur and professional athletic associations.

While the straighteners, the grinder, and the inspector worked in close proximity, only the Straightener A and inspector were dependent on each other. Typically the grinder and the Straightener A had a backlog of weapons ahead of them, so that they could do their jobs without waiting for the Straightener B. The inspector almost never had a backlog.

For nearly six weeks prior to September 22, Frank Staiger, the Straightener A, was absent because of illness. As a result, Hugh Lovell, the Straightener B, was transferred temporarily to Staiger's work, and a relatively new man was placed on Lovell's job — operating the press. Since the Straightener A's job required considerable experience and an expert touch, Staiger's job was rated higher than Lovell's, and Staiger's higher hourly rate was assigned to Lovell for the time he was on the job. However, Lynn Peters, the replacement on the straightening press, was considerably slower than Lovell, and the group's incentive earnings fell drastically. Members of the crew complained repeatedly to Foreman Roy Anderson, in an effort to have the incentive rate adjusted while Peters developed his skill on the job. As an alternative the men asked for a guaranteed minimum rate equivalent to their average earnings before Staiger became ill.

On the morning of September 25, Mr. Lovell, who had been most vociferous about the poor incentive earnings since Staiger's illness, reported to the plant nurse complaining of headaches. He had told his foreman that he did not think he could continue work that day. Roy Anderson, the foreman, promptly notified the union steward that if Lovell left the plant the other three men on the incentive team would have to be laid off. Heeding Lovell's complaints, the nurse sent him home at 11:00 a.m. Anderson then informed David Davies, the grinder, and Robert Douglas, the inspector, that they were being laid off at 12:00 noon for the remainder of the shift which ended at 3:00 p.m. Peters remained at work for the rest of the day to build a bank for the others. Article V, Paragraph 3 of the Collective Agreement, titled, "Seniority," provided for temporary lay-offs as follows:

> Lay-offs for a period of one (1) week or less shall be deemed temporary and shall not be subject to the provisions of this Article, provided there is reasonable justification for such temporary lay-off.

This provision had been negotiated five years earlier and had been part of company-union agreements since then. Davies and Douglas punched out at 12:00 noon, but the next day both men filed grievances, stating that their lay-offs were not justified and demanding pay for the three hours missed. Their Steward, Frank Wiesner, argued that there was not reasonable justification for the lay-offs. At 11:00 a.m., when Lovell left the plant, there was a sufficient backlog of work so that both men could have worked their regular jobs for the remainder of the shift. Wiesner observed that there were plenty of weapons to keep Davies going and that Peters, if necessary, could have switched to Straightener A work in order to keep Douglas, the inspector, supplied.

Foreman Anderson acknowledged that there was enough work in the "bank" for Davies to fill out the shift, but stated that the backlog would have been depleted by morning and then Davies would have had to stand around waiting for Peters. "Furthermore, I had no idea whether Lovell would be in the next day," said Anderson. He continued:

> As for Douglas—his work was closely tied to the second straightener, and he had no backlog that day. Peters never tried the Straightener A work before, and it would've been unreasonable to expect him to gain any competence in the few hours remaining that day.

Steward Wiesner pointed out that other grinders and inspectors in the plant had less seniority than Davies and Douglas and, if the company could justify the need for a temporary lay-off, the lesser-seniority men should have gone out — that Davies and Douglas should have been transferred. Two other grinders, Powell and Kiessling, worked that afternoon on jobs that Davies had done in the past, and both had less seniority. One inspector, Peter Blake, had less seniority than Douglas, and he worked that day on a job Douglas had done in the past.

Anderson said:

> I can't prove it, but you know as well as I that this was one of a long line of incidents by these men to get some padding in the incentive rate. They've had a lush job for years and now — with Staiger gone — they've got to eat hamburgers like the rest of us. All three men — Lovell, Davies, and Douglas have been goofing off lately — taking extra long breaks, long lunch hours, and reporting to the nurse for every ache or pain. I'm not going to switch the whole shop around just to suit their whims.

"I don't know about these men goofing off," said Wiesner, "but if they are, you've got a disciplinary procedure to follow. In this situation you've violated the contract. The temporary lay-off provision was not intended as a substitute for discipline."

Foreman Anderson, after hearing Wiesner's arguments, went to his superior, James Heintskill, Manager of the Weapons Division, and told him what had happened. "I may get stuck," said Anderson, "but if I have to pay these guys for doing nothing everyone in the shop will play us for fools." Anderson said that if Davies had worked on the 22nd and exhausted his backlog and if Lovell had failed to come in the next day, the company would have been liable for four hours' reporting pay. "I sent the two 'blokes' home in order to avoid that possibility," said Anderson.

Article XIII of the Collective Agreement provided for reporting pay as follows:

> An employee who is instructed to report for work and finds his regular work not available, shall be given four (4) hours of work, or four (4) hours' pay in lieu of work, at the employee's current straight time hourly rate, exclusive of shift premiums.
>
> In the event the employee refuses to accept work offered him in accordance with the provisions herein set forth, such employee shall not be entitled to the compensation mentioned above. An employee who is not notified before quitting time on any work day not to report for work the succeeding day is deemed to be instructed to report for work.
>
> If failure to provide work is due to an Act of God or a condition beyond the control of the Company, then the Company shall not be required to pay reporting pay.

"Even if we have to pay the three hours for sending them home improperly," said Anderson, "we've saved ourselves four hours' call-in pay."

Mr. Heintskill, in looking over the Collective Agreement, felt that Article II, titled "Hours of Work," might be partly applicable.

> *A Work Day.* The usual work day is defined as eight (8) hours of work in a twenty-four (24) hour period. Except for any unpaid lunch period provided according to prevailing practice, the hours of the work day are consecutive.
>
> The provisions of this Article shall not be construed as a guarantee by the Company of hours for work to be provided per day or per week.

"This section, plus the section on Temporary Lay-offs, should support us," said Heintskill.

"I certainly don't want to take a position that I'm going to switch people all around the factory just because of a temporary situation. And if we don't apply the temporary lay-off provision in this case, we won't ever be able to apply it."

This was the first time the temporary lay-off provision on the contract had been used. In the past, when emergency situations occurred because of unexpected absences or temporary shortages of material, the workers affected were transferred to other jobs in the same classification or in a lower classification without any reduction in base pay. Mr. Heintskill wondered whether past practices barred use of the temporary lay-off on September 22.

Article V, in addition to the temporary lay-off paragraph, had the following provisions:

For the purpose of Lay-offs in connection with the decreasing of the working force and for the purpose of recalling to work employees so laid off the following factors shall be considered:

a) Ability to perform the required work;

b) physical fitness for the job;

c) length of continuous service.

Where factors (a) and (b) are relatively equal, length of continuous service shall govern.

"Ability to perform the required work," as used in this Article, shall mean that the employee possesses the required skill and ability to perform the work in a reasonably satisfactory manner, without any training, and subject to physical fitness of the employee to perform the job.

YOUNG PRODUCTS LTD.

Young Products Ltd. was a major Canadian consumer products company. The firm's headquarters was in Toronto; to it were responsible three major divisions. One division manufactured and distributed a complete line of home care items, including a variety of cleaning products, waxes, soaps, air fresheners, and laundry detergents. A second division manufactured and distributed a full line of personal care items, including soap, shampoos, and related products such as toothpaste and deodorants. A third division produced a line of proprietary drugs and health care products. Each division had a single manufacturing location. The health care group had its plant in Montreal. The personal care items were manufactured in Kitchener, Ontario, while the home care items were made in Toronto.

The Personal Care Division of Young Products Ltd. was a major employer in Kitchener. The plant employed 500 people on three shifts. Hourly employees in the plant and the adjacent warehouse were represented by the Food and Commercial Workers Union (AFL—CIO/CLC). The plant had been unionized for over 25 years, and although the union-management relationship had been initially somewhat strained, that relationship in recent years had been generally accommodative, and company officials viewed the labour relations climate in the plant as being quite good.

Exhibit I presents a partial organization chart of the Kitchener operation.

On June 20, the plant manager, David Ross, welcomed the Warehouse Superintendent, Ralph Ames, and the Employee Relations Manager, Jim Thompson, into his office at 3:00 in the afternoon. Ames had called in the morning of that day requesting the meeting and suggesting that Jim Thompson also attend since the problem he wished to discuss would merit Thompson's attention as well. As Ames and Thompson settled into chairs in front of his desk, Ross asked, "What's the problem today, Ralph?"

"Well, I think the quickest way to say it is to say that we have a sexual harassment problem in the warehouse," replied Ames.

"What do you mean?" asked Ross.

"It all started when Diane McCarthy got engaged, I guess," Ames replied. "At that point, she decided she didn't like to be pinched anymore."

"Has this woman filed a complaint?" Thompson asked.

Ralph Ames said, "Yes. Maybe it would be better if I just laid out the whole situation for you."

"Go ahead," Ross said.

"Okay," Ames said. "Diane McCarthy is a warehouse employee. She has worked for us for four or five years. She's not bad looking, but . . . , well, I guess you could say she's just too smart. Anyhow, Diane has always been a source of and part of the kidding around and horseplay that occurs in the warehouse, just as it does anywhere in the plant, I guess. Giving Diane a pinch had always been part of this fooling around. There was apparently no problem at all until a couple of weeks ago when she became engaged. Then her attitude changed. One of the

EXHIBIT I

YOUNG PRODUCTS LTD.
PERSONAL CARE DIVISION
KITCHENER PLANT
PARTIAL ORGANIZATION CHART

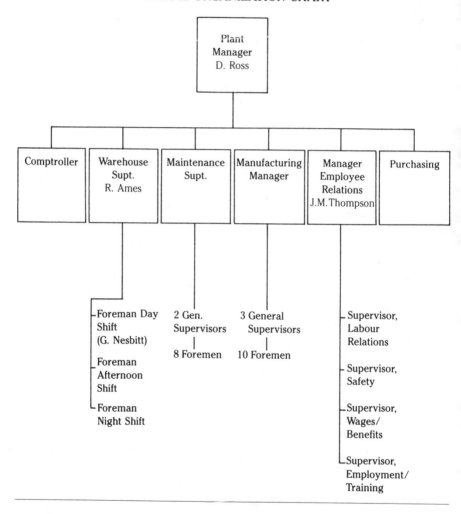

other employees, named Bob Daly, pinched her last week. She warned him not to do it anymore, but the day before yesterday, he forgot and did it again. That night, she was at a party with her boyfriend and her sister, and told them about the most recent incident. Well, after he got home from the party, her boyfriend called up Daly at 2:00 in the morning and told him that if he touched Diane again he'd be sorry. When he came to work this morning, Daly put up a sign on the bulletin board. The sign said, 'WARNING—DON'T PINCH DIANE ON THE ASS ANYMORE'."

"Well, when she came to work and saw it, Diane hit the roof," Ames continued. "She went to her foreman, George Nesbitt, and complained about the sign and complained about the incident. She insisted that the sign be taken down right away, that Daly produce a verbal apology and a published written apology, and that he be subject to some kind of penalty from the company."

"What did you do?" asked Thompson.

"Well, George Nesbitt got the sign taken down right away, and then came to me with the story. After I heard him out, I called you," Ames replied.

"How old are these people?" Ross asked.

"Oh, they're both in their middle to late 20s," Ames said.

"Well," Thompson said, "I don't know whether you know it or not, but the Ontario Human Rights Code has provisions that make it the responsibility of the employer to prevent sexual harassment on the job. We'd better take action on this or face the prospect of a visit from the Human Rights Commission"*

"There's a couple of other things you ought to know," Ames said. "You know that Women's Action Committee which has been getting a lot of attention in the press recently?"

"I sure do," said Thompson.

Ross added, "Aren't they the group that is agitating for stronger laws and stronger police action against sexual harassment and wife beating and rape?"

"Yes they are," said Thompson. "Didn't you see the reports of that big rally they had in the square last weekend? They are really a militant bunch."

"I hate to tell you this, but Diane McCarthy's sister is the president of that group," said Ames. "I think that she's the source of Diane's sudden complaints about the pinching. In fact, I wouldn't be surprised if she put Diane up to making the demands she's made."

"Wonderful, wonderful," muttered Ross.

"Any more bad news?" questioned Thompson.

"There is one more thing. Daly's wife works in the plant too." Ames said.

"Ralph, how much of this girl's story have you checked out?" Thompson asked.

"I had Nesbitt talk to Daly. He admitted pinching her the day before yesterday and admitted putting the sign up. He said he was sorry about the fuss he had stirred up, and said that he certainly wouldn't pinch Diane any more or put any more signs up. Diane McCarthy insists on getting both a written and verbal apology from Daly, and says the company should give him some time off, without pay, as a punishment. She's really in a royal snit and says she was going to demand retribution even before Daly put up the sign."

"Have you talked to the union?" Thompson asked.

"What does the union have to do with it?" David Ross interrupted. "There's nothing in the collective agreement about harassment."

"That's right, but if we attempt to discipline Daly, the union ought to be informed and involved. He has every right to grieve the discipline if he wants," Thompson replied.

*Data about the relevant sections of the Ontario Human Rights Code are in Exhibit II.

"Well, I suspect the union won't be any happier than we are about being involved in this situation," Thompson said. "What about these employees' work records? Are they good employees?"

"They both have clean records. I don't think either of them have even had a verbal warning," Ames replied.

"Jim, what's this about the Human Rights legislation? Why haven't we got an information statement and a policy out on it? I remember hearing something about it at a Chamber of Commerce meeting, but now that I think about it, I haven't seen anything in print here about it," David Ross said pointedly.

Thompson looked a little uncomfortable. "There was supposed to be a meeting at headquarters about it, but for some reason, the meeting got cancelled. That meeting was supposed to work out a policy for general distribution. I guess the answer is that we don't have anything in place at the moment."

"Well Jim, I think we'd better get something in place pretty soon, don't you agree?" Ross said firmly. "Just as soon as we've figured out what we're going to do with this lovely little case. What kind of recommendation do you have?"

EXHIBIT II

SELECTED PROVISIONS FROM THE
ONTARIO HUMAN RIGHTS CODE, 1981

Sec. 9. f) ''harassment'' means engaging in a course of vexatious comment or conduct that is known or ought reasonably to be known to be unwelcome;

Sec. 4. 1) Every person has a right to equal treatment with respect to employment without discrimination because of race, ancestry, place of origin, colour, ethnic origin, citizenship, creed, sex, age, record of offences, marital status, family status or handicap.

2) Every person who is an employee has a right to freedom from harassment in the workplace by the employer or agent of the employer or by another employee because of race, ancestry, place or origin, colour, ethnic origin, citizenship, creed, age, record of offences, marital status, family status or handicap.

Sec. 6. 1) Every person who occupies accommodation has a right to freedom from harassment because of sex by the landlord or agent of the landlord or by an occupant of the same building.

2) Every person who is an employee has a right to freedom from harassment in the workplace because of sex by his or her employer or agent of the employer or by another employee.

3) Every person has a right to be free from:

  a) a sexual solicitation or advance made by a person in a position to confer, grant or deny a benefit or advancement to the person where the person making the solicitation or advance knows or ought reasonably to know that it is unwelcome; or

  b) a reprisal or a threat of reprisal for the rejection of a sexual solicitation or advance where the reprisal is made or threatened by a person in a position to confer, grant or deny a benefit or advancement to the person.

Sec. 7. Every person has a right to claim and enforce his or her rights under this Act, to institute and participate in proceedings under this Act and to refuse to infringe a right of another person under this Act, without reprisal or threat of reprisal for so doing.
    8. No person shall infringe or do, directly or indirectly, anything that infringes a right under this Part.

Sect. 32. 1) The Commission shall investigate a complaint and endeavour to effect a settlement.
    2) An investigation by the Commission may be made by a member or employee of the Commission who is authorized by the Commission for the purpose.
    3) A person authorized to investigate a complaint may,
      a) Enter any place, other than a place that is being used as a dwelling, at any reasonable time, for the purpose of investigating the complaint;
      b) request the production for inspection and examination of documents or things that are or may be relevant to the investigation;
      c) upon giving a receipt therefor, remove from a place documents produced in response to a request under clause (b) for the purpose of making copies thereof or extracts therefrom and shall promptly return them to the person who produced or furnished them; and
      d) question a person on matters that are or may be relevant to the complaint subject to the person's right to have counsel or a personal representative present during such questioning, and may exclude from the questioning any person who may be adverse in interest to the complainant.

Sec. 35. 1) Where the Commission fails to effect a settlement of the complaint and it appears to the Commission that the procedure is appropriate and the evidence warrants an inquiry, the Commission may request the Minister to appoint a board of inquiry and refer the subject-matter of the complaint to the board.
    2) Where the Commission decides to not request the Minister to appoint a board of inquiry, it shall advise the complainant and the person complained against in writing of the decision and the reasons therefor and inform the complainant of the procedure under section 36 for having the decision reconsidered.

Sec. 37. 1) Where the Commission requests the Minister to appoint a board of inquiry, the Minister shall appoint from the panel one or more persons to form the board of inquiry and the Minister shall communicate the names of the persons forming the board to the parties to the inquiry.
    2) A member of the board hearing a complaint must not have taken part in any investigation or consideration of the subject-matter of the inquiry before the hearing and shall not communicate directly or indirectly in relation to the subject-matter of the inquiry with any person or with any party or his representative except upon notice to and opportunity for all parties to participate, but the board may seek legal advice from an adviser independent of the parties and in such case the nature of the advice shall be made known to the parties in order that they may make submissions as to the law.

Sec. 38. 1) The board of inquiry shall hold a hearing,
      a) to determine whether a right of the complainant under this Act has been infringed;
      b) to determine who infringed the right; and
      c) to decide upon an appropriate order under Section 40,

and the hearing shall be commenced within thirty days after the date on which the members were appointed.

2) The parties to a proceeding before a board of inquiry are,
   a) the Commission, which shall have the carriage of the complaint;
   b) the complainant;
   c) any person who the Commission alleges has infringed the right;
   d) any person appearing to the board of inquiry to have infringed the right;
   e) where the complaint is of alleged conduct constituting harassment under subsection 2 (2) or subsection 4 (2) or alleged conduct under section 6, any person who, in the opinion of the board, knew or was in possession of facts from which he or she ought reasonably to have known of the conduct and who had authority to penalize or prevent the conduct.

Sec. 40. 1) Where the board of inquiry, after a hearing, finds that a right of the complainant under Part I has been infringed and that the infringement is a contravention of section 8 by a party to the proceeding, the board may, by order,
   a) direct the party to do anything that, in the opinion of the board the party ought to do to achieve compliance with this Act, both in respect of the complaint and in respect of future practices; and
   b) direct the party to make restitution, including monetary compensation, for loss arising out of the infringement, and, where the infringement has been engaged in wilfully or recklessly, monetary compensation may include an award, not exceeding $10,000, for mental anguish.

4) Where a board makes a finding under subsection (1) that a right is infringed on the ground of harassment under subsection 2 (2) or subsection 4 (2) or conduct under section 6, and the board finds that a person who is a party to the proceeding,
   a) knew or was in possession of knowledge from which he ought to have known of the infringement; and
   b) had the authority by reasonably available means to penalize or prevent the conduct and failed to use it,
   the board shall remain seized of the matter and upon complaint of a continuation or repetition of the infringement of the right the Commission may investigate the complaint and, subject to subsection 35 (2), request the board to re-convene and if the board finds that a person who is a party to the proceeding,
   c) knew or was in possession of knowledge from which he or she ought to have known of the repetition of infringement; and
   d) had the authority by reasonably available means to penalize or prevent the continuation or repetition of the conduct and failed to use it,
   the board may make an order requiring the person to take whatever sanctions or steps are reasonably available to prevent any further continuation or repetition of the infringement of the right.

Sec. 43. 1) Every person who contravenes section 8, subsection 32 (11), or an order of a board of inquiry, is guilty of an offence and on conviction is liable to a fine of not more than $25,000.

2) No prosecution for an offence under this Act shall be instituted except with the consent in writing of the Attorney General.

Sec. 44. 1)   For the purposes of this Act, except subsection 2 (2), subsection 4 (2), section 6 and subsection 43 (1), any act or thing done or omitted to be done in the course of his or her employment by an officer, official, employee or agent of a corporation, trade union, trade or occupational association, unincorporated association or employers' organization shall be deemed to be an act or thing done or omitted to be done by the corporation, trade union, trade or occupation association, unincorporated association or employers' organization.

2)   At the request of a corporation, trade union, trade or occupational association, unincorporated association or employers' organization, a board of inquiry in its decision shall make known whether or not, in its opinion, an act or thing done or omitted to be done by an officer, official, employee or agent was done or omitted to be done with or without the authority or acquiescence of the corporation, trade union, trade or occupational association, unincorporated association or employers' organization, and the opinion does not affect the application of subsection (1).

GLOBE ELECTRONICS LTD. (A)

Globe Electronics was a major multinational manufacturer of electrical products. Its product line included small and large appliances, electrical controls, motors, and communication equipment. Its Canadian subsidiary had its headquarters in Toronto. Two of its five plants were also located in Toronto. The company had three other plants in St. John, New Brunswick, Montreal, and Waterloo, Ontario. Sales and service operations were located throughout Canada.

All of the company's manufacturing operations were unionized, one by the UE (United Electrical, Radio and Machine Workers of America) and the rest by the IUE (International Union of Electrical, Radio and Machine Workers — AFL-CIO/CLC). Production and maintenance employees in both Toronto plants had been represented by the IUE since the early 1950s. In 1975, the IUE also won representation rights for clerical workers in the head office and the adjacent plant located in suburban northern Toronto. The plant produced a variety of electrical control devices and systems. The clerical workers composed Local 544, while the production and maintenance workers were organized into Local 382. The two locals were organizationally distinct and negotiated Collective Agreements separately. Those agreements had expiry dates a year apart, with the two-year clerical agreement due to expire next year, and the production and maintenance agreement ending the following year. The two locals had good lines of informal communication and cooperated wherever possible.

Relationships between the company and the union representing production and maintenance employees had been stormy over the years, and the company believed that the somewhat militant attitudes of production workers had "rubbed off" on clerical employees. The ultimate consequence was the certification of the clerical local.

The company had fought the clerical certification move with every legal weapon at its disposal, including challenge to the inclusion of certain personnel in the bargaining unit, which took nine months of argument and investigation by the Ontario Labour Relations Board before being resolved. Despite the tension caused by the lengthy certification process, the parties managed to negotiate a first agreement without a great deal of difficulty. Since that time, the company's relationships with both unions had been reasonably good, with recent contracts signed with both Local 544 and Local 382 without strike activity. The parties were still clearly wary of each other, but were apparently successfully moving toward a greater degree of accommodation.

The subtle changes in the relationships were reflected in the grievance procedure. The number of formal grievances had been reduced, primarily through an intensive company effort to improve supervision's ability to resolve problems informally. Similarly, the number of arbitrations had declined. The use of arbitration had not been eliminated, however, as neither the unions nor the company had shown any willingness to back down where basic principles were at stake or where either side clearly believed it was right.

On June 24, a third-step grievance meeting was scheduled to discuss two grievances which had been appealed to that step by Local 544. The third step was the last step prior to arbitration. The company was represented at this step by Mr. William Kemp, the Labour Relations Manager, and the union by Mr. John Heminge, President of the local and Chairman of its grievance committee. These individuals would be joined by others who could present both information and argument in an attempt to resolve the dispute prior to arbitration. Generally speaking, indications of agreement or non-agreement were made during the meeting, although the company's formal response to the appeal was made in a letter from Mr. Kemp to the union.

One of the cases to be discussed involved a protest of a promotion decision, and the other a protest of termination of employment.

The promotion appeal involved an employee in the purchasing department in the plant office. On May 13, Katherine Baptista, a clerk-typist in the purchasing department, filed the following grievance:

> I protest the action of the company in not awarding me the position of Procurement Clerk (Expediting), job posting 317-C. I claim the ability to do the job plus greater seniority. I demand full redress.

The company's answer at both steps one and two of the grievance procedure was:

> You have no previous experience in the Procurement Clerk function as required in the job description. Grievance Denied.

The job of Procurement Clerk had been posted on April 3, in accordance with the collective agreement. The job opening existed because of the resignation of the employee holding it. Miss Baptista had bid on the job, but had not received any word on her application from the company. On May 12, a new employee appeared at the desk normally occupied by the Procurement Clerk, which was located only a few desks away from Miss Baptista's own desk. On discovering that the new employee was employed in the position she had applied for, Miss Baptista went immediately to the department manager, Mr. Thomas Morton, and asked why she had not been given the job. He told her that the job description required experience with both the materials ordered and the records kept of those materials, neither of which she had.

After the conversation, Miss Baptista went to her Department Steward, Anne Page. On hearing the story, Page helped Baptista write out the grievance which was then submitted to Mr. Morton.

Section 12 of the collective agreement stated:

> All promotions shall be made on the basis of seniority and ability to do the job. Ability is defined as a sufficiency of skill or competence to satisfactorily perform the work required of a job.

The job description for the Procurement Clerk (which had been posted with the notice of vacancy) read as follows:

CLERK-PROCUREMENT

Job Requirement—Adequate knowledge of the materials handled by Buyers. Good working knowledge of the relevant records. Previous experience in the operation of a materials system, using the "balance forward" system of record keeping. To work from supplied information, with a minimum of supervision, under the direction of the Buyers.

Normal Duties—To post supplied information accurately to the Procurement Record and insert balances.

To assess the status of balances of material and determine availability or non-availability for specific requirements.

To establish and record the quantities of material to be purchased, supplying such basic information from the Procurement Record as may be required by the Buyer to prepare the purchase order.

To reconcile stock quantities found in the plant with quantities reflected by the Procurement Record. To prepare and check documents recording procurement transactions as required by other departments for purposes of distribution of material or costs.

May be required to perform work relevant to Procurement.

In the first two steps of the grievance procedure, the union argued that the job description was obsolete. Since the description had been written, the company had developed a computerized inventory control system. The "balance forward" system of record keeping, which involved maintaining cardex files, was no longer used by Procurement Clerks. Reports on materials on order and material shortages were prepared in the form of computer printouts and were received in the department weekly.

In reality, there were two types of Procurement Clerks in the department. One type, informally called "Materials Control," did the work required to maintain the computerized materials inventory system. Their work closely approximated the statements of the job description, with the significant exception that the computerized system was now in use. The second type of procurement work involved working with the buyers to expedite the ordering and delivery of materials for which purchase orders had been issued by the buyers. These clerks checked and at times completed details on purchase orders, sent them to clerk-typists to be typed, and then made contact with vendors to speed and verify delivery dates. They completed a form which went to the "Materials Control" Procurement Clerks showing which materials and parts had been ordered and when delivery was expected.

Miss Baptista's job as a clerk-typist had been to type the purchase orders for the "Expediter" Procurement clerks. She claimed that she was thus familiar with the basic form used in the Procurement Clerk's work, and from association with these clerks was familiar enough with the job to begin working on it without training. She had worked as a clerk-typist in the department for 8 years.

The union and Miss Baptista were upset because Mr. Morton, the Materials Manager, had not even interviewed her for the job, but simply rejected her application out of hand.

Mr. Morton, on the other hand, insisted that experience in both record keeping and expediting were necessary to do the job. He maintained that he expected Procurement Clerks to be able to do both kinds of work, even though they principally worked with one assignment. Miss Baptista was not familiar with and had had no direct experience with the inventory system—a requirement which was set out in the job description. Mr. Morton maintained that the fact that the system was now computerized was irrelevant.

Mr. Morton said that while Miss Baptista might have gained some insight into the job of Procurement Clerk from her position of clerk-typist, she knew nothing about the materials ordered, and not enough about the meaning of various reports to be able to do the job without a great deal of training. The person he had hired for the job had three years of experience with a computer-based inventory system and had done expediting work as well.

At the second step of the grievance procedure, Mr. Morton proposed that Miss Baptista be given a test about materials, procedures, and records to see if she knew enough about the job to do it. Miss Baptista agreed, and Mr. Morton developed a test with the help of buyers and the chief Procurement Clerk, which was then given to Miss Baptista.

When she was informed that she had failed the test, and that her grievance was thus denied, Miss Baptista objected, saying that the test was unfair since a good deal of the material related to the "Material Control" Procurement Clerks, and she had not applied for that job, but rather for an "Expediter" Procurement Clerk. She said that it really wasn't necessary for her to know the difference between different types of materials ordered by the department. Nor was it necessary to know the size and weight of materials described on the computer printout. In brief, she thought the test was unfair. Besides, Steward Page argued, Morton had made his original decision not to promote her without the benefit of a test, and that decision was the one that was being challenged.

With these arguments, the union appealed the case to step three of the grievance procedure.

The second grievance to be discussed at the June 24 grievance meeting involved the termination of employment of Miss Elizabeth (Betty) Fletcher.

Miss Fletcher was hired by the company in early December of the previous year, as an assembly-line worker in the electrical control manufacturing section of the plant. In early April of this year, she applied for and received a position of clerk in the Shipping Department office. While on the assembly line, she was a member of Local 382, but on assuming the Shipping Department office job, she became a member of Local 544, which represented the clerical employees.

In the Shipping Department office, Miss Fletcher was responsible for typing invoices for outgoing shipments and typing cheques from invoices. She also did filing and was normally expected to answer the department's telephone.

On April 30, after a number of verbal warnings, Mr. Richard Burbage formally warned Miss Fletcher about her lateness. A written warning, signed by both Mr. Burbage and by Miss Fletcher stated that Mr. Burbage was not satisfied with her punctuality, and that unless she could arrive at work on time consistently, he could not keep her in her position as clerk.

On May 27, Mr. Burbage again met with Miss Fletcher. He told her that while her tardiness had improved for a brief while after their last discussion, it had reverted to its prior unsatisfactory level. Because of this, Mr. Burbage said he had no alternative but to return her to her original job on the assembly line.

Miss Fletcher said that her old job was on the night shift (11:00 p.m.–7:00 a.m.) and that she had found that she really could not work those hours. She said that she was unable to sleep well, and believed that her health was affected. Her difficulty in working the night shift was the primary reason she had applied for the office job. She said that if she had to return to the assembly line job, she would quit.

Mr. Burbage told her not to do anything rash, and said that he would arrange to have Mr. Regan, the Personnel Manager, check with her old department to see if her old job was still open, and if there was any possibility of a job on the first shift, although she would have to improve her ability to arrive at work at 8:00 a.m. to merit consideration for a first shift job. He said that he would go with her to meet with Mr. Regan the next day.

On May 28, Mr. Burbage and Miss Fletcher went to Mr. Regan's office. After introducing Miss Fletcher to Mr. Regan, Mr. Burbage returned to his department. Mr. Regan told Miss Fletcher that Mr. Burbage had instructed him to make arrangements to have her transferred back to her old department. He said that the company considered her to be probationary on her Shipping Department job, and had the right to assign her back to her old position since her performance on the clerical job had been unsatisfactory due to her lateness.

Miss Fletcher explained that she had difficulty getting a ride to work that would get her there on time, and that she had found it difficult to use public transit to arrive at 8:00 a.m. She said that she planned to move to a new apartment on June 15 and believed that she would be able to get a ride or to use public transit from that location to arrive at work on time.

Mr. Regan said that Mr. Burbage had been as patient with her as he could be and that she could not remain in the Shipping Department any longer.

Miss Fletcher spoke of her problems with working on the third shift and asked if there were any other jobs available. Mr. Regan told her that the only available job was her old one. Miss Fletcher said that she could not go back to the night shift and that she would resign before doing so.

Mr. Regan told her that the decision was hers, but the only job he could offer her was her old one. At this point, Miss Fletcher signed an exit interview form with the following statement:

> Please accept my resignation to take effect May 28. Reason for leaving: resigned.

At the bottom of the form Mr. Regan wrote:

> Refused transfer from typist job in Shipping Department to Electrical Control Assembly. Employee's health is affected while on 11–7 shift. Employee will return to school or travel.

Mr. Kemp read Miss Fletcher the above statement, said he was sorry she was not staying with the company, and wished her good luck. At this point the meeting ended.

After the meeting, Miss Fletcher talked with Mr. Ed Mortimer, the Steward in her department. Shortly after noon on the 28th, Mr. Mortimer took the following handwritten letter to Mr. Regan's office:

I hereby withdraw my resignation and have no intention of quitting for the following reasons:

1. I was not informed of my rights.
2. I did not have union representation as I am guaranteed by the Collective Agreement — Article 15, Section 2.

(signed) E. Fletcher

GLOBE ELECTRONICS LTD. (B)

MANAGEMENT CONSIDERS THE GRIEVANCES

Mr. William Kemp, Globe's Director of Labour Relations, was the company's official representative at the step three grievance meeting. In preparation for the meeting he met with the management personnel involved in each of the disputes.

As Mr. Kemp put it, "I don't want to make up my mind on the grievance before I discuss it with the union. However, I want a clear understanding of all the facts as seen by the management personnel involved before I go into the meeting. The union isn't above putting up a smokescreen if they think they can get away with it. I also try to get a feel for what the potential impact of the dispute is on the company. Sometimes a grievance will be denied at the first two steps because supervision has their back up about some really insignificant issue. We can concede these without any loss of operating efficiency or management's rights. All we lose is a little management 'face,' which is tough sometimes. On other occasions, real principles are involved, and we've got to be careful to let the union know we're going to hang tough on the thing, or at a minimum, make sure that if we compromise we're not conceding principle or any future flexibility."

Mr. Kemp first met with Mr. Morton, the Purchasing Manager, along with Walter Herbert, the Head Buyer, and George Nash, the Chief Clerk in purchasing to consider the Baptista grievance.

After briefly reviewing the events in the dispute, Mr. Kemp asked Mr. Morton, "Tom, why didn't you consider Baptista for the job?"

Morton: Basically because she didn't have enough experience. That means she doesn't know the work well enough to do it without a lot of training.

Kemp: Are you saying that she didn't know anything about the job?

Morton: No. Her job as clerk would give her some notion of what went on, but she wouldn't be able to jump right in and do the job as Procurement Clerk.

Kemp: But were you able to fill the job with someone who could do it right away?

Morton: We hired someone with experience with a computerized inventory control system, who'd worked with buyers before. It took him a week or so to get totally clued in.

Herbert: He knew a hell of a lot more about purchasing than Baptista. I helped Tom make up the test that we gave her. She didn't know half the answers.

Kemp: Was the test specific to her job as procurement clerk-expediting or did it also involve materials control work too?

Morton: It involved both kinds of work. We expect these people to be able to move between both kinds of work.

Kemp: Do you mean they regularly do both types of work?

Herbert: They really don't on a regular basis. But sometimes they have to fill in for each other.

Kemp: Well, I'd feel better about the test if you had given it to her *before* filling the job. As it is now, the union may argue that the test results are irrelevant — that the decision not to give her the job was made before the test was given to her — in fact, the test wasn't even made up until *after* she filed a grievance.

Morton: Well she still didn't pass it. It shows our decision to give the job to someone else was the right one.

Kemp: We would still be in better shape if you had used the test before and not after. Or if you had even interviewed her.

Morton: Bill, that woman is a hatchet-faced shrew. She won't give you a smile if her life depended on it.

Nash: Hatchet-faced shrew is probably the nicest thing anyone ever said about her.

Herbert: She's a frustrated old maid. I certainly wouldn't want to work with her. She's bad enough where she is now.

Kemp: Look fellows, the contract doesn't say anything about 'hatchet-faced shrews." It says seniority and ability.

Morton: And ability means being able to satisfactorily perform the work. She hasn't got the ability — not without training. That's what our case is all about.

Kemp: OK. I'll accept that, but that has to be our line of argument — not the fact that she's not Snow White.

Morton: Bill, if they win this grievance, we might as well forget about leaving any discretion in promotions. If she's considered to have enough ability just on the basis of holding the clerk-typist's job, then we've always got to fill the clerk's job by promoting the senior clerk-typist, and that's no way to run a railroad. We might as well just give up and turn over the keys to the plant to the union.

Kemp: Now things aren't that bad, Tom, but you certainly do have a point about promotion, or our ability to hire instead of automatically promote.

Herbert: What about the job description? Doesn't it say 'adequate knowledge' and 'working knowledge'? The test showed she didn't have either.

Kemp: The job description is terribly out-of-date. I wouldn't want to lean too heavily on that.

Morton: Don't look at me. Job descriptions are Personnel's responsibility. We can still say that knowledge is necessary, despite the changes in the job.

Kemp: OK, but if this thing went to arbitration, the job description wouldn't be much help.

Morton: They won't take it to arbitration.

Kemp: Who says? It's just as important a principle for them as it is for us.

Morton: Well, if they do, I don't think we should back off.

Kemp: We'll have to wait and see what happens in the third step meeting.

Mr. Kemp met with Mr. Burbage, the Shipping Manager, and Mr. Regan, the Personnel Manager, and Mr. Voltimand, the Plant Manager to discuss the Fletcher grievance.

Kemp: Well I want you guys to know we've got a dilly of a case here.

Voltimand: What's so hard about it? She quit. Seems like a simple matter to me.

Kemp: That's our major argument. If she quit — voluntarily — then she is not an employee from the time of her resignation and the agreement does not apply.

Regan: Well she did quit, of her own accord. She signed the form, and then I wrote in the last part of it and read it back to her and she said, 'fine,' and that was it.

Kemp: Did you pressure her to sign it at all?

Regan: Absolutely not! I told her that the only job available for her was her old one. And she said that she'd quit before going back to the night shift. I told her it was her decision. After a while, I asked her what she wanted to do. And she said, 'Quit, I guess.' And then I gave her the form to sign.

Voltimand: Bill, how about this statement she signed withdrawing the resignation. Does it make any difference?

Kemp: I don't think so. There's a case called Anchor Cap and Closure* that says that two tests are necessary about whether a resignation is genuine. One is intent to resign, and then some act to signify or substantiate the intent. I think signing the form indicates both intent and action. Once an employee has resigned, the employment contract is severed. The contract does not apply because the individual is no longer an employee. There are several arbitration decisions that back that up.

 We clearly did not have time to act on the resignation before she attempted to withdraw it. I mean we didn't hire someone to fill the job, and I expect the union will argue that. In fact, we still haven't filled the job have we?

Regan: No, we're using a girl from Office Overload.

Kemp: Well, I still think we're OK. A resignation is a resignation.

Regan: Why are you concerned then?

Kemp: Well, if you look at the contract clauses about probationary employees closely, you'll see that our right to transfer her back to her old job is far from clear. It is not at all certain that we could justifiably consider her to be a probationary employee. We'd have to try to argue that she was 'hired' for the clerk's job, and not transferred. That might be tricky.

Regan: So?

Kemp: As I say, our only absolutely sure way to win the case is to say it's not arbitrable. If the question of our ability to transfer her back comes up, we're on much more shaky ground.

Voltimand: Well, we'll just say it's not arbitrable.

Kemp: But even then, a board might just decide that it was. That she didn't mean it. Or she was confused. Or pressured. And then we're back to the probationary business. I mean I think we're OK on the arbitrability grounds. In fact, I'm pretty certain, but you never can be sure.

Burbage: Well you can be sure about one thing. She couldn't get to work on time.

Kemp: You did warn her?

*1LAC 222.

Burbage: Lots of times. I talked to her before the written warning and then again after, before I finally told her she was going to be transferred back.

Kemp: How many times did you talk to her?

Burbage: At least half a dozen, besides the time we put it in her file. It got so I hated to do it—talk to her, I mean. The last time I said, 'Betty, I really hate to keep after you like this, but you've got to get here on time.'

Kemp: How often was she late?

Burbage: About every other day. One day she'd miss the bus. Then she'd sleep in. Then she'd miss her ride. She always had excuses. Usually, because she'd missed a bus. But she was 15 or 30 minutes or even an hour late.

Kemp: What's this about moving to a new apartment?

Burbage: Well, she said something about that but I think she's had plenty of chances. Too many, in fact. Aren't we setting a bad precedent if we take her back?

Kemp: Probably. And we probably can win this one, if we want to try. . . .

GLOBE ELECTRONICS LTD. (C)

THE UNION CONSIDERS THE GRIEVANCES

John Heminge, the Union President, also served as Chairman of the local's grievance committee, which was comprised of all the shop stewards. The full committee voted on the disposition of all grievance cases — whether to appeal them to the next step of the procedure or not. Under the local constitution, a grievant whose case was dropped by the committee could appeal that decision to the full membership. In practice, the use of the grievance committee to screen grievances helped to take individual stewards "off the hook" politically with constituents. They could say that the grievance had been dropped by the committee, rather than refusing as individuals to handle cases.

Heminge believed that this step was important. "We really can't afford to take every complaint to step three or four — or even to just second step," he said. "When we have a real beef we want it listened to. If we bring all the petty bitches up, the real complaints and problems won't get the attention they deserve."

Heminge took some time to ensure that the union had all of the relevant facts before it went to step three meetings. "Every so often a Steward or a grievant will 'forget' to tell you some important detail," Heminge said. "Then you go to the meeting and management brings it up and you look like a fool. That doesn't help your general position one bit."

In preparation for the third step meeting on June 24, Heminge met with both grievants and their shop stewards. He started the meeting on the Katherine Baptista grievance by asking the grievant, "Katie, did Morton ever talk with you about this job?"

Baptista: Not until after he had given it to someone else. He never said one word to me!

Heminge: What did he say when you asked him why you didn't get the job?

Baptista: He said I didn't have enough experience to do the work.

Page (Shop Steward): And that's bullshit! The job primarily has to do with checking and filling in purchase orders. Katie's been typing those things for seven years. The only other part is filling in the form to show that the materials had been ordered and when delivery was expected — and you get delivery dates from the vendors. What's hard about that?

Baptista: Nothing. I can do that job! Morton doesn't like me because I'm a strong union supporter! And probably because I'm a woman, too!

Heminge: Is that why they refused the grievance?

Page: I think there's some of that in there. But I think that they want to be able to pick and choose who gets the clerk's job. They don't want to go by seniority. They want to be able to reward their friends and punish anyone who asks questions.

Heminge: Has the guy who got the job joined the union?

Page: No. I asked him, and he said he didn't believe in unions.

Baptista: See?

Heminge: What about this test they gave you?

Baptista: It was unfair. They asked a lot of questions about Material Control Work, like, 'which of these parts can be air-freighted in?' and 'what part does this number stand for?' I think it was put together to justify their decision.

Heminge: Well, we've got a really good argument there. The test doesn't have any bearing on the decision Morton made. He can't argue that you didn't get the job because you didn't pass the test. I think we will just refuse to let them bring up the issue of the test at all, let alone whether it was fair or not.

Page: And their arguments about the job description are worthless, too. The thing is so out-of-date it's ridiculous. It doesn't prove a thing.

Heminge: I think you're right there. If we had to, could we get someone to testify in an arbitration hearing about how the job has changed?

Page: Sure. Tony Mark has been here for 25 years. He's seen all the changes. They haven't got a leg to stand on as far as the job description is concerned.

Heminge: The big thing is that they didn't even consider you or talk to you about the job, Katie. They just turned your bid right down.

Baptista: He's gonna be sorry.

Heminge: I hope so. Suppose they offer you a training program or consideration for the next opening. Would that satisfy you?

Baptista: No! I deserve the job now! Why should I wait? Whose side are you on anyhow?

Heminge: Calm down, Katie. I was just seeing how you'd react. We'll get you that job, or try our darndest. I can't see how they can hope to win this one.

Later Heminge met with Betty Fletcher and Ed Mortimer to discuss the second grievance to be heard at the meeting.

Heminge: Betty, let me ask you a question. Did you voluntarily sign that resignation form?

Fletcher: I guess I did.

Heminge: Regan didn't force you to sign?

Fletcher: No. But he told me I had to either go back to assembly or quit. Ed says that's not true. So Regan lied to me. I was really confused and frustrated. So I signed the paper.

Mortimer: She didn't have representation like she's supposed to. He really pulled the wool over her eyes. Have you read the contract? I don't think she was still on probationary status and I don't think they had the right to transfer her back.

Heminge: I think you're right. The contract's not really clear on that. When it talks about 'recent date of hiring' it can't apply to this situation. Betty wasn't hired for the office job. She was transferred. How soon after you signed the resignation did you withdraw the resignation?

Fletcher: An hour or so.

Heminge: Well they didn't have the time to hire anyone. I can't see how allowing the resignation to be withdrawn would hurt them.

Mortimer: It wouldn't hurt them one bit. Regan's just an S.O.B.

Heminge: We've still got a problem. If someone is not an employee the contract doesn't apply. And when Betty resigned she technically wasn't an employee.

Mortimer: Yeah, but the circumstances under which the resignation was made are really questionable. Betty wasn't informed of her rights. She was given a fast shuffle right out the door.

Heminge: Betty, if we get your job back, do you think you can do better about getting to work on time?

Fletcher: Oh, yes, I moved to a new apartment where it will be easier to get the bus. I don't like being late—honest. I really like working in the office. The third shift was terrible. I couldn't sleep in the daytime. And I had no social life.

Heminge: Do they know about her move?

Mortimer: Yes. Regan said it was too late.

Heminge: He *is* an S.O.B., isn't he?

Mortimer: We can't let them get away with this.

Heminge: We'll try not to. Betty I wish you had gone back to assembly under protest—filed a grievance. We'd be in better shape than we are with you having resigned. But I think we've got a good case and we'll see what we can do. Do you want to come to the hearing?

Fletcher: No, unless you absolutely want me there. I'd just as soon not talk to them any more.

Heminge: I'll think about it. You probably won't have to be there. If we should go to arbitration you'd have to attend that. Would you be willing to do that?

Fletcher: Yes, if it will help me get my job back.

Heminge: OK. Keep your chin up. You'll be hearing from us.

GREAT LAKES IRON AND STEEL (A)

JOB ASSIGNMENT DISPUTE

At 1:00 p.m. May 22, 1975, Mr. F. J. Oliver, Superintendent of Employee Relations, was about to leave his office for a quick lunch. Earlier in the day, a meeting with the union had been held to clear up a dispute in the Cold Rolling Department which had precipitated a two-hour walkout the day before. Mr. Oliver was concerned that the dispute had not been fully resolved. In fact, it had been brewing for over two months. It concerned a change in job assignment.

As he left his office and headed toward the cafeteria, Mr. Oliver saw Tom Sanderson, Superintendent of the Cold Rolling Department, coming toward him. Sanderson stopped abruptly and excitedly barked, "The day shift boys just cleared out — walked off and left the plant."

BACKGROUND: PARTIES

Mr. Oliver was employed by Great Lakes Iron and Steel Corporation (Glisco) of Islington, Ontario, a major steel producer. As Superintendent of Employee Relations, he was responsible, in consultation with the mill supervision, to make labour relations decisions. In carrying out his duties, he worked constantly with the supervisors of the various work areas and the employee representatives: union stewards and delegates.

Glisco produced all types of steel products, mainly for the domestic market (20 percent was exported). Of these, about 50 percent were flat rolled steel products (the balance being mainly structural and rails). Since 1971, Glisco, like many other Canadian corporations, had been caught in a profit squeeze. Glisco management, including D. Mallory, Vice President Administration — Oliver's superior — realized that they must lower the cost of their products and encourage productivity gains to stay profitable and competitive. Costs and earnings figures for the period 1971–1974 are shown below. The first three months of 1975 indicated costs were running at 81 percent of sales, earnings at 9 percent.

	Costs of Products % of sales	Earnings % sales	Earnings Per Share
1971	79	7.0	1.22
1972	74	10.4	2.14
1973	70	12.6	2.66
1974	70	12.2	2.38

The majority of the 6,000 members of the workforce at Glisco belonged to the United Steel Workers of America (USWA), Local 2807. Ted Arless was the president of the local bargaining unit. Jim Parker was the international representative for USWA serving the Islington area.

During the past three years, Glisco had suffered from a number of strikes, work stoppages, and slowdowns. Many of these work stoppages were illegal wildcats prohibited under Section 54 (1) of the Ontario Labour Relations Act.[1] In 1972 a work stoppage which the union denounced closed one department for 27 days. The dispute was over a reassignment of work which was performed only once a week for a few minutes.

BACKGROUND: STEEL MAKING

The steel making operation at Glisco had five basic steps. First, the company received refined limestone, iron ore, and raw coal from the mines. The coal was made into coke. Then the three raw materials were made into iron in a blast furnace. The molten iron was then used to produce molten steel either in open hearth furnaces or in huge rotating vessels (the Basic Oxygen process). After this, the molten steel was poured into ingots, then cooled and rolled into blooms, billets, or slabs. Blooms and billets are bar-shaped pieces of steel: billets are narrower than blooms. Slabs are thick, flat sheets.

In the final operations blooms and billets were further rolled and processed into structural shapes, bars, and rails. The slabs were used primarily to produce flat rolled products called plate, sheet, and strip.

Rolling constituted the major finishing operation. This process involved passing steel between two rolls revolving in opposite directions at the same speed. It resembled the passing of a towel through a clothes wringer. The opening between the rolls was smaller than the thickness of material being rolled. Thus the process shaped the steel by reducing it in cross sectional area and elongating it. The temperature of the steel and the amount of rolling varied according to the end product specifications.

The sheet and strip departments had two major processes. First, the slabs were reheated and rolled while hot, producing sheet and strip. Some sheets were then cold rolled. This involved passing them while cold through a pair of rolls and resulted in accurate thickness and glasslike smoothness. Products requiring cold rolling were usually the thinner sheets and strips.

COLD ROLLING DEPARTMENT[2]

The Cold Rolling Department (C.R.) received sheets which had been hot rolled and then rolled them into still thinner sheets and strips for use mainly for automobile bodies, refrigerators, and stoves.

The department consisted of four rolling mills. Different mills were used depending on the product specifications. It was often necessary to change the rolls in the mills for these operations. These rolls were heavy, tempered steel

---

[1]Sections of the Ontario Labour Relations Act referred to herein were those in effect at the time of this case.

[2]Also known as Cold Mill. In steel operations, the word mill often had three meanings: the actual machine which rolled the product, the department containing many mills, and the building housing mills. In this case, mill means only the machine which rolled the product. Department refers to the division of work areas, e.g., Cold Rolling Department.

cylinders which squeezed down upon the steel sheets much like washing machine rollers on a towel. The individual mills had to be shut down while the rolls were being changed. Putting the rolls in was a delicate operation requiring the use of a crane.

One-hundred-and-fifty men worked in the Cold Rolling Department. There were approximately fifty on each of three shifts. Twenty shifts operated each week. A wide variety of occupations worked in the department. There were production people (machine operators), labourers, cranemen, and maintenance people. The maintenance group included millwrights, pipefitters, and electricians.

Wage rates depended on one's classification and were based largely on skill. Cranemen received about $5.51 per hour, which was roughly the average rate in the department. Millwrights were considered highly skilled workers and received $6.40 per hour. Catchers were mill helpers whose principal job was to assist a Roller (salaried employee) in ensuring good quality. Catchers held classifications slightly above those of cranemen. They received $5.64 per hour.

BACKGROUND TO DISPUTE

In October of 1974, a new 20-ton electric overhead crane (E.O.C.) was installed to service the cold mill roll shop,[3] located at one end of the building containing the rolling mills. It was placed on the same tracks as a 100-ton crane which had been used since C.R. Department opened in 1972 to service all four mills. The 100-ton crane was operated solely by an experienced craneman. A few years after installation it became overloaded with work.

The 20-ton E.O.C. could be operated either from the ground by use of a portable pendant control console or from an overhead cab. If operated from the cab a craneman was required. Both the pendant and cab controls were equipped with a 'dead man' safety device. This stopped the operations of the crane when the operator's hand left the control. The 20-ton E.O.C. was located so that it could service the roll shop and the 30″ temper mill, both at the extreme end of the building. As a result, it could be used to change rolls on the 30″ mill when the 100-ton E.O.C. was otherwise occupied. For a diagram of the area see Exhibit 1.

Initially, the roll shop people and millwrights objected to using the small crane, claiming that they should wait until an experienced craneman was free to do the job. However, they finally accepted the assignment.

THE GRIEVANCE

On March 16, 1975, the 100-ton E.O.C. was not available so the catchers were told to use the 20-ton E.O.C. to change rolls in the 30″ temper mill. Catchers had not used the crane previously and objected, claiming that this was a craneman's job. After some argument they did consent to use it, but one of them filed a grievance claiming that operation of the crane was not part of his duties and it should have been assigned to a craneman. The grievance was denied at both step one and step two of the grievance procedure. The company asserted that

[3]The roll shop was the area where rolls were stored and reground to restore surface smoothness at a lesser diameter so that they could be reused in another capacity.

EXHIBIT 1

DIAGRAM OF THE ROLLING MILL AREA

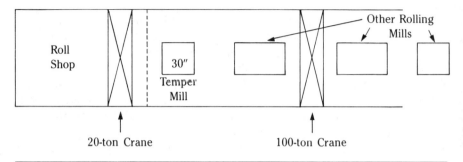

the 20-ton crane would only be used by catchers when the 100-ton crane was unavailable. The union did not seek arbitration of the case immediately but instead asked for permission to extend the time limits set out in the contract which required filing a case within 15 days of the step two answer in order for it to retain its validity. The company agreed to extend the limit to May 30.

NEW TRAINING PLAN

Mr. Sanderson, the Superintendent, was interested in clearing up the dispute so that the catchers would operate the crane. He was certain that their assistance in changing the rolls would reduce down time and increase production. Consequently he developed a new training program in early May.

Since the 30″ temper mill would be down for three or four shifts in the near future, he felt this would be an opportunity to train the catchers. On May 14, he met with the union delegate for the Cold Rolling Department, Bill Marshall. Sanderson informed Marshall that while the temper mill was down, catchers would be scheduled to practise using the 20-ton crane.

Sanderson emphasized to Marshall the key points of the training program:
— it was only for training purposes
— the 20-ton crane would only be used when the 100-ton crane was not available
— the catcher would not be responsible if he damaged a roll during training
— when the 20-ton crane was used, delays through inexperience would be accepted, and
— catchers' training would be supervised by a qualified person (a craneman).

Bill Marshall reminded Sanderson of the grievance and the reasons given for objecting to the assignment of crane work to a catcher. The two argued for some time. Marshall concluded with the following remarks.

> Tom, I have nothing against the training idea — but the boys do. The know it's just a step toward catchers doing a craneman's job. They won't buy it. Take my advice — the whole thing is not worth the trouble it's going to stir up.

DISPUTE

On May 20, four catchers were assigned to train on the 20-ton crane. They refused. They were immediately suspended for insubordination.

The following day, at 10:30 a.m., supervisors of the Cold Rolling Department, the Employee Relations Department, and representatives of the union met to discuss the suspensions. Nothing was resolved at this meeting. The union argued that the work should have been assigned to the craneman. A second meeting was scheduled for the following morning, May 22nd. The employees of the department were informed of the meeting late that afternoon.

At 5:00 p.m. on the 21st, all 47 of the 3:00 p.m. to 11:00 p.m. shift Cold Rolling Department employees left their jobs and went to the welfare room. This room housed lockers, showers, and a washroom. It was located nearby in the building. The men said that they would not return to work until the four suspended employees were put back on the job. They insisted on an immediate answer, claiming that they would not wait until the meeting scheduled for the following morning.

Mr. Oliver heard about the walkout at 5:15 p.m. He phoned Ted Arless, the union president, and insisted that he speak to the men. He reminded Arless that it was his responsibility to help enforce Article 16:01 of the contract which outlawed such work stoppages. Oliver further cited his option to have the strike declared illegal under Section 54 (1) of the Ontario Labour Relations Act (Exhibit 2). Arless promised to take whatever action he could under the circumstances.

EXHIBIT II

Section 54(1) of the Ontario Labour Relations Act (OLRA) declared that:

> Where a collective agreement is in operation, no employee bound by the agreement shall strike and no employer bound by the agreement shall lock out such an employee.

A company could apply to the Labour Relations Board to have a strike declared unlawful. If the board agreed and declared the strike unlawful, then the company could receive consent to prosecute the offenders. It was possible for the company to apply for consent to prosecute under Section 74 of the OLRA.

Under the terms of the Act (Section 57), any person or organization that engaged in an unlawful strike or did anything that would cause another person to engage in an unlawful strike could be liable to fines.

Under the Act (Section 69), individuals could be fined up to $1,000 per offence and organizations such as unions or companies up to $10,000 per offence. The Act stated that each day constituted a separate offence.

Arless and Bill Marshall, union delegate for the department, arrived at the welfare room at 6:00 p.m. The workers had already been off work for about one hour. It took another hour to convince them to return to their jobs. Finally, at 7:00 p.m. they returned to the work area of the rolling department.

MAY 22 MEETING

Management announced that penalties would be levied on the 47 employees who staged the two-hour walkout. However, the company and union met as planned the following morning at 10:30. At this meeting, the company agreed to recall the four suspended employees immediately without any further penalties.

The company also agreed, after some discussion, to impose no penalties on the workers of the three-to-eleven shift who had engaged in the work stoppage the day before. The union, as representative of all the workers, agreed that the catchers would operate the 20-ton crane.

Bill Marshall was present. He agreed to meet with the employees and tell them about the agreement which had been reached. With the permission of the company, the department operations were shut down for ten minutes at 12:30 for this purpose.

WALKOUT

Nevertheless, Mr. Oliver's earlier uneasiness was well founded. The workers decided not to stick with the agreement their representatives had reached with the company. They walked out at 1:00 p.m.

Oliver returned to his office with Sanderson and arranged to have sandwiches sent in. He began to discuss the issues with Sanderson.

Oliver: Do you think the men felt we backed down when we rescinded the penalties this morning?

Sanderson: I'm not sure, but I wonder whether the men are really heated up about this issue or the union is pushing it.

Oliver: I wonder how they would react if we applied discipline now.

Sanderson: The thing that worries me is whether the next shift will show and whether we'll get any production out. I can't run the mill without my skilled people on the job.

Oliver: It's an illegal strike and I could go to the Labour Relations Board but it doesn't produce steel unless the men come back.

Sanderson: Here are the sandwiches.

Oliver: I've really lost my appetite actually.

Sanderson: I know what you mean — we have to decide something quickly.

GREAT LAKES IRON AND STEEL (B)

WALKOUT REACHES CLIMAX

The morning shift of the Cold Rolling Department had walked off their jobs at 1:00 p.m. on May 22, 1975 over a job assignment dispute. The employees had staged a two-hour sit-down the day before to dispute the suspensions against the four catchers who had refused to perform the assignment. Now the employees were walking out in disagreement with the accord reached between the union representatives and management in the morning. The agreement repealed the suspension to the four workers and imposed no penalties for the sit-down the day before. However, it directed the catchers to perform the duties assigned. The workers did not accept this resolution of the problem and chose to walk out.

All members of the morning shift were given penalties for walking out. They ranged from warning notices to a discharge for one employee. The variations in penalties were due to the past records of the men. The one who was discharged had numerous warnings and suspensions previously.

The afternoon shift reported for work at 3:00 p.m. as usual. However, less than 15 minutes elapsed before they walked out. Only ten night-shift workers reported. Since there were not enough men to operate the department, the ten men were assigned to the shipping department. This caused them to leave.

From this point, about 30 of the 150 regular workers of the department reported each day. Employees from other departments were transferred to the Cold Rolling Department. Nevertheless, it was not possible to find sufficient men familiar with and skilled in the mill's operations. Consequently, most units were able to run only 10 of the normal 20 shifts per week.

The employees who did report for work after May 22 were continually threatened and harassed outside the plant by the strikers. They and their families received threatening phone calls. Their cars were damaged and there were fights.

Immediately after the walkout, the company began proceedings to have the strike declared illegal by the Ontario Labour Relations Board under Section 54(1) of the Ontario Labour Relations Act. Such a declaration by the board would open the door for Glisco to begin legal action against the employees participating in the strike. Under the terms of the Act any person or organization that engaged in an unlawful strike, or did anything that would cause another person to become involved, could be liable for heavy fines. Individuals could be fined up to $1,000 per offence. The Act stated that "each day constituted a separate offence." On May 24, the company applied to the Labour Relations Board for consent to prosecute the striking employees.

The company also filed a grievance against the union for violation of Article 16:01 of the contract, claiming costs. Article 16:01 provided that there should be no strikes or lockouts during the term of the agreement.

The union approached Mr. F. Oliver, Superintendent of Employee Relations, on

May 28 to ask what the penalties would be if the employees returned to work. Mr. Oliver informed them five employees with particularly poor past records would be suspended pending discharge, while the others would receive varying time-off penalties depending on their overall personnel records.

On May 30, 1975, a hearing was held before the Labour Relations Board to investigate the company charges. A few days later, on June 2, the board declared the strike to be illegal. Pursuant to this, the board sent its decision to all the strikers.

During this period, the union president, Ted Arless, repeated his request that the company guarantee no discharges. However, Oliver, in consultation with other company executives, refused.

On June 2, Mr. Oliver met with the foremen of the Cold Rolling Department. He informed them of the board's decision and subsequent notification which had been mailed to the employees involved. The foremen were firmly resolved that the men who walked out were in the wrong. Because of this, they felt certain that the mill workers would soon give in and come back to work. They further expressed the concern that they, as foremen, should not get shoved around by the union as much as they felt they had been in the past. Therefore, they expressed the belief that a warning telegram should be sent to bring the workers back.

Consequently, the next day, June 3, telegrams were sent to each striking employee telling him what his next scheduled shift would be and informing him that he would be discharged if he failed to report.

However, on June 4, when the shifts were scheduled, none of the strikers reported to work. The Employee Relations Department phoned each employee informing him that he was discharged.

Two days later, on June 6, 1975, 25 strikers began distributing pamphlets (Exhibit I) to other workers at the gates. No picket signs were present initially. However, signs appeared by 10:00 p.m. that night. Ted Arless, president of the local, went on radio and told all workers to report to work. All other employees did report.

EXHIBIT I

PAMPHLET FROM STRIKERS, JUNE 6

This newsletter has been prepared by approximately 150 men who, very recently, formed the working force of the Glisco Limited's Cold Mill Department.

In this letter, we wish to inform our brothers, friends, and the general public about the reasons that have made us face the misery of unemployed and accused men.

For a long period of time, the management of the mill has been re-evaluating the reach of many established jobs in the mill by adding new commitments to them. Each added commitment has inflamed our mind because there has been no corresponding increase in wages. Instead, there have been lost opportunities of employment for additional men. All grievances filed have been fruitless — dissatisfaction with such forced conditions has been growing steadily but not secretly, and the management of the mill has been kept informed of the situation.

Starting on May 20, the catchers of the 30" temper mill were asked to operate a crane, in addition to their usual commitments, to change rolls in the mill. Four of them refused to perform the assignment, and as a result, were suspended. This was done while all means of continuing operations as before were there.

The recklessly rough manner used in the attempt to get the men to agree did raise the irritated mood the men had, to the breaking point. On May 21, all units of the mill were shut down by the crews for two hours, and an inquiry into the state of affairs of the suspended men was made.

Once more, the management of the mill was warned by a proper party that considering the mood of the men, it would be wrong to try to use force and intimidation in settling the antagonism. A key member of management brushed the warning aside by stating that the men were asking for, and the company was going to give "a lesson to them." This action constitutes, in our opinion, a direct violation of Section 57 of the Labour Relations Act which states, in effect, that no person shall perform an act if he knows or ought to know that as a probable and reasonable consequence of the act, other persons would engage in an unlawful strike.

The remark about the "lesson" is a perfect example of a premeditated lawbreaking by a member of the management of Glisco Steel. Next day, the officials of the company agreed to recall the four suspended men, but not before they had made the men, under threat of immediate dismissal, accept all requested additional work assignments. Men who had stopped working for two hours were to get the following penalties: one man suspended; one man 20 days off; four men, 10 days off; and 42 men were to get warning notices.

On the 22nd of May, as soon as the 7–3 crews had learned about the penalties, they decided to stop working and walked out of the mill. They were followed by incoming crews. Soon, instead of trying to reason with the men, the company announced more penalties which included four more suspensions.

We knew very well that by walking out of the mill, we were violating the Labour Relations Act. But, so did the company when its officials violated the same Act before us. We knew that our step would be declared unlawful, and the lie inserted into the testimony of the company's representative before the Labour Relations Board was unnecessary to achieve the decision. It may help us to uncover the fitting story behind the drive to stamp us down.

In recognition of our technically unlawful step, we have offered to return to work if the company would forget about the suspensions and would divide other penalties equally among all men who participated in the walkout. The suggestion made by the company's spokesman that we go through a grievance procedure is ridiculous. The company officials had no moral right to ask that we return to work with the future of our five fellow-workers on our conscience. We think that our offer is not an ultimatum but a gift to the Great Lakes Iron and Steel Corporation. Maybe it is the guilty conscience of the officials of the company that prevents them from accepting our gift.

We have lost our means of income, but we have kept our integrity. Without integrity a man ceases to be a man. Are our brothers in the rest of the plant going to allow this to happen to us? WHAT IS YOUR STAND???? When you are finished with this, please pass it on to a brother who hasn't seen it *YET.*

Then at 7:30 p.m., June 9, the union held a general membership meeting. Arless informed Oliver afterwards that the membership decided to support the strikers. Oliver could not ascertain if Arless personally supported this decision. Oliver wasn't sure now if he should be negotiating with the union president or the members.

At 2:00 p.m. the following day, a large crowd gathered outside the main gates of the plant. Only 60 percent of the 3–11 shift for all departments reported to work. Many were prevented from entering the plant by the crowd.

The company sought an injunction immediately. At 9:30 p.m., June 10, Judge O'Brien issued an ex parte injunction against the picketing. The injunction made all violators (the picketers) liable for prosecution for contempt of court.

Nevertheless, that evening, June 10, witnessed an even larger crowd at the gates of the plant. Violence began to break out. The city police, present to enforce the injunction, left the area of the gates at 11:00 p.m. The police feared that their presence would cause an incident and possible violent disruption.

However, violence occurred anyway — cars damaged, rocks thrown, fires built in the street, bottles smashed, etc. This continued through the night and by 6:00 a.m. the throng had closed all entrances to the plant. At 7:00 a.m., shutdown procedures commenced. It would take five days to shut the plant down properly. Boats were used on the river adjacent to the plant to get food and supplies in to those inside involved in shutting down the plant.

At 11:00 a.m. on Thursday, June 11, D. Mallory, Vice President of Administration, and J. Parker, International Representative for the USWA, met to discuss the stalemate. Mr. Mallory, speaking on behalf of top management, stated that his interests were to maintain production and avoid violence. At that point, Mr. Parker proposed a settlement along the following lines:

a) No employees to be discharged;
b) No penalties to exceed 30 days;
c) The application to the Labour Relations Board to prosecute employees to be dropped;
d) The grievance against the union, for damages, to be dropped;
e) Catchers would operate the cranes in the future.

7

BUILDING AN INDUSTRIAL RELATIONS SYSTEM

Industrial relations systems reflect the personalities of those who work within them. Many union-management relationships are the products of careful, step-by-step planning and are extensions of the beliefs and attitudes of the principal administrators. Many others are characterized by uncertainty and lack of direction. There may be a hodgepodge of rules and regulations, a plethora of grievances, a union which seems to be constantly fighting against management — a state of mutual distrust. The latter type of relationship is often the product of top administrators who believe that industrial relations matters are unimportant and not particularly worthy of top management's attention.

Now, with North American businesses experiencing severe competitive pressures from abroad, particularly from Japan, and with increasing discontent among members of the workforce regarding the quality of life, many union leaders and company managers are being forced to re-evaluate their industrial relations system. Unions are coming to realize that it takes more than a high wage and an occasional kick in the pants to build job satisfaction and acceptable productivity. Both unions and management are coming to realize that improved productivity is essential for the survival of North American enterprises and that the achievement of improvements is a joint responsibility.

Quality of Work Life (QWL) is a phrase that has emerged as an umbrella term for describing a number of efforts to improve organizational effectiveness. As such, QWL is a term that has many definitions, and many activities and programs have been installed under the rubric of QWL. QWL programs need not be directly tied to efforts to improve productivity; but very often such programs are undertaken as a deliberate attempt to improve productivity, and even where no direct links are made, increased productivity is often the result of the implementation of a QWL programs.

QWL efforts have been characterized as generally having three elements:

employee involvement, job enrichment, and participative management.[1] Another writer has identified seven elements as parts of a QWL effort:
1. Worker control and autonomy;
2. Recognition of employees for their contributions;
3. A feeling of belonging;
4. The opportunity for self-development and accomplishment;
5. Appropriate external awards — pay, benefits, status;
6. Decent working conditions;
7. Dignity.[2]

QWL efforts have been conducted under a variety of names: participative management, worker involvement, quality control circles, job enrichment, Scanlon plans, autonomous work groups and socio-technical systems. A number of efforts at the latter have been well documented and publicized; among these are the systems used at Saab-Scania and Volvo in Sweden and at General Foods in the U.S.[3]

In Canada, QWL efforts have been undertaken in a number of locations, including Shell Canada, Polysar, Canadair, Hayes-Dana, Bell Northern Research, Budd Canada, General Motors, Steinbergs, CGE, the federal government, and others.[4] Ontario has established a Quality of Working Life Centre which publishes, consults, and holds conferences on the subject.

UNIONS AND QWL

Unions have played a variety of roles in QWL efforts. In some, they have actively cooperated with management.[5] In other settings, they have acted as careful observers or "watchdogs," while in other settings they have actively resisted management's efforts to establish programs. Jean-Claude Parrot's reaction to efforts at Canada Post has probably been the best publicized example of the latter. Historically, unions have had reasons to feel ambivalent about QWL. On one hand, QWL improves working conditions for employees, which unions seek, and on the other hand, QWL attempts to have workers identify with management goals, which some unions may object to since this may reduce union loyalties. Indeed, QWL has been promoted at times as a way of combatting unions.[6]

Several studies have shown that worker interest in QWL issues, such as job design and product quality, is as high as that in traditional "bread and butter" issues.[7] At the same time, there is some evidence that QWL activities do not reduce union loyalties.[8] Clearly, interest in QWL activities is increasing, and unions are a part of that process. QWL is a way to provide work and working conditions that are part of the changing expectations of the workforce.

Sucess in QWL activities can help lead the way to a more cooperative, less adversarial relationship. Nevertheless, contracts will still have to be negotiated and grievances handled. The way will not be smooth, nor will managing such activities and relationships be easy for either management or unions. The move to the kind of flexibility in work rules and job arrangements that QWL aims at will be particularly difficult for unions, and developing a receptivity to worker input on traditional management decisions will be difficult for many managers.

The case which follows is but one example of an attempt to install a QWL program in the workplace. It does illustrate some of the difficulties involved, though, and should help to underscore the problems attendant to the implementation of such a program.

Notes

1. Dennis N. T. Perkins, Veronica Meva and Edward E. Lawler III, *Managing Creation*. Toronto: John Wiley & Sons, 1983, p. 3.

2. Barry A. Stein, *Quality of Work Life in Action*. New York: American Management Associations, 1983, pp. 12–13.

3. See, for example, P. G. Gyllenhammer, "How Volvo Adapts Work to People," *Harvard Business Review*, July-August, 1977, pp. 102–113; and Richard E. Walton, "How to Counter Alienation in the Plant," *Harvard Business Review*, November-December, 1972, pp. 70–81.

4. For some details on these arrangements, and others, see: Research Branch, Ontario Ministry of Labour, *An Inventory of Innovative Work Arrangements in Ontario*. Toronto: 1978; *QWL Focus*, (The News Journal of the Ontario Quality of Working Life Centre); David A. Peach, "The Canadian I.A.M. Productivity Improvement Plan, *Relations Industrielles/Industrial Relations*, Vol. 37, No. 1, 1982, pp. 177–198; Ron Eade, "Dignity in Workplace Led Turnaround of Budd's Labor Strife," *The Financial Post*, May 12, 1984, p. 6.

5. For example, see Robert H. Guest, "Quality of Work Life: Learning from Tarrytown," *Harvard Business Review*, July-August, 1979, pp. 76–87; and B. A. Macy, "The Bolivor Quality of Work Life Program: A Longitudinal Behavioral and Performance Assessment," *Proceedings, Thirty-Second Annual Meeting Relations*, Industrial Relations Research Association. Madison, Wisconsin: I.R.R.A., 1980, pp. 83–93; and the Ron Eade article mentioned in the previous footnote.

6. David Jenkins, *QWL—Current Trends and Directions*. Toronto: Ontario Ministry of Labour, Quality of Working Life Centre, 1981, p. 31.

7. Thomas A. Kochan, David B. Lipsky and Lee Dyer, "Collective Bargaining and the Quality of Work: The Views of Local Union Activitists," *Proceedings, Twenty-Seventh Annual Meeting*, Industrial Relations Research Association. Madison, Wisconsin, I.R.R.A., 1974, pp. 150–162; Thomas A. Kochan, Harvey C. Katz and Nancy R. Mower, "Worker Participation and American Unions: Threat or Opportunity?", Working Paper, Alfred P. Sloan School of Management, Massachusetts Institute of Technology, February, 1984, p. 8.

8. Kochan, Katz and Mower, pp. 15–20.

DARTHOM INDUSTRIES LTD. (A)

BACKGROUND

THE MERGER

Nearly seven years ago Dartmouth Paper Co. Ltd. of Canada merged with R. J. Thompson Products Company to form Darthom Industries Ltd., one of Canada's largest companies in the pulp and paper industry. Within four years after the merger, Darthom had diversified into other fields and was rapidly becoming one of Canada's most important companies. The company stretched from New Brunswick to British Columbia, with its greatest concentration in the prairie and western provinces of Canada. It also extended into the northwestern United States. In January of last year over 16,000 people were employed by Darthom Industries Ltd. Corporate headquarters were in Vancouver, B.C.

Under terms of the merger two shares of Darthom preferred stock were exchanged for one and a half of Thompson Products preferred shares. Common shares were exchanged at the rate of four Darthom to one Thompson. Stockholders voted overwhelmingly in favour of the exchange, and six months after the merger all shares were exchanged for new ones carrying the new name: Darthom.

PRESIDENT'S VIEWS ON THE MERGER

Both Dartmouth and Thompson Products Company had recognized the need for diversification to lessen the impact of economic cycles on their businesses. These cycles were most severe in the paper products and container plants of Dartmouth, and in pulp producing plants operated by Thompson. Commenting on these two phases of the business Mr. Fredrick A. Genrich, president of Darthom, said:

> In an industry like the pulp, paper, and container industry, size allows for greater utilization of the forests' natural resources and lowers the company's vulnerability to economic cycles.

About 18 months after the merger Darthom called on Scudder, Fenner and Hamilton, well known management consultants, to advise on the appropriate organization, the design of corporate strategy, and the setting of implementing policies. Eight months later Scudder, Fenner and Hamilton completed their work and submitted recommendations — most of which were accepted for prompt implementation. Commenting on the consultants' report, Mr. Genrich said:

> We are now in the shakedown period. All the decisions have been made, and we simply have to make them work.

Organization

The reorganized company was directed by a management team reporting to the

EXHIBIT I

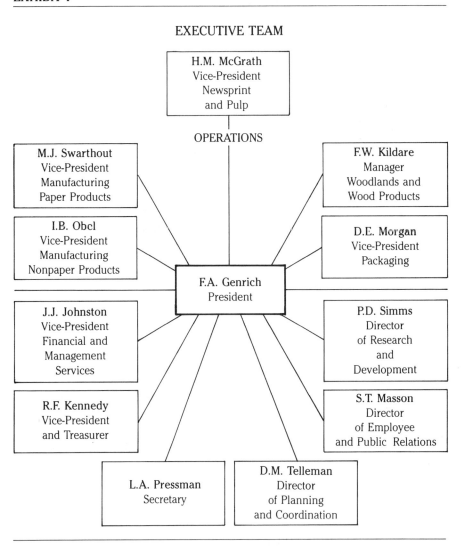

EXECUTIVE TEAM

H.M. McGrath
Vice-President
Newsprint
and Pulp

OPERATIONS

M.J. Swarthout
Vice-President
Manufacturing
Paper Products

F.W. Kildare
Manager
Woodlands and
Wood Products

I.B. Obcl
Vice-President
Manufacturing
Nonpaper Products

D.E. Morgan
Vice-President
Packaging

F.A. Genrich
President

J.J. Johnston
Vice-President
Financial and
Management
Services

P.D. Simms
Director
of Research
and
Development

R.F. Kennedy
Vice-President
and Treasurer

S.T. Masson
Director
of Employee
and Public Relations

L.A. Pressman
Secretary

D.M. Telleman
Director
of Planning
and Coordination

president, each member with responsibility for a segment of the business. The executive team is shown in Exhibit I.

Mr. Genrich believed in centralized control and, while he encouraged discussions among his executives, he reserved prerogative to make final decisions.

> The team members do not have a vote on every issue. I have never believed in committee management of anything.

Company Performance

Four years after the merger, sales had risen to $1.3 billion. Earnings were $53 million, and Darthom's total production of paper products was divided as follows:

66.3% newsprint
22.1% containerboard
 6.3% kraft paper
 5.3% boxboard

Mr. Genrich termed the performance of the past five years in the paper products business "disappointing." He referred to the following factors by way of explanation:
1. World overcapacity in newsprint, containerboard, and market pulp manufacturing facilities;
2. higher wages and rising material costs which had not yet been fully offset by productivity improvements or higher selling prices;
3. high interest charges arising from heavy capital expenditures and other expansion projects which were not yet contributing their potential to earnings.

"Our successes in the non-paper fields have kept us reasonably healthy," said Genrich, "Proving once again the value of diversification."

Pulp and Paper Industry Situation

In the last decade Canadian pulp and paper companies had been caught in an over-capacity squeeze. Massive increases in capacity came on-stream at a time when demand growth temporarily halted. For the next two or three years Canadian mills would most likely be operating at approximately 83 percent of capacity. Industry problems were attributed to three factors:
1. Rising competition in the United States market;
2. over-expansion in Canada;
3. extraordinarily high start-up costs.

No major improvements were foreseen for at least five years, and industry experts were anticipating major shutdowns in most Canadian pulp and paper operations during the next year or two.

Mr. Genrich predicted there would be no significant improvement for Darthom Industries for five years, but he expected dramatic improvement from then on. Genrich expressed the belief that Darthom's wealth of resources, its sound product planning, and its extensive research programs would ensure excellent long-term performance.

Winnipeg Corrugated Container Plant

Darthom had ten Canadian plants that manufactured corrugated containers, three in British Columbia, two in Alberta, and one each in Saskatchewan, Manitoba, Ontario, Quebec, and Nova Scotia. The newest of these plants was located near the Inkster Industrial Park in the northwest portion of metropolitan Winnipeg. It was built at a cost of $7 million and started production two years ago. The plant was attractive, well designed, and had equipment and machinery to match any competitor.

Competition

The southern Manitoba region was serviced by three large and firmly established competitors: Consolidated Bathurst in St. Boniface, Domtar in St. James, and McMillan Company in Brandon. St. Boniface and St. James were considered part of greater Winnipeg — St. Boniface directly across the river to the east, St. James in the western outskirts of the city. Brandon was located 135 miles to the west. About three years ago the officers of Darthom Industries decided that the fast-growing southern Manitoba region could support one more producer of corrugated containers. None of their existing plants were close enough to do an effective job in competing with firms located in the market area.

Customers

Some of the principal customers for Darthom's Winnipeg plant were Canada Packers, Labatt's Brewers, and Eaton's. Any company manufacturing or selling products that could be shipped in a carton was a potential customer.

Market Share

By the end of its first full year of operation, Darthom at Winnipeg had reached an annual sales volume of $7.5 million, approximately 11 percent of the southern Manitoba region. In the past three years there had been an overall market growth of four to five percent per year. Last year the market share breakdown for sales was:

Consolidated Bathurst	34%
McMillan	33%
Domtar	18%
Darthom	11%
Others	4%
	100%

Last June the Darthom plant's share of the southern Manitoba market amounted to approximately 16 million square feet of production per month.

Plant Organization

The management organization for the Winnipeg plant is shown in Exhibit II. Exhibit III, following, shows the position of the Winnipeg manager in the total company's organization.

Mr. Gerald Weatherby, the Winnipeg plant manager, commented about the scope of his position within the total organization:

> The divisional plants run their own operations with very little interference from head office in Vancouver. Only large capital expenditures, for example greater than $10,000, require approval from the head office. Decisions are made at the local level, and we stand or fall on them. Budgets are established by the plant manager and the sales manager. Every nickel has to be accounted for in the budget. Of course, should something be vital, we can deviate from our forecast provided we obtain head office approval. My performance is measured on results versus budgets.

Production Process

The production process at Winnipeg is described as follows: Large rolls of liner

EXHIBIT II

MANAGEMENT ORGANIZATION CHART
WINNIPEG PLANT, MARCH 1966

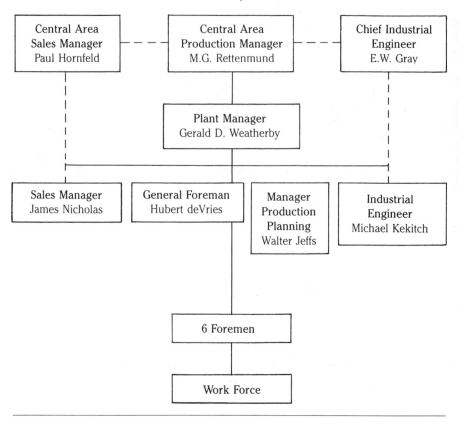

board and corrugating medium were received at the corrugated container plant from the company's pulp and paper mills. The rolls were fed into a box-plant corrugator which fluted the medium or centre portion of the board and glued it to two sheets of paper called "kraftliner," to form corrugated board.

The corrugated board was then transferred to a machine called a "printer slotter." Here it was cut and scored for eventual forming into boxes. In addition it was usually printed with customer and product identifications.

As a final stage in the manufacturing process some of the slotted, printed board was sent to the finishing department for closure. This process was accomplished by taping, gluing, or stitching. The final product was then stacked, tied, or strapped, and shipped to the customer.

The corrugator performed the key operation in the plant. All products went through it, then branched off to other operations depending on the customers' needs.

EXHIBIT III

POSITION OF WINNIPEG PLANT MANAGER
IN TOTAL COMPANY ORGANIZATION

President
Frederick A. Genrich

Vice-President
Packaging Products
D.E. Morgan

Vice-President
&
General Manager
F.G. Elwell

Central Area
General Manager
R.L. Satriano

Central Area
Production Manager
M.G. Rettenmund

Production Manager
Winnipeg
Gerald D. Weatherby

Plant capacity was rated at 30 million square feet of production per month on a two-shift basis. However, since start-up, the plant had operated almost solely on one shift. Production had reached a maximum of 19,500 MSF in August of last year, and had ranged from there to a low of 12,500 last year.

Mr. Weatherby said that the plant had operated well both during and after start-up.

> Almost none of the hourly workforce had any industrial experience prior to working here. Thus we had to train them all for the low-to-medium-skilled jobs available. Nevertheless, performance has been so good that we are far ahead of our projected production schedule.

Six hourly and twenty salaried (sales, management, and clerical) people made up the initial workforce. Within two years, the force had grown to 89 hourly and 36 salaried personnel. Approximately one-third of the hourly employees were women. Turnover rates were high (see Exhibit IV).

EXHIBIT IV

WINNIPEG TURNOVER FOR LAST 6 MONTHS

Labour Force	Month	% Turnover	(voluntary) Quits
80	Jan.	2.5	1
82	Feb.	3.7	1
83	March	2.4	2
86	April	4.7	2
84	May	3.6	3
89	June	6.7	6

Unionization

About five months after the Winnipeg plant began operations, the International Woodworkers of America (IWA) organized the plant's production employees, forming Local 3–400. The company did not resist the organization, because most of its workforce in other locations was represented by some union, and all Darthom production workers in the Prairie Provinces were represented by IWA. Unionization in this industry in this area of the country was viewed as inevitable.

The newly formed local negotiated its first contract in September, about six months after operations began. Its provisions were retroactive to June 20 and would terminate two years later on June 19. The hourly wage scale ranged from $5.50 to $10.00. While incentive plans characterized all other Darthom corrugated container plants, no incentive scheme was incorporated at the Winnipeg plant. Both management and union agreed that an incentive scheme based on time standards would be impractical in view of the newness of the plant and the inexperience of the employees. Methods of production were likely to change often while men and machines became acclimatized.

Union-Management Relations

Union-management relations were reasonably cordial in the early days. During those days when adjustments were being made workers were not held to rigid performance standards, and disciplinary regulations were not tightly enforced. There were few grievances and no arbitration cases. While a labour-management committee had been formed to air differences and suggest improvements, union leaders expressed the belief that little, if any, constructive changes resulted from these meetings.

Toward the end of the first contract term relations became more strained. Female employees complained that they were not receiving equal pay for equal work. They compared their rates of pay with pay rates of men working in competitor plants on identical jobs. Men on the Titan strippers and semi-automatic stitchers were receiving .50¢ to $1.00 more in basic hourly pay.

The female employees also complained of having to pay for hospitalization and insurance benefits when most were already covered on policies held by their husbands. Take-home earnings for women at McMillan and Consolidated Bathurst, including incentive premiums, averaged $1.00 per hour more, and this caused still more dissatisfaction at the Winnipeg plant.

Fourteen months after the first contract was signed, Mr. Ian Britney was elected President of Local 3–400 on a platform dedicated to closing the earnings differential between Darthom and competitor plants. Management representatives characterized Britney as considerably more militant than his predecessor. Aside from his "parity" objective he was concerned about lack of interest in union affairs, and sought to stimulate greater participation. Turnout for Local 3–400's monthly meetings was poor, averaging 10 to 15 percent of the total membership. Ian Britney, when questioned about union support, said:

> We don't have quantity but I think that we do have quality in those that actively support the union.

Within the union there were at least three discernible factions. The female employees formed the most demanding and vocal group, but their complaints were often viewed as "petty" by the males. The non-production hourly employees — four maintenance men, two rubber die makers, one truck driver, and two stationary engineers — formed a second faction. Members of this group had wage rates equivalent to those of McMillan and Consolidated Bathurst's non-production employees. Consequently they were more interested in fringe benefits, job security, recognition, and prestige. Males in the production force constituted the third major group. They were primarily interested in obtaining earnings comparable to those at competitor plants.

The Second Contract

The first collective agreement for Darthom's Winnipeg plant was to expire on June 20. However, negotiations for a second contract began more than nine months before the expiration date, as union leaders of the IWA locals at Darthom's four corrugated container plants in the Prairie Provinces expressed their desire to bargain for a master contract covering all locations. These were at Calgary and Medicine Hat in Alberta, Moose Jaw in Saskatchewan, and Winnipeg. The two agreements in Alberta were to expire in November, and the one in Moose Jaw in March, three months before the Winnipeg agreement. The final master agreement would not be signed until agreements had been reached for all locals, but newly-agreed-upon provisions would be applied to the various locations as their contracts expired. Ostensibly all locations were involved in all talks, but there were occasions when talks progressed without any representatives from the Winnipeg plant.

One of the coordinated demands put forth by the union was that all incentive programs then in existence be abolished. The union wanted the companies to buy out the plans. The company, in spite of problems with the incentive programs, balked, because other companies in the industry had suffered serious productivity losses when they had eliminated their incentive programs.

After lengthy bargaining the various incentive plans were retained and Darthom's Winnipeg plant, which till then had no incentive program, became committed to one. However, there was some feeling that a better, more realistic incentive scheme could be devised instead of the traditional MTM piecework used in the other plants. Consequently, the form of the Winnipeg plan was not decided. Section 13D of the new contract simply called for some form of incentive scheme for Darthom's Winnipeg plant by January 1 of the next year, giving the parties several months to explore various alternatives.

Section 13D   It is agreed that incentives will be applied by January 1, or alternatively a committee will be established to study and recommend some other type of plan. If the existing plan of the Corrugated Division is implemented it will apply to the existing machine centres:

> TWO EXISTING PRINTING PRESSES
> SCORING MACHINE
> MANUAL STITCHER
> S & S AUTO TAPER
> TWO SEMI-AUTO TAPERS
> WARD DIE PRESS
> TITAL DIE PRESS
> SCRAP SLITTER
> PARTITION SLOTTER
> CORRUGATOR
> SEMI-AUTO STITCHER

In the event of the existing program being decided upon and not implemented in the above-noted machine centres, a penalty clause as outlined in the master agreement Incentive Clause will apply to employees in these machine centres.

The reopener on the incentive clause in respect to the Winnipeg plant will be at the mid-point of the contract between the date of signing and termination.

The master agreement penalty clause called for a payment to all employees of 10 percent of their hourly base rate during the first 60 days in which no incentive plan was in use. The initial 10 percent was to be increased by a 5 percent payment for each additional 30 days in which no incentive plan was installed, to a maximum of 25 percent.

Mr. David Wilson

Mr. David Wilson, Darthom's Industrial Relations Manager for pulp and paper products, was instrumental in the formulation of Section 13D. Mr. Wilson had joined Darthom in April and was only superficially involved in the negotiations. However, he took a special interest in the Winnipeg plant. Here was a relatively new factory with excellent prospects for growth. The workforce was young and the plant was small enough for each employee to see how his or her contribution affected the final product. In addition, there were many opportunities for improvement. Given the proper atmosphere, Mr. Wilson believed that men and women in the shop would contribute to these improvements. They might be receptive to a relationship that Mr. Wilson termed "Quality of Work Life." QWL featured employee involvement, job enrichment, and participative management.

Many companies had successfully implemented participative management pro-grams and Mr. Wilson had read extensively about their experiences. He was particularly interested in companies using Scanlon plans, expressing the belief that a Scanlon-type plan might be appropriate for the Winnipeg plant. Contract Section 13D could open the way to such a plan.

Mr. Wilson hoped that if successful at Winnipeg, the participative manage-ment plan could be transferred to other plants. If Darthom output per manhour could be improved by such a plan, it would give the company an advantage over its aggressive competition and, at the same time, result in a highly motivated workforce.

With these thoughts in mind, Mr. Wilson tested some of his ideas on members of management. He circulated articles on QWL and the Scanlon plan throughout the executive levels of the Darthom organization.

Meanwhile he sought the advice of a labour relations consultant experienced in the installation of participative management schemes. After several phone calls, Mr. Wilson was referred to Dr. James Forsyth, Professor of Labour Law at Winnipeg's St. Francis University. He told Dr. Forsyth about the current negoti-ations, described Section 13D and its purpose, and asked if Dr. Forsyth would be willing to meet with Darthom's management to look at the Winnipeg plant and offer his opinion on the possibility of installing a workable scheme.

Dr. Forsyth accepted the invitation. During the telephone conversation he explained to Mr. Wilson that participative plans require considerable maturity on the part of both labour and management. He stated that such maturity often depends on the parties having enjoyed a relatively long relationship. However, the elements of youth and newness, plus the strong desire of both union and management to avoid problems associated with piecework systems, might make the Winnipeg plant an exception. Certainly it was worth exploring.

On June 27 Dr. Forsyth visited the Winnipeg plant. He was met by Edward Gray, Chief Industrial Engineer for the Winnipeg plant, and Michael Kekitch, Industrial Engineer. Messrs. Gray and Kekitch had done a considerable amount of reading about the theories of QWL and specifically about the Scanlon plan. They intended to discuss these plans with Dr. Forsyth and to show him the Winnipeg operations. They wanted Dr. Forsyth's opinion on whether ideas from such schemes were applicable to their plant. Both Mr. Gray and Mr. Kekitch were experts in piecework plans, but they had been instructed to postpone in-stalling piecework standards at Winnipeg during the exploration of alternative systems. Experience with piecework plans at other Darthom locations had been bad. People were taking home pay cheques in some locations that bore little relationship to their work effort. There were out-of-line rates and excessively high numbers of grievances. Furthermore, productivity levels at these plants were disappointing.

The Walkout

June 27 was the scheduled date for formal signing of the new contract. Union and management representatives from each of Darthom's four corrugated con-tainer plants in the Prairie Provinces had gathered at Winnipeg's Fort Garry

Hotel, along with Industrial Relations Manager for pulp and paper products, David Wilson, to affix their signatures. Gerald Weatherby, the Winnipeg Plant Manager, was ill that day, so he designated General Foreman Hubert deVries to attend on his behalf. Local 3–400 was represented by Ian Britney, President, William Linton, Vice President, and Samuel Harwood, Secretary.

Although the formal signing was scheduled for 11:00 a.m., some members of the Winnipeg plant's workforce had other ideas. At 9:30 a.m., coffee break time, the entire production operation at the Winnipeg plant shut down. The workers had staged a protest walkout.

Soon after the walkout, Walter Jeffs, Manager Production Planning, phoned Mr. Kekitch in the conference room where Kekitch was meeting with Messrs. Gray and Forsyth. He said that all the workers were outside in front of the plant and that newspaper reporters had arrived on the scene. The meeting ended while steps were taken to find out what was wrong.

Walter Jeffs and Michael Kekitch were the highest-ranking members of management at the plant. They decided that Kekitch and George deHaviland, Senior Foreman, should go outside, talk to the workers, and try to find out what had caused the walkout. They suspected it was a protest against the union leaders; consequently, they were reluctant to issue any ultimatums or warnings. Kekitch soon confirmed the suspicions, and a decision was made to telephone the union leaders and Mr. deVries at the Fort Garry Hotel.

When word of the walkout reached the Fort Garry Hotel the contract-signing was postponed. Hubert deVries, Ian Britney, and the other Local 3–400 officers made plans to drive back to the plant immediately. Meanwhile the workforce stayed outside in the sunshine, talking to reporters. Gray, Kekitch, and Dr. Forsyth resumed their conversations, then took a tour through the quiet, abandoned plant. Dr. Forsyth expressed doubt at that time whether any form of participative management program could work. There appeared to be a lack of communication within the union, as exemplified by the walkout, and a communications gap between management and the members of the workforce, as exemplified by management's surprise when the walkout occurred. Nevertheless, the men agreed to explore the situation further, paying particular attention to the outcome of deliberations when Messrs. deVries and Britney returned.

Ian Britney and the other Local 3–400 officers arrived back at the Winnipeg plant before 11 o'clock. They talked briefly to the workers standing in front of the plant, and arranged to meet later in the afternoon. The turnouts at this and a subsequent meeting that evening were reported to be the "best ever." Members aired their complaints about the contract, and officers explained their positions. The most significant complaint reported by the *Winnipeg Free Press* was that the membership had not been kept informed about the progress of negotiations. The *Free Press* article, dated Friday, June 28, is reproduced on page 383.

On Friday, the 28th, all the workers reported back to their jobs. No disciplinary action was taken against any of the employees for staging the walkout, and no changes were made in the contract. The Local members were far from satisfied, however, as reflected by their subsequent 26 to 7 vote against ratification.

UNION REVOLT

Strikers Protest Lack of Contract Information

Jerome Hilton, Free Press Labour Reporter

WINNIPEG — Hourly-rated employees at the Darthom Industries corrugated container plant here walked off their jobs Thursday, shortly before a contract was to be signed at the Fort Garry Hotel by union and company representatives.

The workers, members of Local 3–400, International Woodworkers of America, were protesting a lack of information on the new contract.

The workers — about 40 on the day shift left their jobs — said they were not informed about the full contents of the contract.

"There's been a breakdown in communications between the union, the company and the membership," a worker said.

"There are only three guys who know what's going on," another worker added, after pointing out Local 3–400 president Ian

Britney, vice-president William Linton and secretary Samuel A. Harwood were to sign the contract without informing the membership of its details.

The workers said some contract agreements were reached at a Wednesday meeting between union and company representatives and the membership was not informed about them.

"We want to know exactly what the contract consists of, we have the right to know," a female worker said.

"We went out because we want equalization and incentive standards," another female added.

The contract at the Winnipeg container plant, which has about 70 local 3–400 workers, expired June 20.

Nevertheless, the contract became effective, because the majority of the workers in the four plants affected by its terms voted in favour.

Ian Britney had commented to reporters on the day of the walkout that the contract was a good one — blaming the misunderstanding on "people who don't go to union meetings (blowing) it all out of proportion." Sometime later Britney said that he was not particularly happy with the agreement and expected that there would be a return to local bargaining the next time. According to Britney: "the coordinated approach did not work very well from our point of view."

The new contract became effective on Friday, the 28th, retroactive for the Winnipeg plant to June 20. It would run for two years. Section 13D had been incorporated in full, causing Messrs. Gray and Kekitch to express a desire to meet further with Dr. Forsyth. A diary of the subsequent meetings follows:

JULY 4

Dr. Forsyth returned to the Winnipeg container plant and talked with Michael Kekitch and Hubert deVries. He wanted to see the plant in operation and to learn more about the intra-union problems that caused the June 27 walkout.

The precipitating cause of the walkout had been a remark made by Ian Britney when he was preparing to leave for the Fort Garry Hotel on June 27. A union member had asked "where are you going?" Britney replied "downtown to sign the contract, but don't tell anyone!" It wasn't long before everyone in the shop knew of the comment. When Britney returned on the 27th and explained the contract terms, the women objected vehemently. The new contract called for them to receive $5.50 on labouring jobs—$5.75 below rates for men on comparable jobs. In addition, when they compared themselves to workers in other plants on similar jobs, they found they were receiving less money. For example, in Moose Jaw the two men operating semi-automatic finishing machines were classified as operators and received identical pay. Both men worked on all phases of the job. The new contract called for one man and one woman to operate similar machines in Winnipeg. The woman, classified a feeder, was specifically assigned to feed product into the machine. The man, called an operator, took the product from the machine and bundled it. He also adjusted the machine for the new runs and filled the glue pots. During the setup time for a new run, the feeder was usually idle. In Winnipeg, feeders received $8.00 per hour while operators received $9.00.

Dr. Forsyth's skepticism about a participative management scheme for Winnipeg was aggravated further when he saw the organization chart for Darthom Industries. Mr. Weatherby, the plant manager, was located five levels below the company's president (see Exhibit III of Case A); and, apparently, his decision-making authority was severely restricted. Nevertheless, Dr. Forsyth agreed to continue discussions. He said that the apparent savoir faire of Messrs. Kekitch and deVries, coupled with their desire to begin laying the groundwork for change, gave him some amount of encouragement. Both men, according to Dr. Forsyth, seemed to recognize that the proper atmosphere for such a plan might not exist for several years—well past the January 1 deadline for implementation of Section 13D.

Dr. Forsyth briefly described the kind of atmosphere that would have to exist in order for participative management to work. It would require a new concept of the roles that representatives of management and union would play. Managers would solicit the complete involvement of workers in decision making. When new machines were contemplated, workers to be affected would be consulted. When new products were considered, workers would be informed. If orders were cancelled or cut back, workers would receive an explanation. Eventually, under such a system, employees and management would develop confidence that both their best interests were served when they cooperated for the well-being of the firm. Evidence that the system was beginning to work would be observed in reduced absence and turnover rates, in fewer grievances, in reduced lateness, in plant-wide concern for company production problems, and in heated but constructive arguments between workers and members of management over problems that in the past were considered strictly the prerogatives of management.

The role of union leaders would also change dramatically under such a system. Without sacrificing their own need to police the contract and represent employees in grievances, the leaders would find themselves becoming concerned with long-range planning and would participate in decisions involving new acquisitions, employment policies, and marketing practices.

Dr. Forsyth explained that participative management schemes usually centre around some sort of bonus-sharing scheme. Bonuses are based on improvements in performance and are paid on a group basis. Such schemes must be simple, easily understood by all, and derived from union and management working together. At all times, however, it should be clear that the bonus-sharing scheme is only a gimmick, a device around which new attitudes are built and genuine participation obtained.

Dr. Forsyth then expressed a desire to meet with leaders of Local 3–400, to see whether they would be receptive to such a scheme. Arrangements were made for a meeting to take place on July 10. Meanwhile, Michael Kekitch agreed to accumulate company performance figures for the past two-and-one-half years, so that he and Dr. Forsyth could make some preliminary calculations toward development of a bonus-sharing plan.

JULY 10

Meeting with Union Representatives

Dr. Forsyth met with officers of the union: Ian Britney, President, William Linton, Vice President, Samuel Harwood, Secretary, and Linda McArthur, Steward. Dr. Forsyth explained that he had been invited by company representatives to offer advice on implementing Section 13D of the contract. He asked the union representatives what they expected to realize as a result of this section. Mr. Britney said, "We want a plan that will guarantee us a 25-percent increase!" Dr. Forsyth asked why they hadn't negotiated this. Britney replied, "We tried!" After further discussion Mr. Britney conceded that his real desire was to obtain a plan that the union could police and that was fair to the workers.

Then Britney talked briefly about piecework plans, expressing his desire to avoid problems that seemed to accompany such plans. When asked about his reaction to a group savings-sharing plan, Britney and the others showed interest. Dr. Forsyth cautioned that such plans had not, to his knowledge, been tried in the paper products industry, but then described several company-union situations in other industries where such plans had been successfully introduced. All involved close union-management cooperation and called for union involvement in management decision making. Mr. Britney expressed doubt whether Darthom management would go along with such a plan. He cited some earlier experiences with a labour-management committee, a group formed to consider suggestions for improvement. Mr. Britney said that several suggestions had been considered by the committee, but not one had been implemented. Furthermore, no explanations had been given for the failure to implement the suggestions. The union representatives agreed that for all practical purposes the union-management committee was ineffective.

JULY 6

Design of a Formula

Michael Kekitch and Dr. Forsyth met twice, July 6 and again July 13, to study the company performance figures gathered by Mr. Kekitch, and to design a tentative bonus-sharing formula for consideration by the parties.

Messrs. Kekitch and Forsyth used the following criteria to guide their work:

1. The bonus plan should be simple, one that all workers could understand.
2. The plan should reflect, as closely as possible, conditions that could be influenced by the participants.[1]
3. The plan should be based on a realistic standard, and improvements on that standard should be shared on a group basis.
4. The plan should be flexible enough to reflect changes in product mix.
5. It should be possible to change standards with relative ease if it becomes obvious that they are out of line — at least in the early stages.

After agreeing on the criteria, Messrs. Kekitch and Forsyth made a sample bonus calculation which related labour costs to production output. For illustrative purposes they compared the months of May and June as follows:

	May	June
Production in 000 sq. ft.	15,732	16,985
Direct labour cost	74,605	72,912
Indirect labour cost	8,035	8,090
Factory supervision	24,005	22,932
Total labour cost	106,645	103,934

The total labour cost per square foot produced in May was $.0068 (106,645 ÷ 15,732,000). If May were used as the base month, the $.0068 figure would become a standard to be applied in all future months. In June the actual production was 16,985,000 square feet. Applying the $.0068 standard we would expect a labour cost of $115,498 (16,985,000 × .0068). The actual labour cost for June was $103,934, a saving of $11,564 over the base. This saving would be divided among participants.

Messrs. Kekitch and Forsyth believed that a fair, attainable standard could be derived through this sort of comparison and that improvements on that standard should be shared by those who made the improvements possible.

They recognized that the formula they had been considering did not reflect changes in product mix. These changes were not controllable by the labour force and did influence the degree of difficulty with which production could be accomplished. To include a factor reflecting product mix changes would result in a more accurate standard but would cause two problems: one, it would make it impossible to calculate a standard in advance, so participants could know the goal at which they were shooting; and two, such inclusion would complicate the formula. Kekitch and Forsyth were convinced that a fair standard could be derived which would take into account various product mixes over time. Such a standard would be known in advance and attainable, but parties would retain the flexibility to change it if it was obviously out-of-line. However, Messrs.

[1]This criterion ruled out profit sharing plans, because profits are sometimes dependent on matters over which men in the shop have little control, such as changes in depreciation rates. It also ruled out any plan based on shipments, because management sometimes decides to produce for inventory.

Kekitch and Forsyth believed that maximum benefit from the plan would be derived if everyone participated, including foremen, the general foreman, the industrial engineer, and the plant manager. They felt they were now ready to present their ideas to company and union representatives.

JULY 17

Dr. Forsyth met with Gerald Weatherby, the plant manager. Dr. Forsyth described the proposed formula for bonus sharing and the concepts and agreed to attend a meeting with union representatives later that day in order to show his support.

Dr. Forsyth had translated the actual performance figures into hypothetical figures for illustrative purposes. However, he sought permission from Mr. Weatherby to disclose the actual figures to the union representatives if such disclosure seemed appropriate. Professor Forsyth said he doubted whether they would be requested but pointed out the importance of demonstrating a policy of complete disclosure with the union, starting immediately. Mr. Weatherby, while supporting the concept of full disclosure, said he could not give permission, that such permission would have to come from someone else in the organization.

It was with some trepidation, then, that Messrs. Kekitch and Forsyth entered the meeting with the union. The meeting could not wait, because union leaders might interpret a delay as another example of management's insincerity, thus ruining the chances of any participative management scheme before it got started.

Professor Forsyth, using hypothetical figures, described the bonus-sharing plan tentatively devised by himself and Mr. Kekitch. The bonus calculation related direct labour costs to production, thereby avoiding reference to indirect and supervisory costs.

Sample Bonus Calculation
given to Union Representatives on July 17

Assume, based on past experience, that it has cost the company $3.50, on average, to make 1,000 square feet of finished product.	
Assume in month X the following:	
Actual production	10,000,000 sq. ft.
Actual direct labour cost	$30,000
Employees	50
Bonus Calculation:	
Expected labour cost (3.50 × 10,000)	= $35,000
Less: Actual labour cost	30,000
Difference	5,000
Share per person (5,000 ÷ 50)	100

Dr. Forsyth showed how the bonus calculations could be made and posted on a cumulative daily basis. He then cited two matters that required caution.

1. There would be some months when actual costs would exceed the standard. Past experience showed that January, February, and March had been typically poor. It would be important for everyone to know that no bonus could

be paid in such months, and it would be advisable, in Professor Forsyth's opinion, to set some money aside during bonus months to offset loss months. The company should not be expected to absorb the complete loss in poor months if participants expected to receive the total gain in good months.

2. The union leaders should be careful not to oversell the bonus plan. Employees' expectations should not be inflated beyond what could be realistically expected. In fact, figures used for illustrative purposes should be intentionally deflated. Thus actual performance would hopefully yield a bonus in excess of the examples, and the plan would be looked upon favourably by the employees.

Mr. Weatherby attended part of the session and expressed his support of the concepts. The union leaders expressed a considerable amount of enthusiasm and said they were anxious to translate the proposal into something workable.

Dr. Forsyth cautioned against proceeding too rapidly. He suggested that Mr. Kekitch and other management representatives derive a realistic standard. They might consider an experimental dry run of two months before making any final determination. Dr. Forsyth gave the union representatives several matters to think about and suggested they be prepared to put forth their views at a future meeting. These matters included the following:

1. Who should share in the plan: supervisors? service employees? probationary employees?
2. How should bonus shares be calculated? Should everyone share equally? Should shares be based on a worker's present wage? Should those who work only part of a month receive the same as those who work the whole month?
3. Under what conditions should the base be changed?
4. How much should be set aside in good performance months to compensate for months when performance fails to meet the standard?

Dr. Forsyth stressed again that the bonus formula was only a small part of a total participative management plan. The more important part would be union participation in management decision making. A suggestion committee consisting of union representatives and management would replace the so-far-ineffective union-management committee. The new committee would consider ideas for improving performance and would have power to implement suggestions, within certain as-yet-undefined limits. Union members were urged to consider how the committee members would be appointed and within what limits the committee would operate.

Union representatives indicated some preliminary sentiments about the plan. They seemed unanimous in their desire that *everyone* participate, stating that through full participation members of management would symbolize their interest in making the plan work.

The representatives agreed that a two-month trial period would be advisable, and there was general agreement that September and October would be the best months for such a trial. This way various "bugs" which showed up could be ironed out well in advance of the January 1 deadline.

As a final matter, the union was asked to designate two people who would work along with Michael Kekitch and Hubert deVries of the company to formulate a detailed experimental plan based on the ideas already discussed.

Following the July 17 meeting, members of management and Dr. Forsyth expressed optimism. Both management and union appeared sincere in their desire to work together.

Hubert deVries suggested that the foremen be informed of what had happened and arranged a meeting for Dr. Forsyth to speak with them that same day. Dr. Forsyth outlined for the foremen the various events that had transpired since his involvement. Then he illustrated the bonus-sharing plan as he had done earlier with the union representatives. Dr. Forsyth cautioned that the bonus-sharing plan was only a gimmick, a symbol of a new relationship. An important key to the success of the new relationship were the first line supervisors. The foremen, under such a system, would be expected to manage. Clerical duties would be done by clerks. Foremen would be responsible for education of the workers, for placing them in jobs, seeing that conditions were ideal for top performance, and soliciting new ideas. Foremen would be judged not only on their budget performance, but also on how well they stimulated and successfully implemented members' new ideas that would improve performance.

The foremen responded enthusiastically to the meeting, expressing a strong desire to be active participants in the bonus-sharing plan. Some of them expressed personal thanks for having been informed about the progress of discussions and said they hoped they would be informed of future developments.

Following the meetings on July 17, Messrs. Kekitch and deVries met with Edward Gray, the company's Chief Industrial Engineer, in an effort to derive a realistic standard from which a monthly bonus could be calculated. They encountered difficult problems in deriving such a standard, because the plant had only operated for two-and-one-half years. No consistent pattern was apparent from past performance records. Furthermore, the frequent changes in product mix, caused by factors over which the workforce had no control, apparently had a direct effect on output. From month to month they could cause variations in the bonus. Nevertheless, the men were optimistic and expressed that optimism to management in Vancouver — men who eventually would be called upon to approve or disapprove any participative management plan. With this in mind Edward Gray contacted David Wilson, the company's Industrial Relations Manager for Pulp and Paper products, and the two men arranged a meeting for July 23 to review the status of the plan. Dr. Forsyth was asked to attend.

JULY 23

The following were in attendance:
David Wilson, Industrial Relations Manager, Pulp and Paper Products
Edward Gray, Chief Industrial Engineer
Stanley Lehroux, Director of Manufacturing Services
Marvin Rettenmund, Central Area Production Manager
Dustin Nickerson, Manager of Production Control
Jack Owens, Assistant Industrial Relations Manager

Gerald Weatherby, Manager, Winnipeg Plant
Michael Kekitch, Industrial Engineer, Winnipeg
James Forsyth, Consultant

After being introduced by David Wilson, Dr. Forsyth gave a chronological summary of the meetings that had taken place since June 27. He expressed optimism that a participative management plan could work but cautioned that short-run dramatic results probably could not be expected. "My greatest concern," said Dr. Forsyth, "is whether management can be open-minded and flexible enough to adjust to the form of management needed to make the program work." Dr. Forsyth stated he was echoing doubts expressed by the union leaders. An important symbol of management's sincerity could be the prompt and effective implementation of an experimental bonus-sharing plan. The figures would be posted, but no payments would be made. He noted that Messrs. Kekitch and deVries, along with two designees from the union, were planning meetings to derive an acceptable formula.

Dr. Forsyth pointed out that Darthom was embarking on a plan that was different. They would be pioneers. There would be frustrations, but the returns in job satisfaction and improved performance could be huge.

During the discussion which followed the bonus-sharing formula illustrated on July 17 to the union members was reviewed. Mr. Lehroux expressed some doubt whether the union would accept any plan which called for setting aside an amount as a contingency against losses. Dr. Forsyth stated his belief that this was an important feature of the plan — that all participants should be continually reminded that the company, in instituting a plan of this nature, was assuming greater-than-normal risk. There was the risk that labour costs, by virtue of no ceiling, would sky-rocket or that performance, by virtue of no controls, would drop. And there was the further risk of management frustration, as the traditional rights to manage without interference would be encroached upon.

Dr. Forsyth expressed confidence that the union leaders had already accepted these concepts, provided they could be assured of management's sincerity in making the plan work. He thought an important symbol of this sincerity would be wholehearted participation in the plan by all members of the Winnipeg plant's workforce, including management personnel.

When the members of the meeting appeared to be reasonably well acquainted with the ideas behind the proposed plan, Dr. Forsyth outlined a four-step action plan which he said should be implemented as soon as possible in order for matters to proceed.

1. Gain complete understanding of the proposed plan, its strengths and its weaknesses.
2. Give approval, in principle, to the scheme so that local management and union people could proceed with implementation on an experimental basis starting in September.
3. Take whatever steps were necessary to allow local management autonomy to implement suggestions promptly and conduct its industrial relations program without having to check each item with the head office.

4. Give approval in advance to the concept of complete participation in the plan — everyone from plant manager to labourer.

Commenting on the final point, Mr. Lehroux said that an incentive plan for all management personnel was presently under consideration at corporate headquarters. He expressed reservations about recommending that Winnipeg plant managers participate in two plans. "After all they *are* managers," said Mr. Lehroux, "and deserve separate treatment from members of the factory force. Furthermore we don't want to get ourselves into the position of giving Winnipeg managers preferred treatment."

Mr. Lehroux expressed additional concern about the degree of autonomy that should be given to the local manager. He noted that Mr. Weatherby presently had authority to approve and implement all capital expenditures of less than $1,000. Anything over that needed head office approval.

Dr. Forsyth suggested that the members in attendance resolve these issues as soon as possible and made it clear that he believed complete participation and considerable autonomy for local managers were important ingredients of success. The members agreed that, while head office pondered these questions, Messrs. Kekitch, Gray, and deVries would proceed with designated union members to design an experimental plan. They were given a tentative deadline of September 1.

Following the management meeting Michael Kekitch, Hubert deVries, and Dr. Forsyth met with Ian Britney, Samuel Harwood, Linda McArthur, and Susan Randall of the union to report on the results of the management meeting. When she arrived in the conference room Mrs. McArthur asked Dr. Forsyth, "Well, did the shit hit the fan?" Dr. Forsyth replied, "No, not really. We think we made some progress." Then he described what had happened, pointing out the two areas of apparent concern. He reported that agreement had been secured to continue with the experimental plan. The union had decided that Mr. Britney and Mrs. McArthur would work with Messrs. Kekitch and deVries to design a plan for a trial run in September.

DARTHOM INDUSTRIES LTD. (B)

Union and management personnel at the Winnipeg corrugated container plant of Darthom Industries Ltd. expressed considerable optimism after the July 23 meeting. Two company and two union representatives were designated to devise an experimental bonus-sharing plan that would undergo a trial period during the months of September and October. The test would allow the parties to work out problems in the plan and to decide on its acceptability well in advance of the deadline date of January 1.

A union-management committee was formed to consider suggestions for improvement under the plan. This committee would meet monthly starting immediately. The company representatives would include Mr. Jason Keller, Industrial Relations Representative for the four corrugated container plants in the Prairie Provinces.[1] Union designees would come from all principal work centres in the Winnipeg plant.

During August Messrs. Stanley Lehroux, Marvin Rettenmund, and Edward Gray sought answers to some of the questions raised by Dr. James Forsyth at the July 23 meeting.

1. Should supervisory people participate in the bonus plan?
2. How much authority would be given to Winnipeg managers to accept and implement suggestions?
3. Would top management support the concept of a bonus-sharing, participative management program?

While these questions were being asked, Michael Kekitch, Hubert deVries, Ian Britney, and Linda McArthur waited. Company representatives wanted approval from corporate headquarters before proceeding with the design of a detailed plan. The approval never came. Rather, members of management expressed a desire to investigate the situation further and arranged another meeting in Winnipeg for September 4.

Meanwhile, Edward Gray and Michael Kekitch contacted a company in Janesville, Wisconsin — the Parker Pen Company — to arrange a visit for themselves and, perhaps, one or two union members. Parker, whose workers were represented by the United Rubber Workers, had instituted a Scanlon-type participative management plan in the early 1950s which had been immensely successsful. Messrs. Gray and Kekitch thought it advisable to see such a plan in operation and talk with people who worked there. The visit never took place.

MEETING OF SEPTEMBER 4

The meeting of September 4 was attended by the following:
   Fabian Elwell, Vice President and General Manager, Packaging Division,
   Stanley Lehroux, Director of Manufacturing Services,
   Robert Satriano, Central Area General Manager,

[1]Mr. Keller's regular responsibilities included administration of the labour contract with the corrugated container plants in Medicine Hat and Calgary, Alberta, Moose Jaw, Saskatchewan, and Winnipeg.

David Wilson, Industrial Relations Manager, Pulp and Paper Products,
Marvin Rettenmund, Central Area Production Manager,
Gerald Weatherby, Manager, Winnipeg plant,
Hubert deVries, General Foreman, Winnipeg plant,
Michael Kekitch, Industrial Engineer, Winnipeg plant.

Dr. Forsyth was asked to attend, but a prior engagement prevented him from doing so. However, the formula devised by Dr. Forsyth and Michael Kekitch for sharing in cost savings was discussed. Mr. Kekitch, using last April as an arbitrary base, presented figures that indicated bonuses would have been paid under the proposed formula during the past year as follows:

	Total	Per Person
January	$14,802	$176.21
February	(2,662)	no bonus
March	(7,382)	" "
April	base month	
May	13,255	157.80
June	23,955	285.18
July	6,455	76.84

According to Mr. Kekitch there would be a 10-percent reduction in each bonus month to build a reserve against which loss months would be charged.

Some concern was expressed regarding the stability of bonus payments. Mr. Satriano, in particular, said he felt weight should be given to various product mix factors which contribute to higher labour costs. Mr. Kekitch and Mr. Gray were directed to work with a company accountant, Mr. Frank Cunningham, to come up with a more refined formula and present it at a meeting scheduled for September 18.

Accordingly Messrs. Kekitch, Gray, and Cunningham made a further study of production figures, converting all of them to reflect the maximum labour costs caused by adverse product mix: double facing, extra partitions, heavy weight boards, and water proofing. They concluded that the effect of all this was negligible. The reason for losses during February and March was inefficient plant operation attributed to low volume, not adverse product mix. According to Mr. Gray volume was a "great leveller."

Mr. Gray said that he had worked through another, more sophisticated, formula by which he calculated an average cost per thousand square feet of production on each machine in the plant. He added these costs for a two-month period, selected arbitrarily, to form a standard direct payroll. Then he added indirect payroll, load transfer costs, and training costs. He then computed actual costs and compared them to the standard. He said that the results were exceptionally close to the ones put forth by Mr. Kekitch at the September 4 meeting.

Evidence notwithstanding, management remained concerned about product mix variations. In addition they were concerned about the possible effects on productivity of major capital investments in labour-saving machinery. Consequently a management consulting firm was contacted and introduced at the September 18 meeting. The consultants were Sears-Horton and Partners,

Darthom's auditors, and were represented by Dr. John Taylor and Mr. Robert Cumper. Dr. Taylor, while advocating a simple formula, said he wished to see the Winnipeg plant and learn about production problems: machine downtime and the like. It was subsequently decided to employ the Sears-Horton firm, and Mr. Kekitch resumed methods studies at the Winnipeg plant for possible application of MTM standards. Apparently, then Mr. Kekitch had resumed the work he had abandoned more than seven months earlier.

One month later, in mid-October, Mr. Wilson expressed concern that while Sears-Horton and Partners were studying the plant situation at Winnipeg the human factors and educational factors — so strongly emphasized by Dr. Forsyth — had not been considered. Wilson was especially concerned that the company had reneged on its promise to the union that there would be dummy runs in September and October so that adjustments could be made before any bonus-sharing plan was implemented. The union leaders had simply been informed that "things had been delayed."

Soon thereafter Mr. Fabian Elwell, Vice President and General Manager of the Packaging Division, appointed his special assistant, Mr. Blair Hardman, to work with the Sears-Horton people and oversee the installation of a workable incentive plan for the Winnipeg plant as soon as possible.

WINNIPEG PLANT UNREST

While Dr. Taylor and other Sears-Horton people were working with Mr. Kekitch and before Mr. Hardman came upon the scene, a management decision was made at the Winnipeg plant which caused considerable chagrin among union leaders. Without prior notification to the union, a temporary second shift of 42 new workers was added. This created difficulties within the union ranks as members raised questions which the local leaders could not answer, such as: How long would the second shift be needed? Would some of the existing members be required to move to the new shift? Would the new people share in the group bonus plan — if we ever have one? By the way, what ever happened to the bonus plan?

Amid the consternation caused by addition of the second shift, a surprising event occurred in the ranks of the office workers at the Winnipeg plant. The clerks, typists, and stenographers formed a union. Management had not been aware of the organizing efforts until they received formal notification of a certification hearing.

SEARS-HORTON AND PARTNERS

Dr. John Taylor, a partner of Sears-Horton and Partners, requested a meeting with Darthom management representatives in Vancouver on November 7. Dr. Taylor, in conjunction with other members of the firm, had designed an incentive plan for the Winnipeg plant, using the results of Mr. Kekitch's studies, and he was ready to unveil it. The plan was described by Dr. Taylor as a group incentive plan based on accumulated MTM standards. Members of Darthom management who attended the meeting were:

Blair Hardman, Special Assistant to Mr. Elwell,

Lee Calhoun, Corporate Industrial Relations Director,
George Meyer, Industrial Relations Manager, Pulp and Paper Products,[2]
Edward Gray, Chief Industrial Engineer,
Gerald Wheatherby, Manager, Winnipeg plant,
Michael Kekitch, Industrial Engineer, Winnipeg Plant.

Even though Sears-Horton's plan was only in its preliminary formulation stages, the people in attendance expressed the feeling that it had sufficient merit so that preparation should be started promptly for its eventual introduction. Thus the following decisions were made:

1. Mr. Calhoun, the company's Industrial Relations Director, would head a company negotiating team to draft a contract clause which would incorporate the Sears-Horton plan into the existing collective agreement.
2. A brochure would be prepared explaining the plan. The union would be offered an opportunity to assist in its preparation so that language used would be understood by all. Sears-Horton would prepare a draft of the brochure first. Then the draft would be presented to the union for comments.
3. Messrs. Keller and Kekitch would inform the union that the plan would be presented to them in the near future and give the union a brief outline of its features. They would explain, in addition, why the company had delayed so long in presenting something to them and they would leave a number of questions with the union that were still pending resolution:
   Who would participate in the plan?
   What would be the frequency of payments?
   Would reserves be set aside for months when performance did not meet standard?
   How often would the standard be subject to revision?

   All these questions had been given to the union in August by Messrs. Kekitch and deVries. At the time the union representatives responded to them, and their responses were communicated to Mr. Elwell at Darthom's head office in Vancouver. However, so far the responses apparently had been ignored.
4. Sears-Horton would be responsible for converting the principles of the bonus sharing into figures for later presentation to the union. In addition, Sears-Horton would determine the effects of various product mixes on incentive opportunities, comparing the best and worst examples of product mix variations from past experience.
5. Sears-Horton would arrange clerical, accounting, and other procedural details required to implement the plan.
6. Weekly labour-management committee meetings at the Winnipeg plant would be scheduled to "create the atmosphere of discussion." These would be considered a "part of the implementing procedure."
7. Management would insist that problems arising from implementation of the bonus-sharing plan be considered separate from the contractual grievance

[2]Mr. Meyer succeeded Mr. David Wilson as Industrial Relations Manager, Pulp and Paper Products on October 15, following Mr. Wilson's resignation.

procedure. While many potential grievances would likely arise in meetings concerning the bonus plan it was important not to confuse the two.

8. There would be an attempt to re-establish contact with Dr. James Forsyth of the St. Francis University Law School. While he had not been involved since July, there was a feeling that his presence could help assure acceptance of the plan by the union.

On November 11, Blair Hardman contacted Dr. Forsyth to request that he attend a meeting with Dr. John Taylor of Sears-Horton and Partners and offer his comments on the newly devised bonus-sharing plan. Mr. Hardman explained that the new plan was similar to the one prepared earlier by Messrs. Kekitch, Gray, and Forsyth, but in order that the plan have transfer value to other Darthom corrugator plants the standards had been recalculated.

Dr. Forsyth asked whether the union had been informed of the Sears-Horton studies and involved in preparation of the new plan. Mr. Hardman said they had been informed but not involved, causing Dr. Forsyth to express considerable doubt regarding the union's receptivity. "Non-involvement could cause non-commitment," said Forsyth, "and without clear commitment from all parties the plan would be doomed."

In spite of his doubts Dr. Forsyth accepted Mr. Hardman's invitation, and he met with Mr. Hardman and Dr. Taylor on November 20.

Dr. Taylor explained that Sears-Horton and Partners had been studying the Winnipeg plant's operations for several weeks and had devised a cost-savings sharing plan similar to the one proposed to the union during July. It differed in only one respect: the standard, rather than being a labour cost figure based on historical data, was a composite of Methods Time Measurement (MTM) standards for the principal work centres in the plant, weighted to reflect the relative contribution of each work centre to the total output. Fourteen separate work centres were listed, each with an MTM standard:

	Standards*
1. Corrugator	.119
2. Printer Slotter	.129
3. Tital Die Press	.023
4. Ward Die Press	.005
5. Semi-automatic finishing	.080
6. Automatic taping/gluing	.054
7. Manual stitcher	.017
8. Partition slotter	.011
9. Partition Assembly — Manual	.045
10. Partition Assembly — Automatic	.006
11. Slitting and Scoring	.037
12. Automatic Unitizing	.043
13. Hand Unitizing	.035
14. Indirect: Shipping, Die Mounting, Maintenance, Boilerman	.196
TOTAL	.800

*Standards were expressed in hours per thousand square feet of production (MSF). They were based on the average product mix for the most recent five months.

A bonus would be calculated each month to reflect improvements on the standard. While Dr. Taylor had not prepared sample bonus calculations, this is how one might have looked for the month of November.

> If the plant produced 16 million square feet in 12,000 man hours in November and the payroll for the month was $75,000 the standard would call for expenditure of 12,800 hours (16,000 × .800). Thus the November performance would yield an improvement of 800 hours (12,800 − 12,000), or 6.67 percent. By applying this percentage to the monthly payroll the bonus amount would emerge. In this case the bonus would be $5,000, to be divided among participants.

There would be an additional factor to reflect changes in product mix from the base months. However, it was still uncertain how the product mix factors would be calculated.

Dr. Taylor said further studies would be required in the Winnipeg plant before he could be sure that standards for all 14 work centres were proper. This would take several more weeks. Meanwhile, he and Mr. Hardman were anxious to proceed by meeting with management and union representatives at the Winnipeg plant and explaining what had been done so far. They asked for Dr. Forsyth's comments.

Dr. Forsyth said he believed the basis for calculation of the standard was sound and that the plan could be sold, even at this late date. Although the new plan was similar in its derivation to the one considered by the union the previous summer, it was somewhat more complicated. Consequently it would be necessary to explain it with care, making certain that everyone understood it perfectly. He cautioned a mere statement by someone that he understands would not be sufficient. Assertion of understanding *could* be an indication of ignorance or unwillingness to admit non-understanding.

Dr. Forsyth advised that the union members would understand best when the plan was explained to them by the use of sample bonus calculations. Until then, it was likely to be meaningless. He suggested postponing a meeting with them until such calculations had been worked out.

Mr. Hardman ruled out the possibility of further dèlays, saying the company was obligated to present something to the union promptly if there was any hope of meeting the January 1 deadline. "Mind you," said Hardman, "this plan is not negotiable. We expect to install it January 1 whether or not the union agrees. Naturally we'll try to *sell* it, but if we're not successful we'll go ahead anyhow."

Then Mr. Hardman asked Dr. Forsyth if he would be willing to accompany himself and Dr. Taylor to the Winnipeg plant the next day for preliminary talks regarding the new plan. Dr. Forsyth declined, saying his presence could create the impression that management wanted to stuff the plan down the union's throat. "This may be the blunt reality," said Forsyth, "but I don't want to be a part of it, and management would be well-advised to avoid creating such an impression." Forsyth did express a desire to be kept informed about the forthcoming events and a willingness to help where he could if there seemed to be hope that the plan would be well received.

Mr. Hardman and Dr. Taylor went to the Winnipeg plant the next day and explained the plan to members of management. In addition they made arrangements for a subsequent meeting at which principal members of Darthom's top management would be introduced to the Sears-Horton plan.

NOVEMBER 21 MEETING

Those in attendance:
   John Taylor, Sears-Horton and Partners
   Robert Cumper, Sears-Horton and Partners
   Blair Hardman, Special Assistant to F. Elwell
   James Forsyth, Consultant
   Gerald Weatherby, Manager, Winnipeg plant
   Michael Kekitch, Industrial Engineer, Winnipeg
   Hubert deVries, General Foreman, Winnipeg
   Lee Calhoun, Corporate Industrial Relations Director
   Jason Keller, Industrial Relations Director, Prairie Provinces
   George Meyer, Industrial Relations Director, Pulp and Paper Products.

Blair Hardman opened the meeting with the statement that the next day, November 22, the Sears-Horton cost-savings sharing plan could be revealed to the union. He reviewed the history of the plan and explained that the plan's formulation had been delayed since July to provide the company with time to perfect details.

Hardman said that the plan depended for its success on enthusiastic acceptance by management and union members alike. If it succeeded in Winnipeg, it could form the basis for elimination of antiquated incentive plans throughout the company.

> The purpose of this meeting is to explain the plan. No one should leave here without a good idea of where we now stand and how the plan will work.

Dr. Taylor and Robert Cumper of Sears-Horton and Partners stood ready with a viewgraph projector and 15 transparencies designed to illustrate the Sears-Horton plan. However, the meeting was thrown open for comments and questions, and the presentation was momentarily delayed.

Dr. Forsyth was asked to explain the philosophy behind a participative management scheme. He replied that the plan to be illustrated by Taylor was a symbol, a tool around which participative management could develop. He said he believed that an atmosphere could be developed that would allow the plan to point the way toward greater job satisfaction and greater profitability. Dr. Forsyth stated that outward symbols of job satisfaction would likely be slow in developing but they would include the following:
— dramatic reductions in absences, lateness, and turnover rates;
— reduction of time taken for coffee and lunch breaks;
— reduction in grievance rates;
— workers helping each other;
— suggestions to management for improvements;
— conversations around the plant centring on matters of importance to the

company's well-being, such as its profits for the last month, new capital acquisitions, and reasons for returned shipments.

Dr. Forsyth described a few other companies where participative management schemes had been introduced and pointed out that the majority of them had failed. Those which succeeded owed their success to strong management and union leaders: men who understood that participative management required some dramatic adjustments in traditional ways of thinking. Managers had to open communication lines and be receptive to ideas from everyone, even those who were critical.

Union leaders had to adopt dual roles. On the one hand they had to be antagonists, fighting vigorously during negotiations for the best possible contract, and fighting with equal vigour to prosecute legitimate grievances. On the other hand union leaders had to actively share management's concerns — to help create conditions of prosperity, efficiency, and growth so that the company could afford to pay top dollar in negotiations. Not many union leaders were able to balance these two roles successfully, but any diminution in either would significantly reduce the likelihood of success.

Lee Calhoun, the Corporate Industrial Relations Director for Darthom, said that he had taken some initial steps to obtain cooperation of the union. He had met earlier that day with IWA International representatives to describe the company's objectives at the Winnipeg plant and obtained assurance that the International would not interfere with the Winnipeg local while the plan was being explained and finalized. The IWA representatives expressed special interest in the possible transfer value of the Winnipeg plan, if it was successful, to other corrugated container plants. Like Darthom management, the IWA was generally opposed to traditional piecework incentive plans.

Mr. Calhoun then asked Gerald Weatherby, the Winnipeg Plant Manager, if he felt that local management would be able to adjust to a participative-type scheme. Mr. Weatherby responded that his management was capable of adjusting but that the adjustment would be easier if plant foremen were included as participants in the plan.

Messrs. Kekitch and deVries strongly supported Mr. Weatherby's views. Hubert deVries voiced two reasons for the inclusion of the foremen:

1. They expected to be included;
2. some of the foremen were receiving less take-home pay than their hourly employees. This was a serious source of irritation among foremen and would have to be corrected before their support could be expected.

Others at the meeting, including Mr. Hardman, voiced opposition to foremen participating. Mr. Hardman said that these men were members of management and would be included in a separate management plan. He was anxious that their status as management representatives not be diluted. Mr. Hardman ended the discussion by saying:

> As the plan is presently constituted the foremen are not included. I hope that you who would hold other ideas will defer them until later. There will be an extra burden on top management if they're included. Tomorrow no mention will be made to the foremen about their participation in the plan.

Dr. Taylor then started the viewgraph projector to begin his presentation but was interrupted by Jason Keller. Mr. Keller asked whether members of the support staff such as maintenance people would be included and, if so, on what basis. He pointed out the importance of effective and prompt maintenance in realization of any long-term improvements in productivity and urged the inclusion of these people. Mr. Keller's points were generally accepted, but the question of how the support staff should participate was left unanswered. Dr. Forsyth stated that he agreed with Mr. Keller, but he pointed out that there were certain attendant dangers associated with their inclusion. One such danger might be the tendency to cut back on maintenance people in order to reduce the total number of participants sharing in the bonus. Such a tendency could result in short-run gains but would sacrifice the company's long-run well-being.

Finally, after more than an hour of waiting, Dr. Taylor began his viewgraph presentation. He reviewed the progress of the plan from the date the contract had been signed, last June 28. Dr. Taylor recapped the early meetings of Mr. Gray, Mr. Kekitch, Dr. Forsyth, and members of the union. He then described the process from which the Sears-Horton plan had been derived. Dr. Taylor listed the 14 work centres, explained various means by which periodic performance results could be reported, and suggested ways in which a bonus could be calculated, but he was not prepared to put forth examples.

Dr. Taylor said that daily results could be posted. However, there would be a three- or four-day lag because of the time required for the central computing facilities in Vancouver to receive and convert information from the various work centres into meaningful information.

Dr. Taylor emphasized that standards might be inaccurate and, although he did not anticipate having to alter them, it was important to retain the flexibility to do so. He also explained that improvements in methods as a result of suggestions by participants would not influence the standards if their effect on the total MTM value was less than three percent, unless they required an expenditure of capital funds. Changes introduced by management could result in immediate alteration of the standards.

While nearly all those in attendance expressed an interest in attending the next day's meeting with the union representatives, it was decided to restrict the number to minimize the impression that the plan was something that management intended to ram down the union's throat. To further minimize this impression, Dr. Taylor was requested to make his presentation from notes and to abandon the viewgraph. Blair Hardman agreed that management should not give the union the impression of inflexibility but reiterated his view that the plan was not negotiable. The union would help to decide such issues as how various workers would participate and how often changes in the standard would be made. Aside from these points, there would be no infringement of management prerogatives.

At this point Gerald Weatherby stated that he would be unable to attend the next day's meetings because of a pre-arranged medical appointment. It was decided then that Michael Kekitch would introduce the various persons in attendance, and Dr. Taylor would then make his presentation. In addition to

Weatherby, only George Meyer, Robert Cumper, and Dr. Forsyth — of those at the evening meeting — would not be in attendance the following day.

NOVEMBER 22 MEETING

The next day, the Sears-Horton plan was presented to the Union Committee of Ian Britney, Walter Jones, Linda McArthur, and Roy Biggar. Mr. Jones represented maintenance, rubber die, and shipping employees, and Mr. Biggar was a member of the union-management committee then meeting on a weekly basis. After an opening apology from Michael Kekitch abut the delay in getting back to the union, Lee Calhoun discussed the events that led to the meeting. He explained the delay by stressing that the company at first glance had a great fear of installing a scheme as radical as the one designed in July and then submitted to the head office. This plan was a completely new idea from Darthom Industries. However, the company had thoroughly studied it with help from Sears-Horton and Partners and found it to be feasible. Management had agreed to try the plan at the Winnipeg plant. Mr. Calhoun stated that there were still some problems to be solved but expressed confidence that there was sufficient time to finalize an acceptible plan by January 1.

After being introduced, Dr. Taylor began his presentation by congratulating the Winnipeg personnel on their progressiveness. He said that the plan he was about to explain was basically the same as the one they had considered earlier in July. According to Dr. Taylor, Sears-Horton and Partners had been employed in order to help develop a standard that would be fair to both union and management. He said the plan considered in July, which related labour costs to production, likely would have resulted in a large proportion of loss months for reasons that could not be influenced by members of the workforce. Consequently, the Sears-Horton proposal used a standard based on the relationship between man hours and production. There would be a constantly changing standard reflecting changes in product mix. When certain product mixes created greater-than-usual labour hour demands, the standard would be loosened, and vice versa.

Dr. Taylor explained that standards had been set to allow for a 25-percent earning opportunity. He then outlined the plan, as he had done the night before with management representatives.

Dr. Taylor apologized for not having figures available to illustrate the plan. Nevertheless, he asked members of the union to accept the plan in principle and requested that they raise any questions they wished.

Mr. Britney said that the members had already considered several matters concerning the scheme and that in their view participation should be limited to union members, and bonuses should be paid equally to all participants.

Taylor said he believed participation should be based on a man's existing salary because this reflected his relative worth to the enterprise. However, he did not pursue his differences with Britney, and the meeting proceeded. Consensus was reached on several points:
1. Probationary employees would receive 50 percent of the regular bonus.

2. A pool would be established in profit months in order to have something available for loss months.
3. Bonuses would be paid on a monthly basis.
4. A board would be installed in the plant to keep employees informed about the status of their bonus on a day-to-day basis.

Mr. Hardman then took the floor. He said that work had been started on a pamphlet to describe the plan. He invited union members to proofread the draft copies when they were ready and to submit any comments they might have for improvement. Hardman then stated that the bonus-sharing plan, as put forth by Dr. Taylor, was only a small part of the total plan. The union-management committee, then meeting on a weekly basis, was the real guts of the plan, because through this committee ideas would be exchanged and improvements would be nurtured. Ian Britney asked Mr. Hardman if the committee would have "full say" regarding proposals from members of the workforce. He said he was worried about management taking action without union consultation. Some such actions would dilute the individual bonuses. Addition of a new shift was an example.

Mr. Hardman told Britney that the union-management committee would consider all matters that might affect the plan. He stated that the plan's success depended on attainment of a "team" relationship.

Further conversation developed about the concepts behind calculation of the bonus. Mr. Britney indicated he was not clear how the new plan differed from the bonus scheme presented by Dr. Forsyth in the summer. Hardman said that he believed Dr. Forsyth would be willing to meet with the union to help clarify the new plan. He stated that Dr. Forsyth was well acquainted with it and suggested that the union contact him if they so desired.

Soon after the meeting ended, Mr. Hardman phoned Dr. Forsyth to relate what had happened and to inform him of the likelihood of a phone call from the union. Mr. Britney would ask that he attend a union meeting to answer their questions about the plan. Dr. Forsyth replied that he would be willing to attend a union meeting but wanted Mr. Hardman to understand that he, Forsyth, had grave doubts whether the new plan could succeed, because the union had not participated in its formulation and because even now at this late date no one had seen a sample bonus calculation. Beyond this, Dr. Forsyth said he did not believe that Winnipeg management was either capable or in favour of trying to make the plan work. Forsyth said he would tell the union this and would urge them not to go along with the plan until they were clear beyond doubt how it would work and were convinced that it was in their own best interests. In view of these doubts he asked Hardman if he still wanted him to meet with the union. Hardman said "yes," he did.

Later that same day Dr. Taylor and Mr. Hardman met with the Winnipeg foremen and talked about the same matters covered earlier with the union. The foremen asked a few questions but saved their important comments till later. The comments, reported by General Foreman Hubert deVries the next day, were strongly negative. They expressed keen disappointment that they would not participate in the plan. Aside from the likelihood of receiving added income the plan would have given them a sense of "belonging" — something that, till then, had been lacking. Assurances by Mr. deVries that another plan was being formulated for supervisory personnel failed to assuage them. "We want something more than promises," said one.

THE UNION MEETING

The next day Ian Britney contacted Dr. Forsyth and invited him to attend a special union meeting which had been called for the following Sunday, the 25th. Britney indicated that the union representatives who had attended the November 22 meeting with management were not satisfied that they understood the Sears-Horton and Partners bonus plan. He said further that most Local 3–400 members were unfamiliar with incentive plans, participative management plans and the like, and asked if Dr. Forsyth would try to explain these and answer questions. Forsyth said he would be there.

There were 18 union members, including officers, in attendance at the November 25 meeting. Without ceremony Mr. Britney explained briefly the purpose of the meeting and introduced Dr. Forsyth. Dr. Forsyth said there were two reasons for his being there:

1. To try to explain the Darthom bonus plan formulated by Sears-Horton and Partners, as he knew it; and
2. to explain the philosophy of improvement-sharing concepts.

He said that traditional piecework plans suffered because they are breeding grounds for grievances. When new rates are applied to jobs the incumbents often seek to increase those rates by arguing that standards are too tight. Since standard setting is largely subjective, arguments often result. Many times concessions are made, opening the way to even more bickering as subsequent standards are set and then compared with those in existence.

The proposed plan would largely avoid grievances over incentive standards. It was based on the philosophy that the man on the job knows it best. He can put forth ideas for improvements better than any time-study or methods man, and he should be encouraged to do so. The plan itself was designed to create an atmosphere for bringing forth these ideals. Individuals would benefit through bonus earnings, and the company would benefit by using the increased knowledge gained from members of the workforce to improve efficiency. In a competitive industry like this one, efficiency is vital for survival.

The proposed plan would hopefully motivate everyone from Gerald Weatherby to the newest second shift employee to work together for common benefits. While some persons are interested mostly in making some money, others complement this interest with a desire for recognition for doing a good job. Still others are motivated by working together, putting forth new ideas and seeing those ideas implemented. This plan was designed to appeal to all these people, because it had elements in it that called for generation of ideas, for group work toward common objectives, toward improvement, toward recognition for doing a good job, and toward more money!

Dr. Forsyth described the Sears-Horton bonus-sharing plan but pointed out that, so far, no figures had been put forth to show how the plan would affect each man's pocketbook. Forsyth demonstrated various means by which a bonus could be calculated from the standards as proposed, but he warned union members to be certain that management explained the plan to their satisfaction before they approved it. He said they should insist on definite answers to three questions:

1. How will bonus dollars be related to performance?
2. Under what circumstances will the standards be changed?
   — will the union have a voice in the changes?
   — how often will changes be made?
3. What kind of decisions can the labour-management committee influence?

Questions were then requested from the union members. From the questions Dr. Forsyth concluded that there was general understanding of the theoretical concepts around which a group participation plan should be built and a good understanding of the bonus plan as put forth by Sears-Horton. However, there was a definite mood of skepticism among the members: skepticism about whether management could pay any more than lip service to the concepts they had talked about.

THE BONUS SHARING PLAN

In early December Sears-Horton and Partners finally delivered a plan which converted their concepts into dollars and cents.

The bonus would be calculated by comparing actual performance to standard performance each day, accumulating the daily comparisons, and making payments at the end of each month whenever actual performance exceeded standard. The standards were based on 13 production centres plus five support functions. These standards were derived from MTM studies, the results of which were compared for reasonableness with equivalent operations in other Darthom corrugated container plants. This comparison led to a conclusion that actual performance at Winnipeg was generally less efficient than in other plants. Some areas were as much as 40 percent less efficient. Consequently most of the Winnipeg standards were changed to reflect the differences.

PRODUCT MIX FACTOR

Of the 13 production centres, five were considered most important. Factors were assigned to each of these five to represent the difference between product volume for a day, week, or month under consideration and the volume for an agreed-upon base period. To start, this period consisted of the five months of June to October. If the difference exceeded seven percent, the standard for the centre involved would be adjusted up or down.

Each of the five centres, with their standards and respective weights, are shown in Table 1 with variance factors for the month.

Thus in November the standards for Station 2 and 4 were changed since the

Table 1

Section	Description	Base standard in man hours (from page 396)	Variance factor	Revised standard
1	Corrugator (1)	.119	105.4	.125
2	Presses (3)	.129	91.3	.118
3	Semi-automatic tapers, gluers, and stitchers (5)	.080	102.0	.082
4	Automatic gluers/tapers (2)	.054	81.5	.044
5	Manual Partitioners (6 operators)	.045	100.0	.045

product mix factors caused a variation of more than seven percent from the base. All other stations retained the base period standard.

The process of evaluating product mix would take place on a cumulative daily basis for all five work centres. No adjustments would be made in standards assigned to the other eight centres except by mutual agreement between the company and union. Central computer facilities at the company's head office were programmed to handle the necessary calculations, and a large chart would be prepared for the Winnipeg plant to show the accumulated bonuses or deficits daily, with a three- to four-day lag caused by transfer of information to and from the central computer.

Bonuses would be paid monthly on an equal basis to all participating employees (50 percent to the probationary employees). Rejected production and returned product would not be credited toward total production. If performance in a given month fell below 100 percent the deficit would be carried forward and charged against bonus earning months. An accumulation of deficit beyond 15 percent would be ignored.

The basic standard would be changed as a result of methods changes if improvements generated by the company reduced total labour requirements by over three percent. If methods changes were generated by employees and there was no capital expenditure there would be no immediate change in the standard. However, the cumulative effects of such changes in methods could result in changes in standard at the end of designated periods of time. Six months was suggested as appropriate.

The plan would commence on January 1, and continue in full force until the expiration of the labour agreement, June 19, the following year. There would be a meeting of union and management to evaluate it at the end of six months.

Two committees would be established: a production committee and a steering committee, each consisting of representatives of union and management. The production committee would meet monthly to discuss ways and means of increasing production and improving efficiency.[3] The steering committee would be responsible for all facts and figures used in calculation of the bonus.

[3]This was the committee already in existence.

The proposed Sears-Horton and Partners plan was named the Darthom Employee Earnings Plan (DEEP) and presented to union and management representatives on December 13, as an addendum to a memorandum from Mr. Blair Hardman. Management hoped for the union's approval, but plans were laid to commence implementation, with or without approval, starting January 1.

Issues for Discussion

1. Comment on the Sears-Horton and Partners final plans with special attention to:
   A. derivation of standards
   B. the product mix factors
   C. changing of standards
   D. reporting of bonus
2. How would you appraise the prospects of success for Darthom's participative management plan for the Winnipeg plant?
3. Assume a new manager has been appointed to the Winnipeg plant with full authority to devise strategy and to implement it. As advisor to the new manager what plan of action would you recommend to him for the next year?

INDEX

Note: Page references in *italic* indicate
material in case studies.

Accommodative relationship, 17
Addington Chemical, *208-209*
AFL-CIO, 11, 34
Alexander Bert, Ltd., *270-281*
All-Canadian Congress of Labour, 28
Apex case, *282-285*
Arbitrability, 246-247, *332-333, 334, 354*
Arbitration, 142-145, 242-253; clauses,
  135, *291-292, 314-315*; decisions,
  277-280; forms of, 242-244; hearing,
  244-247; judicial review, 252-253;
  powers of arbitrators, 247-248,
  291-292, 332-333; precedent, 249. *See
  also* Grievances.
Asbestos strike, Quebec (1949), 40
Attitudinal structuring, 150-151

Bargaining process, 145-151; negotiation
  practice, 151-164
Bargaining structure, 11-12, 138-140,
  162
Bargaining units, 62, 64-65, 66
Basic elements of industrial relations
  system, 1
Beavair case, *286-288*
"Best evidence" rule, 248
Blacklists, 37-38
Bonus-sharing, *385-406*
Boulwarism, 148-149
Bucklin Corporation, *289-297*
Business unionism, 14

Canada Labour Code, 48
Canadian Congress of Labour (CCL), 28
Canadian Federation of Labour, 9-10, 35
Canadian Labour Congress (CLC), 9, 10,
  34, 35
Canadian Labour Union (CLU), 24-25
Canwest Life Assurance Co., *298-305*
Certification of unions, 62, 64-69;
  decertification, 70-71
Checkoff, 136-137
Closed shop, 136
Collective agreements: administration
  of, 240-267, *see also* Grievances;
  coverage by industry group, 4;
  exclusions from, 137-138; interpre-
  tation of, 249-251; mandatory
  inclusions in, 135-137; negotiating, *see*
  Negotiation of collective agreements.
Collective bargaining, 79-80. *See also*
  Bargaining process; Negotiation of
  collective agreements.
Collusive relationship, 17-18
Combinations in restraint of trade, 46
Conciliation, 55, 140-142, 157-161, *197,
  198, 201-207*
Conflict relationship, 16
Containment-aggression relationship,
  16-17, 240
Cooperative relationship, 17, 240
Craft unions, 7, 26; v. industrial unions,
  30-36
"Culminating incident" doctrine, 255

407

Darthom Industries, *372-406*
Decertification of unions, 70-71
Discipline, 253-256, *270-281, 291-292, 298-305, 318-322, 326-334, 349-351, 353-355, 357-358*
Dispute resolution, *see* Arbitration; Conciliation.
Distributive bargaining, 146-149

Employer associations, 11
Employer resistance to unions, 37-38, 76-77, *82-133*, 144; illegal actions, 79
Employers' rights, 77-79. *See also* Grievances.
Environmental Factors, 12-14

Federations of unions, 7, 9-11
Final offer selection, 143

Globe Electronics, *346-358*
"Good faith" bargaining, 135
Government, 12, 25; intervention (8 stages), 45-55. *See also* Legislation.
Great Lakes Iron and Steel, *359-368*
Great Northern Telephone Co., *306-310*
Grievances, 240-253; arbitration of, 242-253, *277-280, bona fide*, 246; cases, *270-281, 282-285, 286-288, 298-305, 306-310, 311-317, 318-322, 323-325, 335-338, 346-358, 359-368*

History of Canadian labour relations, 22-43
Hours of work, 260-262, *311-317, 323-325*
Human Rights Code (Ontario), *342-345*

Ideology, 14-15, 26-36
Incentives, 259-260, *282-285, 335-338, 379-380*; demoralized, 260. *See also* Bonus-sharing.
Industrial unions, 7; v. craft unions, 30-36
Injunctions, 49-50, 55, *210, 215, 368*
Interpretation of contract, 249-251
Integrative bargaining, 149
International unions, 6-7, 26-30, *212-213*
Intervention by government, 45-55
Intra-organizational bargaining, 150

Job assignment, 265, *297, 347-349, 352-353, 356-357, 359-368*
Job classification, 262-265; administrative problems, 264-265, *326-334*
John Hemstead & Sons, *311-317*
Jones and Smart, Ltd., *220-239*

Knights of Labor, 27, 30

Lay-offs and recalls: seniority in, 258-259, *335-338*
Labour relations boards, 61, 69-70
Labour spies, 38
Legal framework: for labour relations, 44; for negotiation, 134-138; for union organization, 61-71
Legislation, 44-60; in Canada (outlined), 56-57; exclusions from, 62, 63; postwar (Canada), 54-55; public sector, 55, 56-57, 58, 137-138, 145; social, 51; U.S., 48-51, 53-54, 55; wartime (Canada), 52-53
Local unions, 5, 6
Lockouts, 135-136, 141, 142, 162, 164

McDonald Containers, *168-207*
MacIntosh Metal Co., *318-322*
Management rights, 251-252, *332, 333*
Mediation, *see* Conciliation.
Modified union shop, 136
Muskoka University, *82-133*

National unions, 6-7, 35
Negotiation of collective agreements, 134-167; bargaining process, 145-151; bargaining structure, 11-12, 138-140, 162; case studies, *168-207, 212-214*; dispute resolution, 140-145; legal framework, 134-138; negotiation practice, 151-164
Norris - LaGuardia Act, 49-50, 55

Ontario Labour Relations Act (1943), 52
Open shop, 136
Organizing of unions: case study, *82-133*; legal framework, 61-71; techniques, 71-80
Overtime, 261-262, *311-317, 323-325*

Participative management, 370, *380-406*
Personal Paper Co., *323-325*
Picketing, 156, 157, 208, 210-211, *214, 215, 220-239, 298-305*
Policies of unions and management, 18-19
Political parties, 15
Port Erie Hydro, *326-334*
Power in bargaining, 147-148
Pre-hearing vote, 66-67
Printers' strike, Toronto, 23-24
Proof, in arbitration cases, 245, *279*
Public image of labour, 36-37
Public sector: bargaining structures in, 139-140; legislation, 55, 56-57, 58, 137-138, 145

Quality of Work Life (QWL), 369-371, *380-406*
Quebec: bargaining structures in, 139, 140; labour movement in, 27, 38-41

"Raids," 69
Rand formula, 53, 136
Relationship between union and management, 15-20, 240, 241. *See also* cases.
"Reserved rights" theory, 251
R.G. Williamson Co., *335-338*

Sabotage, 267
Safety, *289-297, 318-322*
Scanlon plans, 370, *381*
Seamen's dispute, 29-30
Seniority, 256-259, *326-334, 335-338*
Settlement stage of negotiations, 160-163
Sexual harassment, *339-345*
Sign-ups of union members, 73-75
Slowdowns, 266
Standards: hours of work, 260-262; job classification, 262-264; production, 259-260
"Status quo" theory, 251-252
Stewards, *289-297*
Strikebreakers, 156-157
Strikes, 135-136, 141, 142, 148, 162, 164, 265; cases, *208-219, 220-239, 291*; deadline, and negotiations, 155-156; employee groups forbidden to strike, 143; preparation for, 155-156, 197-198, *208-212, 216, 217*; wildcat, 266, *359-368*
Successor rights, 71

Taft-Hartley Act, 54
Technological change, and job evaluation, 264-265
Toronto Electric Commissioners v. Snider, 48
Trades and Labour Congress (TLC), 27, 28

Unfair labour practices, 69-70
Union politics, 19-20
Union pressure tactics, 265-267. *See also* Sabotage; Slowdowns; Strikes.
Union security provisions, 136-137
Union shop, 136
Unions in Canada: craft, 7, 26; federations, 7, 9-11; industrial, 7; international, 6-7, 26-30, *212-213*; legal status, 25-26; locals, 5, 6; membership, 2-3, 5, 8; national unions, 6-7, 35; organizing, *see* Organizing of unions; organization, 5-11; and QWL, 370-371, *384-406* passim; relationships with management, 15-20, 240, 241, *see also* cases.
United States: labour law in, 48-51, 53-54, 55

Violence, 30-31, 32, 33, 36-37
Voluntary recognition, 70-78
Wagner Act, 50-51, 54
Wildcat strikes, 266, *359-368*
Winnipeg General Strike, 31-33
Women in the labour force, 13-14, *378-379*; sexual harassment, *339-345*
"Work-to-rule," 266

Yellow-dog contracts, 37
Young Products Ltd., *339-345*